MOTHER OUTLAWS

MOTHER OUTLAWS

THEORIES AND PRACTICES OF EMPOWERED MOTHERING

Edited by

Andrea O'Reilly

Women's Press
Toronto

Mother Outlaws: Theories and Practices of Empowered Mothering
edited by Andrea O'Reilly

First published in 2004 by
Women's Press, an imprint of Canadian Scholars' Press Inc.
180 Bloor Street West, Suite 801
Toronto, Ontario
M5S 2V6

www.womenspress.ca

Canadian Scholars' Press/Women's Press gratefully acknowledges financial support for our publishing activities from the Government of Canada through the Book Publishing Industry Development Program (BPIDP).

National Library of Canada Cataloguing in Publication

    Mother outlaws / edited by Andrea O'Reilly.

Includes bibliographical references.
ISBN 0-88961-446-6

    1. Motherhood. 2. Mothers. I. O'Reilly, Andrea, 1961-

HQ759.M669 2004   306.874'3   C2004-901875-2

Cover design by AF Design
Cover photo by Keith Reicher/istockphoto.com
Text design and layout by Brad Horning

04 05 06 07 08   5 4 3 2 1

Printed and bound in Canada by AGMV Marquis Imprimeur Inc.

Canada

DEDICATION

To my Girlfriend "Mother Outlaws" who sustain and inspire me:

Linda Agasucci
Angela Bosco
Jennifer Conner
Christina Cudahy
Vicky Brown
Suzie Gatrell
Jane Hofstetter
Carol Lemen
Dorothy Liptrot
Kitty McKonnell
Siobhan McEwan
Marie Murphy
Linda O'Neill
Sandie Primeau
Christie Taylor
Patty Welsh

"I'm not a good mother. I'm not a good wife. I don't want to be. I'm [me] and I still love to dance."

—Margaret Laurence, The fire dwellers

Table of Contents

Acknowledgements xiii

Introduction
    Andrea O'Reilly 1

Section One: Feminist Mothering

Chapter One
Feminist mothers: Successfully negotiating the tensions between motherhood as "institution" and "experience"
    Fiona Green 31

Chapter Two
Resistance as a site of empowerment: The journey away from maternal sacrifice
    Erika Horwitz 43

Chapter Three
"We were conspirators, outlaws from the institution of motherhood": Mothering against motherhood and the possibility of empowered maternity for mothers and their children
    Andrea O'Reilly 59

Chapter Four
The (male) advantage of a feminist mother
    Juanita Ross Epp and Sharon Cook 75

Chapter Five
Telling our stories: Feminist mothers and daughters
    Christina Baker 95

Chapter Six
From perfect housewife to fishnet stockings and not quite back again:
One mother's story of leaving home
    Petra Büskens 105

Section Two: Lesbian Mothering

Chapter Seven
Imag(in)ing the queer lesbian family
    Jacqui Gabb 123

Chapter Eight
Our kids in the hall: Lesbian families negotiate the public school system
    Rachel Epstein 131

Chapter Nine
Lesbian mothers and the law of custody, access, and child support
    Joanna Radbord 145

Chapter Ten
Lesbian nonbiological mothering: Negotiating an (un)familiar existence
    Dawn Comeau 155

Section Three: African-American Mothering

Chapter Eleven
A politics of the heart: African-American womanist thought on mothering
    Andrea O'Reilly 171

Chapter Twelve
Black women's mothering in a historical and contemporary perspective:
Understanding the past, forging the future
    Erica Lawson 193

Chapter Thirteen
Community mothering: The relationship between mothering and the
community work of black women
    Arlene E. Edwards 203

Chapter Fourteen
"You'll become a lioness": African-American women talk about mothering
  Trudelle Thomas 215

Chapter Fifteen
Reflections on the mutuality of mothering: Women, children, and
othermothering
  Njoki Nathani Wane 229

Section Four: Mothers and Daughters

Chapter Sixteen
Across the divide: Contemporary Anglo-American feminist theory on
the mother–daughter relationship
  Andrea O'Reilly 243

Chapter Seventeen
The global self-esteem of an African-American adolescent female and her
relationship with her mother
  Barbara Turnage 263

Chapter Eighteen
Don't blame mother: Then and now
  Paula Caplan 275

Chapter Nineteen
Mother of mothers, daughter of daughters: Reflections on the motherline
  Naomi Lowinsky 285

Chapter Twenty
A daughter's praise poem for her mother: Historicizing community activism
and racial uplift among South African women
  Dolana Mogadime 293

Section Five: Mothers and Sons

Chapter Twenty-One
In black and white: African-American and Anglo-American feminist
perspectives on mothers and sons
  Andrea O'Reilly 305

Chapter Twenty-Two
Bringing our boyz to men: Black men's reflections on their mothers'
childrearing influences
Wanda Thomas Bernard 329

Chapter Twenty-Three
Swimming against the tide: Feminists' accounts of mothering sons
Alison M. Thomas 341

Chapter Twenty-Four
Raising relational boys
Cate Dooley and Nikki Fedele 357

Chapter Twenty-Five
A mom and her son: Thoughts on feminist mothering
Andrea O'Reilly 387

References 401
Contributors' notes 433
Copyright acknowledgements 439

ACKNOWLEDGEMENTS

Birthdays, for many of us, are a time for pause and reflection. Having recently celebrated my forty-third birthday, I found myself reflecting upon my life journey thus far and, in particular, upon the decisions and choices I had made along the way. In so doing, I soon realized that in each area of my life—career, relationship, and children—I came upon these life events in quite a happenstance manner. I ended up in graduate school because I couldn't figure out what else to do, I met my life partner when he joined a conversation I was having after overhearing and disagreeing with a point I was making, and our three children—born within five years when I was an undergraduate and later a graduate student—were all "birth control" babies. It would seem that what matters most in my life came to be not by choice or design, but by chance and, dare I say, destiny.

I open these acknowledgements with this reflection upon design and destiny because this beloved volume, *Mother outlaws*, likewise came into being, as with my kids, work, and partner, because it was, from the very beginning, meant to be. For the last couple years I had wanted to edit a collection on empowered mothering but I was busy and distracted by other projects. Fortunately, destiny intervened: the table I was staffing for the Association for Research on Mothering at the National Women's Studies Conference in June 2003 was located beside Women's Press. In the quiet times when participants were in session we got to talking, and by weekend's end this book, title and all, was conceived. However, *Mother outlaws* would have remained an idea had it not been for Women's Press's unwavering belief in, and commitment to, this book. The book, while conceived happenstance, came into being only through the trust and grit shown by the staff at Women's Press. I would like to thank Renée Knapp for her initial belief in the project, Christian Vernon for creating order from computer chaos,

Rebecca Conolly for getting the book into production under impossible deadlines, and finally, and most deeply, Althea Prince, who othermothered this book through each and every one of its labour pangs. Appropriately, *Mother outlaws* goes to press nine months after the idea was first conceived: thank you to each of you for making the birth of this book possible. Thanks also to Cheryl Dobinson, my intellectual/spiritual/emotional midwife, who kept me breathing through it all. And to the students in my WMST "Mothering–Mothering" course: this book exists because of them. I would also like to thank the contributors of this volume, for their research on empowered mothering, and for allowing me to reprint their chapters for the volume. And, as always, I would like to thank my children, Jesse, Erin, and Casey O'Reilly-Conlin. Once again, they have graciously shared their childhood with one of my books. In particular I thank them for their love that has sustained me in my goal of empowered mothering. And finally, thank you to my life partner of twenty-two years, Terry Conlin, who makes possible my empowered mothering.

INTRODUCTION

Andrea O'Reilly

In *Of woman born*, Adrienne Rich, when discussing a vacation without her husband one summer, describes herself and her sons as "conspirators, outlaws from the institution of motherhood" (195). She writes:

> I remember one summer, living in a friend's house in Vermont. My husband was working abroad for several weeks, and my three sons— nine, seven, and five years old—and I dwelt for most of that time by ourselves. Without a male adult in the house, without any reason for schedules, naps, regular mealtimes, or early bedtimes so the two parents could talk, we fell into what I felt to be a delicious and sinful rhythm … [W]e lived like castaways on some island of mothers and children. At night they fell asleep without murmur and I stayed up reading and writing as I had when a student, till the early morning hours. I remember thinking: This is what living with children could be—without school hours, fixed routines, naps, the conflict of being both mother and wife with no room for being simply, myself. Driving home once, after midnight, from a late drive-in movie … with three sleeping children in the back of the car, I felt wide awake, elated; we had broken together all the rules of bedtime, the night rules, rules I myself thought I had to observe in the city or become a "bad mother". We were conspirators, outlaws from the institution of motherhood; I felt enormously in charge of my life. (194–195)

However, upon Rich's return to the city, the institution, in her words, "closed down on us again, and my own mistrust of myself as a 'good mother' returned, along with my resentment of the archetype" (195).

Rich's reflections on being an outlaw from the institution of motherhood and the references she makes to being a "good" and "bad" mother are drawn from the distinction she develops in *Of woman born* between motherhood and mothering. Central to *Of woman born*, and developed by subsequent motherhood scholars, is the key distinction Rich makes between two meanings of motherhood, one superimposed on the other: "the *potential relationship* of any woman to her powers of reproduction and to children," and "the *institution*," which aims at ensuring that that potential—and all women—shall remain under male control" (13, emphasis in original). The term "motherhood" refers to the patriarchal institution of motherhood which is male-defined and controlled, and is deeply oppressive to women, while the word "mothering" refers to women's experiences of mothering which are female-defined and centred, and potentially empowering to women. The reality of patriarchal motherhood thus must be distinguished from the possibility or potentiality of gynocentric or feminist mothering. To critique the institution of motherhood therefore "is not an attack on the family or on mothering *except as defined and restricted under patriarchy*" (Rich, 14). In other words, while motherhood, as an institution, is a male-defined site of oppression, women's own experiences of mothering can nonetheless be a source of power.

In patriarchal culture, women who mother in the institution of motherhood are regarded as "good" mothers, while women who mother outside or against the institution of motherhood are viewed as "bad" mothers. In contrast, Rich argues that mothers, in order to resist patriarchal motherhood and achieve empowered mothering must be "bad" mothers, or more precisely, "mother outlaws." Therefore, and in opposition to the dominant and accepted view on motherhood, Rich defines empowered mothers as good mothers and patriarchal mothers as bad mothers. It has long been recognized among scholars of motherhood that Rich's distinction between mothering and motherhood was what enabled feminists to recognize that motherhood is not naturally, necessarily, or inevitably oppressive, a view held by many early second wave feminists. Mothering, freed from the institution of motherhood, could be experienced as a site of empowerment, a location of social change. However, as I examine in my edited collection *From motherhood to mothering: The legacy of Adrienne Rich's Of woman born*, there is no discussion of empowered mothering or how its potentiality may be realized in Rich's book, with the notable exception cited above. While this absence has puzzled scholars, most agree that—as mothering is not described or theorized in *Of woman born*—the text, in distinguishing mothering from motherhood and in identifying the potential empowerment of motherhood, has enabled feminists to envision empowered mothering for women. And for many scholars, this is the true legacy of Rich's work.

This book was developed in response to Rich's call for a theory and practice of outlaw mothering. While most feminist scholars now distinguish mothering from motherhood and recognize that the former is not inherently oppressive, mothering has not been theorized in feminist literature. Numerous publications document why and how patriarchal motherhood is harmful, indeed unnatural, to mothers and children alike. In contrast, no book, to my knowledge, considers how women may experience mothering as a site of empowerment and a location of social change. A few books examine feminist mothering, most notably the edited collection *Mother journeys: Feminists write about mothering* (1994), and Tuula Gordon's book, *Feminist mothers* (1990); however, both of these works are now over a decade old, and only look at feminist mothering, not at the more general concept of empowered mothering.

This book grows out of my third Women's Studies course, "Mothering and motherhood," a course I designed in 1991, and have taught at York University since 1992. The first semester of the course examines patriarchal motherhood, while empowered mothering is the focus of term two. Four themes of empowered mothering are explored in the second term: Lesbian Mothering, African-American Mothering, Mothers and Daughters, and Mothers and Sons. In the second term, with no book on empowered mothering available, articles from various issues of *The Journal of the Association for Research on Mothering* are read, as well as selected chapters from two of my edited books: *Mothers and daughters: Connection, empowerment and transformation* and *Mothers and sons: Feminism, masculinity and the struggle to raise our sons.* The volume *Mother outlaws* thus was initially designed so that my students would have a second term textbook, a move that would save both time and expense. However, as I selected the chapters for this volume, it became increasingly evident that the larger community of feminist scholars on motherhood would benefit from a collection on empowered mothering. In reflecting upon the need for a book on empowered mothering I recalled a comment made by Toni Morrison: "I wrote the books ... I wanted to read" (as quoted in interview with Sandi Russell, 43). *Mother outlaws* was the book I had always wanted—and needed—to read.

Mother outlaws examines practices and theories of empowered mothering under the four themes from my course noted above, as well as under the new topic of "Feminist mothering." The first three sections of the book, "Feminist mothering," "Lesbian mothering," and "African-American mothering" analyze mothering as a site of power for mothers while the final two sections, "Mothers and daughters" and "Mothers and sons," examine mothering as a location for social change. The chapters in this book were selected from various volumes of *The Journal of the Association for Research on Mothering* and my edited books on motherhood. For the new section on feminist mothering I included an article by Erika Horwitz, as well as two chapters from my recent edited collection *From motherhood to mothering: The legacy of Adrienne Rich's Of woman born.* As well, I included a revised chapter on African-American mothering from my book *Toni Morrison and motherhood: A politics of the heart*, a chapter that I use in the course for my introductory lecture on African-American mothering. Selecting the chapters this way—developed from and for a course on the subject matter—invariably will lead to some duplication and replication, particularly in the instance of my articles.

Empowered mothering, or what may be termed "outlaw mothering" or "mothering against motherhood," has yet to be fully defined, documented, or dramatized in feminist scholarship on motherhood. Rather, we know what empowered mothering is by what it is not: namely, patriarchal motherhood. A central aim of this collection is to develop, by way of theory and practice, a definition of empowered mothering. However, since empowered mothering is formulated and practiced in resistance to patriarchal motherhood, patriarchal motherhood itself must be studied. This is the focus of the first term of my course and the topic to which I now turn.

Patriarchal motherhood

I open my Mothering-Motherhood course by asking students to define "good" motherhood in contemporary culture. What does a good mother look like; what does she do or not do? Students have commented that good mothers, as portrayed in the media or in popular culture more generally, are White, heterosexual, able-bodied, married, and in a nuclear family with usually one to two children. Words such as altruistic, patient, loving, selfless, devoted, nurturing, and cheerful were frequently mentioned. Good mothers put the needs of their children before their own, are available to their children whenever needed, and if the mother works outside the home, her children rather than her career are at the centre of her life. Good mothers are the primary caregivers of their children; care other than that provided by the mother (i.e., daycare) is viewed as inferior and deficient. Children and culture at large do not see mothers as having a life before or outside of motherhood. As well, while students agreed that our culture regards mothering as natural to mothers, it simultaneously requires mothers to be well-versed in theories of childrearing. Several students remarked that good mothers today are concerned with their children's educational and general psychological development. Thus, good mothers ensure that their children have many varied opportunities for enrichment, learning, self-growth, and so forth. And, of course, mothers are not sexual!

"We all know the ideal of the good mother," Susan Chase and Mary Rogers (2001) argue in their book *Mothers and children: Feminist analyses and personal narratives*:

> Above all, she is selfless. Her children come before herself and any other need or person or commitment, no matter what. She loves her

children unconditionally yet she is careful not to smother them with love and her own needs. She follows the advice of doctors and other experts and she educates herself about child development. She is ever-present in her children's lives when they are young, and when they get older she is home everyday to greet them as they return from school. If she works outside the home, she arranges her job around her children so she can be there for them as much as possible, certainly whenever they are sick or unhappy. The good mother's success is reflected in her children's behaviour—they are well mannered and respectful to others; at the same time they have a strong sense of independence and self esteem. They grow up to be productive citizens. (30)

The above description refers to mothering as it practiced in the patriarchal institution of motherhood. Moreover, patriarchal motherhood, as the dominant ideology, becomes the mode of motherhood by which all mothers are regulated and judged.

This mode of mothering, what I term "sacrificial motherhood," however is not a natural condition; rather it a style of mothering that emerged in the middle of the twentieth century. "The patriarchal institution of motherhood," Rich (1986) explains, "is not the 'human condition' any more than rape, prostitution, and slavery are" (33). Rather motherhood, "has a history, it has an ideology" (33). Motherhood operates as a patriarchal institution to constrain, regulate, and dominate women and their mothering. "[F]or most of what we know as the 'mainstream' of recorded history," Rich writes, "motherhood as institution has ghettoized and degraded female potentialities" (13).

Feminist historians agree that motherhood is primarily *not* a natural or biological function; rather, it is specifically and fundamentally a cultural practice that is continuously redesigned in response to changing economic and societal factors. As a cultural construction, its meaning varies with time and place; there is no essential or universal experience of motherhood. Patriarchal motherhood, as described by students and in the quotation above, is neither natural nor inevitable. In my upcoming book *Reconceiving maternity: From sacrificial motherhood to empowered mothering*, I develop this concept further to argue that the institution and ideology of good motherhood is rewritten whenever a social reorganization is desired, particularly in the realm of gender roles and behaviour. Numerous works detail how the modern image "full-time stay-at-home" mother—isolated in the private sphere and financially dependent on her husband—came about as result of industrialization. Industrialization took work out of the home and repositioned the domestic space, at least among the middle-class, as an exclusively nonproductive and private realm, separate from the public sphere of work. In this century, at the end of World War Two, the discourse of the "happy homemaker" made the "stay-at-home" mom and "apple pie" mode of mothering the normal and natural motherhood experience. The view that stay-at-home motherhood is what constitutes good motherhood emerged only in the post-war period to effect a social reorganization and, more particularly, to redesign feminine gender behaviour and roles. During World War Two there was an unprecedented increase in women's employment, which included White middle-class mothers who had previously not been engaged in full-time employment. Thus, during the war period, mothers were encouraged to work and celebrated, particularly in the propoganda films and literature, for doing so. With the end of the war and the return of the soldiers, women were forced to give up their wartime employment. This was orchestrated and facilitated by an ideological redesign of what constitutes good motherhood. Buttressed by the new psychological teachings, notably Bowlby's attachment theory, two beliefs emerged: (1) children require full time "stay-at-home" mothering, and (2) children, without full-time mothering, suffer from what was termed "maternal deprivation." According to Bowlby, as noted by Shari Thurer (1994) in *The myths of motherhood: How culture reinvents the good mother*, "maternal deprivation was as damaging in the first three years of life as German measles in the first three months of pregnancy: 'mother love in infancy is as important for mental health as proteins and vitamins for physical health'" (276).

Sacrificial motherhood, as described by my students, thus emerged as the dominant view of good mothering in the post-war period approximately sixty years ago. Sacrificial motherhood is characterized by three central themes. The first defines mothering as *natural* to women and essential to their being. It is conveyed in the belief, as Pamela Courtenay Hall (1998) notes, that "women are *naturally* mothers, they are born with a built-in set of capacities, dispositions, and desires to nurture children [... and that this] engagement of love and instinct is utterly distant from the world of paid work [...]" (337). Second, the mother is to be the central caregiver of her biological children. Third, children require full-time mothering, or in the instance where the mother must work outside the home, the children must always come before the job. This model of mothering, as Sharon Hays (1996) explains in *The cultural contradictions of motherhood*, "tells us that children are innocent and priceless, that their rearing should be carried out primarily by individual mothers and that it should be centered on children's needs, with methods that are informed by experts, labor intensive, and costly" (21). Hays calls this style of motherhood "intensive mothering" and argues that is has been the dominant mode of mothering since the Second World War. She emphasizes that intensive mothering is "a historically constructed *cultural model* for appropriate child care" (21, emphasis in original). "Conceptions of appropriate child rearing," she continues, "are not simply a random conglomeration of disconnected ideas; they form a fully elaborated, logically cohesive framework for thinking about and acting toward children [...]. [W]e are told that [intensive mothering] is the best model, largely because it is what children need and deserve. This model was not developed overnight, however, nor is intensive mothering the only model available to mothers" (21).

Sharon Hays argues that intensive mothering emerged in the post-war period. I contend, in contrast, that while the origins of intensive mothering may be traced back to this time, intensive mothering, in its fully developed form, came about in the 1970s. Hays argues, as noted above, that intensive mothering is characterized by three themes: "first, the mother is the central caregiver"; mothering is regarded as more important than paid employment"; and that such "mothering requires "lavishing copious amounts of time, energy, and material resources on the child" (8). I would suggest that while the first two characterize mothering from post-war to present day, only mothering of the last thirty years can be characterized by the third theme: namely that children require copious amounts of time, energy, and material resources. As I argue in my book *Reconceiving maternity: From sacrificial motherhood to empowered mothering,* while the post-war discourse of good motherhood demanded that mothers be at home full time with their children, it did not necessitate the intensive mothering expected of mothers today. I see the post-war discourse of motherhood as covering the period between 1946 to the mid-1970s, the time when children of the baby boom generation were being raised, and before they themselves were mothers. I term the post-war discourse on motherhood, "custodial mothering" or "the flower pot approach," and see it different from intensive mothering. Intensive mothering, in contrast, emerged in the 1970s, and is practiced by the daughters born in baby boom years—1946 to 1962—who become mothers in the 1970s, 1980s, and 1990s. While intensive mothering emerges from custodial mothering, I emphasize that it is a distinct motherhood discourse specific to its historical period. Most research on motherhood does not distinguish between the two; rather both are characterized as post-war mothering or more generally twentieth century mothering. To fully understand how patriarchal ideologies of "good" motherhood function as culturally constructed practices, ones that are continuously redesigned in response to changing economic and societal factors, we must, I suggest, distinguish between custodial and intensive mothering because these two discourses emerged in response to two very different cultural transformations.

The ideology of "good" motherhood in the post-war era required full-time mothering but the emphasis was on the physical proximity of mother and child— i.e., the mother was to be "at home" with the children, with little said regarding a need for the mother to be continually attuned to the psychological, emotional, or cognitive needs of her children. My mother, for example, remembering the early 1960s, recalls "airing" my sister and me on the front porch each morning while she tended to the housework. Domesticity—keeping a clean house and serving well-prepared dinners—was, more than children, what occupied the post-war mother's time and attention. As well, in the 1950s and 1960s, there was a clearer division between the adult world and the world of children. Children would spend their time out in the neighbourhood playing with other children; seldom would children look to their parents for entertainment or amusement. And rarely were children enrolled in programs, with the exception of the occasional Brownies or Club meeting in the school-age years.

Today, the ideology of good motherhood demands more than mere physical proximity of mother-child: contemporary mothers are expected to spend, to use the discourse of the experts, "quality time" with their children. Mothers are told to play with their children, read to them, and take classes with them. As the children in the 1950s and 1960s would jump rope or play hide-and-seek with the neighbourhood children or their siblings, today's children dance, swim, and "cut and paste" with their mothers in one of many "moms and tots" programs. And today, children as young as three months old are enrolled in a multitude of classes from water-play for infants, French immersion for toddlers, karate for pre-schoolers, and competitive skiing, skating, or sailing for elementary school children. (An article I read recently also recommended reading and singing to your child in utero.) Today, though they have fewer children and more labour-saving devices—from microwaves to takeout food—mothers spend more time, energy, and I may add, money, on their children than their mothers did in the 1960s. And the majority of mothers today, unlike forty years ago, practice intensive mothering while engaged in full-time employment. Mothering today, as in the post-war era, is "expert driven." However, mothering today is also, under the ideology of intensive mothering, more child-centred than the "children should be seen but not heard" style of mothering the characterized the post-war period. Toni Morrison's (2003) novel *Love* delineates well the differences in these two styles of mothering. Vida, a mother and grandmother in the story, reflects:

> [Her grandson's generation] made her nervous. Nothing learned from her own childhood or from raising [her own daughter] Dolly worked with them, and every where parents were flummoxed. These days the first thought at Christmas was the children, in her own generation it was the last. Now, children wept if their birthdays weren't banquets; then the day was barely acknowledged. (148–149)

The ideology of intensive mothering, as Hays (1996) notes, "advise[s] mothers to expend a tremendous amount of time, energy, and money in raising children" (x). However, as Hays continues, "In a society where over half of all mothers with young children are now working outside the home, one might wonder why our culture pressures women to dedicate so much of themselves to child rearing" (x). Again to quote Hays, "Today, [...] when well over half of all mothers are in the paid labor force, when the image of a career women is that of a competitive go-getter, and when the image of the family is one of disintegrating values and relationships, one would expect a de-emphasis on the ideology of child rearing as labor-intensive, emotionally absorbing work" (3). Indeed, one would expect to locate the ideology of intensive mothering in the post-war period when middle class mothers, engaged in full time motherhood, had more time and energy to devote to childrearing. Instead, the emergence of intensive mothering parallels the increase in mothers' paid labour force participation.

Theorists of motherhood and mothers alike offer various explanations to account for the emergence of intensive mothering over the last twenty-five years. Sharon Hays, for example, argues that "the ideology of intensive child rearing practices persists, in part, because it serves the interests of men but also capitalism, the state, the middle class and Whites. Further, and on a deeper level, [...] the ideology of intensive mothering is protected and promoted because it holds a fragile, but nonetheless, powerful cultural position as the last best defense against what many people see as the impoverishment of social ties, communal obligations, and unremunerated commitments" (xiii).

Elsewhere I have explored how the ideology of intensive mothering emerges in the 1980s in response to changing demographics of motherhood. Today, for the majority of middle class women, motherhood is embarked upon only after a career is established, when the woman is in her thirties. For these mothers the hurriedness of intensive mothering is a continuation of their busy lives as professional women; where once their daybooks were filled with business lunches, office meetings and the like, as intensive mothers, home with their children, gymboree classes and "moms and tots" library visits schedule their daytimers. Often these professional, highly-educated women, unfamiliar and perhaps uncomfortable with the everyday, devalued, invisible work of mothering and domesticity, fill up their days with public activities that can be documented as productive and visible work. With fewer children, labour-saving devices, and household help, childrearing—or more accurately, the enrichment and amusement of the one beloved child—becomes the focus of the mother's time and attention; as opposed to cooking and cleaning as it was in my mother's generation. And when these professional women return to their careers, intensive mothering, as practiced in the evenings and weekends, is the way a working mother, consciously or otherwise, compensates for her time away from her children; it bespeaks the ambivalence and guilt contemporary working mothers may feel about working and enjoying the work they do. As well, intensive mothering, in its emphasis upon enrichment—toys, books, games, activities, programs, camps, holidays, theatre and so forth—emerged in response to mothers earning an income of their own, and having a say on how household money is to be spent. Mothers, more so than fathers, are the consumers of items children need and want; as a mother's earnings and economic independence increases, more money is spent on children. Finally, some argue that just as custodial mothering emerged in the post-war period in response to new psychological theories that stressed the need for mother-child attachment, intensive mothering in our time came about in response to the new scientific research that emphasizes the importance of the first five years of life in the intellectual, behavioural, emotional, and social development of the child. Whatever the economic or social explanation may be, the ideology of intensive mothering measures good mothering in accordance with the amount of time, money, and energy a mother expends on childrearing. Raising one child today, as my mother frequently remarks, demands more of these than the raising of four in the post-war period. Indeed, the demands made by society on mothers today are unparalled in our history.

Today's intensive mothering is also, as was custodial mothering in the post-war era, an ideological construction that functions as a backlash discourse. Like all backlash discourses, it functions to regulate women, or more specifically in this instance, mothers. In my current book, drawing upon Naomi Wolf's (1991) theory of the beauty myth, I explore how the current discourse of intensive mothering emerged in response to women's increased social and economic independence: increased labour participation, entry into traditionally male areas of work, rise in female-initiated divorces, growth in female-headed households, and improved education. It seems that just as women were making inroads and feeling confident, a new discourse of motherhood emerged which made two things inevitable: that women would forever feel inadequate as mothers, and that work and motherhood would be forever seen as in conflict and incompatible. I believe that the guilt and shame women experience in failing to live up to what is, in fact, an impossible ideal is neither accidental nor inconsequential. Rather, it is deliberately manufactured and monitored. Just as the self-hate produced by the beauty myth undercuts and undermines women's sense of achievement in education or a career, the current discourse of intensive mothering gives rise to self-doubt or, more specifically, guilt that immobilizes women and robs them of their confidence as both workers and mothers. "The image of [perfect] motherhood," as Sheila Kitzinger notes, is a false one. "A woman who catches sight of herself (unmasked as it were) sees a very different picture. And the message is clear: she is a failure" (as quoted in Maushart, 8). Given that no one can achieve intensive mothering all mothers see themselves as failures. This is how the discourse works psychologically to regulate—i.e., paralyse—mothers, via guilt and shame. And, some mothers, believing that perfect motherhood—i.e., intensive mothering—could be achieved if they "just quit work," leave paid employment. This is how the discourse regulates on the level of the social and the economic.

The ideology of intensive mothering dictates that: (1) children can only be properly cared for by the biological mother; (2) this mothering must be provided twenty-four hours a day, seven days a week; (3) the mother must always put children's needs before her own; (4) mothers must turn to the experts for instruction; (5) the mother is fully satisfied, fulfilled, completed, and composed in motherhood; and finally, (6) mothers must lavish excessive amounts of time, energy, and money in the rearing of their children. Each demand is predicated on the eradication or, at the very least, sublimation of mother's own selfhood; in particular her agency, autonomy, authenticity, and authority. The discourse of intensive mothering becomes oppressive not because children have needs, but because we, as a culture, dictate that only the biological mother is capable of fulfilling them; that children's needs must always come before those of the mother; and, that children's needs must be responded to around the clock and with extensive time, money, and energy. "Infancy and early childhood *are* periods of high emotional and physical dependency and, moreover this is not a pure invention of patriarchal science." However, as Petra Büskens (2001) continues, "*The problem is not the fact of this requirement but rather that meeting this need has come to rest exclusively, and in isolation, on the shoulders of biological mothers*" (81, emphasis in original). Yet, as author Toni Morrison commented: "If you listen to your children and look at them, they make demands that you can live up to. They don't need all that overwhelming love either. I mean, that's just you being vain about it" (Morrison, 2003: 270–71). While sacrificial motherhood and, in particular, intensive mothering, requires the denial of the mother's own selfhood in positioning the children's needs as always before her own, there are other ways to mother, ways that do not deny a mother her agency, autonomy, authenticity, and authority, thereby allowing her both her selfhood and power. This is the subject of this volume.

The patriarchal ideology of motherhood makes mothering deeply oppressive to women because sacrificial motherhood, both custodial and intensive, requires the repression or denial of the mother's own selfhood; as well, it assigns mothers all the responsibility for mothering but gives them no real power from which to mother. Such "powerless responsibility," to use Rich's term, denies a mother the authority and agency to determine her own experiences of mothering. Mothering, in other words, is defined and controlled by the larger patriarchal society in which a mother lives. Mothers do not make the rules, as Rich reminds us, they simply enforce them. Whether it is in the form of parenting books, a physician's advice or the father's rules, a mother raises her children in accordance with the values and expectations of the dominant culture. Mothers are policed by what Sara Ruddick (1989) calls the "gaze of others." Under the gaze of others, mothers "relinquish authority to others, [and] lose confidence in their own values" (111). "Teachers, grandparents, mates, friends, employers, even an anonymous passerby," continues Ruddick, "can judge a mother and find her wanting" (111–112). Ruddick calls this an abdication of maternal authority. "Fear of the gaze of others," she continues, "can be expressed intellectually as inauthenticity, a repudiation of one's own perceptions and values" (112). In *Of woman born*, Rich remembers her mother locking her in the closest at the age of four, for "childish behaviour—[her] father's order, but [her] mother carried them out—and being kept too long at piano lessons when she was six—again, at [her father's] insistence, but is was [her mother] who gave the lessons" (224). The "powerless responsibility" of patriarchal motherhood is predicated upon such abdication of maternal authority and inauthentic mothering. However, the denial of authority and authenticity demanded in both the mandate of powerless responsibility and in the discourse of sacrificial motherhood, in particular intensive mothering, is neither natural nor inevitable. There are other discourses and modes of mothering, ones that afford mothers agency, autonomy, authenticity, and authority. To this discussion I now turn.

Empowered mothering

"The institution of motherhood," Rich writes, "is not identical with bearing and caring for children, any more than the institution of heterosexuality is identical with intimacy and sexual love. Both create the prescriptions and the conditions in which choices are made or blocked; they are not 'reality' but they have shaped the circumstances of our lives" (42). "To destroy the institution is not to abolish motherhood," Rich continues. "It is to release the creation and sustenance of life into the same realm of decision, struggle, surprise, imagination and conscious intelligence, as any difficult, but freely chosen work" (280). And while we may not yet know completely what empowered mothering looks like, we, in interrupting and deconstructing the patriarchal narrative of motherhood, destabilize the hold this discourse has on the meaning and practice of mothering, and clear a space for the articulation of counter narratives of mothering.

A counter narrative of empowered mothering is concerned with imagining and implementing a view of mothering that is *empowering* to women as opposed to oppressive. Alternatively called authentic, radical, feminist, or gynocentric mothering, this mode of mothering positions mothers, in Rich's words, as "outlaws from the institution of motherhood." The theory and practice of empowered mothering recognizes that both mothers and children benefit when the mother lives her life and practices mothering from a position of agency, authority, authenticity, and autonomy. Second, this new perspective, in emphasizing maternal authority and ascribing agency to mothers and value to motherwork, defines motherhood as a political site wherein the mother can effect social change. She can do this by challenging traditional patterns of gender acculturation through feminist childrearing, and by challenging the world at large through political-social activism. This book will examine how mothers and theorists of motherhood seek to imagine and implement a theory and practice of mothering that is *empowering* to women as opposed to oppressive. While this new practice of mothering is frequently termed "feminist," I prefer the more general term "empowered" because such is more inclusive, and embraces all styles of empowered mothering, including empowered mothers who may not identify as feminist.

In *Of woman born*, Rich writes: "We do not think of the power stolen from us and the power withheld from us in the name of the institution of motherhood" (275). "The idea of maternal power has been domesticated," Rich continues, "In transfiguring and enslaving woman, the womb—the ultimate source of the power—has historically been turned against us and itself made into a source of powerlessness" (68). The aim of this book is to examine how mothers can and do reclaim that power, or more specifically the empowerment denied to them in the institution of motherhood. The first three sections of *Mother outlaws* examine three modes of empowered mothering—Feminist, Lesbian, and African-American—wherein mothering is positioned as site of power through which mothers have agency, authority, autonomy, and authenticity. The first three sections, in exploring how motherhood may be redefined as a site of power, are concerned with the mother role in terms of the mother herself—her experiences of it, the meanings she attaches to it—while the final two sections, "Mothers and daughters" and "Mothers and sons," focus upon the mother's role in relation to her children, and the manner in which she raises them. In other words, as the first three sections explore how empowered mothering affords mothers' agency, the final two sections examine how empowered mothering, in emphasizing maternal power and ascribing agency to mothers and value to motherwork, enables mothers to effect social change through the socialization of children, particularly in terms of challenging traditional patterns of gender acculturation. While this book distinguishes between the mother and the process of childrearing for the point of discussion, the two are, of course, interconnected and overlapping. As well, and as I explore further in chapter three, the two are interdependent: we cannot effect changes in childrearing without first changing the conditions of motherhood. To paraphrase Adrienne Rich, what children need are mothers who want their own freedom and ours (247). In other words: only an empowered mother can empower children, and children can only be empowered by an empowered mother.

In the above section on the patriarchal institution of motherhood I argued that patriarchal motherhood, particularly as it is expressed in the ideology of intensive mothering, oppresses women because of six key factors. As well, patriarchal motherhood, as noted in the above section, assigns mothers all the responsibility for mothering but gives them no real power from which to mother. Such "powerless responsibility," along with the six demands of good motherhood, denies a mother the authority, autonomy, authenticity, and agency to determine her own experiences of mothering.

The articles in the first three sections on Feminist, Lesbian, and African-American Mothering explore the many and diverse ways empowered mothers resist patriarchal motherhood. In particular, empowered mothering as practiced by feminist, lesbian, and African-American mothers challenges the six attributes of good—i.e., intensive—motherhood and the mandate of powerless responsibility. Empowered mothering does not assign full responsibility of childcare to the biological mother nor does it regard 24/7 mothering as necessary for children. Feminist mothers look to friends, family, and their partners to assist with childcare while lesbian mothers often raise their children with an involved co-mother. Likewise, in African-American culture, othermothering is frequently practiced. As well, in most instances, lesbian, feminist, and African-American women combine mothering with paid employment and/or activism, and so the full-time intensive mothering demanded in patriarchal motherhood is not practiced by these mothers. As well, many of these mothers call into question the belief that mothering requires excessive time, money, and energy, and thus they practice a mode of mothering that is more compatible with paid employment. As well, empowered mothers see the development of a mother's selfhood as beneficial to mothering and not antithetical to it as is assumed in patriarchal motherhood. Consequently, empowered mothers do not always put their children's needs before their own nor did they only look to motherhood to define and realize their identity. Rather, their selfhood is fulfilled and expressed in various ways: work, activism, friendships, relationships, hobbies, and motherhood. Empowered mothers insist upon their own authority as mothers and refuse the relinquishment of their power as mandated by the patriarchal institution of motherhood. Finally, for many empowered mothers, motherhood is understood to be a location or site of power wherein mothers can effect social change, both in the home through feminist childrearing and outside the home through maternal activism. Motherhood, in the dominant patriarchal ideology, is seen simply as a private; more specifically, an apolitical enterprise. In contrast, mothering for lesbian, feminist, and African-American women is understood to have cultural significance and political purpose. Building upon the work of Sara Ruddick, the chapters in the section on "Mothers and daughters" and "Mothers and sons" explore how mothers have redefined motherwork as a socially engaged enterprise that seeks to effect cultural change through new feminist modes of gender socialization and interactions with daughters and sons.

With the chapters on mothers and daughters, the counter-narrative of mother–child relations and roles has been scripted as mother–daughter connection and feminist mothering. These writers explore how mother–daughter connection, or what Naomi Lowinsky, in chapter nineteen, terms "the motherline," empowers mothers and daughters alike and gives rise to the transformation of patriarchal culture. These writers insist that mother-daughter connection is at the heart of emancipatory care and is essential for the empowerment of daughters, particularly in adolescence. The chapters identify and challenge the cultural practices that work against mother-daughter attachment, and seek various strategies of connection. Feminist mothering, the second theme explored in this section, is concerned with mothers modeling and mentoring female empowerment through "outlaw"mothering, in particular, through non-sexist childrearing.

The final section, on mothers and sons, examines how empowered mothers of sons have reconfigured the mother and son relationship, as well as masculine gender socialization. The first theme challenges the assumption, both lay and academic, that sons must separate from their mothers to achieve psychological wellness and maturity. The authors in this section argue that it is mother/son *disconnection* that harms men psychologically. The later theme examines the various ways feminist mothers seek to dismantle, destabilize, and deconstruct normative patterns of male socialization and traditional definitions of masculinity. With each, these writers, like the mother-daughter theorists, seek cultural change through new modes of mothering and mother-child relations.

The above themes of empowered mothers and empowered mothering may be found in the chapters that follow. However, not *every* empowered mother practices each theme of empowered mothering. The overall aim of empowered mothering is the redefinition of patriarchal motherhood in order to make mothering less oppressive and more empowering for mothers. Or, more specifically, empowered mothers seek to fashion a mode of mothering that affords and affirms maternal agency, authority, autonomy, and authenticity, and which confers and confirms power to and for mothers. However, such mothering, it must be emphasized, is practiced in a culture wherein patriarchal motherhood is the norm. In other words, empowered mothering, as it seeks to challenge patriarchal motherhood, remains defined by it. Consequently, while empowered mothering, in theory, may be clearly defined and realized, empowered mothering, in practice, is far more contested and elusive, achieved and expressed through negotiation with the institution of patriarchal motherhood that it resists. Many of the chapters in the collection examine this theme of negotiation.

Five modes of empowered mothering

Feminist mothering

The first section, on feminist mothering, opens with Fiona Green's chapter, "Feminist mothers: Successfully negotiating the tensions between motherhood

as 'institution' and 'experience'". Fiona Green argues that still missing from
scholarship on motherhood is an examination of Rich's monumental contention
that motherhood can successfully be a site of empowerment and potential
activism. Green's chapter, developed from interviews with self-identified feminist
mothers, considers how mothers successfully negotiate the tensions between
the "institution" and "experience" of motherhood. This study shows, Green
contends, that mothers can, and do, find opportunities within motherhood to
explore and cultivate their own agency, and to foster social change, through
their children and others. Some openly resist the pressures to live by the patriarchal
script of "good" motherhood, while others consciously use their socially-sanctified
role of motherhood in a subversive way to raise their children to be critically
conscious of, and to challenge, various forms of oppression.

The following chapter, by Erika Horwitz, investigates how a group of mothers
redefined mothering as a site of empowerment in a process of resistance to the
dominant discourse on mothering. The mothering literature has documented
thus far that women live under the oppression of a dominant discourse that
expects them to be perfect, all-loving, ever present, fulfilled, and sacrificial.
However, as Horwitz found while conducting her study, not all women subscribe
to the beliefs and expectations of the dominant discourse to the degree that they
are promoted and perpetuated in Western society. In this chapter she explores
how the mothers in her study resisted and how, by resisting, most of them
experienced a sense of empowerment even though they faced certain challenges.
These women exercised agency and positioned themselves as critical, independent
thinkers. Resistance by these women occurred in degrees along a continuum. In
other words, mothering involved both resisting and complying with different
aspects of the dominant discourse. Finally, not all the women who participated
in the study identified themselves as feminist even though all of them drew from
feminist discourse to construct their mothering beliefs and practices.

The chapter, "'We were conspirators, outlaws from the institution of
motherhood': Mothering against motherhood and the possibility of empowered
maternity for mothers and their children," written by me, focuses upon the
formulation of a female-defined and -centred experience of mothering, and the
development of a feminist practice of gender socialization. While the two aims
seem similar, the first is concerned with mothering in terms of the mother herself—
her experiences of mothering, the meanings she attaches to it—while the second
theme focuses upon the mother's relation with her children, and in particular the
manner in which she raises them. It has been long recognized that Rich was one
of the first feminist writers to call for non-sexist childrearing and women-centred
practices of mothering. What has been less acknowledged, and what will be the
focus of this chapter, is how the two are intrinsically linked, in so far as the goal
of non-sexist childrearing depends upon the abolition of patriarchal motherhood

and the achievement of feminist mothering. I argue that non-sexist childrearing—a challenge to traditional practices of gender socialization for both daughters and sons—depends upon motherhood itself being changed; it must become, to use Rich's terminology, mothering. In other words, only when mothering becomes a site, role, and identity of power for women, is feminist childrearing made possible.

In the following chapter, "The (male) advantage of a feminist mother," Juanita Ross Epp and Sharon Cook present an analysis of the responses of sons when questioned about the impact that their mothers' feminism had on their lives. The participants were the authors' sons, and data collection was done within and across the two families. The authors' fears that an overtly feminist stance on their mothers' parts might have caused difficulty for their male children appeared to be unfounded as the boys reported that the knowledge and outlook provided by feminist mothers worked to their advantage in understanding social issues and personal relationships

In "Telling our stories: Feminist mothers and daughters," Christina Baker discusses the findings described in her book *The conversation begins: Mothers and daughters talk about living feminism*. The book probes one of the most intimate and complicated relationships of a woman's life. Baker asked feminist pioneers of the second wave and their grown daughters to talk about their relationship as they attempt to live their feminism. In this chapter Baker examines the generational "passing down" of the feminist legacy and the "cost of combining motherhood with a career." Baker maintains that daughters overwhelmingly embraced their feminist inheritance but that the second question proves to be far more complicated. Mothers and daughters alike expressed how difficult it was to combine motherhood with their feminist careers. The women interviewed spoke of their struggles while trying to do both in a culture that assigns the responsibility for childcare and domesticity exclusively to mothers while not supporting or valuing the motherwork that they do. However, each woman spoke to the centrality of each in their lives and called for a redefinition of motherhood and work so that both could be lived more fully and happily.

In the final chapter of this section, Petra Büskens argues that contemporary motherhood is characterized by these two themes: (1) ambivalence and contradiction with regards to the dual institutions of "intensive motherhood" and "individualism"; and (2) an ongoing, profound inequality in the domestic division of labour. Taken together, we see women across the social strata are still structurally disadvantaged through the "institution of motherhood" (albeit, to varying degrees across race, class, and sexual divides). Assuming this as her point of departure, Büskens's chapter examines the social and sexual position of the "mother who leaves" based on empirical research conducted with fifteen Australian mothers. Seeking specifically to explore the political and symbolic ramifications of an overt "outlaw" to the institution of motherhood, she charts the trajectory of "Lillith" as she moves from a conventional maternal position through to leaving and reclaiming her "self," and then, finally, to a return and reinvention of her mothering role. Like all the women in this project, Lillith returned to mothering her children after an initial period of separation. Using the insights of "the mother who leaves," Büskens aims to render visible and problematic the position of "the mother who stays." Büskens contends that Lillith *did not leave her children,* rather she left the hegemonic institution of mothering which dictates that women relinquish their autonomy for the sake of familial others. Lillith creatively challenged this system, and the Madonna/Whore dualism inherent within it, by actively breaking and ultimately reinventing her familial role. Leaving is therefore read as a strategic withdrawal on the mother's behalf geared to disrupt and reorganize the terms on which parenting is organized. Implicit in this reading is the methodological claim that feminist maternal theorists need also make an analytic shift from the "institution of motherhood" to creative instances of subversion and recreation. Feminists, Büskens concludes, need to examine the agency of mothers contesting and remaking motherhood in their own image. The mother who leaves *and returns* is thus one potent "outlaw" to the institution of motherhood.

Lesbian mothering

Jacqui Gabb, in the chapter "Imag(in)ing the queer family" that opens the section, explores how queer mothering challenges prevailing notions of the family, and in particular the patriarchal script of "good" motherhood. In Western culture, motherhood and lesbian sexuality are perceived as antithetical to each other. Using illustrations from her own and others' lives, Gabb endeavors to reconcile the paradox of the lesbian family, by destabilizing traditional categories of the sexless mother and the sexually-deviant lesbian. Her chapter explores how lesbian mothers appropriate and queer the traditional language of the "family." She then moves on to an analysis of "family snapshot" photography and how it, in her words, "sanitizes lesbian sexuality." In contrast to such normalization of lesbian mothering, Gabb suggests the strategy of "visibility"; "imag(in)ing ourselves in ways which simultaneously illustrate our maternal and sexual identities." Gabb concludes that the aim should not be to defend or justify the lesbian mother, rather it should be to "move the debate on to consider the transgressive potentialities of our lesbian maternal selves."

In the chapter "Our kids in the hall: Lesbian families negotiate the public school system," Rachel Epstein explores some of the issues facing lesbian families (parents and children) in the Toronto public school system, drawing on twenty formal interviews conducted with lesbian parents between 1992 and 1997, as well as on many conversations with lesbian parents about the public school system as a source of fear, anxiety, and disempowerment. The chapter is organized around three theoretical assumptions: (1) that schools not only *reproduce* dominant cultural norms such as homophobia, sexism, and heterosexism, but are important sites for the *production* of sexual and other identities; (2) that understandings of the meanings and practices that make up broader student cultures around issues of sexuality and family are crucial to developing pedagogical and administrative practices that effectively challenge dominant norms; and (3) that the experiences of lesbian parents and their children are not monolithic, but intersect with other complex and contradictory issues of knowledge, power, and identity. In a postscript, the author raises some methodological issues about the uses and limitations of "realist" research, about the interpolation of researchers into the role of "experts," and about the possibilities contained in research perspectives that allow space for "not-knowing."

The third chapter, "Lesbian mothers and the law of custody, access and child support," by Joanna Radbord, discusses the law in Canada, particularly in the province of Ontario, with respect to custody and access for lesbian mothers. As well, it examines child support rights and obligations of lesbian parents. At least one-third of lesbians are mothers. Whether lesbians raise children from previous heterosexual relationships, or have babies as lesbian mothers, the law, Radbord argues, currently fails to support lesbian families. Discussing custody and access after the breakdown of a heterosexual relationship, Radbord reviews early court decisions that viewed "homosexuality" as a negative factor. While many of these lesbian mothers won custody of children, they had to closet their identities as lesbians to do so. And while many lesbians today do win custody, they, as a result of heterosexism and homophobia, have yet to achieve substantive equality in custody and access determinations. In the conclusion, referencing the 1999 Supreme Court of Canada decision that held that the wholesale exclusion of same-sex couples from the justice of family law was discriminatory, Radbord suggests that with such changes, equal rights and obligations for lesbian families may be finally recognized in and before the law. And with this, as Radbord concludes, "the best interests of the children" will, for the first time, be truly acknowledged and acted upon.

Dawn Comeau, in the final paper of this section, examines the role of the co-mother in lesbian relationships, in particular, the struggle of co-mothers to be recognized as parents. In "Lesbian nonbiological mothering: Negotiating an (un)familiar existence," Comeau examines how co-mothers who embody such a position of nonrecognition negotiate relationships with their children, partner, family of origin, and community. Two central questions inform her research: (1) How does the nonbiological co-mother in a lesbian family develop and build a solid foundation from which to negotiate her role in the public realm? and (2) How does her role shift when she returns home to the private sphere? Comeau discovers that, while co-mothers are able to define their identity in the realm of home, her role is misunderstood, questioned, and invalidated in the larger society, which perpetuates heterosexism and refuses to recognize the legitimacy of lesbian families both socially and legally. The co-mothers interviewed by Comeau, as they describe how invalidation and invisibility are obstacles to the creation of family, likewise emphasize their commitment to their families, and their determination to have them socially and legally recognized as such.

African-American mothering

My chapter that opens this section, "A politics of the heart: African-American womanist thought on African-American mothering," explores African-American mothering as a counter narrative of empowered mothering. Drawing upon the writings of many Black feminist writers including Patricia Hill Collins, Patricia Bell-Scott, Carol Stacks, bell hooks, Gloria Wade-Gayles, Alice Walker, Wanda Thomas Bernard, and Joyce Ladner, the chapter explores how the African-American womanist thought on mothering redefines mothering as a site of power and empowerment. I explore five themes in this redefinition that serve to dismantle intensive motherhood, and that position mothering as an identity and role of empowerment. The African-American tradition of motherhood centres upon the recognition that mothering, in its concern with the physical and psychological well-being of children and its focus upon the empowerment of children, has cultural and political import, value and prominence, and that motherhood, as a consequence, is a site of power for Black women. The chapter examines this tradition of African-American mothering under five interrelated topics: "Othermothering and community mothering," "motherhood as social activism and a site of power," "Matrifocality," "Nurturance as resistance: Providing a homeplace," and "The motherline: Mothers as cultural bearers." Next it examines this tradition in the context of mothers' relationships with their children, specifically considering how daughters seek identification or connection with their mothers due to the cultural centrality and significance of the mother role, and how this connection gives rise to a daughter's empowerment in African-American culture. Finally, the chapter explore how African-American mothers remain, contrary to the normative scripts of mother-son relation, involved in their sons' lives and how this involvement fosters their sons' physical survival, psychological well-being, and overall empowerment.

Erica Lawson, in the following chapter, "Black women's mothering in a historical and contemporary perspective," explores how sexuality, reproduction, and mothering are socially constructed and monitored in the interest of the nation-state. It argues that black and white women are differently positioned in the way the nation is imagined; such that the former is exploited re/productively while the latter is encouraged to reproduce the nation and the idealized nuclear family. The racialization of motherhood, mothering, and female sexuality is prevalent in

Western countries. Yet, despite the fact that black mothers and their children are treated as a burden on state resources, black women find political empowerment and expressions of resistance in mothering. Indeed, community-based mothering is a site of self-actualization for many black people who live in oppressive circumstances. This essay explores these points by briefly assessing how mothering is taken up in Toni Morrison's *Beloved*; by examining state interventions to discourage black women from having children in Dorothy Roberts' *Killing the black body: Race reproduction and the meaning of liberty*; and by drawing on the author's memories of growing up in a rural community.

In "Community mothering: The relationship between mothering and the community work of black women," Arlene Edwards distinguishes between othermothering—an acceptance of responsibility for a child not one's own—and community mothering—taking care of the community. Edwards explores how both developed from West African practices of communal lifestyles and the interdependence of communities. The practices of othermothering and community mothering remain central to the African-American tradition of motherhood and are regarded as essential for the survival of black people. In this chapter, Edwards explores how community mothering evolves from othermothering; in particular, she examines the community work performed by black Clubwomen, church mothers, and civil rights women. Her study reveals that the repeated references to mothering as a theme in the language used shows that mothering remains the motivating factor for doing community work for contemporary Black women. The article explores various themes under the larger topic of community mothering, including direct mothering, indirect mothering, mentoring, being a role model, and doing this work without expectation of gratitude.

The next chapter, "You'll become a lioness: African-American women talk about mothering," is developed from the author's interviews with six college-educated African-American women who were mothers of children under age twelve. Trudelle Thomas identified four themes in this study. First, the women spoke candidly about the pleasures as well as the difficulties of raising children. They delighted and took pride in their children. Difficulties included the physical challenges of pregnancy, financial responsibility, isolation caused by inadequate social support, and fears about raising children in a hostile environment. Second, the women spoke about the importance of setting an example of full human development for their children. This included being a caring, nurturing mother as well as a self-reliant, capable, and determined provider. They accepted outside-the-home employment and flexible gender roles as givens for their lives and did not feel guilty about working outside the home. Third, all reported that motherhood had led to a deepened spirituality and an expanded sense of self. Though their relationships with organized religion had been strained and disappointing, all continued to see religious faith as an essential source of strength and comfort. Finally, the essay ends with several suggestions on how religious groups (congregations) can respond to the practical and spiritual needs of mothers. Throughout the chapter, African-American views of motherhood are contrasted with the Euro-American "cult of true womanhood" and the self sacrificing "Giving Tree" ideal.

In the section's concluding chapter, Njoki Nathani Wane examines the community mothering performed by female elders who mother both adults and children, as well the leadership role they assume as consultants for their community. One aim of the chapter is to illustrate and underscore how women interweave motherhood and other aspects of their lives. As well, Wane explores how the principle of African collectivism, particularly as manifested through women's mutual groups, enables women to combine motherhood with work and/or education. She explores this tradition, what she terms "Harambee spirit," in pre-colonial and colonial societies, as well as in contemporary Black communities.

Mothers and daughters

The section opens with my chapter "Across the divide: Contemporary Anglo-American feminist theory on the mother–daughter relationship." The chapter describes the course I designed and taught entitled "Mothers and daughters: From estrangement to empowerment" at York University in the early 1990s. The course aims to identify and expose the cultural practices that underpin the patriarchal narrative of mother-daughter estrangement—sanctions against mother-daughter closeness, daughter-centricity, mother-blame, cultural devaluation of motherhood, matrophobia, inauthentic mothering, fear of maternal power, and normative maternal discourses. As well, it offers various strategies—motherline, maternal narratives, and feminist mothering—through which mothers and daughters may deconstruct the patriarchal narrative, so they can write their own stories of motherhood and daughterhood, ones scripted from relationships of empowerment as opposed to connection.

Barbara Turnage, in her chapter "The global self-esteem of an African-American adolescent female and her relationship with her mother," explores the radicalizing power of the mother-daughter connection for adolescent African-American girls. Turnage's research examines the interrelationships among the daughter's global self-esteem, ethnic identity, appearance evaluation, and trust of her mother. Turnage concludes that girls' relationships with their mothers have a direct bearing on their global self-esteem. Modeling and presenting empowering images of Black womanhood, instilling a love for African-American-oriented features—mothers prepare their daughters to enter society with a positive self-esteem. The significance of the research, Turnage emphasizes, cannot be overstated: "These girls as, they grow into Black womanhood, grow with the knowledge that they can accomplish their goals, that they are worthy of love and respect."

The following chapter, "Don't blame mother: Then and now" by Paula Caplan, opens with the author's personal observations on how mothers are always held responsible for everyone else's problems. She describes aspects of girls' and women's socialization that create or exacerbate disconnection between mothers and daughters, as well as strategies used to repair these rifts. As Caplan explains, there are bad mother myths that are used as evidence against mothers while the important work they do as mothers goes unnoticed. As well, there are good mother myths that set impossible standards to live up to. She argues that these myths, which are mutually exclusive, give rise to mother blame and cause mother-daughter disconnection. Using excerpts from a theatrical play she has written, Caplan exposes and dismantles these good and bad motherhood myths, and advises readers to do the same in their everyday lives. Let us vow, she concludes, "that at every possible opportunity we will protest, we will educate, even interrupt as we would a sexist or racist 'joke' when anyone in any setting utters or implies any of the dangerous myths about mothers."

The chapter "Mother of mothers, Daughter of daughters: Reflections on the motherline" begins with Naomi Lowinsky's description of the primal experience of giving birth as the universal connection of the origin of all human life to the woman's body. Grounding her research in her own personal experience as mother, Lowinksy positions her younger self in her children and her older self in her mother. Although the concept is elusive and hard to explain, she uses the term motherline to refer to the sacred experiences of the embodied feminine mysteries. She goes on to point out that these feminist mysteries are not honoured in our culture and clash with societal views of mastery over nature. However, for Lowinksy, knowledge of our motherline stories is essential to women's well-being, psychologically and spiritually. And "while these stories are all around us" Lowinksy argues, "we don't hear them because our perception is shaped by a culture that trivializes 'women's talk' and devalues the passing down of female lore and wisdom." Finally, Lowinsky believes that, in reclaiming our motherline stories, the wounds of disconnection between mothers and daughters may be healed.

In the section's final chapter, "A daughter's praise poem for her mother: Historicizing community activism and racial uplift among South African women," Dolana Mogadime explores her parents exile from South Africa in 1963, a protest against the apartheid military regime. In particular, the chapter is an enquiry into her mother's life so that Mogadime is able to, in her words, "remember, mend, and reconnect with a South African family, history and cultural identity." Mogadime explores the importance and centrality of mothers in resistance; as well, she emphasizes their key role in recording and passing on these stories of resistance.

The chapter goes on to explore the oral tradition of praise poetry, and to consider how praise poems of mothers serve to honour the merits and achievements of our mothers' work, and reaffirm an ethic of group connectedness and cultural accountability. Mogadime concludes with a consideration and celebration of the Black mother and daughter dyad, and Black women's connection with each other as community workers. In so doing she shows how women in these roles nurture and sustain the community struggle for social justice.

Mothers and sons

The final section, "Mothers and sons," opens with my chapter "In black and white: African-American and Anglo-American feminist perspectives on mothers and sons." The chapter examines three schools of feminist thought with respect to mothers and sons to determine how women's maternal role/identity and the mother-son relation are represented in each. The chapter opens referencing the ancient myths of Jocasta/Oedipus and Clytemnestra/Orestes. These patriarchal narratives, both in their ancient forms and in their modern renditions, enact maternal erasure and enforce mother-son separation. The chapter goes on to argue that maternal erasure and disconnection were central to early Anglo-American feminist thought on mothers and sons, which tended to downplay and devalue women's role and identity as mothers. The chapter considers how recent Anglo-American feminist writings on mothers and sons call into question the patriarchal and early feminist perspective on maternal displacement, in order to emphasize mother and son connection. Finally, the chapter reviews recent African-American feminist thought on mothers and sons to explore both its emphasis on maternal presence and involvement and its specific, racially determined mode of rearing sons. These new feminist perspectives—Anglo-American and African-American—the chapter concludes, by highlighting maternal agency and authority, and in foregrounding the mother-son connection, have imagined and made possible a truly feminist narrative of mothers and sons.

In "Bringing our boyz to men: Black men's reflections on their mothers' childrearing experiences," Wanda Thomas Bernard cites the findings from *Survival and success: As defined by black men in Sheffield, England and Halifax, Canada*, which showed that black women, as mothers, grandmothers, and othermothers, have been important, significant, and meaningful in the lives of *successful* black men. Using the voices of black men who reflect on their experiences with their mothers, grandmothers, and othermothers, the author weaves the stories of influences that these women have on the lives of the men who have managed to survive in societies where they are expected to fail.

Alison Thomas' chapter, appropriately entitled "Swimming against the tide: Feminists' accounts of mothering sons," examines the aims and challenges of feminist mothering of sons. Drawing upon the findings of qualitative research study, Thomas identifies three salient themes in contemporary feminist thought on mothering and masculinity. The first topic, "[mothers'] efforts to encourage an alternative and more positive style of masculinity" details the many ways mothers, in the words of Elsie Jay, writing in the special issue *Feminism and Psychology*, "[seek] to create] a new man—sensitive, expressive, nonviolent, respectful, and loving of women." Social and, at times, familial—fathers, grandparents—resistance to this maternal aim is the second topic identified by the mothers in the research study and explored by Thomas. These mothers, aware that they are, as one participant described it, "going against the grain of the dominant culture," discuss how their feminist mothering is continually being countered and undermined by the school system, peer ground pressures, the mass media, and for some, the influence of the boy's father. The final theme, defined by Thomas as "the risks in sabotaging masculinity," examines the mothers' own ambivalence and anxiety about raising a boy feminist. The mothers wondered whether they were, in the words of one woman, "compromising [the son's] masculinity" and worried, as Thomas explains, "[that in] making their son *too* different [he would be] expos[ed] to potential ostracism from his peers." The final section of the chapter considers the father's role in this redefinition of masculinity

The fourth chapter in this section, "Raising relational boys" by Cate Dooley and Nikki Fedele, draws upon relational theory to develop "a model of parenting-in-connection." In their work with three thousand mothers of sons, as well as adult sons and couples, Dooley and Fedel find that "boys with secure maternal connection develop stronger interpersonal skills and enjoy healthier relationships as adults." However, the world in which our sons live, first as boys, and later as men, demands both disconnection and domination. Boy culture, as it is defined by Dooley and Fedele, among others, straightjackets boys into specific and rigid gender identities that discourage, if not disallow, sentiments of care and relations of connection. In opposition to boy culture, and to counter its dictates of disconnection, mothers and fathers must practice what they term "parenting-in-connection." "The goal," as Dooley and Fedele explain, "is to enhance connection and to circumvent distance and separation" and "to move toward reconnection when disconnection does occur, as it invariably will. Mothers must model and teach to their sons specific behaviours and strategies that will enable them to stay in connection." The chapter concludes by looking at four stages in the mother-son relationship—early years, middle years, teenage years, and college/adult years—in order to identify the cultural dictates of disconnection found in each stage, and to detail the various ways mothers may "counter these cultural influences and keep sons on the path of relational development."

The chapter that closes the section is my chapter "A mom and her son: Thoughts on feminist mothering." In this narrative I reflect upon how feminism shaped the mothering of my son, and how being a mother of a son redefined my feminism. When raising my son, Jesse, I did not overtly or consciously set out to impart feminist teachings. However, as discussed in this chapter, I did practice what I term "radical mothering," or more specifically, resistance to the traditional practices of male socialization that mandate both mother-son disconnection and "macho" masculinity for boys. In nurturing a connected and close relationship with my son, and in allowing and affirming the strong feminine dimensions of his personality, my son grew up with the knowledge that it was all right to be a sensitive boy, and that it was indeed quite normal to need your mother. The chapter also considers how my feminism was rethought, reworked, and redefined in and through the mothering of my son, most significantly in terms of the way I understood gender difference. Being the mother of a "good" son I came to came realize that the masculine is not inherently evil, as I had believed in my pre-mother of son, radical feminist days. I explore how, through this realization, I was able to discover and honour the so-called masculine dimensions of my self that were before unacknowledged or unaffirmed.

Conclusion

A central theme of this book, introduced above and explored at length in the chapters that follow, is that empowered mothering—in affirming maternal agency, authority, autonomy, and authenticity—makes motherhood more rewarding, fulfilling and satisfying for women. Such mothering allows women selfhood outside of motherhood and affords them power within motherhood. As well, the practice of othermothering or co-mothering, the ability to combine motherhood with work (paid employment and/or activism), and limiting the time, energy, and money spent on children relieves women of much of the isolation, dependency, boredom, and exhaustion experienced in patriarchal motherhood. It is evident that empowered mothering is better for mothers. Such mothering is also, as argued above and shown in the collection, better for children. We understand that mothers content with, and fulfilled by, their lives make better mothers. Likewise, we recognize that children raised by depressed mothers are at risk.

I want to suggest as well that empowered mothers are more effective mothers. Anyone who has been in a plane knows the routine if oxygen masks are required: put on your mask and then assist children with theirs. This instruction initially seems to defy common sense; children should be helped first. However, the instruction recognizes that parents must be masked first, because only then are they able to provide real and continued assistance to the child: unmasked they run they risk of becoming disoriented, ill, or unconscious due to lack of oxygen, and then of course would be of no use to the child. I see this instruction as a suitable metaphor for empowered mothering. Mothers, once empowered, are able to better care for and protect their children.

In her recent book, *A potent spell: Mother love and the power of fear*, Janna Malamud Smith (2003) references the myth of Demeter and Persephone to illustrate this theme; children are better served by empowered mothers. Demeter, Smith argues "is able to save her daughter because she is a powerful goddess who can make winter permanent and destroy humankind" (59). "Demeter," she continues, "possesses the very qualities that Mothers so often have lacked—adequate resources and strength to protect their children— particularly daughters" (59). Therefore, and contrary to patriarchal or more generally accepted wisdom, what a child needs most in the world, Smith argues, "is a *free and happy* mother" (167, emphasis added). Smith explains:

> [W]hat a child needs most is a free mother, one who feels that she is in fact living *her* life, and has adequate food, sleep, wages, education, safety, opportunity, institutional support, health care, child care, and loving relationships. "Adequate" means enough to allow her to participate in the world—and in mothering—[....] A child needs a mother who has resources to enable her to make real choices, but also to create a feeling of adequate control—a state of mind that encourages a sense of agency, thus a good basis of maternal well-being, and a good foundation on which to stand while raising a child. Surely, child care prospers in this soil as well as, if not better than in any other. What is more, such a mother can imagine a life of possibility and hope, and can so offer this perspective to a child. [Finally] a child needs a mother who lives and works within a context that respects her labor, and that realistically supports it without rationalizing oppression in the name of safety, or substituting idealization or sentimentality for resources.

Ann Crittenden, who is cited by Smith, elaborates further: "Studies conducted on five continents have found that children are distinctly better off when the mother possess enough income and authority in the family to make investing in children a priority" (230). "The emergence of women as independent economic actors," Crittenden continues, "is not depriving children of vital support; it is giving them more powerful defenders. Depriving mothers of an income and influence of their own is harmful to children and a recipe for economic backwardness" (230). To return to the story of Demeter: "It is only because Demeter has autonomy and independent resources," as Smith explains, "that she can protect Persephone" (241). Conversely, "when a culture devalues and enslaves the mother, she can [not] be like Demeter and protect her daughter" (244). Therefore, and as Smith concludes, "If we are really interested in improving the lot of children, our best method would be laws and policy that support mothers and mothering" (187). It is indeed remarkable, as Smith notes, that "[n]o society has ever voluntarily turned its laws and riches toward liberating mothers" (168).

The free mother valued by Smith and recognized as essential for the well-being of children however will be not found in the patriarchal institution of motherhood or in the practice of intensive mothering. Patriarchal motherhood, as explored above, robs women of their selfhood and power, and intensive mothering, in its emphasis on excessive time, attention, and energy, makes it difficult, nay impossible, for mothers to be autonomous and independent. Empowered, or to use Smith's term, free mothering thus only becomes possible in and through the destruction of patriarchal motherhood. Such mothers can better protect and defend their children. As explored in this volume, empowered mothers can make real and lasting changes in society through social-political activism and in the way they raise their children. More specifically, empowered mothers challenge and change, in the home and in the world at large, the gender roles that straightjacket our children. They challenge the harm of sexism, racism, classism, and heterosexism. I want to suggest, as I conclude this introduction, that patriarchy resists empowered mothering precisely because it understands its real power to bring about a true and enduring cultural revolution. Indeed, it will be mothers, empowered and united, who will create the just and caring society, that "feminist new world" we seek for ourselves and all our children.

Section One

FEMINIST MOTHERING

Chapter One

FEMINIST MOTHERS

SUCCESSFULLY NEGOTIATING THE TENSIONS BETWEEN MOTHERHOOD AS "INSTITUTION" AND "EXPERIENCE"

Fiona Green

> Throughout this book I try to distinguish between two meanings of motherhood, one superimposed on the other: the *potential relationship* of any woman to her powers of reproduction and to children; and the *institution*, which aims to ensure that that potential—and all women—remain under male control.
>
> Adrienne Rich, *Of woman born* (emphasis in original)

Adrienne Rich is the first person to have acknowledged that motherhood is a complex site of women's oppression and a potential location for women's creativity and joy. In *Of woman born*, Rich provides a detailed discussion of the social construction of motherhood, and a critical analysis of how motherhood functions within patriarchy. Since its publication over twenty-five years ago, feminists have been inspired to research many aspects of motherhood outlined by Rich. Early scholarship explored the ways social definitions and restrictions make motherhood an institution, and examined various ways in which women are constrained by the socially-accepted ideology of mothering. More recent discourse continues to unravel the complexities of motherhood by focusing on the multiple issues and experiences related to class, ethnicity, sexuality, and ability. Yet, still largely missing from the increasing dialogue and publication around motherhood is discussion of Rich's monumental contention that even when restrained by patriarchy, motherhood can be a site of empowerment and political activism for women.[1]

This assertion, that motherhood is simultaneously oppressive and potentially liberating, is reflected in my own experience as a feminist mother. Since giving birth to my son in 1988, I have consciously lived with, and managed, the tension between the oppressive and the emancipating components of motherhood. I continue to experience social pressure to conform to a standard of motherhood that feels restrictive and, at times, damaging. In particular, I find the expectation that I will, without question, follow and replicate "conventional" standards of motherhood and raise a son who will comply with the patriarchal expectations of masculinity offensive and harmful to my child, to myself, and to our family.[2] At the same time, however, I revel in the personal connection and relationship I have with my son. This unique relationship, one that I have yet to share with another person, offers moments when I experience my full potential as a human being. I believe this is partly because I try to be open to our mother/son relationship, and I continually analyze the power dynamics within it. In addition to nurturing both my son's and my own growth within the arena of motherhood, I am able to actively undermine the institution of motherhood and challenge patriarchy. Rich's theory rings true for me; I can and do negotiate the tension between societal expectations of motherhood and my personal experiences of mothering.

While conducting my PhD research in Winnipeg during the mid-1990s, I interviewed sixteen self-identified feminist mothers about their realities of being feminist mothers. Without exception, these women identify and experience both restrictive and liberating elements of motherhood. They also unanimously view their mothering as feminist because they actively challenge patriarchal assumptions about motherhood while parenting. Motherhood for these women is, as Rich proposes, certainly empowering and liberating.

The institution of motherhood

Before addressing the ways in which some of these feminist mothers manage the tension between the onerous and the emancipating elements of motherhood, I want to first explore the meaning of the institution of motherhood according to Rich, and how this is understood by the feminist mothers in my research. Rich describes the institution of motherhood in this way:

> When we think of the institution of motherhood, no symbolic architecture comes to mind, no visible embodiment of authority, power, or of potential or actual violence. Motherhood calls to mind the home, and we like to believe that the home is a private palace .... We do not think of the laws which determine how we got to these places, the penalties imposed on those of us who have tried to live our lives according to a different plan, the art which depicts us in an unnatural serenity or resignation, the medical establishment which has robbed so many women of the act of giving birth, the experts—almost all male—who have told us how, as

mothers, we should behave and feel. We do not think of the Marxist intellectuals arguing as to whether we produce "surplus value" in a day of washing clothes, cooking food, and caring for children, or the psychoanalysts who are certain that the work of motherhood suits us by nature. We do not think of the power stolen from us and the power withheld from us, in the name of the institution of motherhood.[3]

Like Rich, the feminist mothers I spoke with understand that motherhood is part of our patriarchal society and, conversely, that patriarchy is highly incorporated within motherhood. While respondents do not specifically use the term "institution" when they speak about motherhood, they illustrate an understanding of this concept in their interviews. For instance, they speak of how motherhood is restrictive, and at times, oppressive because of the expectations placed on them to conform to and replicate an ideal of motherhood that prescribes particular behaviors.[4] They note the widespread use of messages about the virtues of the stereotypical "good" mother, and warnings about the dangers of "bad" mothers. Television and radio talk shows, newspaper and magazine articles, and popular movies illustrate commonplace standards for both the exemplary and incompetent mother.[5]

We can all picture the ideal mother. She is a heterosexual woman who stays at home with her children while her husband, the father of their children, works in the labour force to support them financially. Because of her "innate" ability to parent and her "unconditional love" for her husband and children, the idealized mother selflessly adopts their wants, needs, and happiness as her own. Her willingness to participate in her children's schooling or in community activities is an extension of her maternal love. The perfect mother always has a connection with her children, never has an ill feeling towards them, and is completely responsible for caring for and nurturing all of her family members. The ideal mother never gets angry; she finds parenting to be the most meaningful aspect of her life. Providing love and care for her family fills her with boundless happiness and self-fulfilment.[6]

While this ideal is far removed from the reality of many women's lives,[7] the presentation of the "ideal mother" seen in mainstream media, advertising, and entertainment is nevertheless held out for mothers to strive for, and is considered, to some degree, as the "legitimate" standard to which mothers are compared. The "perfect mother" is there for all to see; she becomes an ideal to believe in, and one that people both expect and internalize. The participants in my research often hear comments from social workers, law and justice officials, teachers, medical professionals, and clergy about the legitimacy and predominance of the ideal mother and the righteous downfall of the "bad" mother. Peers, co-workers, family, and friends also perpetuate concepts and expectations of motherhood that uphold patriarchal notions and expectations through commentary, free advice, or personal judgement. The message is clear: there is a correct way to be a mother, and those women who do not meet this standard are "bad."

Being labeled "bad" or "deviant" for not adopting the idealized standard of motherhood means living with very real consequences. The feminist mothers I interviewed know from personal experience how women are subjected to external pressure to conform to the dominant image of the ideal mother, and are punished when they do not. They spoke of suffering from feelings of inadequacy and guilt for not being "good" or "real" mothers when they have been unable to replicate, or find happiness in, the idolized stereotypical role of mother. Many verbalized feeling personally responsible for not obtaining the ideal, even though they are fully aware that it is both socially constructed and unrealistic. To illustrate, participants cite examples of raising their voices to their children, of not providing homemade baking for a social gathering, of not meeting teachers when requested to do so, and of not being able to attend a child's sporting event due to study or work commitments.

These feminist mothers also spoke of how characteristics and expectations associated with the ideal mother set them up to fail. The patriarchal definition of motherhood places women in a "no win" situation; the standard of motherhood is impractical and unreasonable, punishing those who fail to meet its criteria. Since their lives do not fit the prescribed mould of mother, many women experience painful consequences. For instance, mothers who are not partnered with men, who are financially impoverished, or who work for a living, are often judged by others to be "unfit" mothers.

Neire, a forty-one year-old lesbian of European and Jewish heritage, understands the realities of patriarchal motherhood. Recently divorced from her husband, the father of their teenage daughter and their ten- and six-year-old sons, Neire provides a critique of how patriarchal notions of motherhood set mothers up to lose:

> I think that society still sees mothers as being women who totally devote themselves to their kids. If the kid has a problem, you are completely tuned into that kid. And I mean, any variation on that is still seen as not being acceptable. In other words, the mother is still very much responsible for her kids and their actions and their behaviours and their whole being. And when your kid does something wrong, the mother is still blamed. That's still very prevalent.
>
> I think it boils down to this whole ideology surrounding the family; that the family has two people, opposite sexes, and the children. And they're fully enclosed, a supposedly fully-functioning family unit. And our society is still predicated on that. So if a woman finds herself in a position where she's not within that structure, the society only pays lip service to supports and that kind of thing.

But I think, given that this patriarchal model is still very much in existence, there are still a lot of women who are falling into this trap, and it just creates a hell of a lot of conflict and a hell of a lot of guilt, you know? I think it's very damaging. It's definitely damaging to mothers because it erodes our self-esteem and our self-confidence in our ability to be good mothers.

Like Rich and the other participants, Neire understands how the weight and "legitimacy" of patriarchy is able to dictate a standard of motherhood, and able to punish those who do not conform to its narrow definition and practice. Punishment is often devastating: the self-esteem and self-confidence of women and children can be shattered. Women often devalue themselves in order to put their children and families first. They may also profoundly limit their options due to abnegation. Many women endure isolation because they are unable to speak of the shame and guilt they experience for not living up to these unreasonable standards. Consequently, they can suffer depression and, in extreme circumstances, complete mental breakdowns and suicide attempts. As we know, children are often removed from mothers who are considered "bad" or "unfit" by government and other agencies.[8]

Liberating experiences of motherhood

The pressure to conform to the dominant model of motherhood and the consequences for non-compliance are very real. However, as Rich posits, patriarchal motherhood is not completely oppressive; there is room for women to practice agency, resistance, invention, and renewal within this institution:

What is astonishing, what can give us enormous hope and belief in a future in which the lives of women and children shall be mended and re-woven by women's hands, is all that we have managed to salvage, of ourselves, for our children, even within the destructiveness of the institution: the tenderness, the passion, the trust in our instincts, the evocation of a courage we did not know we owned, the detailed apprehension of another human existence, the full realization of the cost and precariousness of life. The mother's battle for her child—with sickness, with poverty, with war, with all the forces of exploitation and callousness that cheapen life—needs to become a common human battle, waged in love and in the passion for survival. But for this to happen, the institution of motherhood must be destroyed.

The changes required to make this possible reverberate into every part of the patriarchal system. To destroy the institution is not to abolish motherhood. It is to release the creation and sustenance of life into the same realm of decision, struggle, surprise, imagination, and conscious intelligence, as any other difficult, but freely chosen work.[9]

Feminist mothers live Rich's emancipatory vision of motherhood. Driven by their feminist consciousness, by their intense love for their children, and by their need to be true to themselves, to their families and to their parenting, they choose to mother in ways that challenge the status quo. By consciously resisting the restrictions placed on them by patriarchal motherhood, these feminist mothers put Rich's theory into practice. Some women, for example, openly reject the pressures and expectations placed upon them to reproduce the ideal of motherhood by parenting in ways that openly challenge conventional standards of motherhood. Others consciously use their socially-sanctioned position as mothers in subversive ways to teach their children to be critically conscious of, and to challenge, various forms of oppression that support patriarchy. Regardless of the strategies invented and utilized by these women as they live with the tension between the "institution" and "experience" of motherhood, they successfully challenge and bring about social change as Rich advocated more than a quarter century ago.

i. Overt strategies of resistance

Willow, a thirty-seven-year-old lesbian and lone parent of a ten-year-old girl, provides an example of how feminist mothers use strategies that openly and boldly challenge patriarchal motherhood. For Willow, mothering has meant making "conscious decisions and actions of dissidence." The act of birthing and solely raising a child, without any connection to a man, is a deliberate act of resistance to dominant conceptions and practices of mothering. Willow explains:

> I mean basically, in order to do this, I broke all the rules and I went about this in the most conscious manner that I knew at that time. Although, to be honest with you, because my consciousness has changed, I'd probably go about it differently now. But back ten years ago, I broke all the rules by making a choice to be a mother. Nobody told me I had to be a mother because I was married or that I had to get married in order to do this. I made choices for myself. So in the late 1980s and 1990s there are particular ways that you're suppose to be a mother and they include either: be married to somebody who is relatively wealthy and can allow you to stay home, or putting the kid in day care at the age of six weeks or as soon as your maternity leave runs out, and paying attention to the money issue more than to anything else and run out to work. And I did not do that.

I did not let myself be subjugated, as it were, by men. I'm not married now, and I never have been and no man ever called the shots in my home, nor did a man ever support me in any way. So that is really breaking the rules in the patriarchy. It is clearly the most holistic act of resistance that I have ever done and the most difficult.

By consciously choosing to become a mother and raise her daughter alone, Willow has experienced hardship, as well as great pleasure. Because she wanted to raise her child without the interference of others and was without the financial means to do so, Willow lived on social assistance for a few years. She often bartered with others, exchanging childcare and reading or singing lessons for goods and services. When her daughter reached school age, Willow chose to educate her at home, partly because she believed home schooling was the best option for her daughter at the time and partly because, as a certified teacher, she was qualified to do so. Willow returned to work part-time in the labor force when her daughter, at the age of eight, entered the public school system after expressing a desire and demonstrating a need to do so.

When I last spoke with Willow in 1998, she was still openly challenging patriarchal notions of the motherhood. Finding it difficult to deal with some of her pre-teenaged daughter's behavior, she decided to call upon her network of friends for support. With the help of a close friend, who is also a feminist mother, Willow was able to effectively deal with the unwanted behavior of her daughter. For a few months the two women shared mothering responsibilities, allowing Willow and her daughter to remain strongly and positively connected but also providing the space for them to deal with the issue at hand. For a few days, or even a couple of weeks at a time, Willow's daughter would live with her social mother. Since both households were in the same neighborhood and the lines of communication were open, all three were in touch with each other on a regular basis. "Family meetings" were frequently held to discuss the situation and to work through difficulties as they arose. Within four months the disruptive behavior had been dealt with in a loving and effective manner, and Willow and her daughter were living together full-time.

Through successfully creating her own solution to what Willow believed would most likely have been considered a major concern by others, she has kept herself from being labeled an "unfit" mother and from possibly losing her daughter to the state. Willow not only addresses the needs of her daughter while keeping her family intact when she creates an alternative model of motherhood by expanding her family to include another woman/mother when necessary, she also challenges the patriarchal model of motherhood that is made up of the heterosexual, nuclear family. Continually inventing ways to parent outside of the patriarchal standard also means that Willow enjoys a level of "freedom and strength" that she says she would not have experienced had she conformed to patriarchal methods of dealing with a "problem" daughter.

Bringing down patriarchy is clearly a tricky and lengthy endeavor that requires numerous strategies and actions in various locations. For many participants, using their socially sanctioned position as mother is an effective tactic to challenge patriarchal constructs and notions of motherhood. The feminist mothers I spoke with see mothering, as does Rich, as a significant site of resistance to patriarchy. Under the cover of the institution of motherhood, they use the energy, focus, and dedication that women have always used in going to battle for their children to destroy the institution of motherhood. In doing so, their effective and subversive activity both challenges patriarchy and often goes unnoticed.

ii. Subversive strategies of resistance

Deb, a thirty-five-year-old, heterosexual mother of a seven-year-old boy speaks openly about her strategy of using subversive strategies to contest patriarchy when she says:

> Someone can look at me on the surface and go, "O.K. There's a woman who's chosen to be a mother. Good, patriarchy likes that. Good, good." They don't have a clue! I have the ability to transform what I perceive the role to be, to take it on, to claim it, and to just create it. I'm a mother in my own image in the absence of a role model, or someone who's telling me how to do it. I guess the thing that I was amazed at was just how wonderful I find my experience of mothering to be in a non-patriarchal way.

Deb knows she is considered a "good mother" because she fits, to some degree, the conventional notions of a mother being in a monogamous, long-term relationship with the father of her children. She uses this belief in who she is as a mother to her own advantage; she quietly raises a son who is consciously aware of social injustice caused by patriarchy, racism, homophobia, agism, class bias, and capitalism. Deb recognizes that to be able to subvert motherhood she needs to be aware of what patriarchy expects from her as a mother and to have an understanding of how she can effectively manipulate and challenge those same expectations to her advantage.

Carol, aged forty-five, understands patriarchal motherhood and chooses to challenge it in her mothering. While she is the lone-parent of her ten-year-old biological son and her thirteen-year-old adopted niece, she is also actively involved in mothering the three adult children of her previous male partner. Carol speaks candidly about her understanding about the social expectations placed on her as a mother that she developed from her experience of mothering five children:

What they would have me do is raise my girl children and my boy children
in a specific way, so that when they're adults, that's the way they are.
That, to them, is truth. Patriarchal society dictates me to beat their spirit
out of them.

Rather than follow the patriarchal dictate of beating the spirit out of her
children, Carol chooses to help her children develop without forcing gender
stereotypes upon them. She actively encourages the nurturing and non-
competitive tendencies of her son, while supporting her daughter in her pursuits
of maths and science, which are often considered to be "male" subjects. By
showing her children how to follow their own interests and by treating them with
respect, Carol supports their development of autonomy and individuality. Carol
tells me:

I have always shown a great amount of respect for my children because
they've always been human beings to me. Feminism has given me the
freedom to talk to my children as if they were human beings, instead of
"I'm superior."

The patriarchal society is very competitive. Because I'm a feminist I
have absolutely no desire to compete with my children. So, consequently,
I can tell them the secret recipe to the rhubarb pie, because hopefully
they will end up making it better than I do.

I created a world where competition doesn't go on in my house.
They didn't have to fall into that machismo/feminine world, you know.
They have to struggle through it, and it is a struggle, yes. But there's a
different way.

Providing a non-competitive, loving, and respectful environment is the strategy
Carol uses to teach her children that there are different models and ways of
being male and female in the world. By using her power and responsibility as a
mother, Carol provides a milieu that is supportive of her children's personal
development and teaches them alternative ways of being than those demonstrated
in the media, popular culture or in various social institutions.

Like Carol, Beverly rejects the socially-prescribed standards of motherhood
and chooses to raise her children in ways that develop their self-confidence and
self-governance. Beverly, a forty-four year-old bisexual, is the lone-parent of two
daughters in their late teens. She speaks of how she tries to live out her principles
of fairness, equality and openness in her parenting. Rather than replicate
hierarchical power structures presumed to be the basis of parent and child
relationships, Beverly consciously shares the power she has as an adult and a
mother with her two daughters. She notes:

Because of my principles that I hold, I've had to treat my children in a
equal fashion from the beginning so that they have always known that
they have the right to express themselves, that they have the right to
say no, and that we could engage in a dialogue about the issue as opposed
to me wielding power over them, and that's still very important to me.

Not only does Beverly share her authority as an adult with her children, she
also encourages her daughters to see how all people, including themselves, are
accountable for their own choices and personal conduct. This has been most
difficult at times, especially when one underage daughter began to drink alcohol.
This action triggered a number of issues for Beverly because her father was an
alcoholic, and it raised concerns about the illegal behavior of her child. Through
many hours of talking, often late at night and into the early hours of the morning,
Beverly and her daughter came to understand why the drinking had begun and
what it meant to each one of them. Within a few months, and much to Beverly's
relief, her daughter freely chose to stop drinking.

Beverly believes her daughter's decision came about from the open, honest,
and non-threatening communication she continues to have with her children.
Rather than using threats and punishment to try to curve or stop the drinking
behavior, Beverly chose to talk with her daughter until they came to a place of
deep understanding. Holding her daughter accountable for her behavior, both
when she drank and chose to stop drinking, was tough and scary. Beverly believes
showing respect for her daughter's autonomy throughout the entire process of
dealing with the situation, even when Beverly disagreed with the choices her
daughter was making, helped to resolve the problem and allowed her daughter
to become fully responsible for herself.

Carol and Beverly are not alone. All interviewees, including Neire, Willow,
and Deb, speak of the importance of teaching children to take responsibility for
their own conduct, as well as respecting their choices and decisions. In doing so,
power within the family is shared and people are held accountable for their own
actions. This practice directly challenges patriarchal family structures that assume
a hierarchical formation where women and children have less power, voice, and
autonomy than men. By sharing power and exercising personal accountability
within the family, the patriarchal familial structure is no longer present or effective,
and respect for individuals, both within and outside the family, is developed and
practiced.

Within the domain of motherhood, feminists actively engage their children
in critical thinking. For example, they use watching television, going to movies,
and seeing plays as forums to look at and discuss the power dynamics of the
larger world. They also use situations in the media and in the lives of friends and
acquaintances to discuss the ways in which people are oppressed by racism,

class bias, sexism, homophobia, and notions of ability.[10] Bringing issues of poverty, consumerism, and environmental devastation to the attention of children is another way of explaining the complex way in which oppression works. Shopping for groceries brings about conversations on the politics of boycotting products from particular countries because of environmental destruction, the exploitation of migrant labor, or oppressive political regimes. These teachable moments are used by feminist mothers whenever and where ever they arise.

Equally important in the work of challenging patriarchy while within the sanctity of motherhood, is taking risks in more overt ways and exposing children to public and communal political activism. It is not unusual for feminist mothers to take their children to marches organized around "Take Back the Night," "Gay Pride," or "Reproductive Choice." Visiting protest villages at the provincial legislative grounds, being part of collective student action against increasing tuition costs, participating in play-for-peace workshops and other anti-war protests, or showing support for child care workers and universal day care by joining marches are public demonstrations that feminist mothers have ensured their children have been a part of. They believe that because they are feminist mothers they must participate and take their children to these public and collective events.

Regardless of the ways in which feminist mothers parent, they use their positions within motherhood to both overtly and covertly challenge patriarchy by teaching their children to be critical of the power structures and to be aware of the damage social injustice does to the lives of people. By doing so, they raise the consciousness of their children and challenge patriarchy.

Conclusion

Feminist mothers recognize, as Rich theorizes, how motherhood is both an institution and an experience. In honoring their commitment to feminism and to raising their children from that perspective, they successfully negotiate the tension between the two. Whether like Willow, who calls upon others in her community to help her when she is unable to effectively parent by herself, or like the other women who use the cover of motherhood to connect with and to consciously educate their children, these feminist mothers, as Rich suggests, are actively destroying the institution of motherhood with their "conscious intelligence" and feminist praxis.

Notes

1. Some writers—such as Patricia Hill Collins, *Black feminist thought: Knowledge, consciousness and the politics of empowerment* (New York: Routledge, 1991); Marjorie Hill, "Child-rearing attitudes of black lesbian mothers" in *Lesbian psychologies: Explorations*

and challenges, edited by Boston Lesbian Psychologies Collective (Chicago: University of Illinois Press, 1987), and Sandra Pollack, "Lesbian parents: Claiming our visibility in *Women-defined motherhood*, edited by J. Knowles and E. Cole (London: Hawarth Press, 1990)—do address how those women who are marginalized due to racism and heterosexism find empowerment in mothering.

2. These restrictions also influence my partner and the father of our child. For the purpose of this chapter, however, I restrict my discussion to the influence of motherhood on mothers and children.

3. Adrienne Rich, *Of woman born: Motherhood as experience and institution* (New York: Norton, 1967: 274–275).

4. Ann Dally, in *Inventing motherhood: The consequence of an ideal* (London: Burnett Books, 1982), notes that the concept of motherhood first originated in the Victorian era and has since developed to include the doctrine of the idealized mother, wife, and woman. Shari Thurer, in *The myths of motherhood: How culture reinvents the good mother* (New York: Penguin, 1994) and Betsy Wearing, in *The ideology of motherhood: A study of Sydney suburban mothers* (Sydney: George Allen and Unwin, 1984), also address the social construction of motherhood in their discussion of the ideology of motherhood.

5. Ray Richmond, in *TV moms: An illustrated guide* (New York: TV Books, 2000) profiles over fifty TV moms, both good and bad.

6. Marlee Kline's "Complicating the ideology of motherhood: Child welfare law and First Nation women" in *Open boundaries: A Canadian women's studies reader,* edited by B. Crow and L. Gotell (Toronto: Prentice Hall and Bacon Canada, 2000: 194–204), provides a good description and analysis of the "ideal mother".

7. For example, in Canada (1996), 19% of all families with children were female-headed one-parent families (Statistics Canada: Women in Canada 2000, Catalogue No. 89-503-XPE, 2000).

8. This is especially true of lesbian mothers, racialized mothers, and economically impoverished mothers. See, for example: Katherine Arnup, "Lesbian Mothers and Child Custody" in *Gender and society: Creating a Canadian women's sociology*, edited by Arlene Tigar McLaren (Toronto: Copp Clark Pitnam, 1988: 245–256); Patricia Hill Collins, *Black feminist thought: Knowledge, consciousness and the politics of empowerment* (New York: Routledge, 1991); and Sharie Thurer, *The myths of motherhood: How culture reinvents the good mother* (New York: Penguin, 1994).

9. Adrienne Rich, *Of woman born: Motherhood as experience and institution* (New York: Norton, 1967: 280).

10. The term "patriarchy" and words ending in "ism" are used by some mothers to explain various forms of oppression to their children, while other mothers choose to speak about the concepts and realities of social injustices without using feminist language.

Chapter Two

RESISTANCE AS A SITE OF EMPOWERMENT

THE JOURNEY AWAY FROM MATERNAL SACRIFICE

Erika Horwitz

Many mothers today believe that the word "mother" is synonymous with sacrifice. A close examination of the history of motherhood[1] reveals that mothers have not always been sacrificial, and that the way women have practiced mothering has changed dramatically over the centuries. For example, during the seventeenth century, sending newborn infants to a wet-nurse for up to three years was viewed as beneficial to children. In colonial times, fathers were the ones who rocked, walked, and cuddled their infants, and fatherhood carried the value and importance attributed to motherhood today. It was not until the eighteenth and nineteenth centuries when the responsibility of taking care of children was assigned exclusively to mothers.[2] During the late nineteenth and early twentieth centuries, the Industrial Revolution led to major social changes that drastically changed the traditional structure of the family in which fathers, mothers, and children had worked together in the production of domestic goods.[3] During the Industrial Revolution, large numbers of families moved to urban centres, and fathers stopped participating in home production in order to work in the factories. These changes worried moral reformers who promoted the idea that mothers should continue to remain at home, should avoid paid employment, and should become the main caretakers of children. It was during this historical period that the mainstream image of a mother became that of the "True Woman" who was virtuous, gentle, all loving, devoted, and whose interests were expected to focus on creating the best refuge for her family and on raising her children with extra care.[4] Hence, the current image of the all-sacrificial, dedicated, committed mother whose needs rarely matter was born.

In the past 100 years, the North American social fabric and family life have changed significantly. One might expect that the expectations of mothers would be different now. However, mothers today continue to live under the oppression of a mothering discourse that promotes unconditional love, sacrifice, and the exclusive care of children.[5] The burgeoning literature on the topic of mothering and motherhood has addressed and documented that mothers feel pressured to be "perfect mothers," and that this has an impact on their well being and their lives.[6] Even though some mothers are actively challenging the dominant discourse on mothering, literature that explores this type of resistance by mothers is limited. Although it appears that many mothers (and society at large) continue to believe that they are the best sources of affection and guidance in their children's lives,[7] there are other mothers who are searching for alternatives to this dominant discourse.[8] In this chapter, I discuss how a group of mothers redefined mothering as a site of empowerment in a process of resistance to the dominant discourse on mothering. The chapter borrows from my doctoral dissertation to illustrate how mothers can deviate from the dominant discourse in a manner that, although challenging at times, may be empowering to them. My dissertation was aimed at exploring the experience of a group of women who believed they were resisting the dominant discourse on mothering. I wanted to explore how these women experienced mothering, and how the social context influenced this experience and their resistance.

The framework for the study was based on discourse theory.[9] Discourse can be defined as a specific structure of statements, terms, and categories that are historically, socially, and institutionally specific.[10] Like stories, they "create a communal understanding of power in relationships and appropriate rules of conduct."[11] There are many messages within the current dominant discourse on mothering.[12] This discourse posits that being a mother is all that a woman needs to feel fulfilled. It also suggests that mothers are solely responsible for the physical, spiritual, and psychological well being of their children and, therefore, are held responsible (i.e., blamed) for their children's difficulties.[13] Being burdened with such responsibility puts mothers under pressure to be perfect mothers,[14] and can engender strong feelings of guilt and inadequacy.[15] In addition, the dominant discourse also portrays mothers as icons of sacrifice and unconditional love, which leads to the expectation that they will be ever-present, all giving, and selfless beings.[16] Finally, the working/professional woman discourse also influences mothers to varying degrees.[17] Sharon Hays's study on the contradictions between the discourses of work and mothering suggests that mothers who work are torn by their obligations at work and at home, whereas mothers who stay home often feel inadequate because they are not pursuing a career.[18] Furthermore, the dominant discourse on mothering pressures them to consider their children's needs always before their own so that women who try to integrate their work and mother roles often feel strained.[19] In sum, the dominant discourse promotes an ideal that is impossible to achieve, one that often leaves mothers feeling inadequate, deficient, and guilty.

A close examination of social discourses reveals that there are a multitude of them. Some of these discourses tend to be more dominant and central while others are more marginal or alternative.[20] Because of this multiplicity people are able to note contradictions and gaps within dominant discourses, which allows them to challenge their prevailing messages. Some people are able to resist society's dominant discourses by drawing on alternative discourses. It is in this manner that people are agents in their own lives rather than passive victims of discourses. For example, feminists have engaged in agentic activity by drawing on discourses of equality and human rights to challenge aspects of the dominant discourse. They have critiqued motherhood as an oppressive institution that limits mothers to the private sphere and keeps them from influencing public processes or policies that affect their lives.[21]

Research on the topic of mothering/motherhood suggests that mothers are influenced by a dominant mothering discourse, and that this has significant consequences for them. The dominant discourse, the expectation that mothers should be ever-present and available (whether at home or at work), their paid work obligations, the pragmatic need to support and contribute to their families economically, and the lack of community support, create a tension that complicates a mother's ability to negotiate her way through motherhood without feeling guilty, deficient, depressed, or stressed.[22] However, as I found by conducting this study, not all women subscribe to the beliefs and expectations of the dominant discourse to the degree that they are promoted and perpetuated in Western society.[23] Only a limited number of studies have examined the process of resistance by mothers,[24] and only one, by Tuula Gordon, focused on resistance to the social institution of motherhood. Gordon's ground-breaking study explored mothering from the perspective of feminist mothers. Her study suggests that women do resist the societal expectations set forth by the dominant discourse.[25] However, her study was limited in its focus on women who consider themselves feminist. In this chapter, I intend to build on Gordon's results by exploring how mothers who are resistant, and who may or may not see themselves as feminist, experience mothering.

I interviewed fifteen women whose ages ranged from twenty-three to forty-six years old. Their income levels were between $15,000 and over $75,000 a year. Their educational levels varied from one year of college to PhD student. Three worked full time, seven worked and/or went to school part-time, and five were stay-at-home mothers. All but two were in heterosexual relationships, two were single, and one was gay. The interviews were transcribed verbatim. A hermeneutic, critical analysis was conducted in order to identify the main themes in the participants' narratives. This type of analysis considers behaviour and experience within the context in which they occur. In this chapter, I discuss how these women resisted, how they experienced this resistance, and the implications of these findings in relation to feminist and empowered mothering.

What is resistance?

Some of the mothering literature portrays mothers as powerless victims of the dominant discourse. Many of the publications that offer a critique of the institution of motherhood portray mothers as passive victims who may have no recourse against such a powerful force. However, human beings have historically resisted societal oppression,[26] and mothers are no exception.[27] For the purposes of the study, resistance was defined as the effort of oppressed groups to challenge and act against aspects of the dominant discourse.[28] The women I interviewed perceived themselves as resistant to the common myths (or beliefs) about perfect mothers. They volunteered to share their stories and to describe not only how they resisted but also how resistance impacted upon their mothering experiences. The findings of the study suggest that the process of resistance is complex, and that women who resist the dominant discourse do so to different degrees. Furthermore, the study revealed that a mother's resistance varies not only in relation to how many aspects of the discourse she resists but also in relation to how many aspects of the discourse she adheres to. In other words, some women in the study were more resistant than others. Resistance, then, may fall along a continuum; it does not appear to be a simple process but one that entails the negotiation of many different, and often conflicting, discourses. Finally, the complexity of the process of resistance is also reflected in the degrees of empowerment versus struggle that each participant experienced.

The many faces of resistance

The women who participated in the study resisted the dominant discourse in a variety of ways. Sometimes their resistance was not manifested in their practices but in their ideologies and perception of themselves. It is important to note that the number and types of myths that each participant resisted varied significantly. Moreover, not only the degree and quality of resistance varied but also the extent to which they struggled to resist. Some found resistance to be a relatively smooth process while others found it challenging and difficult.

All the participants in the study expressed that it was important for them to meet their own needs or pursue their own interests. This view challenged the myth that mothers should always be sacrificial. The participants' interests included athletics, graduate school, writing, taking time out, work, exercise, mundane activities, and so on. The degree to which they were able to meet their needs or pursue their interests varied. For example, one of the participants said,

> I think that in order to be whole, you have to be healthy and happy and take care of yourself physically, and mentally, emotionally, before you can give to your spouse, and then as a couple you give to your children.

Others found "community" in friends, family, daycare, and baby-sitting co-ops, which allowed them to pursue their careers or take some time for themselves. Some participants explained that they believed in meeting their needs and pursuing their interests but that they found it difficult to do so because they lacked social supports. In other words, whether these women were able to take care of their needs or not was contingent on the types of supports they had. Those whose partners, family, friends, and/or good daycare providers were involved had more opportunities to meet their needs with greater ease than those who did not.

Furthermore, resistance for this group of women was contingent upon their children not being negatively impacted from the choices they made. In other words, as long as they perceived their choices not to be harmful to their children, these women resisted because it benefitted *them*. As one mother said,

I could continue [to do] what made me happy, because it wasn't in my view, it wasn't affecting them. As long as it wasn't adversely affecting them, it felt OK to do what I had to do.

This is one instance where these women struggled to reconcile the dominant discourse with their alternative views. Furthermore, the complexity of the process of resistance is reflected on how they had also redefined what they believed could be damaging to children. For example, a young mother in the study described how she chose to paint her nails while her baby cried in her crib for a few minutes. She did not believe this could harm the baby. She said,

I have needs and I have wants … in the mornings when the baby is crying, I paint my fingernails because I want my fingernails painted. I don't think she is going to go crazy, or become a sociopath because her mom painted her fingernails.

Thus in destabilizing the dominant discourse, these mothers redefined not only their roles as mothers, but also what they believed could be harmful to their children and how their own actions could impact them. Consequently, they were able to develop alternative views of what children need, often seeing them as resilient.

Unlike the myth that posits that being a mother is fulfilling on its own, most participants in the study believed that even though mothering is an important endeavour, mothers also need other experiences to feel fulfilled. Some of them explained that there is no one thing in their lives that is fulfilling on its own, not even their children; they needed variety to feel satisfied. One participant said, "I do not think that any one thing in life makes you whole." Some found that their initial experiences as mothers were so difficult that they found themselves seeking other activities where they felt more competent and fulfilled. For example, a college professional explained that motherhood, particularly in the early stages, did not allow her to feel competent because she was unable to soothe her baby who cried constantly. For her, mothering during that period did not fulfill her needs and, therefore, she returned to work in order to feel competent. She said,

> If I was going to love that baby, have any quality time with that baby, I had to get away from that baby. I had to meet my own needs, and my own needs of being competent.

The women in the study also expressed that being around their children *all* the time was not necessary for their children's well-being or for them to be good mothers. A graduate student said,

> I don't think you have to be with your child constantly for a strong bond to develop. I think as long as you're there frequently and as long as you are loving and consistent … there is going to be a strong bond.

Another participant stated, "I don't think that a mother has to be around 100 percent of the time to be a good mother." Most of them agreed that they wanted to be around for their children but not *all* the time.

These women also resisted the dominant discourse by involving others in their children's upbringing. They did not see themselves as the only possible caregivers in their children's lives, in fact, most of them resisted the idea that mothers are the best and only good caregivers of children. Four of the participants had relinquished the primary care giving role to their husbands/partners. These women were pursuing careers and education while their husbands were at home taking care of their children. In addition, other participants reported that their husbands were equal partners (or co-parents) in raising their children. A single mother who did not have a partner with whom to share the responsibility involved several trusted friends and daycare providers in helping her raise her children. What is unique to these women is that they did not believe they should be the only ones to care for their children, which translated into decreased feelings of guilt when they were not home with their children. For them, sharing this responsibility not only freed them to pursue other interests but also allowed their children to learn from, and be close to, other adult figures.

It is important to note that all but four of the participants did not like leaving their children in daycare centers. These women explained that they preferred to involve friends and family because these people have an emotional and personal investment in the well being of their children. They emphasized that the way society is structured does not allow for a natural community experience that includes various loving adults collaborating in the upbringing of children. These participants explained that this lack of community often leads them to actively seek ways to create community for themselves and their children. An athlete and student explained that because her partner travels "off and on" for nine months of the year, she has had to seek a community for herself and her children. She said, "I believe in community parenting!" For example, she has participated in babysitting co-ops, she often asks her family to help her, and she organizes pot-luck dinners. She explained that she has never paid someone to take care of her children.

A mother of two also emphasized how living within a community where the children could go out and play freely without needing parental supervision at all times was ideal for her. She lived in co-operative housing in Vancouver,

> We lived in a co-op with enclosed courtyards. And it was really like the best possible set up for little kids. Because from a really early age, they would just go out the door. And, I would kind of check in on them, or check up on them. Because they would just be off doing their own thing. And that was the norm, all of us did that. There were so many eyes on the courtyard, and the courtyard was enclosed that, it was fabulous. It was really a nice safe place.

She explained that she experienced how this community environment made her feel connected and supported. Unlike the majority of mothers in this study, this woman explained that she has always felt comfortable leaving her children with others including babysitters: "And from a very early age I left Ian with baby sitters, and always thought that that was a very healthy thing." This instance illustrates the range of beliefs that mothers who practice resistance may hold. It suggests that resistance may be about questioning the status quo and about having choices rather than an about every mother resisting the same discursive myths or making the same alternative choices.

Another key mode of resistance for these women was to actively engage in questioning the expectations that were placed on them by others and by society. For instance, a stay-at-home mother found the initial period of mothering so difficult (her son would not stop crying) that she began searching for ways to make sense of her experience. She read the feminist literature and began to question the social forces that affected her experience (e.g., the lack of community for mothers who choose to stay home, the views that mothers who stay home are "doormats," sacrificial, and so on). She concluded that she is not a "doormat" and that the reason why mothers have to sacrifice so much is because society isolates and burdens them to take care of their children on their own. She said,

"I am not willing to compromise my right to have close and connected relationships with my children," and explained that the only solution to freeing mothers from oppression is to "overthrow patriarchy." Other participants questioned traditional roles for men and women, choosing to depart from them by relinquishing the main caregiver role to their partners and/or by being the main breadwinners. These are two examples of many that illustrate a process of questioning and critiquing the dominant discourse on mothering. For these mothers, this process of ideological work was challenging.[29] Although they derived a sense of empowerment from doing so, their commitment to meeting both their own and their children's needs always entailed reflection and pressure to make choices that were beneficial to both.

Another mode of resistance for a few of these women involved challenging mainstream parenting practices that they considered to be very individualistic. Instead, they chose to practice mothering that was child focused and/or that involved some aspects of "attachment parenting" (attachment parenting is based on the philosophy advanced by Sears and Sears).[30] A part-time school learning assistant, for example, explained that she believes that mothers and fathers should focus their attention on the children for the first five years of life. Interestingly, choosing to parent in this manner led her, as well as others, to practice a higher degree of intensive mothering. They, however, explained that they were not traditional, sacrificial mothers, but that their choices to practice attachment parenting resulted in intensive mothering only because society is not supportive of mothers and because in individualistic societies, mothers are isolated without the help and support of a community. Having access to a close-knit community, they thought, would free them to meet their needs and to have some time away from their children.

In contrast to the dominant discourse that suggests mothers are to blame for their children's difficulties, all the participants stated that they do not feel solely responsible for how their children turn out. Most of the participants felt that they should not take all the credit or blame for their children's behaviours. They believed that mothers are only one of many factors that influence their children's development. For example, a single mother said,

> Some studies are saying, the parents are actually like thirteen percent of control over the future of the kids. I mean, that was the lowest number I saw, but that was the one I liked the best! (laughs) I only have thirteen percent of control.

The other participants shared similar beliefs. They believed that, among other factors, a human being's biological makeup is a strong influence on how children interact with the world. For instance, a stay-at-home mother stated that her son had been diagnosed with ADHD and that she did not feel responsible for that. Many echoed another participant who said, "Nature is so much ingrained, they will develop the way they are going to develop." These women clearly challenged the idea that mothers are to blame for anything that goes wrong with their children. They had freed themselves from some of the burdens that society had placed on them by acknowledging the complexity of human development.

Finally, in challenging the idea that the only emotion mothers ever feel toward their children is love, some participants expressed that, although they love their children deeply, they did not feel loving towards them *all* the time. One participant explained that when her first son was small she shared her frustrations with other mothers at a parent/baby group:

> It's kind of like a play group but much more organized. And, it was one of those groups, then I looked at everybody, I looked at the parents, and instructors, and I said, "You know, I don't like to be a mom all the time." The myth that mothers are all wonderful and all loving, I mean I think it is possible to love your child completely. It's completely possible to love your child unconditionally and to be loving, and not necessarily act in a loving way all the time, you know what I mean?

Some explained that children can be very difficult to care for at times, and they acknowledged that they do not always feel or have felt loving towards their children. Furthermore, for some it became important to resist by breaking the silence about the negative aspects of motherhood. They felt that by speaking about the dark side of motherhood, they could help other women normalize this aspect of being a mother.

This section summarized the most significant ways in which these women resisted the dominant discourse on mothering. The findings of the study further suggested that these women's experiences as mothers were impacted by the choices they made and the ideologies they adhered to. In every case, seeing themselves as resistant was empowering and beneficial. The next section describes how resistance impacted this group of mothers.

Resistance as a site of empowerment

The choice to resist resulted in an experience of empowerment and liberation for these women. This empowerment manifested itself in a sense of pride and conviction, in their experience of added freedom, in feelings of empowerment and integrity, in seeing their children doing well, and in feeling little or no guilt. These women felt good about how they had chosen to mother. They did not believe that they should have to follow the social expectations placed on them as mothers and that, as one participant explained, mothering this way is empowering:

> I had to take care of myself here … to me it has been empowering. I have always thought that it was the right thing to do that. That my needs and my career and my happiness, if I was going to be a good mother, that I have to fulfill that side of me.

These mothers expressed that mothering by resisting the dominant discourse meant they stayed true to themselves, true to who they are, and that this was a liberating and empowering experience for them. This experience of empowerment was connected to a sense of pride and conviction. One of them explained, "mothering this way is true to me, it has come from my essence." Another one said,

> I feel that what I'm doing is making my own path … because if I did it any other way, I'd feel like a complete hypocrite. You know this is how I feel, this is what I believe. If I do it any other way, I would just be buying into fakeness.

Mothering their way led these women to experience a "good quality of life." They felt that making the choices that worked best for them rather than to serve society's expectations was key to their well being. One participant expressed this sentiment well,

> And it's enabled me, I think, to have a higher quality of life than I would have had … because you only live for life, and I have to be happy in that life. I have to mother the way I mother to be happy.

Furthermore, not viewing themselves as the only possible caregivers of their children was a liberating experience for them. For many of these women sharing the parental or caregiver responsibilities with others allowed them to have the guilt-free experience of taking care of their needs. One graduate student mother explained, "it is easier this way than any other possible way because I get the best of both worlds, I get to be a cross between a mother and a father."

In addition, by being convinced in many instances of their choices, many of these women did not experience guilt. A twenty-three year old single mother said,

> I love the freedom that I give myself. I don't have the guilty mamma feeling. You know, I live by my convictions and I am very proud of myself for that.

Many of the participants explained that they have experienced guilt in the past, but that challenging the expectations that society has placed on them and arriving at their own conclusions and choices has, for the most part, freed them from experiencing guilt. Only two participants emphasized feeling guilty in relation to their current mothering but for most of them, guilt was not central to their mothering experiences. Thus, the findings of the study suggest that mothering by resisting the dominant discourse may decrease the degree of maternal guilt that has been reported in the literature.[31]

One interesting finding of the study was that for the women who chose to resist by practicing attachment parenting,[32] mothering resulted in very intensive mothering practices. This finding was surprising given that one could assume that resistance to an oppressive discourse would lead to more freedom. This was not the case for a few of the mothers in the study. What is interesting about these women is that even though they were engaging in a process of intensive mothering, they still derived a sense of empowerment by simply *perceiving* themselves as resistant. This perception was sufficient for them to reap some of the rewards of being resistant, such as feeling good about themselves, feeling pride, conviction, empowerment, and reduced guilt. Furthermore, questioning and holding alternative ideologies led these women to feel they had more power over their lives and to believe that they had choices. In other words, they believed that they did not *have* to follow the status quo and that they were agents who made the choices best suited to them and their families. Thus, it appears that in resisting, the empowerment these women derive from perceiving themselves as resistant influences their sense of self and self-esteem, which may promote further resistance.

At the same time that these mothers found that resistance was empowering, many of them expressed that this process was challenging and entailed ideological work. They often found it difficult to locate themselves within a society that punishes any deviation from the mothering ideal. Interestingly, these women identified other mothers as being the ones who were most critical and judgmental. For example, many of the participants complained about how other mothers in mother–baby groups or in playgrounds were often the ones pressuring each other to conform to the mainstream societal expectations. Given this pressure to conform, resistance often resulted in a certain degree of strategizing for these women. They often found it difficult to interact with those who were opposed to their alternative mothering practices. This strategizing translated on the one hand into activism and speaking up to educate others about their choices, and on the other into isolation and silence to avoid rejection or criticism. Finally, part of the challenge for these women was also to find ways to juggle between meeting their own and their children's needs. Many did not always find it easy to balance between the two, but because they were committed to themselves as much as to their children, they made efforts to avoid always sacrificing their needs, which often resulted in intense ideological work.

Conclusions

In challenging the dominant discourse, these resistant, empowered mothers redefined their roles as mothers and the meaning they attached to motherhood. In order to achieve this goal, they often questioned the status quo in a dialectical process in which they destabilized the hegemonic discourse on mothering by drawing on alternative discourses. Interestingly, while they resisted and redefined their roles as mothers, these women were still being influenced by the dominant discourse on mothering. For instance, they were opposed to leaving their children at daycare, which reflects their belief in the myth that attachment can only occur from those close to the child, and that going to daycare can potentially harm a child's self-esteem. Thus, resisting led these women to navigate between the dominant discourse and alternative discourses in a process that was empowering to them even when some of their beliefs adhered to the dominant discourse.

The type of resistant, empowered mothering that these women practiced involved agentic power; practicing mothering with a sense of personal agency was central to their resistance. These women positioned themselves as critical, independent thinkers who, by drawing on alternative discourses and engaging in ideological work, questioned and critiqued certain social ideas and structures. This process led them to make more satisfying personal and mothering choices while engaging in practices that reflected their agentic power. In other words, these women exercised their social power by actively constructing their own views and, therefore, their own practices.

Furthermore, similar to the feminist mothers in Gordon's (1990) study, these mothers did not see themselves as "downtrodden, depressed victims of circumstances; [or as] passive recipients of society's dictums."[33] However, unlike the women in Gordon's study who drew from feminist theory to construct their ideologies, not all the participants in this study did so, at least consciously. Many of the mothers in the study did position themselves as feminist, but equally, many did not. In many instances, it was the practice of mothering itself, and not a feminist ideology, that drove them to resist. For example, several of the participants found that their initial experience as mothers made them feel incompetent, deficient, and often angry and resentful. In their case, it was this experience that triggered them to question the popular literature on mothering, or the myths that surrounded their mothering experience. This process of questioning and critiquing resulted in the process of resistance for this group of mothers. In other instances, the participants mentioned their mothers as having modeled self-respect and independent thinking, therefore, encouraging them to be critical, independent thinkers. Thus, resistance for many of the participants in this study was not triggered by a feminist ideology but by other factors. It is important, however, to note that even though they may have not identified feminism as being influential, these women's context has inevitably been influenced by it. The power of feminist thought has influenced societal beliefs about women, women's rights, and equality, and references to these discourses were present in most of the participants' narratives.

Finally, resistant, empowered mothering appears to be about an enhanced sense of self. By engaging in a process of questioning and by positioning themselves as critical thinkers and arriving at their own conclusions, these women protected themselves from the degree of self-doubt that other mothers reportedly experience.[34] Seeing themselves as agents rather than victims led them to experience a positive view of themselves as mothers and women. It seems reasonable to suggest that both feminist mothers, as well as empowered mothers who may not consider themselves feminist, may indeed experience an enhanced sense of self.

In conclusion, resistant, empowered mothering is about *the mother*; it is about making herself count as much as her children (when possible); it is about being part of the equation; and about making choices that are not only beneficial to her children but also to *her*. It is essential to consider that empowered, resistant mothering is about choice and not about uncovering the "True," right way to mother. In carrying out my research and in writing about it, I do not intend to promote yet another grand narrative about how women should mother, but rather to suggest that deconstructing the dominant discourse and finding alternative ways of mothering may allow women to release some of the burden that society has placed on them, so they may achieve a sense of agency and empowerment from their experiences as mothers. Furthermore, I would suggest that empowered mothering should not only be about choice but also about acceptance and respect among mothers. It seems that it is often mothers themselves who police other mothers into compliance with a discourse that is both oppressive and limiting. My hope is that as mothers learn to be more accepting of other mothers, a sisterhood of sorts can begin to emerge, and that as a united sisterhood we can continue to challenge societal ideals that are rarely accessible and impossible to achieve.

Notes

1. S.L. Thurer, *The myths of motherhood: How culture reinvents the good mother* (New York, NY: Penguin Book, 1994).
2. K. Arnup, *Education for motherhood* (Toronto: University of Toronto Press, 1994). C.R. Comacchio, *The infinite bonds of family* (Toronto: University of Toronto Press, 1999).

3. C.R. Comacchio, *The infinite bonds of family.*

4. S.L. Thurer, *The myths of motherhood.*

5. S. Coontz, *The way we never were* (New York: Basic Books, 1992); D. Eyer, *Motherguilt: How our culture blames mothers for what is wrong with society* (Toronto: Random House, 1996). S. Hays, *The cultural contradictions of motherhood* (New Haven, CT: Yale University Press, 1996).

6. C. Bobel, *The paradox of natural mothering* (Philadelphia: Temple University Press, 2002). S.E. Chase and M.F. Rogers, *Mothers and children: Feminist analyses and personal narratives* (New Brunswick, NJ: Rutgers University Press, 2001); N. Chodorow and S. Contratto, "The fantasy of the perfect mother," in B. Thorne and M. Yalom (Eds.), *Rethinking the family: Some feminist questions* (Boston, MA: Northeastern University Press, 1992: 54–75); A. Forna, *Mother of all myths: How society molds and constrains mothers*; N. Krause and H.F. Geyer-Pestello, "Depressive symptoms among women employed outside the home," *American Journal of Community Psychology, 13* (1985): 49–67; S. Maushart, *The mask of motherhood: How becoming a mother changes our lives and why we never talk about it* (New York, NY: Penguin Books, 2000); G. Ranson, "Paid work, family work, and the discourse of the full time mother," *Journal of the Association for Research on Mothering, 1.1* (1999): 57–66; A. Rich, *Of woman born* (New York: W.W. Norton, 1986); S. Seagram and J.C. Daniluk, "It goes with the territory: The meaning and experience of maternal guilt for mothers of preadolescent children," *Women and Therapy, 25* (2002): 61–89.

7. S. Hays, *The cultural contradictions of motherhood.*

8. A.E. Edwards, "Community mothering: The relationship between mothering and the community work of black women," *Journal of the Association for Research on Mothering, 2* (2000): 87–100; T. Gordon, *Feminist mothers* (Basingstoke, Hampshire: Macmillan, 1990).

9. M. Foucault, *The Foucault reader* (New York: Pantheon Books, 1984).

10. M. Foucault, *The Foucault reader*; J. Scott, "Deconstructing equality-versus-difference: Or, the uses of poststructuralist theory for feminism," in A. Hirsh (Ed.), *Conflicts in feminism* (New York, NY: Routledge, 1990: 134–148).

11. S. Robinson and L. Robinson, "Challenging the connection of mother-daughter relationships: A deconstruction of the discourse," *Canadian Women's Studies, 18* (1998): 64–65.

12. S.L. Thurer, *The myths of motherhood.*

13 K.M. Baber and K.R. Allen, *Women and families: Feminist reconstructions* (New York, NY: Guilford, 1992); N. Chodorow and S. Contratto, "The fantasy of the perfect mother," in B. Thorne and M. Yalom (Eds.) *Rethinking the family: Some feminist questions.*

14. S. Contratto, "Mother: Social sculptor and trustee of the faith," in M. Lewin (Ed.) *In the shadow of the past* (New York: Columbia University Press, 1984: 226–255); R. Croghan and D. Miell, "Strategies of resistance: Bad mothers dispute the evidence," *Feminism and Psychology, 8* (1998): 445–465.

15. D. Eyer, *Motherguilt: How our culture blames mothers for what is wrong with society* (Toronto, ON: Random House, 1996); S. Seagram and J.C. Daniluk, "It goes with the territory: The meaning and experience of maternal guilt for mothers of preadolescent children."

16. S.L. Thurer, *The myths of motherhood.*

17. S. Hays, *The cultural contradictions of motherhood*.

18. Ibid.

19. Ibid.; G. Ranson, "Paid work, family work, and the discourse of the full time mother."

20. M. Foucault, *The Foucault reader*; D.L. Little, "Independent workers, dependable mothers: Discourse, resistance, and AFDC workfare programs."

21 E.g., A. Rich, *Of woman born*.

22. K.M. Baber and K.R. Allen, *Women and families: Feminist reconstructions*; D. Eyer, *Motherguilt: How our culture blames mothers for what is wrong with society*; S. Hays, *The cultural contradictions of motherhood*; J.M. Stoppard, "Why new perspectives are needed for understanding depression in women," *Canadian Psychology, 40* (1999): 79–90.

23. T. Gordon, *Feminist mothers*.

24. R. Croghan and D. Miell, "Strategies of resistance: Bad mothers dispute the evidence"; T. Gordon, *Feminist mothers*; D.L. Little, "Independent workers, dependable mothers: Discourse, resistance, and AFDC workfare programs."

25. T. Gordon, *Feminist mothers*.

26. M. Foucault, *The Foucault reader*.

27. T. Gordon, *Feminist mothers*.

28. J. Scott, "Deconstructing equality-versus-difference: Or, the uses of poststructuralist theory for feminism."

29. In her book *The cultural contradictions of motherhood*, Sharon Hays uses the term "ideological work" to describe the process of thought that mothers engage in to make sense of the social contradictions that affect their lives. I borrow from her work in order to capture the cognitive work that resistant mothers engage in to reconcile conflicting discourses.

30. W. Sears and M. Sears, *The attachment parenting book* (New York, NY: Little, Brown and Company, 2001). This type of parenting involves maintaining ongoing, close physical proximity to one's children. For example, it recommends breastfeeding, setting up a family bed, and holding and carrying children as much as possible in order to be able to "read" one's baby's cues well.

31. A. Forna, *Mother of all myths: How society molds and constrains mothers*; S. Seagram and J.C. Daniluk, "It goes with the territory: The meaning and experience of maternal guilt for mothers of preadolescent children."

32. W. Sears and M. Sears, *The attachment parenting book*.

33. T. Gordon, *Feminist mothers*, 64.

34. M. Boulton, *On being a mother* (New York, NY: Tavistock Publications, 1983); A. Forna, *Mother of all myths: How society molds and constrains mothers*; S. Seagram and J.C. Daniluk, "It goes with the territory: The meaning and experience of maternal guilt for mothers of preadolescent children."

Chapter Three

"WE WERE CONSPIRATORS, OUTLAWS FROM THE INSTITITION OF MOTHERHOOD"

MOTHERING AGAINST MOTHERHOOD AND THE POSSIBILITY OF EMPOWERED MATERNITY FOR MOTHERS AND THEIR CHILDREN

Andrea O'Reilly

A central theme in *Of woman born*, and arguably the most significant and enduring insight of this landmark book, is the crucial distinction Rich (1986) makes between motherhood as an institution and as a nonpatriarchal experience of mothering. In the foreword to the book, Rich distinguishes "between two meanings of motherhood, one superimposed on the other: the *potential* relationship of any woman to her powers of reproduction, and to children; and the *institution*— which aims at ensuring that that potential—and all women—shall remain under male control" (13). In other words, while motherhood, as an institution, is a male-defined site of oppression, women's own experiences of mothering can nonetheless be a source of power. The oppressive and the empowering aspects of maternity, as well as the complex relationship between the two, has been the focus of feminist research on motherhood over the last twenty-five years.[1] More specifically, many of the themes of contemporary feminist thought on motherhood originate from and have developed in reference to concerns raised by Rich more than twenty-five years ago. Elsewhere I have argued that feminist thought on motherhood, particularly over the last fifteen years, may be characterized by three interrelated themes.[2] The first theme is concerned with uncovering and challenging the oppressive patriarchal institution of motherhood. The second focuses upon the formulation and articulation of a counter discourse of mothering; one that redefines mothering as a female-defined or, more specifically, a feminist, enterprise. This new perspective, in emphasizing maternal power and ascribing agency to mothers and value to motherwork gives rise to the third theme: the view that mothers can affect social change through the socialization of children; particularly in terms of challenging traditional patterns of gender acculturation. While numerous feminists have located these themes in Rich, none have returned to *Of woman born* to consider how these themes were first developed, or to review how Rich's initial insights may aid contemporary theory in its formulation of these three central concerns.

This chapter will focus upon the second and third themes—the formulation of a female-defined and -centred experience of mothering and the development of a feminist practice of gender socialization. While the two aims seem similar, the first is concerned with mothering in terms of the mother herself—her experiences of mothering, the meanings she attaches to it—while the second theme focuses upon the relation she has with her children and, in particular, the manner in which she raises them. It has been long recognized that Rich was one of the first feminist writers to call for anti-sexist childrearing and women-centred practices of mothering. What has been less acknowledged, and what will be the focus of this chapter, is how the two, in Rich's view, are intrinsically linked insofar as the goal of anti-sexist childrearing depends upon the abolition of patriarchal motherhood and the achievement of feminist mothering. Anti-sexist childrearing—a challenge to traditional practices of gender socialization for both daughters and sons—Rich argues, depends upon motherhood itself being changed; it must become, to use Rich's terminology, mothering. In other words, only when mothering becoming a site, role, and identity of power for women is feminist childrearing made possible.

The chapter will first revisit Rich's vision of new modes of childrearing for both sons and daughters. Next it will explore Rich's argument that these new feminist practices of relating with and raising sons and daughters become actualized only through the eradication of patriarchal motherhood and the emergence of feminist mothering. Though more than twenty-five years have passed since the publication of *Of woman born*, Rich remains the only feminist critic, to my knowledge, to recognize and argue that the changes we pursue in childrearing are made possible only through changes in mothering. While feminist mothers today seek to raise empowered daughters and anti-sexist sons, Rich understood, some twenty-five years ago, that this is achievable only *outside* the patriarchal institution of motherhood. Women must, to again use Rich's terminology, mother against motherhood to raise a new generation of feminist children. It is this insight, I argue, that makes *Of woman born* the truly visionary and prophetic book that it is.

Mother and daughters: "As daughters we need mothers who want their own freedom and ours"

Rich was one of the first feminist theorists on motherhood to define mothering as a *socially engaged* enterprise particularly as it seeks to effect cultural change through new feminist modes of gender socialization and interactions with daughters and sons. Two of her chapters in *Of woman born* examine the mother's relationships with her children, and consider how mothers may challenge traditional gender socialization through feminist childrearing. Chapter nine on Motherhood and Daughterhood is described by Rich as the "core of my book" and is the chapter most referenced by maternal scholars. "The cathexis between mother and daughter, essential, distorted, misused," wrote Adrienne Rich in her oft-cited quote, "is the great unwritten story" (225).

Mother and daughter estrangement under patriarchy

However, as Rich noted the absence of mother–daughter stories, she simultaneously argued that patriarchal culture scripts the roles mothers and daughters are expected to play. The patriarchal view of mothers and daughters, according to Rich, is that this relationship, particularly in the daughter's adolescent years, is to be experienced as antagonism and animosity. The daughter must differentiate herself from the mother if she is to assume an autonomous identity as an adult. The mother, in turn, is perceived and understood only in terms of her maternal identity. The mother represents for the daughter, according to the received narrative, the epitome of patriarchal oppression that she seeks to transcend as she comes to womanhood. This is the patriarchal narrative of the mother–daughter relationship as it is enacted in the patriarchal institution of motherhood.

Across cultures and throughout history, most women, as noted in the introduction, mother in the institution of motherhood; that is, women's mothering is defined and controlled by the larger patriarchal society in which they live. Mothers do not make the rules, Rich emphasizes; they simply enforce them. Whether it is in the form of parenting books, a physician's advice, or the father's rules, a mother is expected to raise her children in accordance with the values and expectations of the dominant patriarchal culture. Mothers are policed by what theorist Sara Ruddick (1989) calls "the gaze of others." "Under the gaze of others, Mothers relinquish authority to others [and] lose confidence in their own values" (111). "Teachers, grandparents, mates, friends, employers, even an anonymous passerby," continues Ruddick, "can judge a mother by her child's behavior and find her wanting" (111–112). Inauthentic mothering and the abdication of maternal authority is at the heart of patriarchal motherhood, and is what gives rise to the disempowerment of mothers and the estrangement of mothers and daughters. Daughters, Rich argues, perceive their mothers' inauthenticity and understand the powerlessness that underpins their mothers' compliance and complicity. "Many daughters," Rich writes, "live in rage at their mothers for having accepted too readily and passively 'whatever comes.' A mother's victimization does not merely humiliate her, it mutilates the daughter who watches for clues as to what it means to be a woman. Like the traditional foot-bound Chinese woman, she passes on her own affliction. The mother's self-hatred and low expectations are the binding-rags of the psyche of the daughter" (243). However, as the daughter experiences this rage toward her mother, she is expected to identify with her because as a woman it is assumed the daughter will become a mother/wife as her mother did. The daughter resists this identification because she does not want to live a life like that of her mother's, nor does she wish to be affiliated with someone who is oppressed and whose work is devalued. "Thousands of daughters," writes Rich, "see their mothers as having taught a compromise and self-hatred they are struggling to win free of, the one through whom the restrictions and degradations of a female existence were perforce transmitted" (235). Rich defines this viewpoint as matrophobia: "the fear not of one's mother or of motherhood but of *becoming one's mother*" (236; italics in original). Matrophobia, Rich continues:

> can be seen as a womanly splitting of the self, in the desire to become purged once and for all of our mothers' bondage, to become individuated and free. The mother stands for the victim in ourselves, the unfree woman, the martyr. Our personalities seem dangerously to blur and overlap with our mothers'; and, in a desperate attempt to know where mother ends and daughter begins, we perform radical surgery. (236)

The devaluation of motherhood, the mother's abdication of maternal authority, maternal inauthenticity, and so on, give rise to matrophobia; this in turn frustrates and thwarts understanding and intimacy, empathy and connection between mothers and daughters. "The loss of the daughter to the mother, the mother to the daughter," writes Rich, "is the essential female tragedy. We acknowledge Lear (father–daughter split), Hamlet (son and mother), and Oedipus, (son and mother) as great embodiments of the human tragedy, but there is no presently enduring recognition of mother–daughter passion and rapture" (237). Building upon Rich's insights on mother–daughter estrangement, feminist theorists, particularly since the mid-1980s, have focused upon the importance of mother–daughter connection and closeness to argue that such are essential for female empowerment, particularly in the daughter's adolescent years.

Feminist narratives of mother–daughter connection

Writers as diverse as Paula Caplan, Elizabeth de Bold, Miriam Johnson, Carol Gilligan, Virginia Beanne Rutter, and Mary Pipher argue that a strong mother–daughter connection is what makes possible a strong female self. Rutter (1996), in her book *Celebrating girls*, argues that high self esteem in girls is made possible through close relationships with mothers. "Mothers," writes Rutter, "can raise girls with a vital, intact feminine spirit [...] [The] mother–daughter relationship is the ground for teaching, talking, and sharing the feminine experience and the more we empower that experience, the healthier our girls will be. We need to secure our daughters' sense of self-worth, in their mind and their bodies, so that they will not turn away from us and from themselves" (2, 9–10). These writers maintain that the daughter's empowerment through the valuation of the feminine depends upon a close and vital mother–daughter relationship.

However, Western culture mandates separation from parents in adolescence to enable the emerging adult to achieve an autonomous sense of self. Recent feminist writers call into question this "sacred cow"of developmental theory, and argue that it constitutes a betrayal of both mothers and daughters. "Separation and autonomy are not equivalent," Elizabeth de Bold explains, "[daughters] need not separate from mothers emotionally to be autonomous. [...] Early childhood and adolescence are the two stages of life were separation has been decreed as imperative to the independence and autonomy of children. To mother 'right' women disconnect from their daughters [....] Rather than strengthen girls, this breach of trust leave girls weakened and adrift" (36). What is most disturbing about this pattern of separation and betrayal is its timing. "In childhood," de Bold (1993) writes, "girls have confidence in what they know, think and feel" (11). With the onset of adolescence, girls come up against what she calls *the wall*: "The wall is our patriarchal culture that values women less than men .... To get through the wall girls have to give up parts of themselves to be safe and accepted within society" (12). Daughters are thus abandoned by their mothers when they need them the most. Mothers can aid daughters in their resistance to the wall through sustained and sustaining mother-daughter connection. Drawing upon the ancient Elyeusian rites of Demeter and Persephone first discussed by Rich, recent feminist writings on the mother–daughter relations celebrate mother–daughter connection and explore how such is achieved and sustained through maternal narratives, the motherline, and feminist mothering.[3]

Mothering against motherhood: Empowering daughters through empowered mothers

This recent feminist aim to fashion an alternative mother–daughter narrative modeled on mother–daughter connection has resulted in perceptive and useful literature on how to raise empowered girls. As well, this counter-narrative has gone a long way to destabilize the patriarchal view that positions mother–daughter disconnection as inevitable and necessary. However, I want to suggest that these achievements remain partial because of the failure of this new literature to fully comprehend the connection-empowerment trajectory as theorized by Rich. While Rich champions mother–daughter connection, she recognizes, as these writers do *not*, that connection gives rise to the daughter's empowerment *if and only if* the mother with whom the daughter is identifying is herself empowered. "What do mean by the nurture of daughters? What is it we wish we had, or could have, as daughters; could give as mothers," asks Rich:

> Deeply and primally we need trust and tenderness; surely this will always be true of every human being, but women growing into a world so hostile to us need a very profound kind of loving in order to learn to love ourselves. But this loving is not simply the old, institutionalized, sacrificial, "mother-love" which men have demanded; we want courageous mothering. The most notable fact that culture imprints on women is the sense of our limits. The most important thing one woman can do for another is to illuminate and expand her sense of actual possibilities. For a mother, this means more than contending with reductive images of females in children's books, movies, television, the schoolroom. It means that the mother herself is trying to expand the limits of her life. To *refuse to be a victim*: and then to go on from there. (246, emphasis in original)

Karen Payne's (1983) *Between ourselves: Letters between mothers and daughters* provides a lived example of Rich's mutual empowerment thesis. One daughter wrote: "When Mum finally left Dad she was giving up female martyrdom; she was waving farewell to that womanly virtue of self-sacrifice. And if she could escape that bondage than so could I [....] In setting herself free, [my mother] set me free" (244). In the same collection, renowned sociologist Jesse Bernard wrote to her daughter: "For your sake as well as mine, I must not allow you to absorb me completely. I must learn to live my own life independently in order to be a better mother to you" (272). Or as Judith Arcana (1983), an early feminist theorist whose work was greatly influenced by Rich advised: "We must live as if our dreams have been realized. We cannot simply prepare other, younger daughters for strength, pride, courage, beauty. It is worse than useless to tell young women and girls that we have done and been wrong, that we have chosen ill, that we hope they will be more lucky" (33).

What daughters need, therefore, in Rich's words:

> [are] mothers who want their own freedom and ours [....] The quality of the mother's life—however, embattled and unprotected—is her primary bequest to her daughter, because a woman who can believe in herself, who is a fighter, and who continues to struggle to create livable space around her, is demonstrating to her daughter that these possibilities exist. (247)

Writing of lesbian mothering in *Politics of the heart*, Baba Cooper (1987) describes radical mothers as "involving children in disloyalty to the culture the mother is expected to transmit at the expense of woman-bonding and female empowerment" (238). This radical mothering works *against* the matrophobia that is at the heart of mother–daughter estrangement, and is what makes possible reciprocal mother–daughter empowerment. Whether it be termed courageous mothering, as Rich describes it, or radical mothering, as defined by Cooper, this practice of mothering calls for the empowerment of daughters *and* mothers, and recognizes that the former is only possible with the later. As Judith Arcana (1983) concludes: "If we want girls to grow into free women, brave and strong, we must be those women ourselves" (33). By mothering against motherhood, and becoming, in Rich's words, "outlaws from the institution of motherhood" (195), women obtain power in mothering and thereby are able to model the empowerment the daughter will acquire in and through mother–daughter connection.

Mothers and sons: "Discover[ing] new ways of being men ... As we are discovering new ways of being women"

As with the mother–daughter relationship, Rich emphasized the necessity of interrogating and dismantling the patriarchal institution of motherhood in the raising of sons. In the instance of daughters, Rich argued that in order for mothers to instill agency, authority, and authenticity in their growing daughters, the mothers must model these same attributes in their own daily lives. With sons, Rich likewise argued that mothers must reject traditional motherhood in order to challenge and change normative practices of masculization because the institution of motherhood serves to foster in sons both sexism and patriarchal masculinity. Thus, while the teaching of anti-sexism and undermining of masculine socialization may be the explicit goals of feminist mothering of sons, such depends upon mothers dismantling the institution of patriarchal motherhood.

Contemporary feminist scholarship on mothers and sons may be organized under three interrelated aims or themes: a challenge to traditional masculine socialization, an emphasis upon mother–son connection and, to a lesser degree, a critique of patriarchal motherhood.[4] As with current mother–daughter literature, these mother–son themes may be traced back to *Of woman born*. And similar to her mother–daughter connection through mutual empowerment thesis, Rich argues that in order for sons to become caring and connected men they must likewise be mothered outside the patriarchal institution of motherhood.

Rich's chapter "Mother and son, woman and man," while arguably not as developed as her "Mothers and daughters" chapter, and cited less often by maternal scholars, is arguably the more radical chapter, in so far as Rich was the first—and for the longest time—the only feminist theorist to confront head-on the thorny issue of being a feminist mother of sons, an issue that was, in Linda Forcey's (1987) words "a taboo topic" among feminists until quite recently (2). "Few subjects so provoke anxiety among feminists," Robin Morgan (1993) wrote, "as the four-letter word *sons*" (38). "We've talked about, written and read about, mothers and daughters," Morgan continues, "but with a few notable exceptions we've averted our eyes from The Other Touchy Subject. Yet that subject goes to the heart of practicing what we claim to believe, that 'the personal is political.' It goes to the crux of power and of patriarchy—even though it also grazes the living nerves of love" (38).

Mother and son connection

Central to contemporary feminist thought on the mother–son relationship is a celebration of mother–son connection and a challenge to the belief that mother–son separation is normal, inevitable, and good for our sons. While this concern is peripheral to the "Mother and Son" chapter in *Of woman born*, Rich nonetheless does consider the issue of mother–son separation and ask:

> How *does* the male child differentiate himself from his mother, and does this mean inevitably that he must 'join the army,' that is, internalize patriarchal values? Can the mother, in patriarchy, represent culture, and if so, what does this require of her? Above all, what does separation from the mother mean for the son? (198)

Rich goes on to observe that:

> Across all cultures sons, at the onset of puberty experience a 'second birth' into patriarchal culture. [T]he child-with-a-penis is expected to bond himself with others who have penises. [...] He must still [...] come to terms with the Fathers, the representative of law and tradition, the wagers of aggression, the creators and purveyors of the dominant culture. And his mother, whatever her deepest instincts tells her, is expected to facilitate this. (200)

Since the early 1990s, feminist writers have taken up these questions to emphasize mother–son connection and position it as central to the reconfiguration of traditional masculinity.

The hegemonic narrative of mother and son attachment—as scripted in parenting books, psychoanalytical theory, and popular wisdom—assumes that sons must separate from their mothers in order to acquire a "normal" masculine identity. A close and caring relationship between a mother and her son is pathologized as aberrant, while a relationship structured upon separation is naturalized as the real and normal way to experience mother-son attachment. Olga Silverstein and Beth Rashbaum (1994) write in *The courage to raise good men*:

> [O]ur culture believes that a male child must be removed from his mother's influence in order to escape the contamination of a close relationship with her. The love of a mother—both the son's for her, and hers for him—is believed to "feminize" the boy, make him soft, weak, dependent, homebound ... only through renunciation of the loving mother does the boy become a man. (11)

Feminist theorists on the mother–son relation have begun to challenge this received narrative by calling into question the central and organizing premise of patriarchally-mandated mother–son separation, namely that this process is both natural, hence inevitable, and that it is "good" for our sons. Feminist writers argue that while we may perceive mother and son separation to be a natural process, it is, in reality, a culturally scripted and orchestrated act. "By expecting our sons to cut off from us," Silverstein and Rashbaum write, "we make sure that they do" (159). Whether the son is fully cognizant of this sudden or subtle detachment, he nonetheless experiences it as a profound and inexplicable loss that leaves him feeling vulnerable and alone. To save our sons, who are destined to become detached and wounded men, and to change the patriarchal world in which they and we live, a mother must foreground her presence in the life of her son; as well, she must establish and maintain a close and caring connection with her son throughout his life. By way of this new relationship mothers will dismantle, destabilize, and deconstruct normative patterns of male socialization and traditional definitions of masculinity. These theorists, as with the feminist writers on daughters, seek cultural change through new feminist practices of mothering modelled on connection and concerned with the creation of new modes of masculinity.

Challenging traditional masculinity

Feminist literature on masculinity, written by both men and women, argues that while men learn that they are beneficiaries of power and privilege, they pay a high price for this status. Michael Kaufman (1994), for example, describes masculinity as "an idealized version of what it means to be male ... a collective hallucination ... a state of mind and a story of how to behave" (25, 32, 29). Having been socialised to repress and deny emotions associated with the feminine—empathy, vulnerability, compassion, gentleness—and having been taught to tough it out on their own through our culture's valorization of an independent, individualistic (and fully individuated) masculinity, men grow into manhood deeply wounded and isolated. Masculinity then becomes a facade or a place of refuge, where men seek to convince themselves and others that they are as brave and strong as the idealized version of masculinity purports them to be. Writers on masculinity agree that masculinity, as with femininity, is a cultural construct that exists in a constant state of flux, its meaning continually shifting in response to changing economic, political, and social times. Today, feminist mothers seek a new mode of manhood wherein feminine characteristics such as gentleness, vulnerability, and compassion are emphasized, and the more harmful aspects of traditional macho masculinity are eliminated. However, the work of raising anti-sexist sons has proven to be more difficult and daunting than the task of rearing feminist daughters. Alison Thomas (2001) explains in her article "Swimming against the tide; Feminists' accounts of raising sons":

> [T]here has been a general lack of anti-sexist men willing and able to act as unconventional role models for their sons (at least until recently), and this has again meant that mothers are the ones who are taking responsibility for directing their sons toward resisting traditional forms of masculinity. On top of that, it is clear that for young men "the costs" of challenging conventional masculine roles are much higher—given a society that still does attach considerable prestige to "masculinity"—and when this entails (for example) sharing domestic responsibilities with women, such "costs" are not compensated by tangible benefits. (125)

Numerous feminist writers and scholars have recognized the need to change traditional masculine socialization and have recommended various strategies for anti-sexist childrearing. However, few have acknowledged how truly arduous and contentious a task this is. In *Of woman born*, Rich was the first to appreciate the ambivalence and anxiety mothers often feel in raising a boy feminist. "If we wish for our sons—as for our daughters—that they may grow up unmutilated by gender roles, sensitized to misogyny in all its forms, we also," Rich emphasizes, "have to face the fact that in the present stage of history our sons may feel profoundly alone in the masculine world, with few if any close relationships with other men" (207). "The fear of alienating a male child from 'his' culture seems to go deep," Rich writes, "even among women who reject that culture for themselves every day of their lives" (205). "What do we fear?," Rich asks. "That our sons will accuse us of making them into misfits and outsiders? That they will suffer as we have suffered from patriarchal reprisals. Do we fear they will somehow lose their male status and privilege, even as we are seeking to abolish that inequity?" (205). In identifying this ambivalence and this conflict, Rich was the first to emphasize that the task of rearing feminist sons demands formidable courage of mothers *and* sons; as well it requires that the institution of motherhood itself be eradicated.

Mothering against motherhood: Connected and caring sons and courageous mothers

To truly free our sons, to move beyond a mere critique of traditional masculinity, mothers must become, in Rich's words, "outlaws from the institution to motherhood." In an oft-cited quote, Rich describes her brief exile from the institution of motherhood:

> I remember one summer, living in a friends' house in Vermont. My husband was working abroad for several weeks, and my three sons— nine, seven, five years old—and I dwelt for most of that time by ourselves. Without a male adult in the house, without any reason for schedules, naps, regular mealtimes, or early bedtimes [...] we fell into what I felt to be a delicious and sinful rhythm [...] At night they fell asleep without a murmur and I stayed up reading and writing as I had when a student, till the early morning. I remember thinking: This is what living with children could be—without school hours, fixed routines, naps, the conflict of being both mother and wife with no room for being simply myself. Driving home once after midnight from a late drive-in movie [...] I felt wide awake, elated; we had broken together all the rules of bedtime, the night rules, rules I myself thought I had to observe in the city or become a "bad mother". We were conspirators, outlaws from the institution of motherhood. (194–195)

"Of course the institution closed down on us again," writes Rich, "and my own mistrust of myself as 'good mother' returned" (195).

Rich was the first to recognize how traditional motherhood leads to traditional masculinity. Judith Arcana, a theorist greatly influenced by Rich and the first to write a book on mothers and sons, argues that mothering is about caring for and catering to the needs of children, and nurturing self esteem so that children see themselves as special and deserving; what Sara Ruddick (1989) defines as the second demand of maternal practice, "to foster growth ... sponsor or nurture a child's unfolding, expanding material spirit" (83). However, in the institution of motherhood this nurturance may be, in the instance of sons, according to Judith Arcana (1993), interpreted as privilege and entitlement: "Though children of both sexes put their mothers in the position of servants ... mothers of sons are, whether we feel it in the moment or not, inadvertently reinforcing the sexist premise that women exist to serve men .... Men learn from infancy to expect and solicit selfishness and cherishing care at the hands of women" (101, 102). While "[d]aughters learn from our mothers to *be mothers*, to give in [sic] that disastrously self-destructive way that has been honored by men as true motherhood; sons learn *to expect such treatment from women*" (102, italics in original). Women in patriarchal culture are expected to devote their time and attention to children and men; sons thus, as Arcana identifies, derive double benefits from these patriarchal imperatives as both men and children. Given that women's secondary status is enforced in both the gender arena, service to men, and in the maternal realm, service to children, mothers must, if they hope to raise anti-sexist men who reject traditional masculinity, challenge both patriarchal imperatives: that women are to serve both men and children. Women, Arcana writes, "need to live out of ourselves. We wrong ourselves and our children if we subordinate our lives to theirs" (235). Mothers must, Arcana continues, "[r]eject [the] traditional mother role [and] ... accept [...] our sons into our daily lives" (247). In so doing, the mother will enable her boy child to see her outside and beyond her maternal identity that positions her as secondary to, and in service to, children and men. Coming to know their mothers outside motherhood, sons learn to view and appreciate their mothers as, in Arcana's words, "whole people."

According to Arcana, mothers must, therefore, reject traditional motherhood if they hope to raise non-traditional sons: i.e., men who have renounced patriarchal masculinity and the entitlement and privilege that such accords. No longer can mothers be, or be seen as, "the primary source of praise, encouragement, and selfless service [for sons]" (280). However, as mothers reject this role of selfless service to sons, traditional male socialization, as Arcana explains, teaches boys "that they are to be the beneficiaries of a male culture: they will grow up to power, status, and the admiration and support of women .... [W]hen [a mother] moves to change that pattern with her son, he understands that she wants him to give up power .... [A] boy has to begin by *losing*" (280). In other words, to become more human, the son must become less "male."

Mothers must dismantle the patriarchal institution of motherhood, Rich argues, in order to effect the gender transformations and new relations they wish for themselves and their sons. Audre Lorde (1993) once wrote: "The strongest lesson I can teach my son is the same lesson I teach my daughter: how to be who he wishes to be for himself. And the best way I can do this is to be who I am and hope that he will learn from this not how to be me, which is not possible, but how to be himself" (77). Feminist writers on the mother–daughter relationship argue that mothers must act and speak from truth and authenticity if they hope to achieve empowerment for themselves and their girl children. A mother of sons also must mother from a place of truth and authenticity, and model for her son resistance so that he may, in Lorde's words, "move to that voice within himself, rather than to those raucous, persuasive or threatening voices from outside, pressuring him to be what the world wants him to be" (77). Therefore, as Mary Kay Blakey (2001) concludes, "[while] getting bounced from the game [of Let's Pretend—passing for perfect mothers, living in the traditional version of a perfect family—] into actual life is invariably traumatic, it is better for us and our sons" (34). "What do we want for our sons?" asks Rich. "We want them to remain, in the deepest sense, sons of the mothers, yet also grow into themselves, to discover new ways of being men even as we are discovering new ways of being women" (211). And for Rich this only becomes possible by mothering against motherhood.

Conclusion

Feminist theorists on motherhood call for the eradication of the institution of motherhood so as to make mothering less oppressive to women. Feminist thinkers concerned specifically with the issue of childrearing seek feminist practices of gender socialization and "in-connection" models of mother–child relations so as to raise a new generation of empowered daughters and empathetic sons. However, Rich was the first and, to my knowledge, the only feminist theorist to recognize that the former depends upon the later: we cannot affect changes in childrearing without first changing the conditions of motherhood. A review of feminist thought on motherhood reveals that a critique of the institution of motherhood and a concern with new modes of childrearing have developed independently of each other, and that feminists committed to the abolition of motherhood and the achievement of mothering have seldom considered what this means for the mother *herself*, apart from the issue of childrearing.

In Chapter one, Fiona Green interviews feminist mothers who, in Green's words, "live Rich's emancipatory vision of motherhood." Driven by their feminist consciousness, their intense love for their children and the need to be true to themselves, their families, and their parenting, [these] feminist mothers," Green writes, "choose to parent in a way that challenge the status quo." They do so, according to Green, by way of two different approaches: "overt strategies of resistance" and "subversive strategies of resistance." To illustrate the first strategy Green gives the example of a lesbian lone parent who births and raises a child without any connection to man. "No man ever called the shots in my home," the woman explains, "nor did a man ever support me in any way. So that is really breaking the rules in the patriarchy." According to Green, this is "a deliberate act of resistance to dominant conceptions and practices of mothering."

The second strategy is less overt; with this approach, mothers "under the cover of the institution of motherhood effectively challenge patriarchy, and their subversive activity often goes unnoticed." Green provides examples of two heterosexual married mothers to illustrate this strategy, one who raises a son to make him consciously aware of social injustices, while the second mother "actively encourages the nurturing and non-competitive tendencies of her son, while supporting her daughter in her pursuits of maths and science." The second subversive strategy thus seems to focus on childrearing undertaken by women in the institution of motherhood while the former, the overt strategy, involves a challenge to the institution itself and is concerned with the empowerment of the mother. In the example of overt resistance, when discussing the mother's choice to rear her daughter with an othermother during a difficult time in her daughter's adolescence, Green comments that this mother "enjoy[ed] a level of freedom and strength that she would not have experienced had she conformed to patriarchal [motherhood]."

I refer to Green's research here because I think it illustrates well the argument I have been developing on what make Rich's insights on mothering and motherhood significant and groundbreaking; namely, we must eradicate oppressive motherhood and achieve emancipatory mothering *for mothers themselves*, so that they may be enriched and empowered by mothering. That is reason enough to abolish motherhood. However, in so doing we also invest mothers with the needed agency, authenticity, and authority to affect the feminist childrearing they desire. As well, daughters, in connecting with mothers who model and mentor empowered womanhood, will be empowered, as advocated by writers who advance the connection and empowerment argument. A son with an empowered mother will similarly desire and seek connection with her, and thus will be more likely to develop feminine characteristics as desired by the "new masculinity" writers. In this volume *Politics of the heart*, I discuss how African-American mothering is a site of empowerment for women because it accords mothers power alongside responsibility; as well it eschews the patriarchal selfishness of natural-intensive mothering. In contrast, in Anglo-American feminist thought there is little written on mothering as site of empowerment *for mothers themselves*. Instead, Anglo-American feminists, it seems, seek feminist childrearing *within* the institution of motherhood. Again, and as Rich realized more than a quarter-century ago, this is not enough. While we can never abolish motherhood as Rich wished, her belief that we must strive to do so *for mothers* is what makes *Of woman born* a truly radical and, for those who benefit from patriarchal motherhood, a truly subversive text. I also believe, as Rich did, that mothering, that which invests mothers with agency, authority, authenticity, is better for children as well. In other words and to conclude, in being "bad" mothers—outlaws from the institution of motherhood—we become better mothers for ourselves *and* for our children.

Notes

1. Please visit the Association for Research on Mothering (ARM) website (www.yorku.ca/crm) for a listing of the various topics explored by maternal scholars. ARM, founded in 1998, and now with more than 500 members worldwide, is the first international feminist organization devoted specifically to the topic of mothering and motherhood. ARM hosts two international conferences a year and publishes bi-annually *The Journal of the Association for Research on Mothering*. More information is available on the ARM website.

2. Please see my chapter: "Feminist perspectives on mothering and motherhood: power and oppression" in *Gendered intersections: A collection of readings for women & gender studies*, Pamela Downe and Leslie Biggs (Eds.), (Fernwood Press, forthcoming). See also my book *Reconceiving maternity: From sacrificial motherhood to empowered mothering*.

3. This is examined at length in my articles "Across the divide: Contemporary Anglo-American feminist theory on the mother–daughter relationship," in *Redefining motherhood: Changing identities and patterns*, Sharon Abbey and Andrea O'Reilly (Eds.), (Toronto: Second Story Press, 1998: 69–91); and "Mothers, daughters and feminism today: Empowerment, agency, narrative, *Canadian Women's Studies* 18: 2 & 3 (Summer/Fall 1998), 16–21. See also the introduction to *Mothers and daughters: Connection, empowerment, transformation*, Andrea O'Reilly and Sharon Abbey (Eds.), (New York: Rowman and Littlefield, 2000). The first is reprinted as chapter 16 of this volume.

4. Contemporary feminist theory on mothers and sons may be organized under three interrelated themes: "Mothering and motherhood," "Men and masculinities," and "Mother and son connections and disconnections." Please see "In black and white: African-American and Anglo-American feminist perspectives on mothers and sons" in this volume for a detailed discussion of these themes and how they are featured in Anglo-American and African-American theory.

Chapter Four

THE (MALE) ADVANTAGE OF A FEMINIST MOTHER

Juanita Ross Epp and Sharon Cook

Working mothers have long battled the personal doubts engendered by a society which assumes that women who work outside the home are somehow damaging the children by "abandoning" them to other forms of childcare, whether the alternative childcare is the other parent, another family member, a neighbor, or a daycare centre. In addition, women who profess to be feminists are accused of other equally damaging—although less well defined—atrocities toward their children. For example:

> Feminists have not answered the argument that daycare provides no substitute for the family. They have not answered the argument that indifference to the needs of the young has become one of the distinguishing characteristics of a society that ... exploits existing resources with criminal disregard of the future. (Lasch, 1977: xvi–xvii)

These accusations are even more pronounced if the children happen to be male. As Adrienne Rich described it more than twenty-five years ago:

> I have been asked, sometimes with genuine curiosity, sometimes with veiled hostility, "What do your sons think about all this?" ("All this" being feminism in general, my own commitment to women in particular.) When asked with hostility, the implication is that a feminist must be man-hating, castrating; that "all this" must of course be damaging to my children; it is a question meant to provoke guilt. (My only answer, obviously, is, "you'll have to ask them."). (Rich, 1986: 207)

We have been asked similar questions and in this paper use historical, sociological, and psychological literature as background for an examination of our own sons' reactions to "all this." We thought to augment our sons' perceptions with those of historically prominent males who had feminist mothers, but the term "feminist" created some difficulty for both aspects of the project. Although relatively new, it is deeply mistrusted and misunderstood and has evolved so quickly that the definition has changed from one generation to the next. As Wolf (1993) pointed out, people have difficulty separating out the emotional side issues that have become attached to the feminist movement—such as abortion, lesbianism, single parenting, birth control, pornography, spousal abuse, safe streets, common-law relationships, daycare concerns, child abuse, child poverty, racism, classism, and a host of other issues. All of these are important to most feminists, but disagreement on individual issues has fragmented the feminist movement and led to public misunderstandings about feminists' collective intentions. Our sons identified four types of feminism and were willing to be associated with only one of them. Fortunately, that definition coincided with ours so for the purposes of this paper, a feminist is defined as anyone who believes in and is working toward equity between the genders—a definition based on an expectation of equal pay for equal work and equal sharing of household responsibilities.

Seeking the historical precedent

> For thousands of years, because of her awesome ability to spew forth a child, mother has been feared and revered. She has been the subject of taboos and witch hunts, mandatory pregnancy and confinement in a separate sphere. She has endured appalling insults and perpetual marginalization. She has also been the subject of glorious painting, chivalry, and idealization. Through it all, she has rarely been consulted. She is an object, not a subject. (Thurur, 1994: 299)

Most modern societies attach deep significance to the mother/child bond through the complex process of nurturance. Whatever the religious orientation, political positioning, class, or ethnicity, women are likely to be given the task of interpreting, inculcating and monitoring the socialization of young children on behalf of the wider society. But women have not always had much to do with their growing sons. Until the late eighteenth century in North America, the cultural assessment of women's moral character was essentially negative. Rooted in religious distrust and governance restrictions, women's presumably inborn predilection for instability, emotionalism, and irrationality caused many to counsel the removal of children, especially male children, from their mother's purview as early as was reasonably possible.

Before the nineteenth century, large families and the need for mothers to contribute actively to the family economy denied any one child much individual attention. Many young men were apprenticed or bound out as servants before their mid-teens, effectively removing them from their mother's influence. Colonial Americans, like members of most developing societies, understood their world as "an organic social order in which rights and responsibilities were reciprocal and in which terms like 'individuality' and 'self-reliance' had little place .... A person's identity was bound up in the performance of social roles, not in the expression of self" (Rotundo, 1990: 12–13). One "expression of self" thus denied to most mothers and sons prior to the nineteenth century was the assumption that they would have a personal relationship.

At the beginning of the nineteenth century several factors altered common views of nurturance. Family size declined, permitting mothers to accord more attention to each child. Fathers increasingly worked away from the home as the family based economy slowly gave way to an industrial system. The role of mother had changed:

> The specifically maternal duties of childcare, once defined haphazardly by her round of daily tasks, became a self-conscious enterprise, one that was assigned exclusively to mother, complicated and time-consuming. (Thurur, 1994: 185)

Societal perceptions of women changed from condescension to an equally unbalanced attitude which set mothers up as models of moral rectitude, empathy, industry, self-restraint, and personal purity by which young men were to be both nurtured and uplifted. Fewer sons left the household before their mid- to late twenties, and mothers were expected to mold young men's characters through a blend of easy companionship and high moral purpose which would last a lifetime.

The advice literature for mothers in this period portrayed the ideal mother/son relationship as emotionally charged and almost sexually reverential: "'Oh mother, mother,' he sobbed, 'I wish I had never left you! I'll keep as near to you in heart as I can. I wish I hadn't grown away from you so; but I'll get back again if I can!'" (*Woman's Journal*, October 1890). The author of a pamphlet series directed towards young men in the late nineteenth century rhapsodized:

> One of the beautiful sights I have seen is a lady and her son walking, arm in arm, from church, Sabbath after Sabbath. He was like a lover in his tenderness. It made no difference who saw him, he was just as

considerate as he could have been if she had been radiant with youth
and beauty. (Scott, n.p.)

Mothers were responsible for their sons' physical well-being and their moral
development. They were expected to keep the "hedonism of boy culture" out of
the house and "extend their moral domain into boys' world" (Rotundo, 1990:
49–50). A really good mother would be able to control her boy's response even
if she was not present. A poem made available for Canadian children engaging
in speaking contests sponsored by temperance youth groups between 1916 and
1922 spoke of "A Boy's Promise" to his mother that earns him the ridicule of
his peers. He is undaunted:

> *"Go where you please, do what you will,"*
> *He calmly told the other.*
> *"But I shall keep my word boys, still";*
> *"I can't; I promised mother."*
> *Ah, who could doubt the future course*
> *Of one who thus had spoken?*
> *Through manhood's struggle, gain and loss,*
> *Could faith like this be broken?*
> *God's blessing on that steadfast will,*
> *Unyielding to another,*
> *That bears all jeers and laughter still,*
> *Because he promised mother.*
> (Archives of Ontario, Colbec, n.p)

But this process of mother's uplifting influence occurred—and still occurs
today—against a backdrop of expectation that the son will imminently move
beyond this secure private zone into an intensely competitive and even dangerous
public arena. Here he will be formally educated, socialized through male peers
and authority figures, play male-dominated games, and learn to negotiate a
profoundly male-centred public domain. This public life implicitly and even overtly
denigrates values and behaviours that have come to be associated with women,
and in particular, with the son's mother.

It has been argued that this denigration has often been accomplished through
the "rule-bound structure of organized sports" which provides "a context in which
they struggled to construct a masculine positional identity" (Messner, 1992: 150).
Sports-facilitated masculine identities differ according to class and race (Connell,
1995; Davison, 1998; Frank, 1994; Messner, 1992: 147–163). This denigration
of the feminine was—and is—also necessary to ensure that mothers will not
prevent their sons from serving in the armed forces. Both sports and the military

have been considered male realms, places in which women and women's ideas did not belong. This separation was a complex juncture for mothers and sons: Masculinity and male status is in part expressed in men's successful separation from the subordination of the sphere of women's activity (Smith, 1985: 35).

Sons were expected to honor and love their mothers but to subjugate women in general; mothers were expected to make the transition from authority figure to passive female at the appropriate time in their sons' lives. Thus, much of the literature produced for mothers over the past two hundred years prepared women for the possibility that their best efforts in civilizing sons would be subverted by an exceedingly powerful society of which women were not a part.

Early feminists sought admission to that male world from an extremely disadvantaged position. Few women were allowed any knowledge of mainstream society and were routinely denied education, as well as excluded from realms such as commerce and politics. They had to find entry points into "discourses from which women have for centuries been excluded" (Smith, 1985: 4).

There were feminists who were also mothers; they considered themselves to be active and visible participants in the public realm, but they encountered resistance as they struggled to break down the barriers between the world of men and the world of women. There were those who believed that it was the twentieth century feminists themselves who encouraged the split worlds. As late as 1976, mothers were being admonished for their duplicity as perpetrators of the he-man myth:

> *Most mothers have retained, and further cultivated, the masculinity myth in their sons.* In a sense, they rigidly maintain a schizophrenic world: on one side they clamor for equality and unistandards and, on the other, they teach little boys how to become masculine he-men. (Sebald, 1976: 87, emphasis in the original)

Charting the contours of feminists' relationships to their sons was not easy. We needed access to the mothers' perceptions, the sons' reminiscences, and some input from a third party such as a biographer or another member of the family. Such requirements immediately eliminated all but the famous (which limited the study's generalizability) and/or the rich, who sometimes have little to do with their own children. We found examples of activist mothers who commented on their sons, but few parallel accounts by these sons or by other observers, and vice versa—we were well-supplied with reminiscences by sons but we lacked their mother's perspectives. Activist mothers tended to write about global issues and commented little about their children. Reminiscences by the sons of activists tended to focus on earliest memories rather than on their adolescent years when they would be more likely to understand feminist issues.

The references which do exist in the writings by sons about feminist mothers speak of the difficulty of raising feminist sons, and are full of guilt. For example, in an afterword to his mother's book on parenting sons, Michael Silverstein writes:

[M]y perceptions and memories of certain situations are different from my mother's. She remembers withdrawing from me and characterizes the attic room of my teenage years as "exile," while I remember my own active distancing behavior and recall that room as sanctuary. On the other hand, when she draws from her bank of therapeutic memories the general conclusion that many boys "not only accepted but encouraged this distancing," I see clearly the shadows of our own relationship.

This confirms what we probably all know: making sense of the mother–son relationship is not easy. Rich refers to the relationship between mother and child as "essential, distorted, misused …. The materials are here for the deepest mutuality and the most painful estrangement" (Rich, 1986: 225–226).

The significance of collecting and comparing mothers', sons', and other observers' voices became clear when we eventually found an example fitting our criteria in the form of the relationship between Vita Sackville-West and her son Nigel. There were several biographies, a television series, and collections of her letters. Her son had contributed thoughtful portraits of his mother, edited her correspondence, and published others' accounts.

The marriage of Vita Sackville-West and Harold Nicolson was privileged and unconventional in the extreme, as was their raising of their two sons. Vita was at the same time greatly admired and disparaged in her youth: bisexual, highly-strung, extraordinarily talented, and closely connected to the Bloomsbury Set and in particular to Virginia Woolf. Nevertheless she remained married to the same man for her entire adult life and forged a compassionate and (eventually) stable household within which to raise her sons. In her youth and early adulthood, she was regarded as fiercely independent because she insisted on pursuing her writing career rather than acting as help-meet to her diplomat husband. She was not a feminist in the sense of championing public issues of equity—as a member of the English elite, her social policies can only be regarded as conservative—but she demanded the kinds of lifestyle freedoms and personal equity within the domestic realm which late twentieth century feminists value. It is understandable that there was no expectation that her sons hold particular views on gender or racial equity since this was not characteristic of English feminism until the 1960s, and was anathema to the class-based ideology within which the Nicolson family was enmeshed.

In surveying what Sackville-West divulged about raising her sons, one is struck by her insistence on honesty in the mother–son relationship, and her clear enjoyment of her sons as they were on the verge of adolescence. In a letter to Harold, Vita writes of the boys:

> 26 December 1926 [Ben was twelve; Nigel, ten]
> Ben is in bed in Cranmer's dressing-room—your room!—and I am in bed in Cranmer's bedroom, and we have the door open between us, so that we can talk. I can hear him saying to himself, "the mild continuous epic of the soil," like somebody rolling a sweet round and round his tongue. Niggs [Nigel] is the same little clown, a born comic. He has got his bicycle, and is as happy as a king. His is infinitely serviable, unselfish, and affectionate. Also sturdy, practical, resourceful, independent, humourous. I see no flaw in him, as a character; everybody loves him. I have had to institute scrubbage, as never was there such a little guttersnipe. Otherwise he is perfect; not an intellectual, but we shall have enough to spare of that in Ben. My darling, we are very, very lucky in those two boys. They will, respectively, satisfy all that we could wish for: Ben our highbrowness, Niggs our human needs. Or, at least, so I read them. (Nicolson, 1992: 179)

She was a great proponent of hard work for her sons, and work that stretched them beyond their present abilities. When Ben failed his entrance exams at Oxford, he explained weakly to his mother, "I am bad at being made to do anything which, had I my own way, I would not do." Furious with this self-indulgent attitude, Vita wrote back in exasperation:

> My dear Ben! Really! What do you imagine life is made of? I curse you for being lazy, wasteful (time, not money) and without guts. I curse you for thinking a veneer of culture acquired principally from the conversation of people older, better educated, and above all more hard-working than yourself, is an adequate substitute for real knowledge, real application, real mental muscles .... Veneereal disease, that's what's the matter with you. (Glendinning, 1983: 271)

Three years later, she reported to Virginia Woolf that Ben was writing a book on Seurat: "rather ambitious, I think, but I'm all for the young biting off more than they can chew" (DeSalvo and Leaska, 1985: 399). At the same time as she meted out censure when necessary to her sons, she took enormous enjoyment in their talents and affection.

As a writer, Vita Sackville-West worked exceedingly hard, often most of the night. She was an extremely skilled landscape gardener/artist, pouring her energies into the huge gardens at Sissinghurst Castle by day and writing by night. She fully expected her sons to be literate and artistic, to accomplish mastery of these fields through their own labours, and to distinguish themselves as men of "good character." Her sons both became men of letters. Until his death in 1978, Ben was an art historian and editor of the prestigious Burlington Magazine. Nigel is author or editor of eight books, publisher of many more, and a former British Member of Parliament.

Nigel, apparently on behalf of his brother and himself, has written extensively about his mother. In *Portrait of a marriage* he notes that a gap always existed between mother and sons:

> It had been there since we were babies. When we were at school she dutifully tore herself away from her work to visit us on half terms at Summer Field and Eton, and was always sweet to us, but she could not disguise the effort it cost her to find new subjects to talk about when we had exhausted the garden and the dogs .... Later she always took an interest in what was happening to us, and during the war wrote to us very regularly, but her letters were more constrained than those she wrote to Harold. Her pen had needed pushing, we felt, instead of keeping pace with her thoughts. She was guiltily conscious that she never managed to establish an intimacy with her sons, and thought herself a failure as a mother, but it was as much our fault as hers. We never made the necessary effort to know her well. (Nicolson, 1973: 226)

Clearly, guilt characterizes both sides of this and many other mother–son relationships. Glendinning (1983) suggests, and Nigel himself concurs, that Vita found it easier to nurture Ben than Nigel, to whom she warmed more slowly (272). Nigel expresses regret about his inability to relate easily to Vita: "I feel remorseful about this. I should have taken the trouble to know Vita better" (Nicolson 14). In his *Portrait of a marriage*, Nigel recounts a painful effort on Vita's part to honour her son, and Nigel's life-long regret at his youthful response:

> She paused one evening at the bottom step of her staircase, turned to me shyly and said: "I have written a new poem, and I would like to dedicate it to you." "Oh, don't do that," I replied unthinkingly, "You know that I don't really understand your poetry." She went up the tower without a word, and when she came to dinner I saw that she had been crying. By this incomparably cruel remark I had meant, "Your poetry is the side of you that I have never shared, and cannot claim to share. I

don't deserve the dedication. I would be a form of intrusion." But that was not what I said .... I was then seventeen. (Glendinning, 1983: 272)

This story does little to illuminate the affect of feminist ideals on a son, but it does serve to remind us that what a son may assert at seventeen is not necessarily what he believes in later life.

What, then, can we conclude about and from the relationship between Vita Sackville-West and her two sons? We know some of what Vita hoped for her sons, how she demanded on occasion that they improve themselves, how one of the sons remembers her, and what became of those sons. We know that this mother, who insisted on time for herself and for her own career development, elicited pride, sympathy, and warmth in at least one son, and this the one reputedly more distant from his mother's affections. We have testimony from both mother and son that this unconventional, artistic, proto-feminist mother actively and effectively nurtured her sons, underlining their duties as well as their privilege. We can conclude much about the relationship between mother and sons, and while this relationship seems to have been mutually guilt-ridden, there is no sense at all that the sons regarded their often-absent mother as emasculating, hostile, or non-nurturant.

Sons of second wave feminists

Our sons were born between 1971 and 1981. They were raised by feminist mothers in two-parent homes where the mothers may not have been "in the home" to the same extent as other mothers. There was perhaps more sharing of household responsibilities, and it is likely that the boys had more personal time with their fathers (and less with their mothers) than was usual for other children. These were the physical implications of having an "absent mother." In addition, our sons were also the sons of feminists so they heard feminist rhetoric— ideas which may or may not have been in conflict with information they were receiving from other sources. We have tried to separate the issues associated with the "absent mother" from those associated with the "feminist mother."

When we conducted the research, the sons were twenty-four, twenty-two, eighteen, seventeen, and fifteen. At the outset, we were prepared for nasty surprises; that is, we expected to hear about hidden resentments and unknown hurts concerning the ideological battles that had become a part of our professional lives. Neither of us felt that we had "failed" our children, but the natural doubts of parenthood were exacerbated by the fact that we had chosen not to be "at home" mothers. There was a possibility that disapproving relatives and neighbours might have been right. Perhaps we had damaged our children by our lack of "sacrificial willingness to set personal ambition aside" (Thurur, 1994: 287). There was also the feminist issue itself. Feminism is often misunderstood to mean a belief in female superiority and is often denigrated in popular culture. It was possible that our boys suffered because, in spite of our efforts, they did not understand our stand on equity. There was also the possibility that they had been ridiculed by peers or mistreated by adults because of our activism.

We used "interlocking conversations" similar to those used by Castle, Reynolds, and Abbey (1996). First, the siblings interviewed each other using a set of research questions. Before listening to our sons' interviews, we recorded our own recollections concerning the same questions. Finally, we had family interviews—mothers and sons. After these had been transcribed and shared, we two mothers discussed them, and one mother did a further interview to clarify "absent mother" questions with her sons.

The absent mother

> The new division between the public and private spheres … produced a more dichotomized view of manhood and womanhood, a more elaborate scheme of sex roles. It also made women's positions more precarious as men worked for wages and women performed the unpaid and increasingly devalued work at home. (Millman, 1991: 136)

When neither parent is available to be a "stay at home" parent, there are several integrated issues to be considered: household duties, childcare, child development, and even family finances. The family practice of housekeeping and childcare in a dual career household is dependent upon the family ideology. In families where there is a belief that certain activities are "women's work" there are two possibilities. There may be no change in the wife's household workload, or the man may assume tasks that he does not normally consider his responsibility in recognition of her wage earner status. In a more egalitarian relationship, the jobs may remain segregated with each partner assuming specific responsibilities, or the jobs may be shared in a partnership format (Lein, 1984: 42). Children raised in an egalitarian partnership witness non-traditional work role separation and are more likely to be expected to do all kinds of work regardless of sex stereotyping.

Our sons mentioned almost nothing about household duties or housekeeping routines. One said: "I don't think there ever has been a time when we came home when there wasn't a meal on the table or in the process." The boys had the perception that cooperation in doing household tasks was normal:

> You trade off things. Someone does the dishes, someone does the laundry, someone does the cleaning blah, blah, blah. We do it together.

I think there is maybe a better understanding (now). I don't think there
are many people out there among our friends who would say "I'm not
going to clear" or "I won't cook" or "I'm not going to clean this because
that is not my job." If it comes about, that's sort of a systemic thing that
they don't talk about. I don't think people would just say I don't do
cooking because I'm a guy.

When specifically questioned on this issue they dismissed it as unimportant.
One boy remembered a time when his friend had been surprised to see his
mother driving the car when his father was in the car but other than that he had
no comment on the issue.

In both households, childcare duties were also shared. The dual-parenting
process produced a sort of "integrated parent" in the minds of the children.
They repeatedly used phrases such as "both my parents" or "both you and dad"
rather than centering on one role. They had difficulty sorting out which things
about their childhood were affected by their mother alone, by their father alone
or by this "integrated parent." The integrated parent allowed them to maintain
balance in the absence of an individual full-time at-home parent.

Contrary to prevailing public perceptions, studies of the security, intelligence,
and social adjustment and "masculinity" of sons of working mothers, have
concluded that these sons have emotional and intellectual as well as financial
advantages. Increased interaction with both parents is beneficial to the child.
Children securely attached to both parents showed the greatest interest in other
adults, even more than those who were attached only to their mothers (Lamb,
Pleck, and Levine, 1986: 145). Teachers rated children of employed mothers as
better adjusted, more independent, and peer oriented (Mischel and Fuhr, 1988:
192). Although some studies have shown that sons of employed mothers had
lower IQs, when the same studies were done with children with increased paternal
influence, there was no difference (Mischel and Fuhr, 1988: 193, 198).

Several studies cited by Lamb, Pleck, and Levine (1986: 149) pointed out
that children develop a sense of personal efficacy when parents make appropriate
responses to their signals. Observations in the orphanages of Romania where
children were fed, changed, and cared for according to a timetable, serve as an
example of this. Children who cried were ignored so they learned not to cry.
When outsiders came to the orphanages after the fall of the Communist regime
in 1989, they found three- or four-year-old children who were delighted to accept
rides on a merry-go-round but who would not ask for more nor show any indication
that they wanted more. They were willing to accept what was given but had no
idea that they could intervene to control their environment (*Ideas*, CBC radio,
July 13, 1998). As Lamb et al. (1986) suggested, "Parents who provided stimulation
that is developmentally appropriate and plentiful have more cognitively competent

children" (149). However this stimulation can come from either parent or from other sources:

> The effects of increased paternal involvement on intellectual performance may reflect ... the benefits of having extensive stimulation from two highly involved and relatively competent parents instead of only one. (Lamb et al., 1986: 150)

Stability of the family unit may be more important to the child than the details of who is available to care for them on a day-to-day basis (Stafford and Bayer, 1993: 142–146).

The effects of maternal employment on children may be related to how the mother feels about working. If mothers believe they are doing the right thing and they are happy doing it (whether it be working or not working) then their children are well adjusted. The unhappy stay-at-home mother is more damaging to her children than the unhappy working mother in measures of social and cognitive development (Mischel and Fuhr, 1988: 195).

The positive affects of a working mother are most evident during the teen years. Teenaged children of employed mothers have higher self-esteem, more sense of belonging, and better interpersonal relations both at home and at school (Mischel and Fuhr, 1988: 199). Our sons confirmed this research. As one of them said "I don't think we suffered in any way."

Much "mother blaming" literature is based on a perception that an inadequate mother (or perhaps an overbearing one) will do irreparable damage to her son's masculinity. As Sebald (1976) wrote—in seemingly complete sincerity—in 1976: "If a mother does not identify herself with the feminine role, the boy's masculinity usually suffers and he exhibits more feminine traits" (97). Sebald set out to warn the American public about "Momism," a dreadful condition in which Mom "tries to manipulate the child by extending acceptance and love on a conditional basis" (9). This results in a man who is "absolutely unequipped for making personal decisions ... inclined to marry a woman who will exploit his overdependence ... his wife becomes a substitute Mom—a horrifying prospect indeed" (11). But fathers are not absolved from blame:

> The pivotal point for the boy's feelings of certainty and adequacy is the role his father plays in his life. If this role is salient, strong, and tangible, personality problems for the boy (including Momistic encroachment) can be warded off. (102)

Adrienne Rich counters this perception of the mother:

The "son of the mother" (the mother who first loves herself) has a greater chance of realizing that strength and vulnerability, toughness and expressiveness, nurturance and authority; [they] are not opposites, not the sole inheritance of one sex or the other. (Rich, 1976: 209)

In studies of sex role stereotyping, both girls and boys whose mothers work are less bound by stereotypical sex-role perceptions, and girls in particular, benefit from the increased "flexibility in sex-role perceptions" (Mischel and Fuhr, 1988: 200; Lamb, Pleck, and Levine, 1986: 147). This lack of stereotyping provides expanded career options for both males and females, and has been associated with more creativity and better personality adjustment and total adjustment scores on standard personality tests (Mischel and Fuhr, 1988: 201).

Although those who study the topics prefer to separate "masculinity" from the issue of homosexuality, questions about masculinity in relation to mothering often focus on the sexual preferences of the sons. There is no evidence that mothers or fathers have anything to do with the child's eventual choices. The myth that boys choose other men "either in flight from the power of women, or in protest against the traditional male role" is just as prevalent and unsubstantiated as the myth that a boy may become homosexual "in reaction to his father's khamstvo, his gross abuse of women as sexual objects," or as a replacement for a father who was chiefly absent (Rich, 1986: 211).

Since there is no evidence that working mothers negatively impact their children, and some evidence that increased paternal involvement has a positive affect on growing children, it would follow that the "integrated parent" our children experienced was at least as valuable as having one full-time parent, and possibly more advantageous. Our sons did not feel that they had been disadvantaged; they spoke only of appreciating our parenting styles:

I guess the argument is that (working mothers') children suffer .... I think that this is sort of a conservative backlash statement .... I don't think I have ever suffered in any way.

Instead of feeling neglected by their mothers, our children commented on how having a working mother enriched their lives both financially (because they contributed to the family income) and intellectually (because they were more interesting). When we asked our sons whether or not women should work outside the home, the boys in both families confirmed that for financial reasons, having one partner stay at home was "not a reasonable way to live."

Our experience confirms Chodorow's (1978) contention that traditional views of motherhood are limiting to all concerned. By limiting the role of primary caregiver to women, sons are deprived of the opportunity to develop their capacity for nurturance. By breaking the cycle with a new model of shared parenting "both male and female children become more whole and ultimately more capable of satisfying relations than their parents were" (Cohen and Katzenstein, 1988: 31).

The feminist mother

> What do we fear? That our sons will accuse us of making them into misfits and outsiders? That they will suffer as we have suffered from patriarchal reprisals? Do we fear they will somehow lose their male status and privilege, even as we are seeking to abolish that inequality? Must a woman see her child as "the enemy" in order to teach him that he need not imitate a "macho" style of maleness? (Rich, 1986: 205–206)

Recent feminist literature has looked at the question of the effective nurturing of male sons (Lorde, 1984; Rich, 1986; Silverstein, 1994). The focus of much of their work is based on the perception that feminists consider men to be "the enemy" and therefore must hate them all, even their own children. For most feminists it is the patriarchal system which is the enemy, not the individuals within it, especially not those who do not subscribe to patriarchy. We want our sons to become men who understand the issues associated with male privilege and refute the inequity that they see there. This may alienate them from men who view feminist sympathizers with the same disregard as they view women. Thus the aims of feminists raising sons and daughters are similar. They hope to nurture them in a belief that all people are equal, and to prevent them from being damaged by patriarchy.

> It is absurd to think that women on the path of feminism wish to abandon their sons, emotionally or otherwise .... We wish for our sons—as for our daughters—that they may grow up unmutilated by gender-roles, sensitized to misogyny in all its forms. (Rich, 1986: 207)

In a special 1993 issue of *Ms. Magazine*, feminist mothers wrestled with the question of what constituted feminist nurturant practices of sons. They were concerned with the interrelated issues of teaching children "critical resistance," humanizing the parental–child relationship, and teaching "aggression deconstruction" and self-protection. They saw themselves as agents of change attempting to produce in their sons a critical view of society, intolerant of injustice. They chose to challenge patriarchal norms through daily discussion with their children, providing them with a vocabulary for understanding systemic injustice. But for boys it is harder than it is for girls. As Morgan noted:

The challenges faced by a feminist rearing a daughter are enormous—but at least you can unambivalently (so I imagine) tell her, Go for it! Don't let anyone stop you. With a son, you must somehow erode the allure of male entitlement and communicate a delicate double message: Fulfill yourself to the utmost as a human being—but try to divest yourself of the male power that routinely accrues to you. Be all you can as a person—but don't forget your automatic male advantages are bought at the cost of their denial to female people. If, as in my case, the son is European American, you try to communicate a comparable message about being white in a racist culture. (Morgan, 1993: 37)

This was a part of our own feminist mothering. Our children spoke about feminism as a gateway to understanding other equity issues. When asked "How did it affect you to have a feminist mother?" one son responded:

I saw stuff more unbiased ... because when you are aware of some of the injustices, and are aware that they occur, you see them, not only as those injustices, but also others that don't have to do with feminism but racism and other stuff like that.

Another son made a similar connection when trying to define feminism:

I think it (feminism) must go beyond just looking at equality .... I would say the same about the black people trying to get equality there. It's just basically fairness.

They seemed to think that being feminist and holding to feminist ideals was "a normal process, especially for educated women."

The feminist mothers in the 1993 *Ms.* article indicated that they had fears for their sons: "Because many of us tend to characterize the world of men as predatory, aggressive, ruthlessly competitive, we fear for our sons more than mothers who see the world of men as more benign" (Gordon, 1993: 48). Rich wrote sadly of the possibility of isolating male off-spring from the masculine world:

We also have to face the fact that in the recent stage of history our sons may feel profoundly alone in the masculine world, with few if any close relationships with other men (as distinct from male "bonding" in defense of male privilege). (Rich, 1986: 207)

It was our knowledge of the perceived difficulties of being attached to feminist principles which caused us to be startled by the complete lack of resentment and absence of fear in own children. For them, the "aggression deconstruction" and self-protection needs described by the feminists of the 1970s were not important. For example, they considered themselves either feminist or pro-feminist, and did not hesitate to say so. One said, "Of course I am a feminist, I think I have always been a feminist." The sons identified four different types of feminism at various times throughout their conversations. They agreed with the "equity between men and women" type of feminism. One said: If feminism is the fighting for equality, then sure I would want to call myself a feminist. It's so natural ... I'm a feminist, everybody is feminist. Most intelligent and educated people are feminists." They also understood the sex role arguments:

> Another way (of understanding feminism) is to redefine what is meant by the concept of women and analyze the concept of women. It may not be equality, but trying to change the definition of gender issues and gender roles.

They were not enthused about "intellectual feminism." That is,

> the "Simone de Beauvoir" feminism where there is a constant speaking of "Other" and women are labeled the "Other" with a capital "O" .... I'm not against it but I definitely wouldn't call myself a feminist in that sense .... The language in which they write is so confused .... It is purely intellectual sorts of games. It is really philosophical and interactive.

They were strongly opposed to "Nazi Feminism which says things like 'all sex with men is rape' and things like that."

However, feminism as equity seeking was considered not only normal but beneficial. They intimated that this attitude gave them an advantage over their less enlightened male counterparts. When one son said he was "raised to be pro-feminist," he was asked if that had affected his relationships with his peers. He responded, "Yeah. I'm better than them—socially better." Another commented "I am probably more sensitive to those issues than I would have otherwise been and that's a good good thing." Still another said that it gave him an advantage over other first year university students:

> I think we got it (feminism) from you (his mother) but for most people I don't think they get it from high school .... At least for males, it's sort of a slap in the face if you go to university ... (where) there is strong feminism, and all the -isms and all the "Others," all the "marginalized" people really try to take back their lost power. For certain people, this was a shock, (for) those who have never experienced this before for a lot of

males and a lot of females as well .... a lot of shock tactics were being used.

In a later discussion, he commented on the role of feminism in the university setting where "you tend to run into a lot of women who are experimenting themselves with feminism and you are in that process as well." He did not claim that it made relationships with women easier or better, just that:

> You tend to try to understand that (their feminism) as well. If you bring it back to having a mother who had feminist ideas, I guess I am more aware of these issues than a lot of other people. I didn't think it made me anything; it just made me more aware of it.

None of the boys spoke about difficulties in relating to male peer groups and they did not perceive themselves as being any different from other males their own age. As one son explained it, "I think all of my friends had a positive perspective of women and that they would take equality for granted."

The feminist mothers from the *Ms.* article (and fathers in several of these relationships) seemed to attempt to demystify parental roles and encouraged their sons to see their mothers (and fathers) as real, fallible people. They saw mothering as "a learning process, rather than an interpretive and potentially critical act" (Everingham, 1994: 7).

There are probably as many styles of parenting as there are of feminism so it would certainly be misleading to assume that all feminists adopt a similar style. However, parenting styles can be differentiated according to methods for securing the child's compliance. Parents may demand obedience, use reasoning, or accept non-compliance. Reasoning has been described as the most beneficial:

> "[I]nstrumentally competent" children (those who are friendly, independent, and assertive with peers, and compliantly nonintrusive with adults) are likely to have authorative parents—that is, parents who provide firm and articulately reasoned guidance for their children. Both authoritarian parents (those who fail to provide any rationale for their instructions) and permissive parents (those who fail to provide adequate guidance) have less instrumentally competent children. (Lamb et al., 1986: 152)

Everingham (1994) suggested that mothering should be understood as an interaction: "it is just as important to investigate what happens to the (m)other while nurturing as it is to investigate what happens to the child, since the affective sensations experienced by the (m)other while nurturing structure future patterns of interaction" (46). Thus parenting is not application of rules or even understanding what the rules are before the "game" begins. It is a negotiated relationship in which the parents seek what is best for the child in a rational and sensitive manner. What is right for one child or situation may not necessarily be right for another.

Our own sons felt that non-authoritarian processes had been beneficial to them. One son spoke explicitly about the advantages his parents gave him by providing a model of intelligent conversation:

> I think it was a tremendous advantage to have educated parents, articulate parents who know how to hold a conversation .... Also important is the way we talked through arguments, not like angry but intellectual arguments ... rationally debated.

He commented specifically about his mother's role in teaching him how to articulate rational arguments and to think critically:

> Rational argument and critical thinking—that was always the form that conversations have taken between Mom and I. It has never been a matter of "do this because you have to do it." It may well be done at the end, but it always started out by her explaining why this is the best thing, not just "this is the best thing that you have to accept" and that got my rational views working.

The other mother felt that non-authoritarian parenting produced a questioning attitude in one of her sons that caused his teachers to think he was defiant. He would refuse to do assignments if he thought they were senseless and would do as he was told only if he saw good reason for it. This caused him trouble at school. His mother described it:

> It (school) was just so straight and narrow that there wasn't space for a kid who was a little different .... He felt he was protecting his principles and I kind of agreed with him. I mean, when you teach a kid to be wary of unreasoned authority, this is what you get. I had to side with him, he was just living out to the nth degree the things that I had taught him. It would have been easier if he had been less principled about it, but that was the way he chose to do it and I had to go along with it.

The boy admitted that "(at school) I always had a problem with all the authority and I wouldn't do what they'd tell me." When asked about his mother's involvement with his schooling, he said, "She always came in and went to the office for me because she got called in a whole bunch and she always fought for my side and I always appreciated that. She never took their side over mine."

Parents in pursuit of critical resistance who wish to protect their sons from being damaged by patriarchy are likely to use reasoned conversation in their interactions with their children. This approach is sometimes difficult in a world that does not always value reasoned fair responses and that is often controlled by unreasoned conventions. Our sons did not perceive themselves as disadvantaged by their upbringing and spoke positively about our parenting processes. They have learned to live in the society we have handed down to them and they seem to think that they are not unusual or in any way distinct from their friends because of it.

Another male advantage?

When we started this study we were unsure of the outcome. The best that we hoped for was that we would find out that our sons did not perceive us as having damaged them by being employed feminist mothers. We did expect a few hurts and passing accusations, and we were not prepared for the wholehearted vote of confidence that we received.

Through this work we have been made aware of the complicated morass of interaction that makes up the parent–child relationship. However, we have been able to apply existing literature to our own experience, a process which was made easier when we accepted as discrete those issues associated the working (absent) mother and those associated with the feminist mother.

The working mother was rather easily absolved. In spite of folk wisdom to the contrary, there was no evidence in the literature that supported the notion that a working mother caused damage to her children. If anything, the literature suggested that rather than less outside work for mothers, there should be increased parental input from fathers. Children of both genders with working mothers have advantages in all areas including intellectual development, social adjustment, and career opportunities. Our own sons saw nothing but advantages to having a working mother; in fact, they planned to have working wives.

The effects of a feminist mother on her sons are less obvious. Although feminists were able to identify their expectations for their children as "critical resisters" in a patriarchal world who would perhaps be isolated and punished for their stance, our sons do not perceive themselves as disadvantaged by their acceptance of feminist ideals. They could not remember any negative incidents associated with having a feminist mother, nor could they think of any way in which their awareness of feminism had served against them. They were able to find specific aspects of their upbringing that they particularly valued, such as their understanding of issues of equity and social justice. They suggested that it was useful to have an understanding of feminism but stopped short of saying that it had given them an advantage in forming relationships.

We realize the difficulties of building a theory on our own rather limited experiences and we remain puzzled by our own children's responses to feminism. They seemed almost nonchalant about an issue that we have always considered defining and life shaping. An issue that affected our lives in many ways seems to have coalesced into theirs without any ripples of resentment or emotional discomfort. We know that feminism is not an easy issue for girls to deal with. Could it be so simple for our boys? Perhaps part of the answer is a simplistic acknowledgment of the fact that patriarchy favours men and therefore, as men, they have a positive choice to make. They can choose patriarchy and enjoy the male advantage or they can choose to tolerate feminism and build strong relationships with women, take advantage of a strengthening trend toward equity, and look forward to a wealthier future with a well-employed partner. If this is the case, in an ultimate irony, it seems that feminist mothers may have handed their sons yet another male advantage. Let us hope that they have also raised them to be sensitive enough to use that advantage equitably.

Chapter Five

TELLING OUR STORIES

FEMINIST MOTHERS AND DAUGHTERS

Christina Baker

> Most of what has been, or is, between mothers, daughters, and in motherhood, in daughterhood, has never been recorded, nor written with comprehension in our own voices, out of our own lives and truths.
>
> —Tillie Olsen[1]

As we interviewed feminist mothers and daughters for our book *The conversation begins*, my daughter and I asked each mother and daughter pair to talk about their own relationship as they attempted to live their feminism. During our interviews with more than twenty-five pioneers of feminism's second wave and their now-grown daughters, two questions were uppermost in our minds. First, had these feminist mothers passed down a feminist legacy to their daughters? Second, what were the costs for mothers and daughters of combining motherhood with a passionate commitment to a broader life? The answer to our first question—had feminist mothers passed down a feminist legacy to their daughters?—was a simple yes. Although not all the daughters are activists like their mothers, all are practicing feminists.

Feminist mothers are world changers; they believe in justice. When Tillie Olsen's daughter Julie came home from school one day quoting the old chestnut, "I complained because I had no shoes until I met a man who had no feet," Tillie responded, "Then I hope you complained twice as hard because both conditions are lousy and neither should be tolerated."[2] Journalist Barbara Ehrenreich says that after her children were born she wanted to change the world for them: "I felt I wouldn't be a good mother if I wasn't stopping nuclear war while making a nutritional dinner." But she adds, "You have to be a superparent to raise children and make the world safe for them at the same time."[3]

Feminist mothers conveyed confidence as well as principles to their daughters. Attorney Lori Smeal, daughter of Eleanor Smeal, twice president of the National Organization of Women and current president of the Feminist Majority, learned she was "capable of doing any job ... capable of anything."[4] Nina Beck, physical therapist and daughter of author and professor Evelyn Torton Beck, says, "I was told that if I wanted to be a rocket scientist, nothing would stand in my way. In fact, I think I was expected to be a rocket scientist."[5] Kirsten Wilson, a performance artist, has drawn great strength from the knowledge that her mother, Ms. Foundation president Marie Wilson, loves the rebel in her—"the part that is inappropriate, that is too loud, that says the wrong things." Knowing she is worthy in her mother's eyes means Kirsten can "dare to be different."[6] For daughters of feminists, the idea of equality handed down by their mothers is securely in place.

Answers, however, to our second question—what were the personal costs of combining motherhood and activism?—were more complicated and sometimes troubling. Motherhood is a topic that the women's movement has addressed, when it has done so at all, with ambivalence. Since Betty Friedan's clarion call in *The feminine mystique* for women to leave the "comfortable concentration camp of the home and find added fulfillment in careers,"[7] women have struggled to combine motherhood and feminism, often in lonely silence. Second-wave pioneer and author Alix Kates Shulman recalls motherhood as "one of the great explosive divides"[8] in the women's movement. Barbara Seaman, founder of the women's health movement, remembers "a lot of debate about whether you could be a mother and a feminist."[9] *Ms. Magazine* cofounder Letty Cottin Pogrebin wrote in 1973 that a discussion of motherhood would "shake sisterhood to its roots."[10]

The reason is apparent. Feminist motherhood complicates the role of the emancipated woman. In *The second shift*, Arlie Hochschild tells us "feminism is infinitely easier when you take motherhood out, but then it speaks to fewer women."[11] Bearing and nurturing children remain a fact of life for more than ninety percent of women worldwide. Two decades after Adrienne Rich lamented in *Of woman born* that motherhood remained a "crucial, still relatively unexplored area for feminist theory,"[12] the discussion remains in its early stages.

Despite the second wave's silence on the subject, motherhood and feminism have always been inextricably linked. Tillie Olsen, in her mid-eighties when we interviewed her, declared:

> Motherhood remains central in my life—more than illuminator, instructor of my feminism—touchstone for sustenance, hope, connectedness, self knowledge; human understanding, beauty, and anguish; yes, and wellspring, passionate source for all I am, do, write.[13]

In reality, the experiences of pregnancy and giving birth led many women to feminism. Congresswoman Patsy Mink, who learned in 1976 that she had been issued diethylstilbestrol (DES) two decades earlier as part of an experimental study, led the fight for gender equity in Congress. Barbara Seaman, enraged upon learning that her infant's illness was caused by a routinely administered laxative that had traveled through her breast milk, used her anger to found the National Women's Health Network. Barbara Ehrenreich became radicalized after her doctor, impatient to leave for vacation, introduced the speed-up drug oxytocin into her otherwise normal labor.

Motherhood for feminists remains fraught with problems. "Mothering is so unsupported in our society that every attempt to raise a child is a complex juggling act,"[14] says Shulman. Early childhood specialist Julie Olsen Edwards, who says that mothering is "the hardest thing I have ever done,"[15] still grieves over the things she couldn't do for her children in a political climate that "wages war on children" and where often families have to "go it alone."[16] Marie Wilson agrees: "Mothering should be joyous work, but trying to raise children in isolation is crazy. Children need to connect to caring adults, lots of them." Wilson adds, "We live in a culture that neither appreciates nor rewards parenting, a culture where the difficulty and hard work of constantly being responsible for another life is enormously denied."[17]

Mother-blame still permeates much of our culture. For many women, says Barbara Seaman, "the way you spell mother is G-U-I-L-T." A manuscript that Seaman began writing years ago, entitled "The American Mother: Whatever You Do, It's Wrong," remains unfinished because she felt "too guilty" as a mother.[18] To remain credible, the women's movement must tackle in earnest the question of how to further the advancement of women and, at the same time, create conditions that guarantee the adequate nurturing of children.

History reminds us that women have always worked outside the home. Prior to 1940, most middle-class women did so before rather than after marriage. My own mother, for example, had no choice but to resign her teaching position when she married in 1928; married women were not allowed to teach in North Carolina. During World War II, women demonstrated their competence at jobs normally held by men. Although most women returned home immediately after the war, they began to re-enter the workforce after their childbearing years.

As the century turns, motherhood is no longer the assumed way of life and calling it was around the middle of the twentieth century; rather, mothering competes with career and personal growth as a source of a woman's identity. In 1996, seventy-seven percent of all married women with school-age children were employed or looking for work. For those with preschool-age children, the figure was sixty-three percent—five times what it was in 1950. In addition, more than a quarter of all children live in single-parent families with mothers who work full-time. Society, however, has not yet caught up with this cultural redefinition. Neither employers nor government nor many men recognize that mothers need support if they are to balance what Andrew J. Cherlin calls "their double burden."

Not surprisingly, the gravest health crisis currently facing mothers, according to Seaman, is exhaustion.[19] Despite progress over the past two decades, employed women continue to do between seventy to eighty percent of all housework, including most of the repetitive chores, laboring from dawn to dusk and beyond. In addition to the "second shift" identified by Arlie Hochschild—that of housework, parenting, and emotion work—most women undertake a "third shift."[20] Routinely ignored by policy-makers and analysts, this shift involves the maintenance of community—caring for relatives and friends outside the home by keeping in touch through letters, phone calls, visits, and invitations.

All told, women who work outside the home devote thirty-five more hours per week than their male partners, the equivalent of an extra month each year, to the second and third shifts. Women have reduced the amount of time they spent doing housework in the past two decades (take-out food sales have increased, while floor-wax sales have gone down), but husbands and male partners have been slow to pick up the slack. While men have increased the amount of social time they spend with their children, mothers still do more than eighty percent of the day-to-day physical care. Letty Cottin Pogrebin says that her daughter, television producer Abigail Pogrebin, is honest about the fact that "you can't be a superwoman without help. Something is going to slip or drop."[21] Those fourteen to twenty percent of mothers who can afford to hire outside help do so.

Second-wave feminists who tell their stories in *The conversation begins* testify to their personal struggles with these issues. In 1969, Shulman, a mother of two, saw that the only way toward true equality in marriage was genuine "task sharing." Her defiant manifesto, "A Marriage Agreement," proposed that men and women play equal roles in taking care of their children and their households. After *Life* and *Red Book* published the "Agreement," Shulman was flooded with letters asking how she got her husband to agree. Twenty-five years later, she says, "The answer is, either he agrees or the marriage is over; but I never said so outright. Despite our best efforts, our agreement didn't work very well. I wanted [my husband] to take responsibility; he wanted to escape."[22]

For some men, escape took the form of rationalization. Eager to get back to work after her daughter, Nguyen, was born, Miriam Ching Louie, a grassroots activist, remembers arguing with her husband, Belvin. "We have to figure out if it's worth your going to work because of the cost of child care," he said. "Maybe it's not worth it." Finally, Louie asked, "How come the price of a baby-sitter is deducted from my salary? How come the cost of the sitter is not deducted from both our salaries?" And she returned to work.[23]

The few fortunate women for whom motherhood and feminism did not clash cite supportive partners as the reason. Patsy Mink says, "A supportive husband made it easier. Because I spent so much of my time organizing and attending meetings, John played a large role in raising Wendy .... One of us was there all the time."[24] Smeal's husband made it "immensely easier to do what I did—and probably made it possible. He was always supportive ... able to be fully present when I wasn't around."[25] Deborah Wolf acknowledges the strong framework of support provided by her husband: "Leonard helped enormously. He was more nurturing than I, and in many respects he was a model feminist father."[26] Ehrenreich's husband did "more than half the childrearing." While she worked, he took care of daughter Rosa, and even after their divorce, he came over to cook dinner three nights a week for the children.[27] Yolande Moses, president of City College of New York, notes that her husband has been the primary parent "two-thirds of the time." She also had helpful assistance from a sister and mother, but the efforts of the husband were crucial. "That's how I've been able to do it," Moses concludes.[28]

Some daughters of these feminists thought of their attentive fathers as equal if not prime caregivers in the home. About her father, attorney Lori Smeal says, "He was an unusual father; not only was he always there for my brother and me, he also helped out at home by cleaning, doing laundry, and cooking."[29] Writer Naomi Wolf observes that her parents' egalitarian relationship gave her "a skewed sense of what was normal. I thought the whole world was going to be like that bubble of tolerance and progression I grew up in and was astonished to find it wasn't true."[30] Rosa Ehrenreich, an attorney, says, "Dad was around the whole time I was growing up." Even after her parents' divorce, she says, "We occasionally had bizarre situations where Mom would be out of town, Dad would come over to make dinner, and my stepfather, my brother, and I would join him at the table."[31] Shana Moses Bawek, a college student, underscores the point: "My father has been the primary parent. I would not be the same person if my father hadn't been around as much as he was."[32] College student Nguyen Louie felt closer to her father "because he did things with me."[33]

Whether or not they had supportive husbands, all our feminist mothers needed some form of mother substitute to help them through. Seaman, insisting that her housekeeper, Ann P. Wilson, be included in the photographs of mothers and daughters in *The conversation begins*, says candidly, "Behind every mother you ever heard of there usually stands another woman who propped her up." She adds, "If we don't do more to provide affordable child care and other assistance to mothers, the slow ascent of women toward equality will stall and our children will be in major trouble."[34] Most mothers cannot choose not to work, but until quality child care is available and affordable for all, equality for women remains elusive.

Some mothers were astonishingly candid in retrospect about the conflict between being active in the world and being present for their daughters. Full-time activist Elizabeth Martinez says that she was often not available to her daughter, Tessa; adding that she was there for her only in emergencies or on occasions like graduation.[35] Evelyn Torton Beck recalls being "so preoccupied with discovering her own capabilities" that she wasn't fully present for her children. Beck sometimes wonders "if daughters have a particular way of getting lost when their mothers are trying to find themselves, especially if the daughter is the firstborn."[36] Helen Rodriguez-Trias, an international leader of the women's health movement, regrets "not being more attentive, not taking more time with the kids."[37]

The daughters spell out their responses clearly. Rodriguez-Trias's daughter, nutritionist Laura Brainen-Rodriguez, says, "I was resentful that my mother was gone so much. I always felt she wanted to be the mother of the world, but not my mother."[38] Her sister, psychiatrist JoEllen Brainen-Rodriguez, adds, "I have missed having [my mother] present for me. I told her, 'I want you to be a grandparent to your grandchildren.' I still wish she were more present for me, which is evidence of how powerful childhood longings are."[39] Teacher Shira Seaman says, "I often felt that I had to compete with my mother's work. I felt that other people got her attention and I didn't. She was preoccupied, and I sometimes felt abandoned.[40]

Daughters admit to having sometimes felt abandoned by their feminist mothers. Lauralee Brown, a singer, says her mother, Paula Gunn Allen, was often absent: "I never seemed to be able to get enough attention from her. She had a studio and was painting and writing poetry .... To get her attention was really difficult."[41] Rainy Dawn Ortiz remembers that her mother, poet and singer Joy Harjo, was away on trips a lot: "I know it was part of her career, but it was rough at times. There were times I wished she had been there to help me or could have seen what I was going through."[42]

Daughters' attitudes ranged from resentment to resignation. Kianga Stroud, a student and daughter of activist Nkenge Toure, says, "We were latchkey kids. A lot of times I wished my mother had been at home. I resented her for being away at meetings. I felt neglected, and I missed her."[43] Shana Moses Bawek says of her mother, "The way I see it, she's trying to be perfect, to have a good job and be a mom who is present all the time, but that's impossible. You can't be in two places at once .... I like my mother best when she is just being my mom."[44]

Mothers usually found it easier to integrate one child into their lives. Television anchorwoman Carol Jenkins says, "Elizabeth became my little partner. I took her everywhere I could, including work. She simply became part of my working life. When I did the news, she would stretch out under the anchor's desk and color."[45] Shamita Das Dasgupta, professor and author, carried her daughter with her to classes and demonstrations—wherever she went. "Sayantani was part of me, like my arm," she says. "I couldn't stick my role as a feminist in one compartment and my role as a mother and wife in another." Das Dasgupta believes strongly that you "cannot give quality time if you don't spend quantity time with a child."[46]

Third-wave daughters are beginning to speak out about the next hurdle for feminism: finding a balance between family and career. Abigail Pogrebin says clearly what many pioneers of the second wave are only beginning to admit publicly:

> Women having kids right now are having a tough time. It's not clear how to handle all the demands or the conflicting pulls. There should be some room for addressing the pitfalls of the career-family balancing act—especially for my generation .... Maybe it's not possible to have a husband, kids, career, and toned body all at the same time. There are costs, and I don't think it's terrible to acknowledge that.[47]

Mothering one's own daughters as feminists especially requires rigorous personal honesty. Marie Wilson, a mother of five, notes:

> It is important to tell the truth, that we not pretend to live in these we-can-have-it-all pictures. There are costs .... That we abandoned our children in some ways while we did the work to save them in others is real. It is important not to gloss things over or to slip into the trap that because we are feminists we were perfect mothers who raised perfectly feminist daughters. We learn most from each other when we are honest about our own lives.[48]

Shulman says, "How you parent involves not just your political commitment or ideology but your whole sociological and psychic makeup."[49] Although feminism influences our mothering, it is only a part of the picture.

The way we parent our children stems in large measure from our own personal experiences. Feminists must address the causes and effects of dysfunction in our own lives if we wish to change the world. Paula Gunn Allen points the way:

> If I can unsnarl the dreadful historical tangle of intergenerational dysfunction, then my children will not have to continue the cycle; we can all let go of it and do something else. That is a legacy I would like to leave my children and grandchildren.[50]

Allen's daughter, Lauralee Brown, now in her mid-forties, has arrived at a place of understanding:

> In the sixties and seventies my mother tried to instill in me a self-assurance she didn't have herself at the time. I'd tell my friends, "She's got me believing and behaving in ways that she doesn't even truly believe or behave in yet." She helped forge the way by not breaking down, by going through therapy, and enriching her own knowledge. I know that any action she took and any choices she made when I was growing up were the best she could do .... Certainly some of it was painful for me and I didn't understand it, but she has made every effort to heal that .... She has gone through a lot of recovery and therapy to be a good mother.[51]

That effort was echoed in the experience of other feminist mothers and daughters we interviewed. Forging a new relationship with her daughter, Tessa, Elizabeth Martinez found that "all sorts of emotions and complications" required attention. The night her mother died, Elizabeth went back to her apartment with Tessa, and there they talked until dawn. "Tessa told me about things that had been difficult for her in our relationship, things she had not said before," recalled Elizabeth. "At some point I had the sense just to listen. I didn't even feel defensive, and was glad she talked."[52]

The conversation has begun as we learn from feminist pioneers who have gone before. In the past, mothers everywhere offered their daughters the best love they knew. Today feminism informs and strengthens the mother –daughter bond as we—mothers and daughters together—continue to expand our vision of social justice and deepen our self-knowledge. Therein lies the healing of ourselves, each other, and the world. May the conversation continue.

Notes

1. Tillie Olsen, *Mother to daughter, daughter to mother* (New York: Feminist Press, 1984: 275).
2. Christina Looper Baker and Christina Baker Kline, *The conversation begins: Mothers and daughters talk about living feminism* (New York: Bantam, 1996: 21).
3. Ibid., 253.
4. Ibid., 199.
5. Ibid., 112.
6. Ibid., 229.
7. Betty Friedan, *The feminine mystique* (New York: Dell, 1963: 266).
8. Baker and Kline, *The conversation begins*, 91.

9. Ibid., 135.
10. Quoted in Baker and Kline, *The conversation begins*, xv.
11. Ibid, 12. Adrienne Rich, *Of woman born* (New York: Norton, 1976), xvii.
13. Baker and Kline, *The conversation begins*, 19.
14. Ibid., 95.
15. Ibid., 27.
16. Ibid., 28.
17. Ibid., 223.
18. Ibid., 123.
19. Ibid., 126.
20. Arlie Hochschild, *The second shift* (New York: Avon, 1989).
21. Baker and Kline, *The conversation begins*, 183.
22. Ibid., 93.
23. Ibid., 338.
24. Ibid., 52.
25. Ibid., 196–97.
26. Ibid., 144.
27. Ibid., 255–56.
28. Ibid., 303.
29. Ibid., 201.
30. Ibid., 150.
31. Ibid., 260–61.
32. Ibid., 310–11.
33. Ibid., 343.
34. Ibid., 126.
35. Ibid., 38.
36. Ibid., 108.
37. Ibid., 71.
38. Ibid., 79.
39. Ibid., 77–78.
40. Ibid., 134.
41. Ibid., 216.
42. Ibid., 380–81.
43. Ibid., 365.
44. Ibid., 311, 315.
45. Ibid., 269.
46. Ibid., 318.
47. Ibid., 179, 181.
48. Ibid., 228.
49. Ibid., 95.
50. Ibid., 212.
51. Ibid., 218–19.
52. Ibid., 39.

Chapter Six

From Perfect Housewife to Fishnet Stockings and not Quite Back Again

One mother's story of leaving home[1]

Petra Büskens

First acquaintance: Meeting Lillith via the literature

Lillith is a gregarious yet softly spoken woman whose energy and enthusiasm belie her seventy years of living. She defies every imaginable stereotype I unwittingly hold of an older woman. She is active, articulate, and strong (her gym equipment lies in the corner of the room); she is opinionated and, to my complete astonishment, she is *sexy*. I notice that her eyes sparkle blue *every time* she throws her head back to laugh with an irresistible combination of wisdom and freedom. I have to admit, this woman is utterly compelling.

Lillith is, however, a mother who has left her children, and it is for this reason that I have come to interview her. I simply never expected to encounter such a powerful, centred, and sensuous woman. I am caught off guard with a reprimanding conscience (asking myself why an older woman wouldn't possess any or all of Lillith's traits), and seduced by the novelty of one who does. I am enamoured with the gift of Lillith's story, and humanised by her sheer extraordinariness. When I walk out of Lillith's tiny Tuscan cottage at the end of our interview I feel like a different person

Like the other fifteen women I have thus far interviewed, Lillith found her conventional role in the family—a 1950s suburban Australian family—a stultifying one. She felt trapped, confined, dependent, exploited, unrealised, and ultimately, abused. Like the others, she too decided that conventional marriage and motherhood were unsustainable for her. Not content to accept her "lot," Lillith took a highly transgressive path and chose to leave her family: both husband and children. While this is the route most men take after the dissolution of a marriage, it is certainly not an avenue many women consider. The stigmatisation is simply too great. While we see statistics bursting at the seams with divorce, its main side-effect remains that ever expanding category demographers call the "Mother Headed Household"[2] (ABS, 1999a; 2000). But how does the family change when it is the mother who leaves and not the father? More specifically, what happens to motherhood when it occurs outside the conventional nuclear or single-parent family?

I am interested to answer these questions since they remain largely unexplored in the feminist literature on motherhood, notwithstanding the new focus on "impossibility" (DiQuinzio, 1999), "contradiction" (Hayes, 1996), "ambivalence" (Hollway & Featherstone, 1997), and "deviance" (Ladd-Taylor and Umansky, 1998). From this research, we know mothers are struggling with the contradictory hegemonies of individualism and maternal self-sacrifice. Similarly, research on the domestic division of labour indicates wives continue to perform seventy percent of household tasks and five times more childcare than their husbands—approximately eighty percent of the total (Baxter, 1993; Bittman and Pixley, 1997; Morris, 1990; McMahon, 1999; Delphy and Leonard, 1992; Steil, 1997; Dempsey 1997; Maushart, 2001). This basic division has not changed, even though women across the social strata are now engaged in paid work (albeit, in a highly stratified set of occupations with poorer conditions and salaries on average than men). This remains the case to varying degrees in all of the advanced capitalist countries (Pleck, 1985; Sanchez, 1994; Shelton, 1990; Steil, 1997; Zhang & Farley, 1995).

In her classic study *The second shift*, Arlie Hochschild (1989) argues that the revolution of women out of the home and into the workforce has not been met with a parallel "revolution" of men entering the home and sharing the domestic load. This has amounted to a major burden for mothers[3] who are now very often working two shifts: one at their paid job and then a second when they return home in the evening to find cooking, washing, shopping, cleaning, and the less savoury aspects of parenting awaiting them. As a result, women tend to work part-time after the arrival of children, further impeding their labour market position relative to men in the same educational and social class. Again, it is women who are assigned and/or assume the burden of structural contradictions between home and work (Baxter, 1993; Probert 1993; 1999a, 1999b; Hochschild, 1998). Not surprisingly, extensive research also show that wives and mothers have significantly less leisure time than other members of the same household (Deem, 1986; Green et al., 1990; Wimbush, 1986; Hochschild, 1989; Wearing, 1990; Bittman and Pixley, 1997; Gilroy, 1999).

Contradictions—between home and work, love and freedom, maternity and self-identity—are the logical outcome of this persistent inequality in the family. Motherhood does not equal fatherhood. On the contrary, the two positions are organised hierarchically in terms of institutionalised power relations privileging men over women in the labour market as well as at home. Resistance is difficult within marriage given the pervasive socio-economic structures supporting inequality. Research indicates that women are largely unsuccessful when they attempt to procure egalitarian change from husbands (Komter, 1989; Wearing, 1984; Dempsey, 1997a, 1997b; Steil, 1997; McMahon, 1999).

Increasingly, women are turning to divorce as a solution to their frustrations and problems,[4] however, most of these women, eighty-eight percent to be precise, take their children with them (McDonald, 1995: 22). Australian data suggest that single mothers are currently rearing one-quarter of Australia's children and yet, further consolidating the sexist division of labour, share the care of their children with the biological father in only three percent of cases (ABS, 1999a). Fathers almost always drop off contact with children when they no longer cohabit together, again reinforcing the kind of parenting dynamic already in existence within the familial home. This suggests women are doing "single mothering" both inside and outside the institution of marriage.

When placed in dynamic synthesis, contemporary research (both large scale positivist studies on the division of labour and focused qualitative studies on the experience of marriage and motherhood) create a social profile indicating women's subordinate position in the labour market and in the family. In turn, mothers are struggling with the "cultural contradiction" between a society premised on individualism and the social construction of motherhood as institutionalised self-sacrifice. What we know less of is how mothers are subverting and recreating this script. Where, we may ask, are the "outlaws" to this highly unequal arrangement? In this sense, while contemporary research offers efficacious analyses of women's position *inside* the institution of motherhood (even at its "deviant" margins), it does little by way of illuminating a pathway out of structural and psychological impasse. The time has come for feminist researchers— especially those motivated not merely to document but also to transform the institution of motherhood[5]—to identify and analyse instances of creative subversion. Methodologically, the focus shifts from oppression to resistance and reinvention. My research on mothers who leave is part of this project.[6]

This paper will therefore cluster around the pivotal question "what happens when the mother leaves home," with a particular emphasis on maternal sexuality both inside and outside the institution of motherhood. There can be no generalisation from these findings given the analysis rests on data gathered from only fifteen cases, with Lillith as my paradigmatic example. However, the research does engage with a much larger corpus of knowledge regarding the domestic division of labour, the economic position of women (separate from male partners), and the contradictions faced by all mothers who work (or in other words, who *leave* some of the time). In this sense, the mother who leaves can be situated against the grain of conventional social structure. Her position is necessarily overshadowed in number and kind by normative mothering practices, however, her "voice," by virtue of its location, has insights disproportionate to its size.[7] We can, therefore, reflect on the position of *mothers who stay*[8] via the socio-economic and psychological shifts experienced by *mothers who leave*. My research is therefore an attempt to raise issues and provoke thoughts on the quiet re-invention of maternity enacted by this small group of Australian mothers who have left (and thereby reconstituted) their families.

Madonna and whore, or Lillith as mother and woman

At the close of one of our interviews Lillith presents me with an anecdote that assures me of her peculiar relationship to motherhood. Her story is designed to elicit a contrast between herself and other presumably "good" mothers, yet her self imposed exclusion finds its root (no pun intended) in her sexuality; more precisely, in her refusal to ascend to the restrictions of conjugal monogamy. Lillith invokes a familiar dualism and positions herself firmly to its left: she is the whore, not the Madonna. She recounts:

> Yeah, it would have been in the 1960s, 1965–1966; I was shopping at the local grocery shop. I'd thrown over this very bright sleeveless thing I put over my swimsuit, or over nothing, probably I'd taken my swimsuit off and didn't have anything on [underneath]. And I remember eyeing this guy off in the grocery shop and he was an actor because Channel 4 was up there at that time, and we ended up going to Channel 4 and making love on the floor of the studio. And then I got my groceries [she says, still laughing] and went home again. I mean, I drove up there, I had the car, and I got in my car, came home again, and unpacked the groceries. *So I never felt like a mother, ever.* [emphasis added]

This is the stuff that movies are made of, so it seems fitting that Lillith's adventure would take place with an actor, whom she recalls later in fits of laughter was "revolting, absolutely revolting." This example is entertaining to listen to, and no doubt to deliver, but beyond this it identifies something fundamental to the institution of motherhood itself: the heterosexual monogamy implied in the term "mother" and, moreover, our intuitive, albeit ideological, sense that a good mother doesn't "fuck around." We assume mothers are prudent, asexual beings who selflessly and, most importantly, *platonically*, love others. This shared insight comes from the unspoken well-spring of common sense, or, following Gramsci (1971), what social theorists somewhat dryly refer to as "hegemony." By this account, common sense is the process whereby consensus is achieved between dominant and subordinate groups in favour of the former. In Western societies, we are structured by a dominant belief system promulgating an equation between maternity and selfless (or is that sexless?), devotion (Warner, 1976). This has a long history in religion, culture, and art, while today it is preserved in the dual and interconnected institutions of marriage and motherhood. Maternity in this ideological context is inherently desexualising. Lillith is herself bound by this commonsensical dualism as she explains her alienation from the institution of motherhood on the grounds of her (libertine) sexuality. That is, she views herself as an outlaw to motherhood *because* of her sexual adventurousness.

I would like to explore this dichotomy further and ultimately watch it implode as Lillith's story unfolds; it seems to me that by leaving the family, Lillith manages, after all the pain and destruction, to innovatively synthesise "madonna" and "whore," or, in other words, Lillith finds a novel way of being both a caregiver and a free (sexual) agent. My reading suggests Lillith exhausts the dialectical hegemony of asexual maternity/sexualised freedom by altering the terms and spaces from which she mothers. In this way, she repositions the whore within the madonna, or the woman within the mother, by finding an insulated geographic location for both. She insists on a simultaneity of her identifications (madonna and whore; free agent and caregiver) whilst prising apart the spaces within which she enacts these different facets of her self. By leaving the familial home, Lillith opens up the space to be something other than a mother; she literally has not merely a room of her own as Virginia Woolf promulgated, but rather, a *home* of her own (Woolf, 1929). From this vantage point, Lillith can exercise her autonomy and later she can provide a (part-time) locus for her mothering too. Leaving, then, can be understood as one way of resisting the totalising institution of self sacrificing/desexualising mothering, however much the stigma "bad mother" attaches itself to her actions. (Indeed, we should use the intensity of the stigma as an index of gendered hegemonies.) The fact that a mother who leaves is judged very differently from a father who leaves stands as a chilling reminder of the double standard inherent in parenting; it stands as a reminder of the ideology of maternal self-sacrifice, and it neatly dovetails with the sexual double standard which calls a sexually adventurous woman a "slut" while a man who acts in the same way is a "hero". It is this double standard that Lillith pushes against; first, through her infidelities, and then, most powerfully, through her leaving. Let us explore the particularities of her situation further.

The feminine mystique: ambivalence and oppression

"This was the fifties," Lillith reminds me, " ... it was a time when you had to be the perfect wife and perfect mother .... And so I was absolutely perfect. I mean I was such a bloody martyr. You've got no idea ... I was so perfect and fiercely protective of the children." While Lillith lived up to this ideal for a time she also resented the constraints it imposed on her life. Thus, she tells me in almost the same breath how "bovine" she felt after giving birth to three children in quick succession:

> I felt like a cow ... always pregnant, always feeding for years and years and years .... I felt trapped [and] suffocated, [like] the children were albatrosses around my neck .... I also felt that I'd been sucked dry, that my youth had been taken and quite resentful ... and the juxtaposition with that, of course, was this sort of fierce love.

Lillith's ambivalence is honestly revealed in her struggle to come to terms with the dual and contradictory experience of caring for children under the hegemony of selfless/sexless mothering. It is a familiar account voiced in White maternal writing for several generations now (Friedan, 1963; Lazarre, 1976; Rich, 1977; Nicholson, 1983; Mousehart, 1997; LeBlanc, 1998). The constraints of isolated mothering place an impossible and historically unprecedented burden on modern mothers: one that sequesters them to the home and isolates them from others. As Lillith found, the need (and later, the desire) to work did not change this basic structure of unequal parental demand.

For years she felt like the only available parent for her children and the strain wore at her. She says, "... it was very difficult because I was both father and mother. I mean Adam was absent." In spite of this uneven strain, Lillith worked in "odd jobs" and eventually developed a career in market research during her children's middle school years. She was reasonably successful with this, and it opened up important avenues for self-expression, financial independence, and autonomy (not to mention the odd "lifesaving" affair). However, it also increased the pressures at home as Adam refused to share the load of domestic labour and childcare. Lillith says, "I mean, he said that if I worked he would never pick up a tea-towel. So he did nothing, absolutely nothing. I felt very put upon." Lillith's experience is supported by sociological research, albeit more recent findings, indicating that women's entry into the workplace has not been accompanied by a corresponding movement of men's work in the home.

Thus Lillith's and Adam's marriage became more and more acrimonious over the years escalating, in the end, to physical violence. Adam began beating Lillith, sometimes in front of the children who were now teenagers. This situation worsened finally leading to Lillith's hospitalisation from a particularly severe beating and her subsequent suicide attempt. "Overdosing was the only way I felt I could leave," she recalls. Lillith's perceived inability to escape this situation and her protective tie to her children became a profound double bind. She says,

> I felt if I didn't have the children I could have gone. I'd felt that for years. If the children weren't there, I would have left the marriage ... there was

nowhere I could have taken the children ... And I don't think I wanted them ... I wanted out of motherhood and out of marriage.

Lillith clarifies the angst in this decision further,

> I felt I was responsible for giving them stability in this dreadful marriage .... I felt as though I had no rights. I felt as though I wasn't even a person. You know ... that ... I ... it's a bit like mushrooms growing out of a dead person or something, you know? Like when I'm thinking of it now ... there's a carcass rotting and the other life forms grow up out of it. I felt like a rotting carcass and that's when I left. And it was dreadful. It was wonderful.

Lillith refers to her leaving as a "rebirth" where she guiltily sought a freedom beyond the painful limits of her violent marriage and the selfless monotony of child care. It would be tempting to think it was only Lillith's marriage that she was leaving, to keep intact our image of an otherwise devoted mother, but Lillith stresses several times that it was *both* husband and children she wanted to leave. It was the problematic nexus of these two roles—wife and mother with their seemingly intractable stranglehold over her life—that Lillith wanted to escape. The one cannot be extricated successfully from the other, for this is part of the institution of both (Rich, 1977; Johnson, 1988). Marriage equals motherhood and motherhood equals marriage (if not to an actual man then to a society that systematically prioritises men). The disarticulation of one from the other immediately implies transgression; such is the ideology of femininity. For Lillith, her freedom meant the withdrawal from both sides of the mother/wife coin. While initially Lillith frames her desire to leave the children in terms of the pragmatic difficulties of single parenting in the 1960s, she later qualifies this position by saying she didn't "want them either." This is the point at which Lillith relinquishes not simply her children but also her socially sanctioned status of mother. It is a courageous act of destruction that will earn her a lifelong stigma. She says,

> And I never thought of what was going to happen after. Never thought. It was just ... *relief* that I didn't have them and I didn't want responsibility for them .... I mean because honestly I didn't give a stuff. I mean I *did*, I did.

The morning after: Trading in love and resentment for guilt and freedom

Lillith reminded me that her claim to normal motherhood was merely a veneer. She was, after all, having clandestine affairs throughout the final turbulent years of her marriage. She claims this was the only time she felt "herself," a brief moment when she was—however superficially—appreciated and admired; but, perhaps more fundamentally, this was a moment when she could access that part of her which was *not* a wife or a mother. This was a part of her self that Lillith craved to discover and cultivate. It was the self that her familial role denied her, and it was the self that she pursued more ardently than any extra-marital affair. Indeed, it is likely that her relationship with her own freedom was the most subversive affair of all. This association between freedom and sexuality is made explicitly by Lillith who saw her leaving as simultaneously the loss of familial constraint as well as the acquisition of sexual autonomy. For Lillith this meant the return to a "lost youth" she felt had been "sucked dry." She says,

> Look, I felt sixteen years of age. It was the most wonderful feeling ... I mean I was in my mid-thirties, late thirties, but I would leap up on a street seat and run along the top of it. And I had a lover who was much younger than me and we weren't living together and *just the freedom. It was exquisite. Absolutely exquisite* .... [It was] this wonderful, wonderful going back to my teenage years. Just being so wild and being able to get drunk and go to the pub every night. Oh God, it was so wonderful. [I'd go] dancing at the ... and I'd look around to see if my daughter was there ... [at] the "Stamping Sam", a disco, and wear short skirts, you know mini skirts and net stockings. I was totally ... you know [...] *I didn't have kids.* I didn't have to ... *I didn't have to be a mother.* And I was no longer somebody's wife or somebody's mother ... I was no longer that. I was *me* ... I was my own identity. Not having these encumbrances, you know, these anchors anymore. It was the most wonderful, wonderful freedom ... so for the first time I stood alone. I'd always been my father's daughter, my husband's wife, my children's mother, my sister's sister, my mother's daughter. For the first time I was me, with a career, and just me. [emphasis added]

This freedom obviously set alarm bells off in the heads of Lillith's male acquaintances, who (also) construed her new freedom in explicitly sexual terms. She says,

> Wives didn't leave children. If wives left, they went and lived with mum and took their children with them. And that was really bad. Wives did not leave. This was a terrible, terrible thing I did. Like Adam's friends, because of the work, they found out where I was, would ring me up and want to fuck me. I was a mother ... and then ... became a sexual being. My stepfather, my brother-in-law ... and my husband's Lion's Club friends ... all rang me up and wanted to fuck me. I mean it was disgusting.

The madonna/whore dichotomy had not ceased to wield its influence in Lillith's life; now she was simply on the "wrong" side of the equation. While Lillith's liberation from the familial role opened up new vistas for her autonomy and sexuality, it was also read as a clear sign of her sexual wantonness; her "loose" morals and carefree attitude. In other words, in a culture dominated by the hegemony of selfless/sexless maternity, for a mother to act freely was and is read as sexual provocation *in itself*. A free woman is a "come on," partly because she personifies taboo, partly because she is perceived as "rebellious" or "feisty," and partly because it is assumed—rightly or wrongly—that she *doesn't have a man* (and presumably wants, needs, or should have one). Culture at large finds it hard to cope with autonomy in a woman, even harder to cope with sexual autonomy in a woman, and hardest of all to cope with sexual autonomy in a woman who is also a mother (Dinnerstein, 1976).

Lillith is therefore correct: the autonomy she wrestled from her family was necessarily sexual and sexualising. There are two sides to this, however, which directly correlate to, on the one hand, Lillith's sense of liberation and awakening, and on the other hand, the objectification she encountered from the men in her husband's Lion's Club. These two poles seem to be interconnected phenomena, different ways of living, resisting, and consolidating the hegemony of the selfless-sexless/selfish-sexual dichotomy. For Lillith, however, the simultaneous insistence on a sexed identity *as a mother* was a means to push past the limitations of the dualism. She sought to make synchronous claims on both sexuality and maternity thereby collapsing the dualism itself. Whereas the men in the Lion's club simplistically read Lillith's departure as indication of her "free" (i.e., sexually "loose") attitude, Lillith had herself insisted on something far more complex. But before she could reach this level of complexity she had first to annihilate her former role. This took place, in the first instance, through an intense reclamation of freedom.

"So, yes ..." she says, " ... it was a great relief to be a sexual *being* when I left." In keeping with this newfound sexual identity, Lillith took up with a man ten years her junior. This was a highly charged and immensely enjoyable relationship for her. She recounts in bursts of laughter,

> So I formed a relationship with him and although *he didn't officially live with me* he stayed several nights ... I mean the sex was amazing, we'd have sex before we went to work, we'd have sex as soon as we got home from work and ... I don't know how many times a day we'd hop into bed [laughing]. We'd be all dressed up ready to go to work and ... we'd fall back into bed again. So ... it was very exciting. [emphasis added]

The hedonism and spontaneity of this relationship coupled with her new sense of personal mastery dramatically improved Lillith's quality of life. "It was the joyfulness of life when I'd left them," she says, "I got that back and I'd lost that ... being joyful in life." She elaborates more generally,

> ... and just to be able to knock off work and have a beer, you know? I mean, the things you can't do when you've got children. Or you couldn't do when I had children anyway. You know I had to go home and cook meals. Now it didn't matter a stuff whether I cooked a meal [or] whether I had sardines on toast ... I didn't have to cook for anybody, I didn't have to wash for anybody, I didn't have to listen to bloody homework, I didn't have to take ... listen ... you know, cheer them on at swimming. It was just marvellous, it was just wonderful .... I really like to be in control of my own life and that was the first time that I've ever been in control of my own life.

When I asked Lillith why she had become a sexual being again (in the hope of getting closer to the now ubiquitous equation between freedom and sex) I met with the same equation: "Because I was free," she said. Lillith, it seems, was sexual because she was free and free because she was sexual. It was a circular logic with no external referents. It seems, therefore, that loosening the strictures of mothering—literally leaving home—was not merely a bold, unconventional, or destructive act, it was a *sexual* act. Lillith had acted sexually in her own account and, somewhat differently, in the account she provides of the lecherous hopefuls at her husband's Lion's Club. As with the equation between maternity and selfless-sexless subjectivity, relinquishing conventional maternity similarly equated with selfish-sexual subjectivity. Lillith feels this to be true insofar as she genuinely indulged and expanded her sexual horizons, yet she was also resistant of, and even a little perplexed by, her sexual objectification by outsiders. It is an interesting contradiction at the heart of her story and possibly one she cannot avoid until she has returned to the problem of her mothering.

Thus after several months, the constant worry for and guilt over the children forced Lillith to return to her painful past and find more integrated and personally satisfying solutions. To break out was one part, but reconstruction was the other, arguably more important, task she still faced.

What about the children?

The children were now being taken care of by a combination of their father and her own mother, but Lillith found that her guilt was too great. While she cherished her newfound freedom and the worlds it simultaneously opened and closed, Lillith found that her feelings of responsibility for the children were pushing through the jubilance. Again, this process was not straightforward; she was bedevilled with the same ambivalence characteristic of earlier phases in her mothering. For example, Lillith spent many months of that year without her children, staving off memories and images of them. "And so I was a workaholic," she says. "It was very easy to forget my children when I was at work." More confrontingly, at another point in our interview, she recalls the following,

> So I distanced myself from them that year. I really did not know or want to know about them. Look, if a big box had've swallowed them up I would have been pleased at that stage. That's how I felt. I didn't even want to have them as part of my life.

There is an almost complete absence of maternal sentiment in Lillith's account. Indeed, it is so transgressive as to be jarring, even on my sympathetic ears. She is clear, almost trenchant, about the fact that she had nothing left, no "inner core" as she puts it, from which to care for her children, or anyone else for that matter. But the ambivalence remained, for she also felt a debilitating guilt. She says,

> I didn't care … I really didn't care. But mixed up in that was this dreadful, dreadful guilt, and I mean that's dogged me all my life. It's shocking guilt. I mean women didn't do these sort of things … I still had the freedom even though … I was really guilty about the children, but I didn't want to even know about them.

Nevertheless, her conscience prevailed, and so at the end of her twelve months of being a child-free *sexed* mother, Lillith organised for her daughter (who was the eldest and then, at age sixteen exempt from a custody dispute) to come and live with her (as the daughter had desired). However, the two boys would remain with their father a little longer. As younger teenagers, Lillith would have to apply for legal custody. Adam refused to let them go notwithstanding the boys' requests to live with their mother. Lillith took her case to court and was awarded custody of both boys. While her leaving was looked upon unfavourably, the combination of an admirable employment record and Adam's failure to show up in court determined her success. She recalls, however, having to carefully suppress information regarding her lovers, lest this render her ineligible for custody. Moving into a middle-class suburb and renting a cheap home from a friend, Lillith again set up house with her children. This time, however, her mothering changed.

Reclaiming motherhood: Trading in apron strings for equality

Like the other stages in her mothering, Lillith found this one difficult also. It meant relinquishing some of the freedom she had grown accustomed to, and it meant managing angry teenagers. This was not easy and she found the guilt over her year apart initially clouding her sense of justice. For a brief time Lillith tried to "make it up" to the kids by assuming a martyr-like position in relation to them. She did all the housework, tolerated extreme rudeness from her middle son, and expected little respect or co-operation. Having tasted another kind of life, however, her martyrdom was short-lived. After a weekend away in deep reflection, Lillith decided to reorganise her household along lines more conducive to her own sense of self and quality of life. She now expected her children to contribute to the household. She recounts a particularly dramatic anecdote to illustrate her point:

> And I remember once when Graham didn't wash his dishes, I got all the dishes he was supposed to wash, I got everything—pots, pans, everything that was dirty—I put it in his bed and I put the doona over the top. So I think after that we probably had a more—I don't mean a list up on the fridge, I don't think I've ever done that—but more sharing of household chores.

Lillith encouraged her daughter to take up an opportunity to live in the nurses' quarters, and later encouraged her sons to venture out, taking jobs in distant states and pursuing relationships elsewhere. Her household became an open space for her (near adult) children, one they could return to and live in, but not one where they could expect domestic service. The expectation was one of cooperative adults living in a house together. Lillith clarifies her feelings poignantly:

> I never wanted children on apron strings. I never wanted that role ever. I felt that having children forced a role on me that I never wanted ... [So] I didn't want to be "Mother" any longer. I didn't want to be a mother,[9] I wanted to share a house with responsible adults who ... shared the living and contributed to it.

In view of this return to mothering, it is my contention that Lillith *did not leave her children, rather she left the hegemonic institution of mothering* which dictates that women relinquish their autonomy for the sake of familial others. Lillith creatively challenged this system, and the madonna/whore dualism inherent within it, by *actively breaking and ultimately reinventing her familial role*. This trajectory is remarkably similar for all the women interviewed. Contrary to my initial expectations on "mothers who leave," I discovered that all of the women returned to mothering some or all of their children after an initial period of separation. Most, however, tended to evolve into part-time mothers in combination with the children's father who was then, by necessity, drawn into a much more active parental role. This finding supports much larger-scale studies on "non-custodial mothers" indicating a return to share care in some capacity after leaving the familial home (Grief and Pabst, 1988).[10] Paradoxically, these mothers tend to share their children with male co-parents much more effectively as part-time single parents than was the case when they cohabited in marital relationships. This suggests that "leaving" is, rather, a *strategic withdrawal on the mother's behalf geared to disrupt and reorganise the terms on which parenting is conventionally organised*. Given that both the gendered division of labour and the hegemony of ideologies equating maternity with a selfless-sexless subjectivity prove especially resistant to change, leaving as a mother may be one of the few avenues open to women to disrupt these profound gender inequalities. Having a "home of one's own" simultaneously forces fathers to parent (in the broad sense of this term to include structural reorganisation of one's life to accommodate children rather than simply "baby-sitting" when mum isn't around), and provides mothers with an insulated time-space for the production and cultivation of autonomy. It is my contention, therefore, that Lillith, as with the other women in this project, reinvented mothering along lines more conducive to the acquisition and propagation of autonomy whilst also eliciting, however reluctantly, much more active parenting from their former spouses. Moreover, by seeking to synthesise caregiving with autonomy, mothers who leave also present a noteworthy challenge to the individualism often associated with modern male subjectivity. Given the significant increase in recent years of mothers leaving in Anglo-American countries (Grief, 1997; Jackson, 1994; ABS, 1999b),[11] this might very well be a quiet revolution in process.

Notes

1. This paper was first presented at the "Mothers, sex and sexuality" conference organised by the *Association for Research on Mothering*, York University, Toronto, March 3–4, 2001. Travel to Canada was supported by the Melbourne University Postgraduate Overseas Research Experience Award and the Australian Federation of University Women (WA) Foundation Bursary.

2. According to the Australian Bureau of Statistics, "One-parent families are projected to increase from about 742,000 in 1996 to about 1.1 million in 2021, comprising 16% of all families" (ABS, 2001). In an interesting reversal of the aforementioned trends, however, single father families are projected to increase more rapidly than single mother families (ABS, 1999b).

3. This burden has, however, always been carried by working-class and coloured mothers. It is only since middle-class women have entered the workforce en masse that the "double-shift" has been considered a social problem worthy of investigation and critique.

4. Divorce rates are increasing across the Western world. Current figures in Australia show that almost one in two marriages now end in divorce (ABS, 2000). Sociologists recognise that it

is usually women who initiate divorce. However, it is women who also suffer disproportionate economic losses with the dissolution of marriage. Thus women are typically eager to re-marry. We have, therefore, a high divorce, high marriage culture. Second marriages are unlikely to produce the changes towards equality desired by women (See Bernard, 1982; Delphy and Leonard, 1992; Wallerstein et al., 2000).

5. Epistemologically, such research exists within the paradigm of "critical theory." On the accusation of researcher "bias" given the explicit call for social change, critical theorists have long pointed out that the vantage point of the "oppressed" ("stranger," "deviant," "outsider," etc.) is more "objective" given their socio-structural position *outside* dominant institutions and discourses. While society excludes and oppresses the outsider (within), this very position offers a wider horizon from which to examine what conventionally passes for "truth." As Hegel pointed out: in the "master/slave dialectic" it is the slave who must know the rules, ideas, and expectations of the master, not the other way around. This doubled consciousness expands the horizon of awareness. In terms of social research, this expansion applies to both the researcher and the researched if located on the same social plane (i.e., the category of "Woman," "Black," "Native," "Other," "Slave," "Worker," etc.) (Harding, 1987; Smith, 1987, 1990; Collins, 1990; Hartstock, 1998).

6. My empirical research gathered the stories of fifteen women who identified as mothers who had left. These women selected themselves on the basis of advertisements placed in local newspapers. It was a requirement of the research that mothers had voluntarily left for a period of six months or more (thereby excluding issues pertaining to adoption or refuge status). Participants were interviewed for a period of approximately two hours in their own homes on two occasions. Interviews were tape recorded, transcribed, and checked by participants before final inclusion in the project. Pseudonyms have been used throughout. This research is part of an APA-funded PhD degree in the Sociology program at the University of Melbourne, Australia.

7. There are other mothers who also provide this level of insight and subversion regarding the conventional (oppressive) institution of mothering. For example, African-American women who practice a collective form of single mothering (called "othermothering"), and lesbian mothers (Bell-Scott, 1993; Dunne, 1998). Both subvert the combined effects of contradiction, economic dependence, and male authority; however, both also retain the essential structure of exclusive female responsibility for childcare and suffer the economic and social losses incumbent upon this position.

8. Mothers who stay are a seemingly unproblematic given. However, it is central to the methodology of this research to uncover the category of the *mother who stays* and from here to problematise her position via the insights and innovations produced by the *mother who leaves*. I situate both, therefore, in dialectical relation. The construction of the mother who stays produces the mother who leaves as its own cultural "shadow."

9. I read Lillith here not as saying she literally didn't want to be a mother, rather, that she didn't want to be a mother whose fundamental relation to familial others was service.

10. Goeffrey Grief's and Margaret Pabst's study of 517 North American "non-custodial mothers" indicates that the majority of these women resume or retain contact with children during and

after moving out of the family home. By contrast, non-custodial fathers do not, on average, retain this level of contact after separation (Grief and Pabst, 1988).

11. In a recent article on "non-custodial mothers" in the United States, Geoffry Grief suggests that their numbers are now "close to three million." He writes that "we see no sign that this trend will reverse itself" (Grief, 1997: 46). Based on figures from the early 1990s, Rosie Jackson also suggests that fifteen percent of mothers in Britain, about 150,000 women, are living away from their children (Jackson, 1994: 17). All data rely primarily on statistics pertaining to lone fathers. However, due to the trend of rapid repartnering amongst single fathers, figures were adjusted upwards. Australian Bureau of Statistics data support these findings, indicating that the absolute number of lone fathers increased by fifty-eight percent in the period 1989–1998 (ABS, 1999b).

Section Two

LESBIAN MOTHERING

Chapter Seven

IMAG(IN)ING THE QUEER LESBIAN FAMILY

Jacqui Gabb

Arriving at a London Pride event a couple of years ago, I remember being struck by the slogan on a woman's t-shirt: "Lesbians are everywhere." I looked around and, sure enough, they were. I was in Heaven: they could be counted in the thousands. I then looked back to my own little gathering of myself, partner, and child, and wondered whether others would automatically add us into this number. Obviously if we made some significant display of our lesbian sexuality—a kiss, an embrace, the adornment of a particular badge, or an adherence to a particular dress code—then we might be identifiable. But standing as we were, in our out-of-town casual clothing, holding the hands of our little boy, we were hard to locate. Taking a couple of steps to the right, we could easily blend into the straight onlookers who gazed onto this annual ritual. A couple of steps to the left and we could disappear into the gay crowd. Our sense of dislocation was intense. Of course, we were not the only parents, and once we had settled into the celebrations and met up with others like ourselves, we felt much more at home. But the initial sense of displacement was overwhelming, and is arguably typical of the experience and identities of lesbian families. This article reflects upon this sense of dislocation, and how lesbian parents negotiate the complexity of their identities throughout their familial lives.

Given that motherhood and sexuality are antithetical to each other within Western culture, lesbian mothers are constantly denied any fixity of identity. Always in a state of flux; we are caught in a continual process of becoming. This paper will consider how lesbian motherhood and sexuality have been artificially separated, looking at how this affects our sense of self. Using illustrations taken from my own and others' lives, I will endeavour to reconcile the paradox of the lesbian family, by challenging the traditional categories of the sex-less mother and sexually-deviant lesbian. I begin this research from the basis that, generally speaking, lesbian mothers are good mothers, and thus obviate the need to continually defend our maternal capabilities and/or the ways in which we raise our children. I take for granted that we are like other mortals. We may occasionally lapse into moments of rage or shut ourselves away in selfish isolation, but nonetheless we still love our children unconditionally and care for them to the best of our abilities. I make no attempt to justify our existence but move the debate on to consider the diversity and transgressive potentialities of our lesbian maternal selves.

There is a growing canon of academic research into lesbian mothering (Lewin, 1993; Dunne, 1998) and "families of choice" (Weeks, 1991; Weston, 1991). Other research seeks to "prove" the normality of our children (Kirkpatrick, 1981; Patterson, 1997; Tasker and Golombok, 1997), and/or consider the domestic realities of our lesbian family lifestyles (Heaphy et al., 1997; Dunne, 1999). However, there is a real scarcity of academic research into sexuality within lesbian families. It is as though desire is presumed to disappear upon the arrival of a child. It does not. Our circumstances may radically change, and so might our energies or inclination, but desire is not absent within the family; it merely becomes encoded, as a means to circumnavigate the ever-vigilant surveillance by (familial) others (Gabb, 1999). Using autoethnographic observation of my own "lesbian family," and informal interviews with other parents and their children, I have examined how our familial lives, loves, and sexual identities impact upon each other.[1] This observation and the interviews are accompanied by fictive images of my own and others' families. These images are not documents of our lives, but are constructed to critique the traditional meanings bestowed upon snapshots as candid representations of "normal" family life. They aim to illustrate the contingency of identity: the complexity of lesbian (m)other-ness. They are not used to interpret or illustrate the text, but add another dimension to it. Alongside the text, they attempt to imag(in)e the sexual and maternal identities of the "Queer Lesbian Family."

Queering the lesbian family

The initial premise for my research seemed quite easy: to consider whether one can be both a lesbian parent and queer. However, after some preliminary enquiry into the two categories, I came to question my assertion of the irrefutable status of my lesbian "family." Why did I consider I had to "qualify" for a queer status, but "naturally" fitted into the institution of the family? If queer is any-body, why not my body? As a lesbian—an identity that I will currently leave intact—the domestic situation of myself, female partner, and child surely constitutes a familial relationship. But given all the baggage that accompanies the term, is it truly a "family"? The term "lesbian mother" may also be a site of contestation. For whilst the category may in itself be queer, insofar as it challenges the heterosexual narrative, this does not necessarily mean that lesbian mothers recognise themselves in queer theory or feel at home within the queering of lesbian and gay activism. So is it empirically possible to reconcile the paradox of the "queer family"? I intend to argue that the lesbian family does occupy the cutting edge of queer politics, radically challenging traditional categories of gender and destabilizing the hetero-normative within society. And this location on "the front line" is critical; it not only affects queer politics, but also traditional family structures.

"The family," as a representation of "blood kinship," is still afforded great status within both straight society and the lesbian and gay community. Indeed, the determinant that biology is essentially different to choice is so entrenched within our culture that it is almost impossible to displace (Weston, 1991: 31). It is extremely hard to counter the popular belief that "blood is thicker than water" within a society that is still based upon biological family inheritance. However, if we are to seriously incorporate all familial (kinship) relations within the debate on "the family," then the excess of signification afforded to "blood ties" must be acknowledged as a social and historical construction. It must become evident that the prestige bestowed upon the biological family serves an explicit ideological purpose: that biology is a symbol and not a substance (Butler, 1990).

But living outside this biologically determined paradigm is not easy. It often resigns you not only to a life of social exclusion, but also to one of linguistic absence. Even though marginality is not inherently negative, it may even be embraced as a positive expression of our repudiation of the Western patriarchal state; it is arguably impossible to retrieve any positive reading from the linkage of language to the patrilinear narrative. Lesbians and gay men have to sift the words and syntax of social discourse in order to find an appropriate language that may legitimise our familial relationships. Some of us may choose to describe ourselves as "alternative," claiming a social status for our relationship whilst also wanting to establish its difference. Or we may define ourselves as "normal," "just like any other" family (Arnup, 1995). The problem with both of these positions is that they serve to reinforce the legitimacy of "the family" as an institution and thereby reinstate a biological and procreative imperative within family relationships. To be alternative, one must first have something that "naturally" exists: the nuclear family is thereby reasserted within the social order. Paradoxically, to claim that lesbians and gay men have a different, lesser role in relation to the family, is no more accurate than the assumption that straight people have a "natural" access to it. Any attempts to shore up such myths represent gay men and lesbians as non-procreative, set apart from the rest of humanity, something which my own, and many other lesbians', maternity flagrantly refutes.

Articulating lesbian (m)other-ness

There is an evident need to publicise the fact that lesbian families are neither normal, nor alternative, but essentially different. The gendered relations that exist within our lives construct a radical re-vision of what actually constitutes a family, and examples of this are evident all around us. When Liam, my seven-year-old son, describes his family, he lays claim to its difference. By stating that I am like a mummy and a daddy to him, he is not filling the gap left empty by the absent father/patriarch, so much as redefining what gendered roles mean in relation to his life. The paternal absence is transformed into a negotiated presence of gendered embodiment. His unexpected decision earlier this year, to claim "Father's Day" as my partners' own, further illustrates the inadequacy of language as a means to express the realities of lesbian family life. My partner apparently could not share "Mother's Day" because, he asserted, "she was not his mother." So he claimed the next available—legitimate—space for her. In his actions, Liam was not intentionally queering "the family," he simply expected there to be a recognised special day for his other parent. Who can argue with that! Hence, rather than being lost within an unstable array of gender roles, Liam is in fact "writing the family" in relation to his own familial bodies. And I wish to posit that such semantic (re)configuration is arguably symptomatic of lesbian (m)other-ness.

Without the binary of "the sexes," the "natural" (gendered) division of labour falls apart. The gendered roles within most lesbian families are typically negotiated, reviewed, and reworked (Dunne, 1998; Oerton, 1997). However, this does not imply that individuals merely duplicate the traditional categories of "mother" and "father," but that gendered demarcation and embodiment is forever displaced. For example, when Christine, a lesbian co-parent, was denied access to the Intensive Care Unit where her (non-biological) baby had just been taken, her response was both pragmatic and insightful. Initially thwarted by the ward manager's dogma, that "the Unit was restricted to members of the immediate family," she intuitively located herself within this social discourse, within the only role that was available to her. Given that Margaret, her partner, was the (biological) mother, and that the gate-keeper did not entertain the possibility of a child having two mothers, she asserted herself as "the father." And though she obviously did not embody the materiality of this category, she instead invoked the familial roles that exist within social discourse to realise a "legitimate" identification. Her response not only gained her access, it also queered the naturalising discourses of "the family" and the gendered embodiments that are contained therein.

It is clearly evident that the process of "naming" ourselves holds the most significant of consequences. Within my own family, I have always been a mother to Liam, so whilst knowing my "first name," he prefers to call me "mummy." My partner, who joined our family when Liam was three-years-old, is referred to as

Nick. Though this is her "first name," it has almost come to serve as a noun. She is "a Nick," neither mummy nor daddy, but a complementary individual within our family. Though she may take an equal part in the quality and quantity of childcare responsibilities, neither she nor Liam perceive her as being a "second mummy." Hence the problem of naming lies in the traditional categories that define parenting within the heterosexual (gendered) narrative and, typically speaking, the lesbian and gay community's adoption of these roles. Indeed my own family's process of "naming" may exemplify this adherence to the patrilinear narrative that defines parental categories. But I contest that this fails to challenge the orthodoxy of parental roles, or leaves intact the categories of "mummy" and "daddy" as unspoken "norms" (Bernstein and Stephenson, 1995). Nick's absence of a parental name does not negate her familial role, nor should it be read as affirmation for the naturalising discourses of maternity, which conflate being a mother with having a baby; instead, it is a real response to the practicalities of circumstance and experience. After all, lesbian "life partners" (to use the terminology of *Friends*) may come and go, but being a "mummy" is for life! Thus, to some extent my own and others' reticence at naming our partners as mothers is a defensive reaction to the transience of adult relationships. It may also signify the predication of the mother/child dyad as determinant of familial relations (Beck and Beck-Gernsheim, 1995). It arguably repudiates the patrilinear narrative of "the family," and sets in place a model that does not read gendered parental roles as a consequence of the reproductive (heterosexual) narrative.

However, whilst Nick is currently an equal member of our family, she does remain without a socially defined gender role. But rather than see this as a sign of her outsider status, it is also possible to read it as indicative of lesbian parenting's queering of the traditional family's gendered roles. Nick "names" herself within the masculine; her physical stature can identify her as butch, and yet she is evidently a woman. Her primary role within the family elevates her above the status of "friend," but she cannot be either "the mother"—for reasons already stated—or its complimentary opposite, "the father," because she is not a man. Her (m)other-ness represents a dynamic source of dislocation and belonging, where her social status and sense of self remains forever in flux. I wish to suggest that the constant transformations, which are a consequence of this instability, require lesbian parents to play out a (gender) masquerade. Negotiating social roles and private identities within ever-shifting parameters, we literally queer "the family" and our roles within it. We make evident the artificiality of the naturalising discourses that underpin the myth of traditional family life.

To some extent it is precisely because of our "unnatural" status—our disruption of the reproductive narrative—that lesbians parents pose such a threat to heterosexual society. We signify the performativity (Butler, 1990) of all motherhood, and analogously by our evident (homo)sexuality, we sexualise all parenting. And this potency has made lesbian families extremely vulnerable to criticism and to attack from the institutions that structure and contain family life. Lesbian parents face a constant challenge to their legitimacy through the British legal system. We are primarily only tolerated as "suitable" parents when we are "discreet," agreeing to suppress our (lesbian) sexuality both from our children and society at large (Brosnan, 1996; Lewin, 1993). Faced with this ever-present threat to custody, the opportunity to "disappear" has often felt the best means for survival (Rights of Women, 1986). With a brief exception during the campaign against Section 28(2)[2] the lesbian and gay community has tacitly accepted our invisibility as an inevitable consequence of living within a society that is determined by a heterosexual imperative. It did not become an issue until queer came along, demanding the public celebration of all transgression, desire, and the visible representation of all our sexual identities (Cooper, 1996: 14).

Imag(in)ing our-selves

Queer culture champions the body in all its vagaries, representing a visible physicality that is largely absent from traditional representations of family life. It often refuses the more earnest techniques that have been traditionally associated with feminist arts and media, relying instead upon the constructed "text" and/or parody. But whilst such public displays make visible certain dissident sexualities, they conversely serve to deny the existence of others. Lesbian families have arguably always existed, but such lives are not readily apparent. Given the edict of our judicial system which states that we should be "discreet" to protect our children's innocence (Rights of Women, 1986), and thence deflect the threat to custody, it is not surprising that we contain our private lives, frequently only making them visible within the sleeves of the family photograph album. And though these portfolios may be an implicitly transgressive document of social reality, their format, let alone dissemination, can hardly be described as a spectacular (queer) display. It would be hard to argue that traditional family snapshots represent the cutting edge of queer photography. Therefore my endeavour to queer the lesbian family may, in practice, need to start by locating a suitable means of representation. So is it possible to depict both our motherhood and lesbian sexuality within the family album or merely document our lives (Cade, 1991: 115–119)? Can we "queer the family album"?

Lesbian families and/or motherhood have been traditionally represented by pictures of devotion: the eternal mother, Madonna and child. And though such images may heighten the awareness of lesbian families, they do little to actually represent us; in fact, they arguably obscure our sexuality beneath the shroud of selfless maternal love. Images showing loving embraces, devoted smiles, and wholesome values are great advertisements for "the family" (Ashburn, 1996), but they deny our dangerous (queer) sexuality (Smith, 1991). Of course I do not wish to imply that lesbian families should be without love, nurturing, and caring considerations, but these should not be at the expense of our sexual identities as lesbians. Lesbian mothers do not automatically stop being sexual just because they have given birth. To continue the cultural myth that mothers are the sex-less, self-less others of their needy children, merely perpetuates a patriarchal logic that subordinates women through wifehood (Van Every, 1995). Women transform from sexual object to nurturing subject as we enter into motherhood, being always defined by the reproductive (heterosexual) narrative. Sex becomes productive rather than pleasurable, and our sexuality becomes obscured by the practicalities of parenting. But lesbian conception narratives refute this functionalist imperative. We offer new familial forms that are not reliant upon the binary logic of "the sexes." We challenge the gendered embodiment of parental roles every day of our lives.

But can we (re)present ourselves outside the patriarchal framework of motherhood? Snapshot photography has traditionally been used to document family life (Williams, 1994). And though some feminist photographers have productively critiqued this form, subverting its claim to the normalcy and privacy of the nuclear family unit (Spence, 1995), this has not really impacted upon images of the lesbian family. Texts that visually illustrate our lives are typically "coffee-table" portfolios (Seyda and Herrera, 1998), lacking any of the critical rigour and/or sexual imagery of other lesbian photography collections (Boffin and Fraser, 1991; Bright and Posener, 1996). Lesbian families are still primarily represented within safe, sanitised, conventional poses that replicate rather than challenge the nuclear family form. I wish to suggest that there is now a pressing need to incorporate images that represent likeness and family lineage, alongside ones that signify our desires and sexual identities. If we wish to queer the lesbian family then it must be made visible. Family snapshots that appear quite conservative to us may be quite enlightening to others. Images that capture the love and mundanity of our lesbian family lifestyles, when placed alongside ones that depict the complexity of our maternal and sexual identities, may become more readily transgressive. And this juxtaposition of images does not undermine the security of our home environments, but instead challenges the myth of the a-sexual family. It represents lesbian families as simultaneously loving, nurturing, and sexual environments. The public dissemination of such representations, which defy traditional readings of sex-less family life, might actually serve to queer the snapshot form as well as making evident the sexual nature of "the family" (Fineman, 1995). In this light, the transgressive potentialities of such images may actually make the (queer) family album the most appropriate and arguably apposite place to start a discourse on the Queer Lesbian Family.

Conclusion

Queer is a movement, an activism, and an identity. But unless it wants to initiate its own self-destruction—imploding beneath the weight of its exclusions—then it must be truly inclusive. For although queer declares a welcome to all individuals, it demands that we sign up, unreservedly, to its mandate. Lesbians are openly accepted, but only when they embrace the queer umbrella: being a lesbian is not quite enough to "qualify" you as queer, you must demonstrate your "dangerous sexuality" (Smith, 1991). But what exactly constitutes a dangerous identity, and who decides on its criteria, is unclear. If one accepts that lesbian parents embody a direct challenge to the hetero-normative, then surely lesbian parents "qualify" as dangerous and thereby our queer status is assured. Hence the problem may be less a matter of inclusion than visibility: we must be seen before we can be counted. So to begin, let us make visible our lives, drawing upon the primary call of feminism that "the personal is political"—let us make public the private representations that we create of ourselves. I believe that we must reconfigure the "family album," its contents and its form, opening it out to a far wider audience in order to exhibit both our familial and sexual selves. But if we are to "imag(in)e the queer lesbian family" in this way, then we need reassurance. We must feel that queer truly offers us a secure space that we may call our own; where our lives as parents are not denigrated as "unoriginal" (Turner, 1998), or dismissed as conspiratorial "breeders" Where the potentialities of our lives and those of our children are seen as progressive. It is this queer space that has yet to be created: the Queer Lesbian Family is already here.

Notes

1.   This is part of a broader empirical study that I am currently undertaking as part of a D.Phil. research project into lesbian families with children in Yorkshire, UK.

2.   Section 28 of the British Local Government Act, May 1988, prohibited local authorities from "intentionally promot[ing] homosexuality," including the promotion, by teaching and publications, of homosexuality and "the pretend family" within schools.

Chapter Eight

OUR KIDS IN THE HALL

LESBIAN FAMILIES NEGOTIATE THE PUBLIC SCHOOL SYSTEM

Rachel Epstein

My daughter has two mothers. Shortly before she started kindergarden we tried to prepare her for the fact that having two moms could make her the brunt of jokes or teasing. The possibility was beyond the scope of her imagination. To her, it was not fathomable that anybody would do or say anything to deny the reality of her family. She is in grade two now. Her experiences to date have consisted of daycare teachers who did not know how to answer questions from other kids about her family; a classmate telling her it was weird that she has two moms; and some awkward moments on Father's Day. We are anticipating, however, as an older, more experienced daughter of lesbians puts it, "it gets worse in the grades."

The bulk of this chapter explores some of the issues facing lesbian families (parents and children) in the Toronto public school system. It has grown from eight years of research on lesbian parenting and many conversations with lesbian parents about the public school system as a source of fear, anxiety, and disempowerment. The quotes are selected from twenty interviews conducted between 1992 and 1997.[1] The chapter is organized around three theoretical assumptions: (1) that schools not only *reproduce* dominant cultural norms such as homophobia, sexism, and heterosexism, but are important sites for the *production* of sexual and other identities; (2) that understandings of the meanings and practices that make up broader student cultures around issues of sexuality and family are crucial to developing pedagogical and administrative practices that effectively challenge dominant norms; and (3) that the experiences of lesbian parents and their children are not monolithic, but intersect with other complex and contradictory issues of knowledge, power, and identity. In a postscript at the end, I raise some methodological questions about the uses and limitations of "realist" research, as represented by the first part of the chapter, and about the possibilities contained in research perspectives that allow space for "not-knowing."

Schools as cultural producers

> In effect, schools operate as important public spaces in which young people learn about and construct their sexualities, and come face to face with the different value society places on heterosexual as opposed to gay and lesbian identities ... heterosexualities are put in place, and maintained through complex social relationships which serve to marginalize and subordinate specific social groups (lesbians and gays, girls and women, Black and minority groups, disabled people). (Redman, 1994, 141–43)

The privileging of heterosexuality and heterosexual family structures manifests itself in a multitude of blatant and subtle ways in daily school life:

- The erasure of anything but depictions of heterosexual family life in curriculum materials.
- Lack of acknowledgment of the nonbiological lesbian parent—or other parental figures—in school forms, for inclusion in parent–teacher interviews, and as potential participants in school activities and outings.
- Lack of visibility of other than heterosexual teachers and administrators.
- Lack of support from the school for children and their parents going through a "coming out" process.
- Denial of the reality of children's family structures. In grade one, which seemed to be the big time when everybody learned the straight version of the facts of life, she was constantly told that she had the facts wrong and that she must have had a dad that died, that we weren't telling her the truth, and that kind of stuff. She would come storming home from school and say, "Kathy says you lied to me."
- Rejection by friends and/or the parents of friends.
    > I picked Tanya up one day visiting her friend and she was sobbing, just sobbing. It came out that her friend had called her "faggot," had said we weren't normal. From then on Tanya didn't want to have anything to do with her.

The marginalization of lesbian families is not always experienced as blatant or aggressive homophobia. Often it is experienced as a sense of discomfort in teachers and administrators, a feeling that cognitively they want to deal appropriately with the issue, but are being confronted with challenges to their own deeply held ideas and values about sexuality and family.

> Nobody's calling me a dyke or a lezzie or anything like that, it's all undercurrent, it's all quite insidious and hidden and covered.
> We're talking about a very nice public school with very devoted teachers who like their work ... They were trying very hard to do the right thing and they were very uncomfortable. Their body language and tone of voice were saying: *"I wish you weren't doing this. This makes me very uncomfortable."*

Common in Toronto schools is a reluctance to acknowledge the systemic nature of the exclusion of lesbian and gay families, and a notion that efforts made in areas of anti-bias education have dealt with the "problem," at least at the level of teachers and administrators.

Lesbian families sometimes sense that they are being viewed through a lens that foregrounds their lesbianism, and that sees the ideas, actions, and parenting practices of individual lesbian parents as representative of *all* lesbian parents. A lesbian mom coaching a girl's softball team feels watched and pressured to "be really the best coach they'd ever had" so that "no one can say you're a perverted lesbian trying to seduce children." A lesbian couple that has split up feels exposed and

> that somehow we've failed in this experiment of lesbians having babies .... There was a huge pressure having the kids and then being the biggest role model throughout the school, and then when you split up it's not just like a heterosexual couple splitting up, it's like, you know, "you see what happens to these lesbian families, they can't provide stability."

Particularly salient are issues around gender role behaviours. Lesbians raising boys are frequently confronted with concerns about the "lack of male role models." When there is a difficulty or problem with a student, the issue of male role models is sometimes raised to foreground lesbianism as the possible source of the problem.

> It was grade four, and I don't think this teacher knew how to relate to boys, so she wasn't very creative in terms of how she dealt with a "behaviour problem". So Karl was in the office a lot. At one point she thought that perhaps he was acting out because he didn't have male role models.

Response from lesbian mothers to the "lack of male role model" argument is varied. Some point out the large numbers of children who have unknown, absent (physically or psychically), or abusive fathers. A 1981 study (Kirkpatrick, Smith, and Roy), comparing lesbian mothers to heterosexual single mothers, found the lesbians to be more concerned with providing opportunities for their children to develop ongoing relationships with men. The study also indicated that lesbian mothers had more adult male family friends, and included male relatives more often in their children's activities than did heterosexual mothers.

There's people who believe that a kid has to have a man in their life. I believe it's great for a kid to have good men in their life. There's few children in this world who can say that's true for them. My kids are some of those few.

A more complex argument points out the problematic assumption that mothers and fathers, simply due to biological gender, provide their children with essentially different experiences. Important to consider are the potentially positive aspects of separating "masculine" and "feminine" behaviour from biological gender, particularly given the nature of dominant forms of masculinity.

Max regards my friend Cynthia as his best male role model. If you think of role modeling in terms of behaviours and attitudes, then Cynthia is indeed quite a lovely role model in that she's vigorous and protective and powerful and tender, and likes things like trucks .... To detach certain kinds of behaviours that are seen as "masculine" from what you've got between your legs allows for far more openness and range in deciding how you are going to grow up into a human being.

Each time the child of a lesbian exhibits behaviour outside of what are considered "normal" gender roles, there is the potential for lesbianism to be focused on as the source of the "problem." A good example is the story of Karl, the son of lesbians, who decided to wear a dress and barrettes to daycare. The next day the supervisor of the daycare called, having had a big reaction and complaints from parents, including some who were concerned about transmission of the HIV virus! While the supervisor was not as upset as the parents, she was sympathetic and expressed concern for Karl, worried that his peers would tease him and that he would get hurt. Karl's parents paraphrase her comments as: "You already are lesbians and now you're doing this. This is going to be extra hard on your kid."

Karl's parents, on the other hand, felt that even though there was a possibility that he might get teased, it was more important that he learn to make his own choices based on the reactions he might receive, and they did not want to be the bearers of the message, "boys don't wear dresses."

As a result of the incident, the daycare held a workshop on sexuality where a high level of general discomfort with issues of sexuality and reproduction became apparent. A teacher expressed her discomfort with Karl's level of knowledge about women's periods and reproductive processes. One of Karl's mothers says:

> … because what "normal" is for most children is they don't have that information at the age of four, so the fact that Karl had that information and could articulate it meant that it was "abnormal", and it being "abnormal" was probably related to us being lesbians. So somewhere "lesbian" gets attached to the problem. Even if it's not verbally stated, that was clearly the undercurrent.

The impact of incidents like this one can put pressure on lesbian parents to encourage their children to conform generally, and specifically in terms of gender roles. One parent describes the tension and inner conflict she experiences:

> We're clearly not aiming to fit in and we have this joint role of influencing our children with the message, "Be who you are." There is such pressure on us, as dykes, as weirdos, as outsiders, and you know that anything that goes wrong with these children, somebody's going to blame it on your sexuality and how you're bringing them up. So that puts pressure on you to bring them up as perfectly fitting-in children. And you have to stop all the time and say "no, no, no, no, no." And we're into pretty wild and raunchy sex and leather outfits and all this stuff and how do you go into the world and balance all this? For a while I think I decided "O.K., I'm going to give up that sex stuff, I'm going to become a nice safe academician, couldn't I just get a PhD and I'd be a famous smarty cakes, right" And then I go "no, no, this is the devil talking, you're about to make a really sick deal here, so put back on that leather jacket, get out to that dance, you know, and let the kids see all of that." … I want them to do well academically, that's their survival … but they've got to be them in that, and wear whatever they want to wear, talk whatever way they want to talk, and be sure of who they are inside themselves. That's probably one of the hardest struggles.

Parents deal with this pressure to conform in different ways, and often with mixed feelings and ambivalence, as illustrated by the following quote from another parent of a boy who wanted to wear dresses:

> Bill went through a dresses phase. And I did not let him wear his dress to daycare. I just decided there was already enough stuff around people looking at us and looking at him as the son of lesbian mothers. I thought

"he doesn't need to be exposed to people's reactions that he is not going to think for a moment are coming." But I felt guilty and I feel like something got lost there. I sent him a message and maybe if he'd had the blatant message that we could have talked about, maybe it would have been better.

This tension between conformity and resistance can also mediate parent interactions with school staff. Lesbian parents are often fearful of the negative impact their lesbianism might have on their children's experiences, and, conscious of the tendency for their behaviour to be seen as "lesbian behaviour," sometimes hesitate to make waves.

I find with her teacher, for example, I become this little kid. I won't speak up, which is quite shocking. Neither of us do. Whereas I know other parents who don't get as worried about things like this ... I think it has a lot to do with lesbianism, I think definitely. Because I think it would be easy to discount what we have to say because we're lesbians.

However, many lesbian parents, including the woman quoted above, do often find themselves in a position to intervene on behalf of their children, but find it a complicated process that requires negotiation with their children and awareness of the cultures their children inhabit at school.

Student cultures

The production of gender and sexual identities in schools takes place within the context of student cultures; cultures that differ according to one's positioning in various relations of power (i.e., class, race, gender, age, ability, sexual orientation, etc.). The student cultures inhabited by boys and girls are, as one mother puts it, "like two different worlds." While I am not equipped to fully discuss the implications for lesbian families of gendered student cultures, I can make a few observations.

Perhaps because homophobia is less integral to girls' culture than to boys'; girls, particularly those who exhibit "normal" girl behaviour, seem to experience less direct, brutal forms of homophobia, and certainly less concern from school staff about the lack of men in their lives. Valerie Walkerdine (1986) analyses the ways that, even though they perform better on average at school than boys, girls are often presented as "'passive', 'hardworking', 'helpful', and 'rule following', characteristics seen as antithetical to the 'active, enquiring' nature of childhood (more often exhibited by boys), but compatible with the requirements necessary to join the caring (female) professions" (71–72). Interestingly, one lesbian mother describes her daughter in terms similar to Walkerdine's, and links her daughter's desire to please and to "fit in" with the receiving of less attention, negative or positive:

Tanya is fine in whatever setting she's in, and I think the sexism in all that is that she kind of gets lost in the shuffle. She's perceived as a great student because she's always on top of her school work, she's quiet, she's cooperative, she's very studious, and she really likes to please people. She's all of the things little girls are supposed to be.

Tanya's other mother says:

Karl gets it [homophobic harassment] more than Tanya does. Partly she's younger, partly she's a girl, so the social scene for her is very different.

For Tanya most of the reaction to her lesbian family has come in the form of teasing from friends. Twice she has had friends abruptly reject her because of their parents' reaction to lesbianism. As a result she does not make a lot of new friends, and carefully chooses those she does. Clearly more work is needed on the ways that homophobia and compulsory heterosexuality impact girls at school, and specifically, the daughters of lesbians.

In the process of schooling, boys learn different lessons than girls with regards to gender and sexual identity, the most important being heterosexuality is "normal", and "macho" is the most acceptable form of masculinity. To maintain this sense of "normal" masculinity, boys learn to distance from, render invisible, and subordinate other, less "manly" forms of masculinity, and their association with the feminine. Homophobia, then, is used as a tool to police gender and sexual boundaries, to subordinate behaviour and attitudes not appropriate to "real" men (or boys).

One lesbian mother describes the combination of factors leading to her son Max's harassment on the playground, including name-calling and physical violence:

The playground was a nightmare for him, an absolute nightmare. He dreaded recess; he dreaded the end of school. They were times when he was in danger. First, he's not at all macho, and never was. His gender identity, I'm proud to say, was not rigid in any way. Piece number two is he was identified in first grade as having a learning disability. And for quite a long time he had to wear a patch over one eye.

She goes on to describe her own commitment to non-violent conflict resolution and her attempt to encourage her son to adopt these methods in the schoolyard. Eventually he came home in tears, saying, "Mom, I have to start hitting back." He did, and the violence decreased.

Max deviated from cultural norms of masculinity in several ways—his gender identity was flexible; he was, at least temporarily, physically and learning disabled; and he did not fight back with a tough or macho style. His mother wonders, "how it would have been had he already been a kid who took care of himself in a way that worked, who had that kind of streetwise toughness. He might have got away with the lesbian stuff quite readily, I don't know."

This then, is the context within which boys of lesbians in urban centres live—a student culture that another mother describes as "tough, competitive, you're always working out who's going to trick you, and you know, little gangs form."

In this context, it is a complicated judgment call for parents as to when and how to intervene on behalf of their children, when, in some cases, intervention can make things worse. Also involved in decisions regarding interventions is the belief, echoed by many lesbian parents, that their children need control over the "coming out process" in the school environment.

> I think as adults we can only have the vaguest idea of what life is really like at school. I think a lot of the time we think it's better than it really is. I think we need to listen to our kids and ask our kids and consult our kids, because it's their lives.

Parents express sadness about their inability to protect their children from pain, while also talking with pride about the resources and survival strategies their children develop.

> How do you allow your kid to learn how to live in the world and not be ashamed of who they are, but also negotiate safety all the time around being kids from a lesbian family, from a family that's split up ... all these things, money-wise, class-wise ... I spent a lot of time crying about the fact that I can't protect them all the time and the fact that I can't run into the school every time there's a problem in the schoolyard. They're going to have to negotiate some of these things themselves.
>
> It's actually quite fascinating to watch how they will figure out what to do. Karl was once asked, "Which one is your mom?" He told the kid, "Well, I came out of her body." He wasn't denying his relationship to Barb (non-biological mother) and he told the truth. I thought "That's pretty brilliant." It teaches you a lot about how kids cope with oppression.

The children of lesbians develop a wide range of innovative ways of negotiating their own and their parents' identities through an intricate web of social norms and expectations. Choices regarding "coming out" and the strategies used to manage other children's reactions to their parents' lesbianism are diverse, and vary contextually and at different ages and grade levels. It seems that as one gets older issues get more complex and there is a perceived need for greater caution. Decisions to come out to friends are often based on careful gauging of potential reactions and safety levels. For example, safety is gauged by noting a friend's reaction to a book about lesbian moms, or by noticing who uses the term "faggot" in the schoolyard. One child of lesbians does not have close friendships at school and reserves these for other children of lesbians; another develops friendships with kids who in some way challenge traditional gender roles, more "androgynous types." One boy asks his mother to remove lesbian content from their shared living space so he will feel more comfortable bringing friends over; another makes friends with tough kids as a way of ensuring his own safety; another, expressing fear of teenage boys, asks to go to an alternative school where he hopes to find more like-minded kids and less macho behaviour; and another begins to refer to his "moms" as "parents," to avoid direct confrontation with the issue.

Lesbian parents *and* their children reiterate again and again the difference that the presence of other children of lesbians *and* openly lesbian or gay teachers makes to their experience at school.

However, the identities and experiences of the children of lesbians are multifaceted. The presence of other lesbian families, while clearly important, is not a guarantee that the school environment will meet the needs of a population, who aside from their membership in a lesbian family, are differently located in relation to a multitude of other social identities.

Complex identities

The coming out discourse that emphasizes the need and desirability of coming out to family and friends has been critiqued for failing to recognize the risks, particularly for gays and lesbians of colour, of losing important involvement and connections to communities of families and friends. The discourse of "coming out" is seen to isolate and privilege the gay or lesbian aspect of one's identity, while not recognizing the impact of multiple and intersecting identities. The experience of coming out to family and friends can differ vastly depending on one's location vis-a-vis race, class, age, religion, able-bodiedness, etc.

The children of lesbians have complex identities and there is a danger of defining identity in terms of a single component and offering simplified solutions to problems that are embedded in complex social relations. For example, for Max, the boy mentioned earlier who suffered much playground abuse, his identity as the son of a lesbian was just a small part of a matrix of factors (gender performance, learning disability, physical disability, mother who advocates non-violence) that influenced his experience. His mother wonders how things would have been different had not all these factors been present and, in fact, he now reports that much of the harassment against him ended when he got contact lenses! A perspective that sees him only as the child of a lesbian misses significant aspects of his experience.

Similarly, Karl, the son of a lesbian couple, has not told his friends at school about his family structure, and has recently been reluctant to bring friends home. His parents and sister, however, attribute this to the fact that his best friend's parents are both professionals and have a lot of money, and that Karl does not feel his house is up to the standards of his friend's.

While Karl, who is white, has chosen to attend an alternative school where lesbian families are (somewhat) more easily accepted, his sister Tanya, who is "mixed-race," has stayed in a regular public school where she has more access to friendships with children of colour, something that is increasingly important to her identity.

Important to keep in mind, too, is the fact that the experience of lesbian parents and their children in the schools is not uniformly negative or unproductive. Lesbian parents also describe the ideas, attitudes, and skills their children develop related to the challenges they face as the children of lesbians. These include: skills in negotiating difficult situations; sophisticated understanding of the dynamics of oppression; understanding of complex political issues; and knowledge and understanding of gender issues. Also,

> ... awareness that there are choices, possibilities, that there is a range of behaviour other than the strictly culturally defined one. It means he is growing into his sexuality with a much more open field to play in, and I think that's wonderful.
> ... he has a nose for bullshit and hypocrisy and for not doing stuff because you're afraid of what people will think about it, that I think is unusually acute, and I love that.

Conclusion

School administrators, teachers, and policy makers who want to seriously address the needs of lesbian families must first become familiar with the ways that schools actively produce hierarchically ordered gender identities, sexualities, and family structures. Effective pedagogical and administrative practices will address the power dynamics involved in the marginalization of lesbian families, and will attempt to take the burden of responsibility for transforming these dynamics off the shoulders of lesbian families. One small example is a teacher who, at a parent–teacher interview, took the risk of asking, "Is your partner a man or a woman?" In this way, she opened a space for lesbian existence.

In Ontario, in 1999, attempts to shift school structures to accomodate the needs of lesbian families take place in the context of large-scale budget cuts and a hitherto unseen dismantling of the education system. In the face of the resurgence of conservative "family values," and a lack of anything resembling government commitment to social justice, lesbian families, and others marginalized in the school system, face an uphill battle. The struggle is inevitable, however, as increasing numbers of lesbians choose to make children part of their families. Parent night will never be the same.

Postscript

This work on lesbian families in schools grew out of eight years of researching various aspects of lesbian parenting. My research interests followed my life: when I was pregnant I produced an information kit on alternative insemination; when I had a baby and toddler I explored the division of labour and "roles" in lesbian parenting couples; when someone close to me was denied access to her non-biological child, I interviewed nonbiological parents; and when my kid hit school age, I began to look at what was happening in schools. Thus my research came, not from a place of knowing, but from a place of not knowing, not being sure what my daughter would experience at school, how I could prepare her, where we should send her to school, how much could we/should we intervene?

Yet, with the publication of an expanded version of this paper in a local, left-wing journal about schools (Epstein, 1998), I came to be seen as someone who knows about lesbian families in schools, and I begin to enact the part. I accept the invitations to sit on panels where I present the "truth" about what is happening. I make suggestions about the kinds of thinking and actions people might want to take around these issues. I answer people's questions with authority. Thrust into the position of "knower," I am left with less room not to know, less room for my own questions and uncertainties to exist and propel me, and less room for new approaches to the whole question. Suddenly I see this happening all around me. We live in a world of experts, whose interpolation into that role gets in the way of opportunities to create from a place of not-knowing. I begin to think of my realist tale as something that has plugged up what should be flowing. Like a dam in a river, the realist tale creates energy, produces order, and does useful work. But the dam is not innocent, it blocks the "natural" flow of the river, it impacts on the environment, and it creates dependencies in people. Soon more dams are needed to create more energy and more order, to create the illusion of control. Dams breed more dams, and realist stories breed realist stories in order to maintain the illusion of unified subjects and mastery of a knowable world.

But dams do useful things, and so does this chapter. It is an attempt to stay close to the things lesbian parents said about their experiences in schools, and to make visible and bring to a larger audience's awareness the concerns and experiences of lesbian parents. Given the significance of visibility/invisibility for lesbians generally, and lesbian parents particularly, the article makes visible a group of people and experiences not typically, in fact rarely, foregrounded in mainstream culture. The article stems from my excitement about its contents, and is my attempt to do justice to people's stories by ordering them in a way that makes sense, that communicates some of the subtleties and nuance of their experiences and that fits conventional formats enough to be publishable. Lesbian parents who have read the article have responded positively: that it "captures what it's really like," that it "is both theoretical and accessible," that it "gets at some of the complexities." They are often delighted that someone has put something down on paper about a largely undocumented experience, and they frequently request copies for friends, and for use in schools and daycares. I have used the article in workshops with teachers, including at my own daughter's school, and at other presentations and speaking engagements. The article provides a framework for political direction and concrete demands around which to organize. Yet the story I tell is just one of many that could be told.

An inquiring tale

Last summer, in the context of a graduate course, I used the same data on which I had based the original article (which I refer to as the "realist tale") to experiment with the writing of what I called an "inquiring tale." It was my attempt to carry out research from a place of not-knowing, of uncertainty, from a place that troubles what can be known and the validity of the "real." My inquiring tale looks very different from the original. The text is a collage, an ensemble of juxtapositions of its various parts—my narrative in the middle of the page, quotes from lesbian parents running down the sides and sometimes invading the middle column, a theoretical piece, a set of "discussion questions," and a poem excerpt at the end. The pieces do not fit together neatly. One does not totally explain the other and they do not make a neat package of "sense." These unconventional textual practices were my attempt to make visible the constructed nature of the framework, to surprise and/or shock the reader out of stereotypes and common assumptions, to make apparent my own questions and lack of knowing, to produce a thinking reader and to resist a smooth sail through a nice story.

The inquiring tale begins by recounting a conversation I had with a young South Asian woman. We were talking about children and schooling, and I spoke about a recent decision to move our daughter from the neighbourhood school to a nearby alternative public school, where we anticipated her experiencing less homophobia. The woman I spoke to was clear that "she doesn't believe in protecting her kid from these things." She experienced a lot of racism at school in England, and it was through these experiences that she learned what she knows about oppression and survival, and she does not regret it. She seemed clear in her view that children should not be protected, while expressing some doubt about exactly how she would handle specifics when they arose. The perspective she offered was not new to me, but that evening it had a strong impact. I remembered another conversation, a few years earlier, with a black lesbian mother who described the racism her daughter had endured at school. She also spoke about the good things she had learned as a result. "The more stuff they deal with the better," were her words.

Recalling these conversations led me to think in a different way about the approaches lesbian parents take to their children's school experiences, and to consider a framework that "poses as a problem what has been offered as a solution" (Lather, 1994: 118) by problematizing the tensions between protecting one's children on the one hand, and preparing them for the dangers of life on the other. Perhaps these tensions are illustrated by the two previously described stories of lesbian mothers figuring out how to respond to their son's desire to wear dresses to daycare. This line of thought led me back to Valerie Walkerdine and Helen Lucey's 1989 book, *Democracy in the kitchen,* in which they use transcripts of interactions between four-year-old girls and their mothers to develop theory about middle and working class mothering practices. In their analysis, middle class mothers are more likely to convey the illusion to their children that the world is safe, that it can be known and mastered, and to raise children for whom the belief that they are empowered, autonomous, and free is part of the mechanism of their regulation. Working class mothers, on the other hand, are more likely to prepare their children for survival in a world where relations of power and conflict are visible.

My aim here is not to give a detailed synopsis of Walkerdine and Lucey's arguments, nor to fully develop this tension between protection and preparation, but to point out the instability of data interpretation. My original article offers one interpretation of the data. An exploration of the tensions between protecting/ preparing our children, and of the meanings of "protection" to different parents and different children would offer other interpretations and different conclusions.

Having spent much of my academic life to date unable to find an embodied place from which to write, writing this "inquiring tale" was an exhilarating experience. Allowing my not-knowing the space to live seemed to enlarge possibilities, and I lived and breathed this writing in a way I had previously associated only with creative writing.

Of course, there are dangers associated with this kind of data interpretation and writing—the danger that data can become clay for artists' hands, disconnected from the meanings it has for those who are its source; or that creative presentation and interesting textual performance can substitute for rigorous thinking. Figuring out a way into the portrayal and performance of complexity can take a lot of time and space. The realist tale seems to lend itself more easily to summarizing and categorizing a lot of data. It can draw cohesive conclusions that allow readers to walk away as if they too are now knowers who can choose to adopt the stance and the praxis stemming from the author's interpretations. I wonder, though, if tales of not-knowing were generally allowed more space, whether we might generate some insights and strategies that would poke us out of the tried and true. How can we do research on lesbian mothering that both makes space for and acknowledges the knowing that stems from the experiences and voices of a previously invisible group, and leaves space for our not-knowing to live and breathe?

Thank you to Patti Lather for an exhilarating shift in perspective.

Note

1. These twenty interviews were conducted in the context of three different research projects. In each case the women I interviewed were asked how they identified in terms of class, race, and ethnicity. Their identifications are as follows: working class–9, middle class–11; English, Scottish, or "WASP"–10; Jewish–4; assimilated Francophone–2, French-Canadian–1, African-Canadian–1, South Asian/Black–1, African/English/French/Portuguese Jew–1. They ranged in age from twenty-nine to fifty-five. I located women to interview through personal networks and with the assistance of a Toronto-based support group for lesbian mothers.

Chapter Nine

LESBIAN MOTHERS AND THE LAW OF CUSTODY, ACCESS, AND CHILD SUPPORT*

Joanna Radbord

At least one-third of lesbians are mothers.[1] Whether lesbians raise children from previous heterosexual relationships, or have babies as lesbian mothers, the law currently fails to support lesbian families. This chapter discusses the law in Canada,[2] particularly in the province of Ontario, with respect to custody and access for lesbian mothers. It also touches briefly on the child support rights and obligations of lesbian parents.

1. Custody and access

The term "custody" refers to the rights and responsibilities of a parent in relation to a child, including the right to make decisions about the child. A custodial parent usually has primary care and control of a child. "Access" refers to the right to spend time with a child, and the right to make inquiries and be given information as to the health, education, and welfare of the child. In Canada, all provinces allow custody and access claims by parents, grandparents, step-parents, and same-sex spouses. Most statutes say that custody claims may be made by "any parent or other person," at least where the claimant has "shown a settled intention to treat the child as a family member." In Ontario, "a court may grant custody or access to one or more persons."[3] As in all matters related to children, "the best interests of the child" are the paramount consideration. However, a relationship by blood between the child and the applicant is one statutory criteria used in determining the child's best interests in custody and access proceedings.[4]

(a) Custody and access on the breakdown of a heterosexual relationship

Traditionally, most custody or access claims by lesbians have arisen after the breakdown of a heterosexual relationship. In early decisions, courts viewed "homosexuality" as a problem or negative factor, although not a complete bar to custody. As a result, many lesbians felt forced to remain closeted, "voluntarily" surrendering custody in favour of more generous access rights.[5]

Whatever success lesbians have achieved at the Supreme Court of Canada in pursuing abstract equality rights, lower courts sometimes participate in and reflect the systemic homophobia of our society. I have heard a judge remark about a lesbian parent, "I have no problem with her as a mother, but with her life," and "she chose this lifestyle and she can live with the consequences." In that case, the judge ordered the stay-at-home mother to leave the matrimonial home, the children to be primarily resident with the father, and the mother's limited access time with the children to be held outside the presence of her girlfriend. In other cases, however, judges take a child-centered perspective and progressively advance substantive equality rights.[6] One judge was surprised by my eagerness to present sociological and psychological evidence on behalf of a transsexual client. This judge accepted immediately that gender identity was completely irrelevant to the best interests of the child and looked instead at my client's excellent parenting.[7]

Judges have frequently distinguished between "good" and "bad" lesbian mothers on the basis of whether the mother is closeted and "discreet."[8] "Bad" lesbian mothers are those who are open about their sexual orientation, and who participate in the gay and lesbian community. Arnup and Boyd conclude that openly lesbian mothers "are almost certain to lose custody of their children to their ex-husbands."[9] Of course, any demands of "discretion" require lesbian parents to deny their full personhood, and punish lesbians for participating in cultural and political life. The approach is discriminatory and contrary to the best interests of the child.[10]

There are many examples of judges demanding "discretion" from lesbian and gay parents. In *Case* v. *Case*,[11] a lesbian mother sought custody of her ten-year-old daughter and four-year-old son. The judge determined that the mother exaggerated allegations of bad conduct by the father, finding that the mother was just "slightly hurt" when the father "pushed the mother around," and the father was not abusive but only "soundly spanked the son." Another problem was that the mother slept in the same bed as her female partner and the partner had not been called as a witness at trial. Justice MacPherson stated that Ms. Case's "way of life is irregular" and "... I greatly fear that if these children are raised by the mother they will be too much in contact with people of abnormal tastes and proclivities."[12] She was denied custody.

The Alberta Provincial Court granted custody to a lesbian mother in *K.* v. *K.*[13] on the basis that her relationship was "discreet" and that her sexuality would not be "flaunted." Her sexuality was described as no more of a bar to custody than the father's drug use. In *D. v. D.*, the trial judge regarded the father's "abnormal" sexual orientation as a "problem which may damage the children's psychological, moral, intellectual, or physical well-being, and their orderly development and adaptation to society."[14] However, the father was awarded custody on the basis that he was bisexual, discreet, not an exhibitionist, he did not flaunt his sexual orientation, had married couples as visitors to the home, was not a "missionary" or militant, and was not a member of any gay club. Similarly, in *B. v. B.*, the court was willing to grant custody to a lesbian mother because "any possible ill effects" were minimized because the mother was not "militant," "did not flaunt her homosexuality," and did not seem "biased" about her child's sexual orientation but rather seemed to assume that the daughter would be heterosexual.[15]

In Ontario, the leading case of *Bezaire v. Bezaire*, provides that "homosexuality of a parent is irrelevant, unless it affects the best interests of the child."[16] This approach still implies that gay or lesbian sexual orientation can be a negative factor.[17] Furthermore, the Ontario Court of Appeal did not criticize the discriminatory restrictions imposed by the lower court.[18] The trial judge had initially decided that the mother should retain custody, having had de facto custody of the children for four years. However, the judge barred "any open, declared and avowed lesbian or homosexual relationship." No other person was permitted to reside with Ms. Bezaire without the approval of the court. The father applied for custody after the mother moved in to an apartment with another woman. The trial judge reversed his decision, finding "psychological instability" on the part of Ms. Bezaire. The Ontario Court of Appeal dismissed her appeal. Apparently, the mother then removed the children and disappeared.[19]

A better approach would recognize that children of a gay or lesbian parent are likely to encounter homophobia regardless of which parent has custody. Therefore, the appropriate question should be which parent is better suited to assist the child in dealing with issues of sexuality, including sexual orientation discrimination, in a constructive and supportive manner.[20] A lesbian mother may then be advantaged in being able to help a child to cope with the inevitable realities of intolerance.

Today, many lesbians do obtain custody of their children. Still, lesbians have yet to achieve substantive equality in custody and access determinations as a result of heterosexism and homophobia. Lesbian mothers continue to be denied custody and be granted limited access to their children.[21] The "best interests" test, while appearing to be neutral, is not necessarily applied in a manner that recognizes the requirements of equality.[22] The best interests test must be infused with substantive equality principles to promote justice for lesbians and to ensure the welfare of children.

(b) Custody of children of a same-sex relationship

In a claim for custody or access involving the breakdown of a lesbian relationship, the court could order custody or access in favour of either partner, even though only one spouse is the biological or adoptive parent. Although the court may be tempted to privilege the parent with a blood or legal relationship, any such presumption threatens the guiding principle of child custody: the paramount concern must be the best interests of the child. The best approach is to carefully consider the individual circumstances and needs of the child. Biological connection should not be privileged over daily caregiving and love.[23]

In Canada, a court would be required to consider a range of factors, including the bond between the child and each parent, each mother's parenting abilities, and the biological connection between parent and child.[24] A recent Ontario case involved a non-biological lesbian parent who was seeking sole custody and a declaration that she was a mother of the child.[25] The couple planned for the child's birth together and shared in all aspects of his life. The child called the birth mother "mama" and had her last name. After the parties separated, the non-biological mother moved out and had access to the child. The birth mother was offered a job in Vancouver and wished to move there with her son. Justice Benotto held that, although the non-biological mother was very involved in the child's care, the birth mother was the primary caregiver. It was in the child's best interest to be with the birth mother, and to maintain regular contact with the mother's former partner. Joint custody was impossible given the conflict between the parties. The non-biological mother's claim for sole custody was therefore denied.

There is an unreported Ontario decision in which interim sole custody was awarded to a non-biological co-mother, "L." *Re L. and S.*[26] involved two children, one adopted legally by "L" and the other conceived by artificial insemination by her partner during their relationship. On consent, the court ordered that "L" retain sole custody of the adopted child, joint legal custody of the other child, and that the children would be primarily resident with "L." The Court relied on the *Children's Law Reform Act*, which states that the parties to an application for custody and access in respect of a child shall include a person who has demonstrated a settled intention to treat the child as a child of his or her family.

Known sperm donors may also bring successful claims for custody and access, despite any agreement with the donor to the contrary.[27] Donor contracts, purporting to limit rights and obligations of parentage, are likely unenforceable,[28] and the reality is that donors can and do change their minds, particularly after seeing that first adorable grin of a cute and cuddly baby. Regardless of the parties' original intentions, a sperm donor, particularly one who has a relationship with the child and who has been providing financial support, will very likely be seen as the child's father and will be equally entitled to claim custody. Lesbians who wish to prevent any future claims by a sperm donor should use clinic services for sperm.[29]

(c) Joint custody and adoption to create parental rights

Several Ontario judges have given same-sex parents joint custody where the couple has decided to co-parent the biological children of one of the spouses, and both wish to have rights and obligations as parents.[30] A joint custody order gives non-biological parents a right of access to information from schools and doctors, and the power to give instructions to institutions. Because there is no restriction on who may be granted custody of children, joint custody orders are available to any group of persons who are co-parenting a child. All four parents might be granted custody in co-parenting situations involving a gay male biological father and his partner, and a lesbian birth mother and her partner.

In *Re K.*[31] Justice Nevins amended the definition of "spouse" to include same-sex spouses for the purposes of second parent and stranger adoption. The case involved non-biological mothers who wished to adopt the children born to lesbian partners so that each spouse had status as her child's mother. Second parent adoptions provide the most certainty and equality to same sex parents on breakdown of relationships.

In cases of stranger adoption, only one spouse in a same-sex relationship will be entitled to legally adopt a child, except in British Columbia and Ontario.[32] A constitutional challenge on the basis of sexual orientation discrimination would be required to access joint adoption. On the breakdown of a same-sex relationship in which one spouse has adopted a child, there may be a strong presumption in favour of the sole adoptive parent. In an American decision, a non-adoptive mother, who had been the primary caregiver for the first seven months after the adoption placement, was held to have no right to even commence an action for custody, visitation, and enforcement of a separation agreement providing for access, despite the court ordinarily allowing persons who stand in place of a parent to bring claims for custody.[33]

Absent a joint custody or second parent adoption order, a non-biological same-sex parent has no power to pick up children from school, take them to the doctor, or travel with them. An easy answer to this problem is a letter of authorization or permission from the biological parent. However, this does not provide the best mechanism for long-term legal security for the family.

2. Getting or paying child support

Child support is a contribution to the financial maintenance of a child paid to the custodial parent by the non-custodial parent, usually strictly in accordance with the payor's annual income. British Columbia is the only jurisdiction to expressly include lesbian co-parents in its support legislation. In that province, "parent" includes the step-parent of a child if the step-parent contributed to the support and maintenance of the child for at least one year, and a step-parent includes a person who lived with a parent of the child in a marriage-like relationship for a period of at least two years. Such a marriage-like relationship may be between persons of the same gender.[34]

In Ontario, New Brunswick, Manitoba, P.E.I., Saskatchewan, and Newfoundland, the definition of "parent" includes those who have shown "a settled intention" to treat a child as a child of his or her family[35] or who stand *in loco parentis* (in place of a parent) to a child.[36] A lesbian who cohabits for a length of time with a spouse and children will therefore likely be considered to have a "settled intention" to parent that is sufficient to create child support obligations. In *M.(D.E.)* v. *S.(H.J.),*[37] a Saskatchewan court ordered a lesbian to pay child support of $150 per child, for two children that the couple had reared for five years, notwithstanding the fact that her partner refused to claim support from the children's biological father. *Buist* v. *Greaves*[38] is another case in which a non-biological lesbian parent was ordered to pay child support of $450 per month plus half of access costs.

In those jurisdictions in which only biological or adoptive parents are recognized in child support legislation, this could be challenged as adverse effects discrimination against lesbians and gay men, contrary to the Charter. Another option would be to argue *promissory estoppel*. An Australian lesbian mother successfully relied on this doctrine to obtain child support from her former partner. The former partner had promised to support the birth mother and child. The birth mother reasonably relied on the assurance to her economic detriment, so the former partner was obliged, on the basis of promissory estoppel, to comply with her promise.

3. Conclusion

With its decision in *M. v. H.*[39] in May, the Supreme Court of Canada has given meaning to the Charter's promise of equality for lesbians.[40] The Court held that the wholesale exclusion of same-sex couples from the justice of family law was discriminatory, and could not be upheld as reasonable limit of the equality guarantee in a free and democratic society. In an eight-to-one decision, the court struck down the definition of spouse under section 29 of the *Family Law Act*. The spousal support provisions will have to be rewritten before the court's November 20, 1999, deadline. The legislature has also been invited to consider all definitions of "spouse" that exclude lesbians and gays to allow comprehensive change, rather than piecemeal court reform.

Although the decision applies strictly only to Ontario's legislation, at the time of writing, legislatures across Canada are reviewing their statutes to ensure equal recognition of same-sex spouses and opposite-sex unmarried cohabitants.[41] The next months will likely be marked by significant family law reform, hopefully across Canada. The law is clear that legislatures should now be providing equal treatment of all unmarried couples. This means it is likely that the law will soon, at least on its face, provide equal rights and obligations for lesbian families, and that can only be in the best interests of children.

The author wishes to thank Maretta Miranda, Ida Morra-Caruso, and Martha McCarthy. Martha and the author co-wrote "Family Law for Same Sex Couples: Chart(er)ing the Course" [(1998) 15 Can. J. Fam. L. 101], which served as a starting point for this piece and provides more comprehensive treatment of a whole range of issues facing same-sex couples.

Notes

*   This article was originally published in the *Journal of the Association on Mothering* 1 (2), 1999. It was current as of its initial publication, but has been updated for this volume.

1. Affidavit of Dr. Rosemary Barnes, sworn August 12, 1994, "Expert opinion from Dr. Rosemary Barnes prepared re: M. v. H., August 12, 1994," S.C.C. Case on Appeal, Tab 18, pp. 128–129; K. Arnup, "'We are family': Lesbian mothers in Canada" (1991) 20:3/4 *RFR/DRF* 101–107; F.W. Bozett, ed., *Gay and lesbian parents* (Westport: Praeger, 1987); S. Slater, *The lesbian family life cycle* (New York: The Free Press, 1995), 89–118; C. O'Brien and L. Weir, "Lesbians and gay men inside and outside families," in N. Mandell and A. Duffy, eds. *Canadian families: Diversity, conflict and change* (Toronto: Harcourt Brace, 1995), 127–130.

2. This article includes occasional references to U.S. law. American readers should note that Canada is considerably more advanced in recognizing lesbian and gay equality rights. Practical suggestions for American family law lawyers are provided in M. McCarthy and J. Radbord, "Unmarried couples: Equality and equity in Canada," in *Family law 2000* (Aspen Publishing).

3. *Children's Law Reform Act,* R.S.O. 1990, s. 28 (1).

4. Ibid. s. 24 (2)(q).

5. K. Arnup, *supra* note 1; K. Arnup and S. Boyd, "Familial disputes? Sperm donors, lesbian mothers and legal parenthood," in D. Herman and C. Stychin, eds. *Legal inversions: Lesbians, gay men and the politics of law* (Philadelphia: Temple University Press, 1995), 83; S. Gavigan, "A parent(ly) knot: Can Heather have two mommies?" in Herman and Stychin, eds. *Legal inversions: Lesbians, gay men and the politics of law* (Philadelphia: Temple University Press, 1995); K.A. Lahey, *Are we 'persons' yet? Law and sexuality in Canada* (Toronto: University of Toronto Press, 1999).

6. For a discussion of Canada's substantive equality jurisprudence, please see M. McCarthy and J. Radbord, "Foundations for 15(1): Equality Rights in Canada," in the *Michigan Journal of Gender and the Law.*

7. Evidence on same-sex parenting which might be helpful to judges includes: *Gay and lesbian parents,* F.W. Bozett, ed. (Westport: Praeger Publishers, 1987); *Homosexuality: Research implications for public policy,* J.C. Gonsiorek and J.D. Weinrich, eds. (Newbury Park: Sage Publications, 1991); C.J. Patterson, "Children of lesbian and gay parents," (1992) 63 *Child Development,* 1025–1042; S. Golombok and F. Tasker, "Children in lesbian and gay families:

Theories and evidence," in *Lesbians raising sons*, Jess Wells, ed. (Los Angeles: Alyson Books, 1997), 158; R. Green, J.B. Mandel, M.E. Hotvedt, J. Gray, and L. Smith, "Lesbian mothers and their children: A comparison with solo parent heterosexual mothers and their children" (1986), 15 *Archives of Sexual Behaviour*, 167–184; C.J. Patterson, "Children of the lesbian baby boom: Behavioural adjustment, self concepts and sex role identity," in *Lesbian and gay psychology: Theory research and clinical applications,* B. Greene and G.M. Herek, eds. (Newbury Park, California: Sage), 156–175. Lawyers might also provide judges with the Ontario case of *Re K* (1995), 15 R.F.L. (4th) 129 (Ont. Ct. Prov. Div.). It summarizes an array of expert evidence and provides answers to the common homophobic stereotypes about same-sex parenting.

8. S. Gavigan, *supra* note 5; K. Arnup and S. Boyd, *supra* note 5; K. Arnup, *supra* note 1. See discussion *infra*.

9. K. Arnup and S. Boyd, ibid.

10. The American Psychological Association reports that, by being open with their children about their relationships and by living with their same-sex partners, gay and lesbian parents assist their children to become well-adjusted adults. American Psychological Association, *Lesbian and gay parenting: A resource for psychologists* (District of Columbia, 1995).

11. (1974), 18 R.F.L. 132 (Sask. Q.B.).

12. Ibid., 138.

13. (1975), 23 R.F.L. 58 (Alta. Prov. Ct.).

14. (1978), 3 R.F.L. (2d) 327 (Ont. Co. Ct.).

15. (1980), 16 R.F.L. (2d) 7 (Ont. Prov. Ct.).

16. (1980), 20 R.F.L. (3d) 358 (Ont. C.A.).

17. The Ontario Court, Provincial Division, adopted a more desirable approach in *Steers* v. *Monk* [1992] O.J. No. 2701 (Prov. Ct.) (Q.L.). Justice Wolder stated that the mother's lesbian "relationship should be seen in the same light as if she were living in a heterosexual relationship with another [sic] male person, which could also either be positive or negative, depending on the particular facts surrounding the relationship and the outward conduct of the parties."

18. The case was decided prior to the introduction of the Canadian Charter of Rights and Freedoms and the equality protections received by lesbians and gays in cases like *Egan v. Canada* [1995] 2 S.C.R 513. See also a Quebec case that found that such a restriction would be unconstitutional under the Quebec Charter: *J. v. R.* (1982), 27 R.F.L. (2d) 380 (Que. S.C.).

19. J. McLeod, Annotation to *Bezaire, supra* note 16 citing *London Free Press* (Jan. 17, 1981).

20. Susan Boyd, "Lesbian (and gay) custody claims: What difference does difference make?" (1998) 15 *Can. J. Fam. L.*, 131.

21. *B. v. B., supra* note 15; *Droit de la Famille - 14*, File no. 750-12-002454-82, 22 décembre 1982 (C.S.Q.); *Daller v. Daller* (1988), 18 R.F.L. (3d) 53, 22 R.F.L. (3d) 96 (Ont. C.A.); *Steers v. Monk, supra* note 17; *N. v. N.*, [1992] B.C. J. No. 1507 (Q.L.).

22. In determining the best interests of a child, it may be relevant to consider whether a parent will be able to provide a permanent and stable family unit. The fact that same-sex couples

are denied the right to marry cannot be used against the lesbian or gay parent. Discrimination must not be used to justify continuing discrimination.

23. As the U.S. Supreme Court has observed in *Lehr v. Robertson*, 463 U.S. 248 at 260, 103 S.Ct. 2985 at 2992, 77 L. Ed.2d 614 at 626, (1983): "Parental rights do not spring full-blown from the biological connection between parent and child. They require relationships more enduring" (citing Caban, 441 U.S. at 397, 99 S.Ct. at 1770, 60 L. ED.2d at 297) (Stewart, J., dissenting) and further in 463 U.S. at 261, 103 S.Ct. at 2993, 77 L. ED.2d at 626: "the importance of the familial relationship, to the individuals involved and to the society, stems from the emotional attachments that derive from the intimacy of daily association ... as well as from the fact of blood relationship." It is important to note that months of

> carrying a child to term and giving birth create an initial relationship between the biological mother and child that should be recognized at law. This would be particularly important in a contest between a sperm donor and a birth mother, for instance. However, the status of birth mother is important because of the caregiving bond of reproductive labour, rather than biological connection.

24. In the U.S., some courts deny standing to non-biological mothers, stating that a non-biological lesbian co-parent is not a parent but a "biological stranger." Co-parent mothers are often restricted to extremely limited visitation. In New York, however, a trial court granted full custody to a lesbian non-biological mother. The couple had agreed that one mother would be inseminated and the other would be the primary caregiver. The judge determined that the non-biological mother was the six-year-old girl's "psychological" parent, and that granting custody to her was in the child's best interest. The biological mother was awarded visitation. *Briggs v. Newingham,* Lesbian and Gay Law Notes (Lesbian and Gay Law Assoc. of Greater N.Y., N.Y.) (Summer 1992), 54.

25. *Buist v. Greaves*, [1997] O.J. No. 2646 (Gen. Div.) (QL).

26. File No. 195/89 (Ont. Prov. Div.) *per* Pedlar J.

27. Newfoundland, Quebec and the Yukon are possible exceptions. The provisions of the *Children's Law Act*, R.S.N. 1990, c. C-13, s. 12(1)(6) and the *Children's Act*, R.S.Y. 1986, c. 22, s. 13(1)(6) are identical. They state that a man whose semen is used to "artificially inseminate" a woman is not the father unless he is married to or living with the mother. There is no clear definition of "artificial insemination" so it is unclear whether "artificially inseminated" includes self-insemination. Given this uncertainty, there is a danger that the statutes may be interpreted in a manner so as to allow sperm donors to assert parental rights. In *Jhordan C. v. Mary K.,* 179 Cal. App. 3d 386, 224 Cal. Rptr. 530 (1986, 1st Dist.), the Court held that parties who proceeded with alternative insemination in a manner not contemplated by the terms of a similar statute could not receive its protections. The sperm donor could obtain parental status.

Quebec's Civil Code provides that participation in the parental project of another person by way of a contribution of genetic material to medically assisted procreation does not allow the creation of any bond of filiation between the contributor and the child born of that procreation. A person who, after consenting to medically assisted procreation, does not acknowledge the child, is responsible to the child and mother of the child born of medically assisted procreation. Procreation or gestation agreements on behalf of another person are void. See Art. 538-542 C.C.Q.

28. Parents can never bargain away support or access rights. See for example, *Willick* v. *Willick*, [1994] 3 S.C.R. 670; *Hansford* v. *Hansford* (1973), 9 R.F.L. 233; *Baumann* v. *Clatworthy* (1991), 35 R.F.L. (3d) 200 (Ont. Gen. Div.): "child support is the right of the child, and a parent cannot bargain away the child's right." *Richardson* v. *Richardson*, [1987] 1 S.C.R. 857 at 869, 38 D.L.R. (4th) 669: "Child maintenance, like access, is the right of the child." *Young* v. *Young*, [1993] 4 S.C.R. 3 at 60: "... the right to access and the circumstances in which it takes place must be perceived from the vantage point of the child."

29. Although some Canadian clinics and doctors have a written or unwritten policy that prevents them from assisting single or lesbian women to conceive, this is clearly discriminatory. The refusal to provide insemination services to lesbians has been successfully challenged under B.C. human rights legislation. See, *Benson* v. *Korn,* [1995] C.H.R.R. D/319 (August 4, 1995) (B.C. Council of Human Rights). See also discussion of a case reaching the same result in Australian jurisprudence: A. Stuhmcke, "Lesbian access to *In Vitro* fertilization" (1997) 7 *Australasian Gay and Lesbian Law Journal* 15 at 30, citing Australian news reports, and *Pearce* v. *South Australian Health Commission* (1996), 66 S.A.S.R. 486, which reached the same conclusion in favour of a single woman.

30. To the best of my knowledge, none of these cases are reported.

31. *Re K.* (1995), 23 O.R. (3d) 679 (Prov. Div.)

32. *Adoption Act,* R.S.B.C. 1995, c. 48, s. 29.

33. *In re Z.J.H.*, 471 N.W. 2d 202 (Wisc. 1991) at 204.

34. *Family Relations Act*, R.S.B.C. 1996, c. 128, as am. by *Family Relations Amendment Act*, 1997 (proclaimed February 4, 1998), s. 1(2)(b).

35. *Family Law Act,* R.S.O. 1990, c. F. 3, s. 1(1); *Family Services Act*, S.N.B. 1980, c. F-2.2, s.113, s.1; *Family Law Reform Act*, R.S.P.E.I. 1988, c. F-3, s. 1(a); *The Family Law Act*, S.N. 1988, c. 60, s. 37(1), s. 2(d); *Family Maintenance Act,* S.S. 1997, c. F-6.2, s. 2.

36. *Family Maintenance Act*, R.S.M. 1987, c. F20, s. 36(4).

37. (1996), 25 R.F.L. (4th) 264 (Sask. Q.B.)

38. *Buist* v. *Greaves, supra* note 25.

39. *M.* v. *H.* (1996), 132 D.L.R. (4th) 538 (Ont. Ct. Gen. Div.) (Epstein J.); aff'd (1996), 142 D.L.R. (4th) 1 (C. A.) (Finlayson J.A. dissenting); aff'd (1999), 171 D.L.R. (4th) 577 (Gonthier J. dissenting) (S.C.C.).

40. In *Egan* v. *Canada, supra* note 18, the Supreme Court of Canada held that gays and lesbians are a historically disadvantaged group requiring the equality protections of the Charter.

41. See, *The National Post* (May 21, 1999) A2. At the federal level, it has been reported that the government plans to introduce omnibus legislation redefining spouse to include same-sex couples in *every* federal enactment that uses an opposite-sex requirement. See, Lori Kittelberg and Mike Scandiffio, "Top Liberals discuss omnibus bill," *The Hill Times* (May 30, 1999). The Quebec National Assembly unanimously approved such an omnibus Bill on June 10, 1999. See, Bill 32, *An Act to amend various legislative provisions concerning de facto spouses,* 1st session, 36th Legislature of Quebec, 1999. Note that Quebec provides limited rights and responsibilities to unmarried couples.

Chapter Ten

LESBIAN NONBIOLOGICAL MOTHERING
NEGOTIATING AN (UN)FAMILIAR EXISTENCE

Dawn Comeau

Lesbian mothering is considered by some to be an oxymoron: women who spend their lives with other women, and who don't have sex with men, are thought to be unlikely to have children. Del Martin and Phyllis Lyon, the founders of the Daughters of Bilitis, the first national lesbian rights organization, captured this sentiment in their 1972 book, *Lesbian/Woman*. They wrote:

> Mothers in our society may be odd or strange, but never "queer"—or so most people believe. Lesbians obviously can't have children. Theirs is a "sterile" relationship that is nonprocreative. "Poor things, they will go through life without ever being fulfilled as women—never knowing the joys and heartaches of motherhood," or so the story goes. Well the news is that many lesbians are mothers, and they are raising their children well, or raising them poorly or raising them indifferently, just as their heterosexual counterparts do. (140–141)

Lesbian motherhood came into visibility in the early 1970s because an increased number of lesbian mothers began to fight for custody of their children who had been conceived within prior heterosexual relationships. Because of these origins, much of the early research about lesbian motherhood seeks to convince the public that the lesbian mother is "normal" and that it is in the "best interest of the child" to remain in her mother's custody, regardless of the mother's sexual orientation. As a result, researchers have compared lesbian mothers to single heterosexual mothers. The rationale for this is that if single heterosexual women can successfully raise their children without a father figure in the home, lesbians can too. Consequently, research has intentionally minimized the experiences of lesbians who have co-parented children with other women. These relationships prompt the homophobic question: might the courts interpret the lesbian's intimate relationship as harmful to the child?

Research has also neglected to address the role and identity of the co-mother. Although not biologically connected, she shares responsibility in raising, loving, and economically supporting the child. Her role is particularly complex because without a biological connection many have a hard time imagining her relationship with the child. Therapist, mother, and co-parent Sally Crawford (1987) confirms this cultural ambivalence towards nonbiological co-mothers. She states, "Family is defined in a certain way in this culture, and although this definition is shifting somewhat, the lesbian two-parent family is most likely to be recognized as the single-parent family, and this recognition, conveniently for the larger culture, skirts the lesbian aspect" (201). Even within the small body of literature on lesbian motherhood, the co-mother's beneficial role is often ignored. In addition, race, social class, able-bodiedness, and geography all affect how lesbians are able to form and maintain a family relationship. These factors, too, tend to be overlooked in the literature. The few extant studies inclusive of the co-mother's perspective lack a race and class analysis; most focus upon white, middle-class, educated lesbians.

This overwhelming paucity of material leaves lesbian nonbiological co-mothers without role models or guidance in their day-to-day lives as they negotiate their parental roles. Their struggle to be recognized as parents, impeded by their lack of legal rights, is the impetus for my research. My research examines and explores how a woman who embodies such a position of nonrecognition negotiates relationships with her children, partner, family of origin, and community. This research will contribute to the dialogue on the many experiences of lesbian co-mothers, and inform future studies regarding lesbian families.

Given the scholarly silences regarding the nonbiological parent, I pose two questions in my research; how does the nonbiological co-mother in a lesbian family develop and build a solid foundation from which to negotiate her role in the public realm? How does her role shift when she returns home to the private sphere?

In most cases, lesbian families are able to safely discuss, deliberate, and define their family unit in their private sphere. But, when in public, their relationships are misunderstood or questioned by a society that perpetuates homophobia and heterosexism, and refuses to validate their family dynamic legally or socially. Crawford claims, "Clear boundaries around the heterosexual family are encouraged and respected by the larger system in many significant and little ways. The boundaries around the lesbian family usually are unrecognized, ignored, or reacted to with hostility and negative judgment" (202). In a society that heavily values the biological bond between mother and child, how does a co-mother explain her relationship to uninformed onlookers? To those who believe parents can only be a mother and a father, must the nonbiological mother become the father? Questions from family friends, and strangers, such as "Who is the *real* mother?" symbolize the lack of recognition non-traditional families receive. As one non-biological mother stated, "I get tired of people always asking my partner about our kid. It's almost like I'm not here" (Pies, 1988: 101). Another woman commented, "When I first got pregnant, I had to keep reminding everyone that there were two of us having this baby. Everyone kept talking to me as though [my partner] Leigh wasn't involved at all" (Ibid.). Crawford states the following about the identity of a lesbian co-mother:

> No matter how strong her presence and involvement in the family, it is she who bears the brunt of invisibility. It is she who disappears, it is she who is disenfranchised—by the school, by both families of origin, by the outside world, sometimes (even more painfully) by the children or by the friends in the lesbian network who do not see her as a parent nor understand the unique pressures of her position in the family. (195)

This lack of recognition and language to describe a lesbian family can permeate and damage the relationship between the parents. Pamela Gray, a non-biological co-parent, documents the impact of her partner's privileged status as a biological mother in her journal. Her writing charts her first two years as a co-mother. She wrote, "I was hurt ... when a woman came up to us and asked, 'Well, whose baby is it?' and Kathleen [her partner] said, 'Mine.' I understood why she said that, but it hurt anyway" (Gray, 1987: 135). The rules of hetero-patriarchy that mandate there can be only one mother are embedded even in the minds of lesbians who choose to parent equally together. This is demonstrated by Gray's partner's instinctual reactions to call the baby "mine." Gray writes later, "I still fell awkward and nervous in public, and also so aware of my outlaw status. I have an identity that is completely alien to 99.99 percent of the people who see me with [my child]" (136). Crawford explains, "Lesbian families are often unsure how to describe or explain their relationships to the outside world, because there is no culturally acknowledged language for these connections" (202).

Many couples report feeling a unique pressure—and a sense of being ostracized from both heterosexual and gay communities. Jane Bernstein and Laura Stephenson, a lesbian couple who chose alternative insemination,[1] documented their struggle to negotiate the role of the non-biological mother in "Dykes, donors & dry ice: Alternative insemination" (1995). Bernstein and Stephenson articulated that even the gay and lesbian literature that speaks of "two mommies" inadvertently reinforces that there should be a "mommy" and a "daddy." They emphasize the need to go beyond the "two mommy" and the mom and dad dichotomy. Although it appears to be a dilemma with language, it signifies the rigidity of socially constructed roles. Bernstein and Stephenson stated, "Put plainly, if you are not a 'mommy' or a 'daddy', you are unacknowledged in the public life of a child ... at some point every parent wants to be recognized as the central figure in their child's world—by teachers, neighbors and, yes, total strangers" (12).

In most parts of the United States, current law forbids two people of the same sex from being legal guardians of a child. Therefore, when a lesbian couple chooses to raise children through alternative insemination, one mother—the lesbian non-biological co-mother—is left bereft of any legal rights as a parent. This legal non-recognition is dictated by our dominant society that defines family in heterosexual terms: one mother and one father. This definition challenges the lesbian co-mother's mere existence. Beverly Evans, a feminist scholar and family therapist, states, "The role of the nonbiological mother (the co-mother) is one without legal, cultural and emotional definition" (Evans, 1992: 131). There are an estimated 1.5 to 5 million lesbian mothers who reside with their children (Falk, 1992: 55) and scholarly efforts can contribute to establishing legal, cultural, and emotional definitions for their partners who play an integral role in raising their children.

This research collected personal narratives from lesbian mothers who became parents through their partners' alternative insemination (not heterosexual liaisons or adoption). I have completed four in-depth interviews in San Diego, California. All of my participants have been white, college educated, middle class women. My participants either heard about my study from friends of friends, or from a flyer at a Family Matters conference (the local chapter of a national gay and lesbian parenting organization). This conference was attended by mostly white women, and my respondents reflect this. Three of the participants were thirty-five, and one was forty. Of these four women, three are birth mothers as well as non-biological mothers.[2] My goal is to continue interviewing to attain a more diverse sample. The interviews have lasted from one to two and a half hours, and have taken place in their homes—or in one case, her private office at work. Two of the four women were a couple, and all participants were joined in commitment ceremonies and referred to themselves as "married." Two of my participants have secured legal rights to both of their children through second parent adoption. The other two are still in the process. When I began my study I intended to only interview women who are non-biological mothers. However, at this point, it has been lesbian families in which each partner has borne a child that have responded favorably to being interviewed. I speculate that these families may feel more comfortable discussing the lack of recognition they receive as non-biological mothers because they are also a biological mother and this provides some security. In addition, because each partner experiences both roles, they may relate to each other's feelings more closely. All of my participants reported frustration when dealing with the lack of recognition non-traditional families receive.

Barbara and Leah are a couple who have been together for fifteen years, and married for seven. They are both thirty-five, Jewish, consider themselves a middle class family, and both have a master's degree in social work. Leah had their first child, a girl, who was five at the time of our interview; Barbara had their second child, a boy, who was six months old at the time of our interview. Both Leah and Barbara expressed difficulty with negotiating their role as the non-biological mother. However, Barbara experienced a more difficult time as the non-biological mother. Leah was the first one to have a baby. Barbara was a non-birth mother for four and half years, until she became pregnant herself. Although at the time I spoke with them they were both experiencing both roles—biological and non-biological—it seemed Leah had adjusted to her non-biological status easier because she had carried a child before partnering a non-biological child. They both spoke of Barbara's tumultuous struggle with her role as a parent.

Barbara revealed how Leah continually supported her role as a mother when she was feeling alienated by family, friends, and community. Barbara, conversely discusses how Leah received more attention as the birth mother and this often made Barbara feel left out. As a result, Leah made great efforts to accentuate Barbara's role as a parent. Barbara explained,

> I really have to thank Leah … and credit her on how hard she worked to always include me—even in the grocery store when we received comments like "Oh you're pregnant, what does your husband think?" Or blah blah blah … and then having to sit there and say "I don't have a husband and this is my partner and we're having this baby together …"

Barbara and Leah refer to themselves as an "educational unit" because they constantly correct people's false assumptions about their family. This challenging and exhausting self-legitimization is similar to the findings in sociologist Fiona Nelson's (1996) study of Canadian lesbian families. Nelson explains that in order for lesbian families "to live a 'normal' life, they must constantly tell people that they *are* a normal family," even when "educat[ing] others prove(s) to be a fatiguing process for some women" (127). Throughout my interview with Leah and Barbara, they continually elucidated their efforts to educate those around them.

Even in the safety of their home, and with their immediate family, the non-biological mothers I interviewed expressed many fears and concerns about their lack of biological connection and how that weakened these social relationships to the child. When the baby was first born, Barbara felt confused about her role as a parent and expressed feelings of guilt because she wanted and expected more validation then she received from her partner, extended family, and friends. She recalled:

> It's sort of embarrassing to say this but I think there was probably a part of me that ... wanted to have some of that attention too ... or some of the recognition that, you know ... I kinda felt like behind the scenes I was working my butt off to do this and do that and the stuff you don't see. You don't see my stomach growing [but I'm working just as hard at being a parent].

Her sense of invisibility was ever-present. She continued,

> I think one of the things that happened for me and that I didn't expect was that I was very worried about being left out. And, you know, what sort of happens is this baby gets all of the attention and then the birth parent gets "How ya doing? How ya feeling?" ... and then ... there's this non-birth mother ... I just don't think people knew what to do with me ...
>
> And they would say [to Leah] "Oh the baby looks just like you" and you know all of this stuff. If just felt like, again, I was doing a lot and I wasn't getting any credit for it. Not that I needed that ... I just didn't expect it ....

Barbara's reactions also reflect her doubts as to whether her parents would accept their child as *her* child. As Barbara explains, "I really wanted my family to see that this was my child too ... I really wanted my mom to acknowledge that ... and they have. But we've worked hard at it." Barbara and Leah have made several trips to visit their extended family, and each time they must reinforce to relatives that they are a family unit, and must be treated and accepted like their heterosexual counterparts.

Throughout my interview with Barbara, she repeatedly expressed her need to "get over her ego" and feelings of inferiority. However, after our two-hour conversation, her needs were hardly egotistical or demanding. Rather, her experience demonstrates legitimate feelings of invisibility. I asked her if she spoke of these feelings with Leah. She said:

> I think we talked about it but after the fact and that was probably unfortunate. But I don't think I knew. She'd say, "What's wrong?" and I'd say, "I don't know." And I don't think I knew at the time. I knew I wasn't acting appropriately, or I wasn't feeling like I was acting appropriately ... But I didn't know what to do about it. I really didn't ...

After my interview with Barbara, I spoke to her partner Leah about coping with Barbara's feelings of nonrecognition. Leah revealed:

> Well I think there are major issues. I mean I think there are a lot of things you don't encounter until you actually go through it … [I] don't think you realize how much attention is focused on the pregnant woman. I felt like after I had [the baby] I was continually having to get people to include Barbara in their conversations when they congratulated us … when they had showers … [I had to remind them that] they were having this for both of us … and they needed to validate her being a parent as well …

Balancing their perceived roles as parents created immense pressure for Leah. She feared the psychological implications on their relationship if Barbara was unable to bear their next child. The pressure of an asymmetrical relationship was tremendous, and Leah expressed that she did not want to endure Barbara's emotional turmoil as the non-biological mother a second time.

She explained:

> I felt very challenged … I told myself that if Barbara couldn't get pregnant, I would never try again. I would never … there were so many issues for grieving because she wasn't the birth parent, and I just didn't want to go through that a second time where I had to validate her even more. It was difficult sometimes. I didn't feel like I could totally enjoy nursing and things people said to me because I felt I needed to deflect and have them include her. You know? And people don't.

After struggling for several years, Barbara was able to get pregnant. I questioned Leah about her new role as a non-biological mom. She expressed similar feelings of non-recognition, although she believes her feelings are not as intense as Barbara's because she has experienced giving birth already. On numerous occasions, Barbara is the only one recognized as the parent. For example, she regularly hears people say, "Barbara, good luck to you and your baby." Leah commented, "That is more frequent than not … it's not because people don't realize [we are both the mothers] because we tell people! I think it is because they feel awkward—they don't know what to say." Around the time of Barbara's baby shower, Leah's invisibility was magnified. As she explains, "People would say to me, 'What does she *need* for the baby?' And I'd be like, what does *she* need? We are doing this baby together!" Leah articulated that comments excluding the non-biological mother as a parent come from close family and friends who *should* know better. In the *Lesbian family life cycle*, social worker Suzanne Slater (1995) explains, "In the eyes of most heterosexual people, the nonbiological or nonadoptive parent is simply not a parent at all. With no legal or biological claim to the children her role is widely seen as redundant, since the only parenting role recognized for women is 'already taken' in the family" (97). Clearly, my respondents experienced this feeling.

Anne, a forty-year-old, Caucasian, non-biological mother, encountered similar situations to those detailed by Barbara and Leah. Anne entered her current relationship with a child from a previous heterosexual relationship. However, after being with her partner for five years, they decided that they would have another child and her partner would carry the baby. After much thought and consideration, they decided that they would use sperm from Anne's brother to inseminate her partner. To date, this arrangement is working out fine. Within a year of birth Anne secured rights to the baby through second parent adoption.[3]

The relationship between Anne and her partner is even more complex. Anne's partner is Philippina, and her child is biracial. Anne described prejudicial encounters with strangers in the grocery store. She received questions such as "Oh [the father] must be so proud of him, is the father Asian?" Because her partner is a woman of color, instead of validating her partner's role as a parent, they are quick to assume she is the "hired help." There have been several occasions at the doctor's office when Anne's partner is presumed to be the nanny. Anne said:

When we are both out we will both carry him and I'm sure we confuse people because sometimes they will decide that I am the parent and then I'll pass him over to my partner and she'll start breast feeding him. They must think ... "wow, not only does she have a nanny but she has a wet nurse too!"

For women of color who are non-biological mothers, racism and classism can pervade people's reactions to their parental role and family. Although Anne laughs when she tells this story, she later expresses her concerns for her baby who will grow up biracial and in a lesbian family surrounded by a society that exudes racism, homophobia, and heterosexism. Anne mentions that at one time, the gay and lesbian parents group in San Diego was comprised of ethnically and racially diverse families. However, in the past couple of years the meetings have been attended by mostly white families. She articulates that she knows lesbians of color are having children, but she speculates that they may not feel comfortable at these meetings. This is of great concern to her and her partner, and mirrors what ought to be of greater concern for the gay and lesbian community. Like feminist scholars, members of the lesbian community need to confront racism, classism, and other complex systems of oppression, as well as privileging of biology.

Anne, Barbara, and Leah experience being a biological and non-biological mother simultaneously, and proclaim that there are drastic differences in these experiences. Leah and Anne insist that their experience as a birth mother was more intense. Although they were clear that they love both of their children equally regardless of biology, the formation of the relationships differed. Anne said:

> I found that the process was slower and scarier because there was this deep down fear ... you know ... is this really going to mesh? Is this really going to happen? Am I really going to feel like that is my kid?

> It just wasn't the same visceral, physical, kind of feeling that I experienced when I carried a child. It's taken time and it's taken him growing into his personality. And him, you know, greeting me enthusiastically when I come home ... the little moments when he does ... the physical bonding things like leaning his head on my shoulder and all that ... and the "ahhh" [and she sighs]. Finally the physical feeling has come. But it took much longer. And, there was, you know ... a deep down fear ... a question as to whether it would happen ...

Anne's sentiments resemble the results that clinical psychologist Barbara McCandlish (1992) found in her study on lesbian families. The lesbian non-biological mothers in McCandlish's study "reported searching for cues that the child responded to her ... Without any defined legal and social role, the partner was wholly dependent on the child's response and the biological mother's expectations to give them a place in the family" (147). Like Anne, Leah describes the bond with the child she carried as more intense and physical than the connection she has with the child her partner carried. She said:

> Being a birth mother for the first time, I was so in touch with my baby. I had her with me all day you know? And I would feel her. I mean I would do things like lean up against my desk and she would kick against my desk. I was very, very, very into the whole thing ... I was bonded from the minute I knew she was in there. I was so bonded ...

However her experience as the non-biological mother was very different. She attributes this partially to the fact that she was busy caring for their first child, and that Barbara did not have an easy pregnancy. Leah explained:

> Barbara didn't have a good pregnancy. She felt sick and uncomfortable and I was very much put off by that .... It was hard for me to bear when

the baby was in utero. I mean I was excited, I was glad we were having another baby, but I didn't talk to him much, not much ... there is a different connection.

In addition, Leah believes that the connection differs because she is not breastfeeding Barbara's child, and she is back at work full time. As a result, she has less time to spend with her family, and the time she does have is often occupied by their oldest child.

After hearing my participants talk about the challenges of being a non-biological mother, I asked them if they had discussed the potential conflicts—either with their partner or other lesbian mothers—between being the biological and non-biological mother before the birth of their first child. Barbara stated:

I think we probably needed to talk about it more. But I don't think we knew what to talk about, you know? Leah had a hard time getting pregnant so I think that kinda helped me avoid talking about that ... I don't think it was conscious but it was a kind of avoidance ...

I asked Anne if she had expressed to her partner her concern over being invisible as the non-biological mother. She responded:

Ummmm [long pause] ... I think I did express that but I don't remember very clearly if we spent a lot of time discussing that issue ... I don't think we really talked about that too much ....

Later on in the interview, she came back to this question. She elaborated:

You asked me if I had talked with other gay and lesbian families about the issue and its a good question. My God, really? Why didn't I?

Anne further explained that the topic was often avoided in the gay and lesbian parenting support group. She stated:

... we found out that it was such as difficult topic and that's one of the reasons why it wasn't a frequent topic. And in fact the big joke—by the founder of the group—was that every time we talk about it—couples break up! [Big laugh, and then she quiets down.] Isn't that scary?

Since the lesbian community does not have definitions and language to describe its own families, it is difficult to avoid conflicts and anticipate necessary conversations. Each interviewee had set of close friends who they looked to as a role model for family. Unfortunately, in each case, the "role model couple" had broken up after having their children. This proved discouraging to my participants. In addition, it illustrates why we must continue to promote discussion about challenges and obstacles in lesbian families. Neither Barbara and Leah, nor Anne and her partner had discussed arrangements in case of a break up.

Kathy is a thirty-five year-old non-biological mother of a six-month-old girl. She has been with her partner for five years, and married to her for three years. When I interviewed her, she and her partner were in the process of creating a legal contract that guides their mutual obligations to their child in the event of their separation. Kathy and her partner decided that only one of them would carry all of their children in order to maintain a biological relationship between the kids. Although Kathy expressed some remorse over not experiencing child birth herself, overall she is comfortable in their decision. Kathy emphasized throughout her interview that she believes the bond she is developing with her daughter is as substantial as a biological bond. However, because of the legal system that makes it difficult for two lesbian mothers to gain equal custody, she fears that her role as a non-biological mother can be subverted. At the time I interviewed Kathy, she was in the process of becoming a legal parent to her child through second parent adoption. This process requires her partner to relinquish fifty percent of her rights so that Kathy can be assigned that fifty percent. After their first meeting with an attorney, Kathy's partner revealed that she wasn't sure she wanted to permit Kathy to gain access to legal rights. Kathy painfully recounts hearing this news from her partner:

> She said, "I'm having a hard time deciding if I want to let you adopt." I was ready to kill her … I was getting mad because for me this was really important because if I was a man I would have rights … so I'm like, this sucks … and she has all this power and she can tell me I don't have rights to my child!
>
> [My partner] keeps telling me that she knows I have every right to her but she just didn't know what the bond would feel like … she didn't know how incredible it would be … I told her that it sounds to me like this is a good reason for me to have the next baby.

This specter of "ownership" often divides a couple. Kathy has economically, physically, and emotionally acted as parent, and this news from her partner was devastating. At this point in time, although Kathy believed that her partner would consent to the second parent adoption, she was horrified with her lack of power. She said, "my partner could walk out the door with my baby and I could never see her again. And there is nothing I could do about it." Kathy's vulnerability exemplifies how second parent adoption, while in many cases is an excellent means for lesbians to circumvent the law and become equal parents, is itself flawed and unjust as it is ultimately the birth mother's decision to grant the adoption.

Further complicating the matter is the fact that second parent adoptions are not granted to lesbian couples in most parts of the United States. Maria Gil de Lamadrid (1993), attorney for the National Center for Lesbian Rights in San Francisco, explains, "Second parent adoptions are granted fairly routinely in heterosexual context as stepparent adoptions in families blended through marriage. In a lesbian context, however, where the mother's partner is not legally related to the mother (by marriage), nor is she biologically related to the children, the courts generally do not allow these adoptions" (203). According to Gil de Lamadrid, there are few locations in the United States where the biological mother is not required to relinquish all of her parental rights in order to proceed with a second parent adoption. By implication, most mothers must relinquish their rights in order for the second parent adoption to occur. Note: these legal distinctions vary widely by locale and are constantly shifting. Sometimes they operate informally. The process of determining parental rights can be stressful for lesbian couples after the birth of their child. As exemplified by Kathy, the birth mother has the decision-making power in this process. This is frightening for non-biological mothers who may be unable to predict their partner's feelings and emotions after giving birth. Gil de Lamadrid explains that "Although donor insemination has now been available for some time, lawmakers have not kept up with the new developments and concerns facing lesbian mothers" (206). As increased numbers of lesbians decide to have children and join the lesbian baby boom,[4] a demand for new legislation will continue to coincide. This lengthy and time-consuming process is crucial to solid formation of lesbian families.

In her 1987 article, "On a creative edge," counselor Toni Tortorilla professes the amount of time and patience that it has taken her to understand her role as a non-biological mother. She states,

> I still don't fit into the comfortable niches other parents (including lesbian moms) take for granted. But I live on a creative edge which celebrates a commitment born of love rather than biological imperative .... It has taken me nearly eight years to validate my role in this way, though I have felt bonded [to my daughter] since conception. (174)

"The creative edge" Tortorilla describes needs more exploration. Interviewing non-biological mothers reveals the challenges and obstacles that lesbian families face when struggling to conform to legal and societal systems that regulate families in terms of heterosexuality. Each of the women I interviewed were determined to develop lasting familial bonds with their partner and children. However, devoid of language and legal rights, themes of invisibility and nonrecognition emerge in their conversations and descriptions of family life. These feelings are usually unforeseen, laborious, and threatening to express to both their immediate loved ones, extended family, and members of the gay, lesbian, and heterosexual communities. As these non-biological mothers continue on their tenacious journey through parenthood, their individual and familial identities can evolve through open dialogue and realistic—binding—negotiations.

Notes

1. In the *Lesbian and gay parenting handbook: Creating and raising our families*, April Martin (1993) specifically uses the term "alternative insemination" rather that "artificial insemination" because she believes it is a "less offensive and more realistically descriptive term" (10). Many lesbian mothers express Martin's sentiment. When discussing the process of becoming pregnant with one of the women I interview she exclaimed, "There is nothing artificial about it!" Other women I interviewed preferred the term "donor insemination," and others felt comfortable using "artificial." Although I agree with Martin, I use these terms interchangeably throughout my paper according to the situation I am discussing and which term was elicited at that time.

2. I use the term biological mother to indicate the woman who physically carries the child, and the term non-biological mother to refer to the mother who is equally committed to raising and supporting the child, but in most cases does so without legal recognition due to her lack of biological connection. Cheryl Muzio (1993) discusses the issues with using the term non-biological. She states, "to be identified as a non-biological mother is to be identified in and through a sense of lack" (226). Muzio's interpretation of language is an important one and needs to be more closely examined as we continue to research lesbian motherhood using "non-biological" as a defining term. As Muzio explains, "The linguistic constraints we encounter affect not only our public discourse but our private ones as well" (226). This becomes evident throughout my interviews with non-biological mothers, even though many of them felt comfortable labeling themselves as such. One mother referred to herself as the "non-birth" mother instead. However, this also defines her by what she is not.

3. A second parent adoption can only occur after the birth of the child. In the case of a known donor, the father's rights must be terminated before the non-biological mother is granted equal legal rights to the child. In my study, Anne was the only participant who used a known donor. Kathy, Barbara, and Leah used an unknown donor from a local sperm bank.

4. In *Families we choose*, Kath Weston (1991) describes the lesbian baby boom as a movement beginning on the West Coast in the 1970s, consisting of lesbians between the ages of thirty and forty-fove who began "bearing, adopting, coparenting, or otherwise incorporating children into their lives." According to Weston, "Most of these women were members of the relatively 'out' cohort [who] came of age at the height of the women's and gay movements" (165).

Section Three

AFRICAN-AMERICAN MOTHERING

Chapter Eleven

A Politics of the Heart

AFRICAN-AMERICAN WOMANIST THOUGHT ON MOTHERING[1]

Andrea O'Reilly

"During the early stages of contemporary women's liberation movement," bell hooks writes, "feminist analyses of motherhood reflected the race and class biases of participants" (1984: 133). "Some white, middle class, college educated women argued," hooks continues, that motherhood was:

> the locus of women's oppression. Had black women voiced their views on motherhood, it would not have been named a serious obstacle to our freedom as women. Racism, availability of jobs, lack of skills or education ... would have been at the top of the list—but not motherhood (1984: 133).

Feminist theory on motherhood, as hooks identifies, is racially codified. Drawing upon contemporary womanist thought on black motherhood, this chapter will argue that there exists a distinct African-American tradition of motherhood. Two interrelated themes, or perspectives, distinguish the African-American tradition of motherhood. First, mothers and motherhood are valued by, and central to, African-American culture. Second, it is recognized that mothers and mothering are what make possible the physical and psychological well-being and empowerment of African-American people and the larger African-American culture. Black women raise children in a society that is at best indifferent to the needs of black children and to the concerns of black mothers. The focus of black motherhood, in both practice and thought, is how to preserve, protect, and, more generally, empower black children; so that they may resist racist practices that seek to harm them, and grow into adulthood whole and complete. For the purpose of this discussion, I employ African Canadian theorists Wanda Thomas Bernard and Candace Bernard's definition of empowerment:

empowerment is naming, analyzing, and challenging oppression on an individual, collective, and/or structural level. Empowerment, which occurs through the development of critical consciousness, is gaining control, exercising choices, and engaging in collective social action. (1998: 46)

To fulfill the task of empowering children, mothers must hold power in African-American culture, and mothering must likewise be valued and supported. In turn, African-American culture, understanding the importance of mothering for individual, and for cultural well-being and empowerment, gives power to mothers and prominence to the work of mothering. In other words, black mothers require power to do the important work of mothering, and are accorded power because of the importance of mothering.

The African-American tradition of motherhood centres upon the recognition that mothering, in its concern with the physical and psychological well-being of children and its focus upon the empowerment of children, has cultural and political import, value, and prominence. Motherhood, as a consequence, is a site of power for black women. This chapter will examine this tradition of African-American mothering under five interrelated topics: "Othermothering and community mothering," "Motherhood as social activism and a site of power," "Matrifocality," "Nurturance as resistance: Providing a homeplace," and "The motherline: Mothers as cultural bearers." Next, it will examine this tradition in the context of mothers' relationships with their children. Specifically, the chapter will consider how daughters seek identification or connection with their mothers due to the cultural centrality and significance of the mother role, and how this connection gives rise to the daughters' empowerment in African-American culture. Finally, the chapter will explore how African-American mothers remain, contrary to the normative script of mother–son relation, involved in their sons' lives, and how this involvement fosters physical survival, psychological well-being, and overall empowerment.

Othermothering and community mothering

Stanlie James, in "Mothering: A possible black feminist link to social transformations," defines othermothering "as acceptance of responsibility for a child not one's own, in an arrangement that may or may not be formal" (1997: 45). Othermothers usually care for children. In contrast, community mothers, as Njoki Nathani Wane explains, "take care of the community. These women are typically past their childbearing years" (2000: 112). "The role of community mothers," as Arlene Edwards notes, "often evolved from that of being othermothers" (2000, 88). James argues that othermothering and community mothering developed from, in Arlene Edward's words, "West African practices of communal lifestyles and interdependence of communities" (2000: 88). Consequently, as Patricia Hill Collins has observed, "Mothering [in West Africa] was not a privatized nurturing 'occupation' reserved for biological mothers, and the economic support of children was not the exclusive responsibility of men" (1993: 45). Rather, mothering expressed itself as both nurturance and work, and care of children was viewed as the duty of the larger community. Collins argues that these complementary dimensions of mothering and the practice of communal mothering/othermothering give women great influence and status in West African societies. She elaborates:

> First, since they are not dependent on males for economic support and provide much of their own and their children's economic support, women are structurally central to families. Second, the image of the mother is culturally elaborated and valued across diverse West African societies. [...] Finally, while the biological mother–child bond is valued, childcare was a collective responsibility, a situation fostering cooperative, age-stratified, woman centered "mothering" networks. (45)

These West African cultural practices, Collins argues, were retained by enslaved African-Americans, and gave rise to a distinct tradition of African-American motherhood in which the custom of othermothering and community mothering was emphasized and elaborated. Arlene Edwards explains:

> The experience of slavery saw the translation of othermothering to new settings, since the care of children was an expected task of enslaved Black women in addition to the field or house duties. [...] [T]he familial instability of slavery engendered the adaptation of communality in the form of fostering children whose parents, particularly mothers, had been sold. This tradition of communality gave rise to the practice of othermothering. The survival of the concept is inherent to the survival of Black people as a whole [...] since it allowed for the provision of care to extended family and non blood relations. (2000: 88).

The practice of othermothering remains central to the African-American tradition of motherhood and is regarded as essential for the survival of black people. bell hooks in her article "Revolutionary parenting" (1984) comments:

> Child care is a responsibility that can be shared with other childrearers, with people who do not live with children. This form of parenting is revolutionary in this society because it takes place in opposition to the idea that parents, especially mothers, should be the only childrearers.

Many people raised in black communities experienced this type of community-based child care. Black women who had to leave the home and work to help provide for families could not afford to send children to daycare centers and such centers did not always exist. They relied on people in their communities to help. Even in families where the mother stayed home, she could also rely on people in the community to help .... People who did not have children often took responsibility for sharing in childrearing. (1984: 144)

"The centrality of women in African-American extended families," as Nina Jenkins concludes in "Black women and the meaning of motherhood," "is well known" (Abbey and O'Reilly, 1998: 206).

In African-American culture, the practice of othermothering, as it developed from West African traditions, became a strategy of survival in that it ensured that all children, regardless of whether the biological mother was present or available, would receive the mothering that delivers psychological and physical well-being and makes empowerment possible. Collins concludes:

Biological mothers or bloodmothers are expected to care for their children. But African and African-American communities have also recognized that vesting one person with full responsibility for mothering a child may not be wise or possible. As a result, "othermothers," women who assist bloodmothers by sharing mothering responsibilities, traditionally have been central to the institution of Black motherhood (1993: 47).

Community mothering and othermothering also emerged in response to black mothers' needs, and served to empower black women and enrich their lives. "Historically and presently community mothering practices," Erica Lawson writes, "was and is a central experience in the lives of many Black women, and participation in mothering is a form of emotional and spiritual expression in societies that marginalize black women" (2000: 26). The self-defined and created role and identity of community mother also, as Lawson explains, "enabled African Black women to use African derived conceptions of self and community to resist negative evaluations of Black women" (2000: 26).

The practice of othermothering/community mothering as a cultural sustaining mechanism, and as a mode of empowerment for black mothers has been documented in numerous studies. Carol Stack's early but important book *All our kin: Strategies in a black community* (1970) emphasizes how crucial and central extended kin and community are for poor urban blacks. "Black families in The Flats and the non-kin they regard as kin," Stack writes in her conclusion, "have evolved patterns of co-residence, kinship-based exchange networks linking multiple domestic units, elastic household boundaries, lifelong bonds to three-generation households, social controls against the formation of marriages that could endanger the network of kin, the domestic authority of women, and limitations on the role of the husband or male friend within a woman's kin network" (1970: 124).[2] Priscilla Gibson, in "Developmental mothering in an African-American community: From grandmothers to new mothers again" (2000), provides a study of grandmothers and great-grandmothers who assumed the caregiving responsibilities of their (great) grandchildren as a result of the parent being unable or unwilling to provide that care. Gibson argues that "[in]creasingly grandmothers, especially African-American grandmothers, are becoming kinship providers for grandchildren with absent parents. This absent middle generation occurs because of social problems such as drug abuse, incarceration, domestic violence, and divorce, just to name a few" (2000: 33). In her research study of women in Kenya, "Reflections on the mutuality of mothering: Women, children and othermothering," Njoki Nathani Wane explores how pre-colonial African beliefs and customs gave rise to a communal practice of childrearing and an understanding that "parenting, especially mothering, was an integral component of African traditions and cultures" (2000: 111). "Most of pre-colonial Africa," explains Wane, "was founded upon and sustained by collectivism. [...] Labour was organized along parallel rather than hierarchical lines, thus giving equal value to male and female labour. Social organization was based on the principle of patrilineal or matrilineal descent, or a combination of both. Mothering practices were organized as a collective activity" (2000: 108). Today, the practice of othermothering, as Wane notes, "serves[s] to relieve some of the stresses that can develop between children and parents [and] provides multiple role models for children; [as well] it keeps the traditional African value systems of communal sharing and ownership alive" (2000: 113). Othermothering and community mothering, Wane concludes, "can be understood as a form of cultural work or as one way communities organize to nurture both themselves and future generations" (Ibid.).

Motherhood as social activism and as a site of power

The practices of othermothering and in particular community mothering serve, as Stanlie James argues, "as an important Black feminist link to the development of new models of social transformation" (1997: 45). Black women's role of community mothers, as Collins explains, redefines motherhood as social activism. Collins elaborates,

> Black women's experiences as other mothers have provided a foundation
> for Black women's social activism. Black women's feelings of

responsibility for nurturing the children in their extended family networks have stimulated a more generalized ethic of care where Black women feel accountable to all the Black community's children. (1993: 49)

In *Black feminist thought*, Collins develops this idea further:

Such power is transformative in that Black women's relationships with children and other vulnerable community members is not intended to dominate or control. Rather, its purpose is to bring people along, to—in the words of late-nineteenth century Black feminists—"uplift the race" so that vulnerable members of the community will be able to attain the self-reliance and independence essential for resistance. (1991: 132)

Various and diverse forms of social activism stem from and are sustained by the African-American custom of community mothering. Community mothering, as Arlene Edwards notes, has been expressed in activities and movements as varied as the Black Clubwomen, civil rights movements, and black women's work in the church. Drawing upon the research of Gilkes, Edwards elaborates: "In reporting on Black community workers, Gilkes found that these women often 'viewed the Black Community as a group of relatives and other friends whose interest should be advanced, and promoted at all times, under all conditions, and by almost any means' (1983: 117)" (2000: 88). Bernard and Bernard theorize black women's work as educators as a form of social activism. "Education," they argue, "is considered a cornerstone of Black community development, and as such Black women, as community othermothers, have placed a high value on education and have used it as a site for activism" (2000: 68). Academic mothers, they continue, "also value education, and use their location to facilitate the education of others. [As well] academic othermothers who operate within an Africentric framework, are change agents who promote student empowerment and transformation" (Ibid.). They go on to elaborate:

Collins' definition of othermothers extends to the work we do in the academy. Othermothering in the community is the foundation of what Collins calls the "*mothering the mind*" relationships that often developed between African-American women teachers and their Black female and male students. We refer to this as mothering in the academy, and see it as work that extends beyond traditional definitions of mentorship. It is a sharing of self, an interactive and collective process, a spiritual connectedness that epitomizes the Africentric values of sharing, caring and accountability. (Ibid.)

Collins argues that this construction of mothering as social activism empowers black women because motherhood operates, in her words, as "a symbol of power." "A substantial portion of Black women's status in African-American communities," writes Collins, "stems not only from their roles as mothers in their own families but from their contributions as community othermothers to Black community development as well" (1993: 51). "More than a personal act," write Bernard and Bernard, "Black motherhood is very political. Black mothers and grandmothers are considered the 'guardians of the generations.' Black mothers have historically been charged with the responsibility of providing education, social, and political awareness, in addition to unconditional love, nurturance, socialization, and values to their children, and the children in their communities" (1998: 47). Black motherhood, as Jenkins concluded, "is a site where [black women] can develop a belief in their own empowerment. Black women can see motherhood as providing a base for self-actualization, for acquiring status in the Black community and as a catalyst for social activism" (Abbey and O'Reilly, 1998: 206).

Matrifocality

The African-American model/practice of mothering, according to Patricia Hill Collins, differs from Eurocentric ideology in three important ways:

> First, the assumption that mothering occurs within the confines of a private, nuclear family household where the mother has almost total responsibility for child-rearing is less applicable to Black families. While the ideal of the cult of true womanhood has been held up to Black women for emulation, racial oppression has denied Black families sufficient resources to support private, nuclear family households. Second, strict sex-role segregation, with separate male and female spheres of influence within the family, has been less commonly found in African-American families than in White middle-class ones. Finally, the assumption that motherhood and economic dependency on men are linked and that to be a "good" mother one must stay at home, making motherhood a full-time "occupation," is similarly uncharacteristic of African-American families. (1993: 43–44)

Miriam Johnson, in *Strong mothers, weak wives* (1990), argues that the wife role and not the mother's role occasions women's secondary status in a patriarchal culture. In contrast, matrifocal cultures, such as African-American culture, according to Johnson, emphasize women's mothering and are characterized by greater gender equality.[3] In matrifocal societies, Johnson writes, "women play roles of cultural and social significance and define themselves less as wives than as mothers" (1990: 226). "Matrifocality," Johnson continues,

> however, does not refer to domestic maternal dominance so much as it does to the relative cultural prestige of the image of mother, a role that is culturally elaborated and valued. Mothers are also structurally central in that mother as a status "has some degree of control over the kin unit's economic resources and is critically involved in kin-related decision making processes."... It is not the absence of males (males may be quite present) but the centrality of women as mothers and sisters that makes a society matrifocal, and this matrifocal emphasis is accompanied by a minimum of differentiation between women and men. (1990: 226)

The wife identity, according to Collins, is less prevalent in African-American culture because women assume an economic role and experience gender equality in the family unit. She writes:

> African-American women have long integrated their activities as economic providers into their mothering relationships. In contrast to the cult of true womanhood, in which work is defined as being in opposition to and incompatible with motherhood, work for Black women has been an important and valued dimension of Afrocentric definitions of Black motherhood. (1993: 48)

"Whether they wanted to or not," Collins continues, "the majority of African-American women had to work and could not afford the luxury of motherhood as a noneconomically productive, female 'occupation'" (1993: 49). Thus, the majority of black women do not assume the wife role Johnson identified as that which structures women's oppression. Moreover, in African-American culture, motherhood, not marriage, emerges as the rite of passage into womanhood. As Joyce Ladner emphasizes in *Tomorrow's tomorrow* (1971):

> If there was one common standard for becoming a woman that was accepted by the majority of the people in the community, it was the time when girls gave birth to their first child. This line of demarcation was extremely clear and separated the *girls* from the *women*. (1971: 215–6)[4]

In African-American culture, motherhood is the pinnacle of womanhood. The matrifocal structure of black families with its emphasis on motherhood over wifedom, and black women's role as economic provider means that the wife role is less operative in the African-American community, and that motherhood is site of power and empowerment for black women.

Nurturance as resistance: Providing a homeplace

The fourth way that African-American mothering differs from the dominant model is the way in which nurturance of family is defined and experienced as a resistance. In African-American culture, as theorist bell hooks has observed, the black family, or what she terms homeplace, operates as a site of resistance. She explains:

> Historically, African-American people believed that the construction of a homeplace, however fragile and tenuous (the slave hut, the wooden shack), had a radical political dimension. Despite the brutal reality of racial apartheid, of domination, one's homeplace was one site where one could freely confront the issue of humanization, where one could resist. Black women resisted by making homes where all black people could strive to be subjects, not objects, where one could be affirmed in our minds and hearts despite poverty, hardship, and deprivation, where we could restore to ourselves the dignity denied to us on the outside in the public world. (1990: 42)

Hooks emphasizes that when she talks about homeplace she is not speaking merely of black women providing services for their families; rather, she refers to the creation of a safe place where, in her words, "black people could affirm one another and by so doing heal many of the wounds inflicted by racist domination .... [a place where] [they] had the opportunity to grow and develop, to nurture [their] spirits" (1990: 42).[5] In a racist culture that deems black children inferior, unworthy, and unlovable, maternal love of black children is an act of resistance; in loving her children the mother instills in them a loved sense of self and high self-esteem, enabling them to defy and subvert racist discourses that naturalize racial inferiority and commodify blacks as other and object. African-Americans, hooks emphasizes, "have long recognized the subversive value of homeplace, and homeplace has always been central to the liberation struggle" (1990: 42). Like hooks, Collins maintains that children learn at home how to identify and challenge racist practices; it is at home that children learn of their heritage and community. At home they are empowered to resist racism, particularly as it becomes internalized. Collins elaborates:

> Racial ethnic women's motherwork reflects the tensions inherent in trying to foster a meaningful racial identity in children within a society that denigrates people of color .... [Racial ethnic] children must first be

taught to survive in systems that oppress them. Moreover, this survival must not come at the expense of self-esteem. Thus, a dialectal relationship exists between systems of racial oppression designed to strip a subordinated group of a sense of personal identity and a sense of collective peoplehood, and the cultures of resistance extant in various ethnic groups that resist the oppression. For women of color, motherwork for identity occurs at this critical juncture. (1994: 57)[6]

The empowerment of minority children through resistance and knowledge occurs at home and in the larger cultural space through the communal mothering and social activism spoken of earlier. This view of mothering differs radically from the dominant discourse of motherhood that configures home as a politically neutral space, and views nurturance as no more than the natural calling of mothers.

The Motherline: Mothers as cultural bearers

The motherline, the fifth and final theme, considers the role black mothers play as cultural bearers and tradition keepers. Anglo-American feminist writer Naomi Lowinsky, author of *The motherline: Every woman's journey to find her female roots* (1992), defines the motherline:

When a woman today comes to understand her life story as a story from the Motherline, she gains female authority in a number of ways. First, her Motherline grounds her in her feminine nature as she struggles with the many options now open to women. Second, she reclaims carnal knowledge of her own body, its blood mysteries and their power. Third, as she makes the journey back to her female roots, she will encounter ancestors who struggled with similar difficulties in different historical times. This provides her with a life-cycle perspective that softens her immediate situation .... Fourth, she uncovers her connection to the archetypal mother and to the wisdom of the ancient worldview, which holds that body and soul are one and all life is interconnected. And, finally, she reclaims her female perspective, from which to consider how men are similar and how they are different. (1992: 13)

Writing about Lowinsky's motherline in her book *Motherless daughters: The legacy of loss* (1994), Hope Edelman emphasizes that "Motherline stories ground a ... daughter in a gender, a family, and a feminine history. They transform the experience of her female ancestors into maps she can refer to for warning or encouragement" (1994: 201). Motherline stories, made available to daughters through the female oral tradition, unite mothers and daughters, and connect them to their motherline. Naomi Lowinsky argues that many women today are disconnected from their motherline and have consequently lost the authenticity and authority of their womanhood. For Lowinsky, female empowerment becomes possible only in and through reconnecting to the motherline.

In African-American society the motherline represents the ancestral memory, the traditional values of African-American culture. Black mothers pass on the teachings of the motherline to each successive generation through the maternal function of cultural bearing. Various African-American writers argue that the very survival of African-Americans depends upon the preservation of black culture and history. If black children are to survive they must know the stories, legends, and myths of their ancestors. In African-American culture, women are the keepers of the tradition: they are the culture bearers who mentor and model the African-American values essential the empowerment of black children and culture. "Black women," Karla Holloway continues, "carry the voice of the mother—they are the progenitors, the assurance of the line ... as carriers of the *voice* [black women] carry wisdom—mother wit. They teach the children to survive *and* remember" (1987: 123). Black mothers, as Bernard and Bernard conclude, "pass on the torch to their daughters, who are expected to become the next generation of mothers, grandmothers, or othermothers, to guard future generations" (1998: 47).

The above five themes demonstrate that mothers and motherhood are valued by and regarded as central to African-American culture; as well, mothers and mothering are recognized as making possible the physical and psychological well-being and empowerment of the African-American people and the larger African-American culture. The following section will detail how the centrality and significance of black motherhood gives rise to the empowerment of daughters. Black women, in connection with powerful mothers, become empowered as daughters. "I come from/a long line of/Uppity Irate Black Women" begins Kate Rushin's poem "Family Tree." "And [when] you ask me how come/I think I'm so cute," Kate Rushin replies, "I cultivate/Being uppity,/It's something/My Gramon taught me" (Bell-Scott, 1993: 176–7).

African-American mothers and daughters

In their early but important work *Common differences: Conflicts in black & white feminist perspectives* (1986), Gloria Joseph and Jill Lewis contrast Anglo-American and African-American women's experiences of motherhood and daughterhood. Joseph argues that respect for the mother was a central and organizing theme of the mother–daughter relationships examined. She also found that female socialization centered upon the teaching of survival skills, and on an insistence upon independence:

What was startlingly evident, as revealed in the mother/daughter
questionnaire, was the teaching of survival skills to females for their
survival *in* and for the survival *of* the Black community. Intra-group survival
skills were given more importance and credence than survival skills for
dealing with the White society at large. There is a tremendous amount
of teaching transmitted by Black mothers to their daughters that enables
them to survive, exist, succeed, and be important to and for the Black
communities .... Black daughters are actually "taught" to hold the Black
community together. (1986: 106)[7]

The independence that mothers insist upon for their daughters is to be
achieved through education and effort. This may be contrasted to the dominant
narrative of Anglo-American feminine achievement that scripts marriage as the
avenue through which women will "get ahead." The African-American mothers'
insistence upon independence for their daughters includes a critique of marriage,
particularly the dependency inherent in the wife role. These mothers recognize
with Miriam Johnson that it is the wife role and not the mother role that organizes
women's secondary status. "Through Mom's guidance and direction," comments
Candace Bernard in "Passing the torch" (1998), "I learned the value of hard
work, self-determination, goal-setting, and shared responsibility .... I experienced
empowerment through Mom's ability to survive in a climate that was not conducive
to survival." The daughter adds, "It is empowering to know that I have come
from such a long line of strong Black women .... I feel honored that ... I am able
to carry on the struggle you began a generation ago" (1998: 48–9).

As Barbara Turnage discusses, "The global self-esteem of an African-
American adolescent female and her relationship with her mother," a black
daughter develops high self-esteem through a secure and close attachment with
her mother and knowledge of her African-American heritage. Her study of 105
African-American young women ranging in age from sixteen to eighteen found
that the most significant variable was "trust of the mother": "African-American
mothers play an important role in their daughters self-esteem development. That
is, the young women in this study who had high self esteem also trusted their
mothers to be there for them. The second significant variable for self-esteem
was "acknowledgment of an African ancestry": "For an adolescent African-
American female knowledge of her African heritage helps her define her body
image and structure her expectations" (O'Reilly and Abbey, 2000). The message
of this study, Turnage emphasizes, cannot be "overstated":

The relationship between these African-American young women and
their mothers instilled in them the knowledge that they are competent
and lovable. Based on their trust in their mothers, these young women

believed, when confronted with difficult situations, that they could rely on their mothers' assistance. Thus, as they grow into black womanhood, they grow with the knowledge that they can accomplish their goals and that they are worthy love and respect. (O'Reilly and Abbey, 2000)

These daughters, connected with their mothers and motherline (awareness of heritage), develop a strong and proud identity as black women and secure empowerment.

Contemporary African-American women's writing also celebrates mothers as mentors and role models, and illustrates the power daughters obtain in connection with their mothers and motherline. Readers of black women's literature have long observed a deeply rooted matrilineal tradition in which daughters think back through their mothers. In Marianne Hirsch's words, "[there is] in much of contemporary black women's writing, a public celebration of maternal presence" (1989: 177). In a 1980 article, appropriately entitled "I sing my mother's name" (Perry, 1984), Mary Helen Washington speaks of a "generational continuity" among African-American women in which "a mother serves as the female precursor who passes on the authority of authorship to her daughter and provides a model for the black woman's literary presence in this society" (Perry, 1984: 147). "For black women writers," as Dolana Mogadime observes in "A daughter's praise poem for her mother," "the idea of thinking back through our mothers is rooted in the notion of revisiting and learning about maternal knowledge and female-centred networks as expressions of African continuities in contemporary society" (1998: 87). Respect and gratitude for "women who made a way out of no way" is repeated time and time again in the groundbreaking collection of writings on black mothers and daughters, appropriately entitled *Double stitch: Black women write about mothers & daughters* (Bell-Scott, 1993).

In an introductory section to *Double stitch*, Beverly Guy-Sheftall writes: "In selection after selection, daughters acknowledge how their mothers provided road maps and patterns, a 'template', which enabled them to create and define themselves ... Though daughters must forge an identity which is separate from the mothers, they frequently acknowledge that a part of themselves is truly their mothers' child" (1993: 61). Margaret Walker, in her poem appropriately entitled "Lineage," pays tribute to her grandmothers, who "were strong/... full of sturdiness and singing" (1993: 175). Sonia Sanchez writes: "My life flows from you Mama. My style comes from a long line of Louises who picked me up in the night to keep me from wetting the bed .... A long line of Lizzies who made me understand love .... A Long line of Black people holding each other up against silence" (1993: 25–6). Judy Scales-Trent writes: "my mother opened the door/.... and set me free" (1993: 213). The first stanza of Irma McClaurin's poem "The power of names," reads: "I slip my mother's name on like a glove/and wonder if I will become like her/absolutely./Years number the times I have worn her pain/as a child, as a teenager, as a woman—my second skin—/as she sat, silver head bowed/silent/hedging the storm" (1993: 63).

In her moving autobiographical narrative, *Pushed back to strength: A black woman's journey home*, some of which is excerpted in *Double stitch* (Bell-Scott, 1993), Gloria Wade-Gayles argues that in the segregated south of the 1940s, "Surviving meant being black, and being black meant believing in our humanity, and retaining it, in a world that denied we had it in the first place" (1993: 6). The survival of black culture and black selfhood was sustained by the motherline. "The men in my family were buttresses and protectors," writes Wade-Gayles, "but it was the women who gave meaning to the expression 'pushed back to strength'" (13). Whether named mentor, role model, guide, advisor, wise woman, or advocate, the mother represents for the daughter a sturdy bridge on which to cross over. Even the author Renita Weems, who was abandoned by her alcoholic mother, writes: "Though not as sturdy as others, she is my bridge. When I needed to get across she steadied herself long enough for me to run across safely" (Bell-Scott, 1993: 129).

Alice Walker's classic essay, "In search of our mothers' garden" (1983), is a moving tribute to her African-American foremothers who, in her words, "handed on the creative spark, the seed of the flower they themselves never hoped to see; or like a sealed letter they could not plainly read" (240). "[S]o many of the stories that I write," Walker emphasizes, "that we all write, are my mother's stories" (240). Walker delineates here a theory of creative identity that juxtaposes the male paradigm of literary achievement that demands separation and individuation. I argue that the observations of Dannabang Kuwabong about Africaribbean women's writing are germane to all black female diaspora literature: "the mother–daughter relationship ... is central to the development of identity and voice" (1998: 132). Cassie Premo Steele's observation about Audre Lorde is likewise applicable to many black women writers: "Grounding her narrative in matrilineal history and myth allows Lorde to find and take root: to form her identity" (2000: 8). Black female subjectivity generally, and creativity specifically, are formed, nurtured, and sustained through women's identification with, and connection to, their motherline. As Sylvia Hamilton, noted documentary writer and director, commented in the film *Black mother, black daughter*, "[Our foremothers] created a path for us ... we are bound to something larger than our selves .... I am moved by the example of their lives" (1989).

African-American daughters seek and hold connection with mothers and the motherline; they achieve empowerment through this identification because motherhood is valued by and is central to African-American culture, and because the motherline bestows to the daughter affirming and empowering lessons of black womanhood. In *Not our kind of girl: Unraveling the myths of black teenage motherhood* (1997), Elaine Bell Kaplan, proposes a "poverty of relationship" thesis to account for the high incidence of black unwed teenage pregnancy. "[T]eenage mothers," she writes, "describe being disconnected from primary family relations, abandoned by their schools and by the men in their lives ... at the time of adolescence, when it is most important that they experience positive relationships" (1997: 11). The absence of relationships in the adolescent girl's life, Kaplan argues, results from the loss of black neighborhood and community occasioned by the economic restructuring of the 1970s. In the 1950s and 1960s, a strong sense of family and community prevailed in black neighborhoods; there was also a low incidence of unwed teenage pregnancy. Whether the two are casually related as Kaplan maintains, her argument explicates, albeit inadvertently, the connection-empowerment thesis advanced here. Disconnection, a word Kaplan herself uses, is at the core of the adolescent girl's aloneness and at the center of the community's despair. As African-American women celebrate the power acquired through connection to a strong mother and a strong motherline, Kaplan's words remind us that the very survival of African-American culture may depend on it.

African-American mothers and sons

Most of the writing by African-American women has tended to focus on the mother–daughter relationship; little has been written on the mother–son relationship.[8] The notable exceptions are Elaine Joyce King and Carolyn Mitchell's *Black mothers to sons: Juxtaposing African-American literature with social practice* (1995) and *Saving our sons: Raising black children in a turbulent world* (1995) by novelist Marita Golden.[9] In the introduction to their book, King and Mitchell, explaining their research interest in mothers and sons, write: "Considering the particular vulnerability of black males in this society and the role that mothers typically play as primary nurturers, this focus on black mother-to-son parenting is long overdue" (1995: 2). The initial question King and Mitchell explored in selected African-American fiction and asked of their research participants was: "What have you done to protect your son(s) from society's hostile forces?" (1995: 6). In their study of African-American literature they found that protection was the primary aim of black mothering and manifested itself in two diametrically opposed modes of mothering: "mothers who whip their sons brutally 'for their own good', and mothers who love their sons to destruction through self-sacrifice and overindulgence" (1995: 9). The first strategy is sustained by the belief that, in their words, "a black man-child duly 'chastened' or broken at home will pose less of a threat to a society already primed to destroy him" (1995: 10); while the latter seeks to shield the child from all that is deemed harsh and upsetting. Each position, they argue, psychologically maims the son: the first by breaking the child's spirit, the latter by thwarting the child's maturation to true selfhood. The question black mothers ask in the raising of their sons is, in the authors' words, how can they "help sons develop the character, personality and integrity a black man-child needs to transcend these forces?" (1995: 19).

Golden's book also assumes as its central theme the survival of black men. Dedicated to the black men who have died violently in Washington, D.C., since 1988, Golden explains that she wrote this book "because at this moment there is no subject more necessary to confront, more imperative to imagine. Until I wrote about our sons, I could not speak or think or dream of anything else" (1995: 185). Homicide, Golden tells us, is the leading cause of death for young black men in America. According to Golden, the violence, drugs, crime, joblessness, and killing of black male youth, mark a new kind of Middle Passage. Her book narrates this crossing as it tells the story of her own son's journey into manhood; in this telling and testifying Golden lists possible causes, drafts solutions, and seeks to imagine what, in her words "we will look like, how will we sound, once we are spewed forth from the terrible hold of THIS ship" (1995: 9). "The major challenge ... to a black mother raising sons today," as Claudette Lee and Ethel Wilson explain in "Masculinity, matriarchy, and myth: A black feminist perspective," is "survival ... Racism, discrimination, and oppression define the childhood of an African-American male. Mothering for an African-American woman is defined by fear for her male child. Therefore her approach and relationship with her son must be different" (Lee, 2001: 56–7).

Golden recognizes, as did King and Mitchell, that for parents with the financial means, retreat has become the strategy of choice. Golden withdrew her son from public school in Washington, D.C., and enrolled him in a private boarding school. She and her husband purchased a house in the suburbs. However, in saving a son this way, he is removed from the black community and its history, from the "sites of resistance"—family, community, history—that have traditionally nurtured and empowered African-Americans by creating black-defined narratives and identities. The women of King and Mitchell's study spoke of the "liberating, healing power of family lore, bloodlines and family secrets" (1995: 37). "[K]nowing about ancestors," King and Mitchell write, "strengthens identification with family values that can help a son overcome anger and hopelessness. Such family lore can also develop a son's confidence in himself .... [it] free[s] black males from the diminished definitions of their humanity and self-worth that society offers them" (38). Golden, too, recognizes that the double consciousness of which Dubois eloquently wrote about more than a hundred years ago is, in her words, "draining and sometimes killing our spirits" (1995: 14). With integration came the loss of communities, traditions, beliefs, legends, narratives and rituals, the "sites of resistance," that have long sustained and enriched black American culture.[10] While suburbs and boarding schools may save black sons from the killing fields of the so-called American inner-cities, they also result in the further disintegration of black communities, the very thing that serve to empower African-Americans.

King, Mitchell, the women of their research group, and Golden agree that sons must be taught, in Golden's words, "that the first line of defense against racism is to mold themselves into disciplined, self-respecting refutations of its ability to destroy our souls or ourselves" (1995: 186). Or as James Baldwin wrote in 1971: "[I]t evolves upon the mother to invest the child, her man child, with some kind of interior dignity which will protect him against something he really can't be protected against, unless he has some kind of interior thing within him to meet it" (As quoted in King, 1995: 39). Audre Lorde wrote in "Man child: A black lesbian feminist's response" (1984) that "[f]or survival, Black children in America must be raised to be warriors. For survival they must also be raised to recognize the enemy's many faces" (1984: 75). She goes on to say:

> The strongest lesson I can teach my son is the same lesson I teach my daughter: how to be who he wishes to be for himself. And the best way I can do this is to be who I am and hope that he will learn from this not how to be me, which is not possible, but how to be himself. And this means how to move to that voice from within himself, rather than to those raucous, persuasive, or threatening voices from outside, pressuring him to be what the world wants him to be. (1984: 77)

The aim of the black mothering is thus to nurture and sustain the "soul," "voice within," and "the interior thing" of black sons, so that they are able to transcend the maiming of racism and grow into manhood whole and complete. Mothers of black sons, according to these writers, must negotiate between the need to keep their sons physically safe while simultaneously promoting their psychological maturation.[11] For mothers of black sons this is achieved by grounding sons in their culture of origin, the black community, and connecting them to their African-American motherline.

The presence and involvement of the mother are recognized as crucial and essential to the son's maturation. African-American mothering foregrounds the importance and centrality of the mother in the son's life, for it is she who both provides protection and teaches her son how to protect himself, physically and otherwise, and passes on the important teachings of the African-American motherline. Presence and participation in the sons' lives are emphasized in African-American culture because black boys' lives are at risk. Black mothers must protect their sons to ensure their survival, and to teach them how to do the same for themselves. The son's well-being thus depends upon, as it does with his sister, the presence and involvement of his mother in his life. The emphasis upon maternal involvement with sons and maternal connection for daughters underscores the importance of mothers and motherline in African-American culture. The African-American tradition of motherhood—othermothering, matrifocality, social activism, providing a homeplace and cultural bearing—gives power and prominence in African-American culture. Mothers, from this site of power, empower their children through the above five themes or tasks of African-American mothering; children, in turn, secure this empowerment through connection with their mothers and motherline.

Conclusion

Reflecting upon the themes of this chapter, I am reminded of the chorus from Canadian singer-songwriter Jann Arden's song "Good Mother":

> *I've got a good mother*
> *and her voice is what keeps me here*
> *Feet on ground*
> *Heart in hand*
> *Facing forward*
> *Be yourself.*

African-American motherhood, in the five themes detailed above, bestows upon black children a loved, strong, and proud selfhood. The mother, in fulfilling these tasks of black motherhood, becomes, to borrow the metaphor from the song, "the voice that keeps [the children] here." She is the "heart in the hand" that enables the children to "face forward with feet on the ground and be themselves." Whether it be a connection realized through the mother–daughter relationship or through mother–son involvement, mothering in black culture is what ensures physical and psychological survival and well-being, and is what makes resistance possible.

Notes

1. Alice Walker (1983) defines "womanist" as:

    A black feminist or feminist of color. From the black folk expression of mothers to female children, 'You acting womanish,' i.e., like a woman. Usually referring to outrageous, audacious, courageous or willful behavior. [...] Womanist is to feminist as purple is to lavender.

2. "Childbearing and children are valued by members of this community and black women in The Flats," Stack continues, "unlike many other societies ... feel few if any restrictions

about childbearing. Unmarried black women, young and old, are eligible to bear children, and frequently women bear their first children when they are quite young" (47). Many of these teenage mothers, however, do not raise their firstborn; this responsibility is left to the mother, aunt, or elder sister with whom the biological mother resides. The child thus may have both a "Mama," the woman "who raised him up," and the biological mother who birthed him. The mama, in Stack's terminology, is the "sponsor" of the child's personal kinship network; the network is thus matrilineal and matrifocal.

3. Johnson's argument is that contemporary African-American culture is matrifocal; at no time does she suggest that black family or culture is matriarchal. Nonetheless, any discussion of matrifocality must locate itself in the infamous Moynihan report and the controversy it generated. The report described the black family as dysfunctional, and argued that the mother was to blame for the purported pathologies of the race: "In essence, the negro community has ... a matriarchal structure which ... seriously retards the progress of the group as a whole" (Rainwater and Yancey, 1967: 75). Or as critic Michele Wallace put it: "The Moynihan Report said that the black man was not so much a victim of white institutional racism as he was of an abnormal family structure, its main feature being an employed black woman" (1990: 12). Swiftly and abruptly the report was condemned for its failure to take into account institutionalized racism to explain under/unemployment, family "breakdown," and so forth, not to mention the report's blame-the-mother/blame-the-victim rhetoric. For an excellent discussion of the Moynihan report in terms of the ideological constructions of black womanhood, see Patricia Morton, *Disfigured images: The historical assault on Afro-American women* (1991), particularly chapter nine, "Rediscovering the black family: New and old images of motherhood," 125–35. Morton argues that

> [T]he 1970s saw a veritable revolution in interpretation of the modern Afro-American family ... [with] an emphasis on familial health. In contrast to the old equation of black deviance from white middle-class norms as pathologized and dysfunctional, the new black family studies increasingly emphasized Afro-American diversity—including familial and sexual departures from white norms—as a positive thing. (126)

The revisionist family scholarship set out to debunk the black matriarchy thesis by documenting the poverty and powerlessness experienced by black women. At the same time, the revisionist black family studies argued that it was precisely the strength and resiliency of black motherhood that enabled blacks to remain whole and intact in a racist world. Paradoxically, the new scholarship exposed black matriarchy as a myth while emphasizing the strength of black mothers. This paradox underscores the difference between matrifocality and matriarchy, and points to the ideological impasse of the Moynihan report that linked strength with domination.

Scholars today often downplay the strengths of the black mother so as to appear that they are staying clear of the controversial black matriarchy thesis. This is evident in historical accounts of slavery, particularly the research of Herbert Gutman, *The black family in slavery and freedom, 1750–1925* (1976), where he emphasizes that the slave family remained, for the most part, intact—by which he means father-headed and nuclear. "It may be," Morton writes, "that matrifocality and strong slave women were too akin to the myth of the black matriarchy to be acceptable to contemporary historians" (1991: 133). Such a perspective keeps us locked in the Moynihan framework, pathologizing the very thing that keeps black families viable and resilient, namely black motherhood. Such a viewpoint also curtails honest and appreciative study of black women. For readings in revisionist black family studies, refer to: Andrew Ballingsley, *Black families in white American* (1968) and *Climbing Jacob's ladder: The enduring legacy of African-American families* (1992); Robert Staples and Leanor Boulin Johnson, *Black families at the crossroads: Challenges and prospects* (1993); Harriette Pipes McAdoo, Ed., *Black families* (1981) and *Family ethnicity: Strength in diversity* (1993).

4.   Ladner continues:

> This sharp change in status occurs for a variety of reasons. Perhaps the most important value it has is that of demonstrating the procreative powers that the girls possess. Children are highly valued and a strong emphasis is placed on one's being able to give birth. The ultimate test of womanhood, then, is one's ability to bring forth life. This value underlying child bearing is much akin to the traditional way in which the same behaviour has been perceived in African culture. So strong is the tradition that women must bear children in most West African societies that barren females are often pitied and in some cases their husbands are free to have children by other women. The ability to have children also symbolizes (for these girls) maturity that they feel cannot be gained in any other way. (216)

For white middle-class culture, marriage, rather than motherhood, is what ushers girls into womanhood. The elaborate, ritualized—and I may add costly—customs of the wedding ceremony, bridal showers, bridal shows, wedding service, receptions, and so forth, bear testimony to the place of the wedding in that culture.

5.   bell hooks continues:

> [The] libratory struggle has been seriously undermined by contemporary efforts to change that subversive homeplace into a site of patriarchal domination of black women by black men, where we abuse one another for not conforming to sexist norms. This shift in perspective, where homeplace is not viewed as a political site, has had a negative impact on the construction of black female identity and political consciousness. Masses of black women, many of whom were not formally educated, had in the past been able to play a vital role in black liberation struggle. In the contemporary situation, as the paradigms for domesticity in black life mirrored white bourgeois norms (where home is conceptualized as politically neutral space), black people began to overlook and devalue the importance of black female labor in teaching critical consciousness in domestic space. Many black women, irrespective of class status, have responded to this crisis of meaning

> by imitating leisure-class sexist notions of women's role, focusing their lives on meaningless compulsive consumerism. (47)

7.   Joseph's research—a 1979–1980 survey—revealed that the majority of black daughters (94.5 percent) said that they respected their mothers.

> Joseph's research identified different issues and trends in the Anglo-American mother–daughter relationship. She found a greater belief in romance amongst white mothers, as expressed in the commonly offered advice: "Marry for love." Joseph discovered further that: "the ways in which the White daughters said they feared their mothers disclosed an area that was rarely, if ever, mentioned by the Black daughters. The response was, 'I fear I might be like her. I want to be independent of her'" (1986: 125). Here the Anglo-American daughters bespeak matrophobia first defined by Rich in *Of woman born* (1986). "White women were included" in the survey, but because of "the small number of respondents," Joseph writes, "it was not possible to conduct a comparative study between White subjects and Black ones" (125). Joseph discovered in her analysis that class was an important variable to the degree that working-class white mothers gave responses similar to the black mother's responses.

8.   For a study of black feminist thought on the mother and son relationship, please see Andrea O'Reilly, "In black and white: African-American and Anglo-American feminist theory on the mother and son relationship," in *Mothers and sons: Feminism, masculinity, and the struggle to raise our sons*, Andrea O'Reilly, Ed. (2001).

9.   I refer here to book length studies of African-American mothers and sons. Articles include: Audre Lorde, "Man child: A black lesbian feminist response," *Sister outsider* (1984); Andrea O'Reilly, "In black and white: African-American and Anglo-American feminist theory on the mother and son relationship," in *Mothers and sons: Feminism, masculinity, and the challenge to raise our sons*, Andrea O'Reilly, Ed. (2001).

10. The conflicting demands of protection and nurturance first identified by Ruddick in *Maternal thinking* (1989) become, in the instance of rearing black sons, an impasse, an irreconcilable contradiction. The women interviewed by King and Mitchell all spoke of this paradox in the mothering of black sons; while sons must go into the world to mature socially, psychologically, and otherwise, this same world threatens their very physical survival.

11. This again is the impasse of black mothers; one that is etched on the very bodies of black men, as Golden remarks of her own son: "The unscathed openness of Michael's demeanor was proof that he had been a protected, loved child. But this same quality was also suddenly a liability, one that he had to mask" (1995: 95). Nurturing sons to be confident and proud, mothers recognize that these same traits—because they may be misconstrued as insolence, obstinacy, and arrogance by other black youth, police, or whites—put their sons at risk. Golden realizes, as does King and Mitchell, that this paradox of mothering black sons necessitates a new mode of mothering, one fashioned specifically for black male children.

Chapter Twelve

Black Women's Mothering in a Historical and Contemporary Perspective
Understanding the Past, Forging the Future

Erica Lawson

Introduction

This essay explores some of the historical and contemporary practices that punish black women for daring to become mothers. It offers a critical reading of how the construction of the bad black mother contributes to the realization of "normal" family life and the "ideal" nation-state. To this end, I will briefly examine the struggle of the central character in Toni Morrison's *Beloved* to save her children from the horrors of slavery, and I will consider Dorothy Roberts' *Killing the black body: Race, reproduction and the meaning of liberty*, which focuses on black women's experiences within states that are determined to control their reproduction. I argue that there are striking similarities between Morrison's historical work and Roberts' current research that illustrate the dangers of mothering then and now. This essay also explores community-based mothering as it contributes to self-actualization and community support among black women.

My academic and political interests in writing this paper are anchored in disrupting conventional praxis that pathologize black women in the context of motherhood. I do not write as a black woman who is a mother. For me, economic constraints, the challenges of student and work life, and the prominence of nuclear family patterns in Canadian society, raise critical questions about the feasibility of motherhood. These questions remain unresolved. Rather, I write as the daughter of a Caribbean woman who, like many other mothers, was forced to leave her children behind to work in Canada. I write as someone who has witnessed this woman's determination to fight for her children's education and general well-being and I write as the granddaughter of a man and a woman who raised many of their grandchildren because many of *their* own children were pushed to emigrate to find work in the "developed" world. My evolving perspective on motherhood is therefore informed by the acts of resistance that black women engage in to claim their understanding and expression of mothering; the exploitation of Black women's labour by the state through the immigration system and its impact on parent/child relationships; and by the reliance on extended families and othermothers to help raise children. Furthermore, I read these realities in the context of broad historical and economic forces that shape African mothering in the diaspora through the production of unique yet similarly oppressive experiences.

Motherhood and the state: Policing black women

It is not a surprise that the struggle for sexual freedom within the Western feminist movement in the 1960s did not appeal to African women. The reluctance to join the sexual liberation movement in large numbers cannot be understood without historicizing African womens' political agenda: their fight against racism, their desire to strengthen their communities, and the importance of challenging the view that black people were inherently promiscuous. In addition to founding societies to uplift the Black community, a number of black women engaged in policing the behaviours of other black people to ensure that they adhered to proper family values and codes of sexual conduct. The underlying principles governing the creation of the Victoria Reform Benevolent Society for Social Relief is a case in point. Founded in Chatham, Ontario, in 1853, the Society was open to all women between sixteen and forty-eight years old, and its services were tied to a vigilant show of proper conduct and morality by the recipients. The Society assisted women who were not addicted to alcohol and who did not engage in multiple relationships (Bristow, 1994: 121). Moreover, article 2 of the bylaws stated that: "no member of this society shall be entitled to any relief on account of any disease that she has imprudently brought upon herself" (Bristow, 1994: 121). Women who broke the rules were expelled from the Society.

Similarly, black women in the United States aspired to dispel the myth of promiscuity and inherent indecency. During the era of Reconstruction, black women struggled against the barrage of negative images that defined black womanhood and sexuality (Hooks, 1981), but their attempts to attain some measure of dignity were usually thwarted by white society. Hooks tells us that: "everywhere black women went on public streets, in shops, or at their places at work, they were accosted and subjected to obscene comments and even physical abuse at the hands of white men and women. Those black women suffered most whose behavior exemplified that of a lady" (1981: 55). Black women's articulation of a sexually moral self destabilized white society's views regarding the Black female body as a unit of re/production. That is, the outrage expressed by whites was tied to a fundamental destabilization of the (white) ontological perception of self and personhood as constructed through the subordination of black womanhood. I submit that these two factors: the subordination of Black female sexuality and reproduction to economic interests, and the construction of these bodies as inherently indecent, continue to have currency in Euro-American society. This paper is concerned with examining motherhood as a site where the economic and psychosocial interests of the dominant group are articulated through and protected by the state, and where these interests are contested by black women who undertake motherhood/mothering as an expression of self that is connected to community values and sustainability.

Female sexuality and reproductivity are not free from social and political constraints. Rather, the idealized expression of sexuality, reproduction, and motherhood are anchored within the institution of marriage and the nuclear family structure. In order to understand these constraints, it is necessary to consider the meanings ascribed to "woman/women" in processes of nationalism, colonialism, and imperialism, for particular meanings have ensured that female bodies are the sites upon which aspirations are mapped and desires are projected. Beyond its articulation of femininity as it is socially constructed and understood, motherhood is tied to the longings of the nation-state. Here I use nation-state to mean the exercise of power that allows a dominant group to control its destiny and realize its goals (Collins, 2000: 229). The creation of family life then, as defined by one's ability to produce children who are connected to a family circle, is a reflection and extension of nationalist aspirations, and is therefore subject to state intervention.

The use of the category "woman" shifts in different situations, and the term itself is produced in classist, racist, patriarchal, and sexualized processes of inequalities (Pierson, 1998; Mohanty, 1991). Pierson (1998) tells us that one may become a woman in opposition to other women in cultures where asymmetric race and class relations are organizing principles. From this perspective, motherhood must be seen as intricately connected to these subordinating processes whereby not all women within a nation are equally encouraged to reproduce. Rather, women who are thought to embody the physical, cultural, and mythical ideals of the nation's past, present, and future are likely to be rewarded for producing the right type of children, while others are punished for perceived over-reproductivity.

One of the most powerful scenes in Toni Morrison's widely acclaimed novel *Beloved,* is the central character's determination to kill her four children to save them from slavery. Sethe, the mother, succeeds in killing one child, and is in the process of destroying another when she is stopped. The scene unfolds in a barn wherein:

> ... two boys bled in the sawdust and dirt at the feet of a nigger woman
> holding a blood-soaked child to her chest with one hand and an infant

by the heels in the other. She did not look at them; she simply swung
the baby toward the wall planks, missed and tried to connect a second
time .... Little nigger-boy eyes open in sawdust; little nigger-girl eyes
staring between the wet fingers that held her face so that her head
wouldn't fall off .... (1998: 175)

Set in post-civil war Ohio, the story centres around the dead baby's spirit,
Beloved, who personifies the evils of slavery and haunts her mother's present as
Sethe struggles to throw off the legacy of slavery. Seeing that the wounded or
dead children are of no monetary value to them or the slave economy, the four
horsemen sent to recapture the runaway family,

trotted off leaving the sheriff behind with the damnedest bunch of coons
they'd ever seen. All testimony to the result of a little so-called freedom
imposed on people who needed every care and guidance in the world to
keep them from the animal life they preferred. (Morrison, 1998: 177)

Sethe and her children were valuable to the extent that they were useful re-
producers in the society.

Black women's reproductive capability continues to be regulated and policed
in American society to protect state interests. Over the past decade, an increasing
number of poor black women have been prosecuted for exposing their unborn
babies to drugs. Jennifer Clarise Johnson, a twenty-three year-old crack addict
became the first woman in the United States to be criminally convicted for exposing
her baby to crack while pregnant (Roberts, 1997b: 127). The laws are framed
under the guise of protecting the fetus from abuse that reduces life chances but,
effectively, they are meant to punish black women who become pregnant,
especially if these women are dependent on state welfare.

When a pregnant woman is arrested for harming the fetus by smoking crack,
her crime is determined by her decision to have the baby since the woman can
avoid prosecution if she has an abortion (Roberts, 1997a: 152). In other words,
the "choices" that she faces in front of the judge are: get an abortion and inject
Norplant[1], or remain fertile and go to jail. In addition, if a black woman violates
probation by becoming pregnant she will be sent to jail. Roberts asserts that
black women are targeted for such harsh punishment because of the widespread
belief that they are not suitable mothers or capable human beings. I would also
argue that the legacy of medical experimentation on African bodies lessens
concerns about the devastating side effects of Norplant on many women.
Furthermore, the entrenched belief in the idea of the "strong Black women"
(Collins, 2000; Beckles, 1995) render state representatives incapable of
considering the emotional and spiritual implications of having an abortion for

many black women. What are we to make of the ways in which black women's reproductive capability is used, as described by Morrison and Roberts? And how do their respective works make connections between black women's reproduction in the slave economy and in the contemporary Diasporic context?

Understanding the past to make sense of the present

If we consider the evolution of imperialist cultures through a continuum of emerging historical patterns of unequal social relations, we can begin to make connections between black women's reproductive/mothering experiences in slavery and the challenges they face in today. A close look will tell us that not much has changed. Let us consider these arguments in light of the scene from Morrison's *Beloved* (1998) described earlier. Four white men were sent to recapture Sethe, a runaway slave and her four children. They found her in a barn in the process of killing her children to save them from the slavery. If we shift our gaze to the men, this powerful scene provides insight into how Euro-American male subjects performed their identity and participated in the economy through the exploitation of black female sexuality and motherhood.

First, to the four white men, Sethe personified the bad black mother, and exhibited all the characteristics of the animal-like black woman. That is, Sethe represented everything that the men's white mothers, wives, daughters, and sisters were not. Essentially, her body, and the way in which she tried to save her children from slavery, allowed the men to imagine home. Sethe's unstable and violent world, created by the slave system which the men helped to sustain, marked the boundary between the slaves' world and the orderly, safe white world suitable for bearing and rearing children in a normal family setting. Second, recapturing slaves allowed working class white males to participate in the economy by being paid for their services. Indeed, exercising male power through racism and patriarchy offered working-class white men some measure of compensation for their exploitation in the ruling nation (Callincos, quoted in McLaren, 1997: 39). Third, the element of an emotional and spiritual sense of privilege that the working class derived from policing others cannot be overlooked. After witnessing Sethe's actions, the men ride off, reaffirmed in their belief that it is dangerous to grant slaves freedom because it will inevitably be squandered. This scene reveals that in the slave economy, black female bodies had symbolism: material uses and meanings that allowed American society to make sense of itself. Moreover, it illustrates how white male subjects articulated their identity by participating violence against Black women. But how does this continue to happen today?

Current state laws that allow judges to sentence pregnant black women to jail for smoking crack are similar to the laws that allowed Sethe to be tracked down and recaptured.[2] These laws are connected over different historical periods by the common goal of regulating black female reproduction for the collective good of the white patriarchal capitalist state (see also Augustine, 1997; Williams, 1997). Today, the continued criminalization of black women results in economic benefits for the law and order industry. This ranges from politicians who build careers by promising tougher laws and larger budgets for the police, judges who build reputations by enforcing these laws, to a burgeoning prison system that is increasingly farmed out to private-sector entrepreneurs. Additionally, there is metaphysical value in black women's bodies in that the meanings attributed to these bodies help to organize the physical and moral borders of white social existence.

The ways in which childbearing black women are perceived and treated today is also illustrative of the connections between the slave economy and the current demands of the capitalist state. In slavery, black women were coerced into producing children to replenish the slave population, and each child produced added cash value to the owner's human stock. In the present "new" world economy, however,, in societies that reduces the person to a unit of consumerism, black women and their children, especially poor ones, are disposable. This is a reality that contributes to the devaluation of mothering in the African diaspora.

Community-based mothering

Mothering plays a crucial role in communal sustainability and self-empowerment for black women. To understand the complexities of how this occurs, it is necessary to consider the importance of community in the lives of African people who are severely constrained in imperialist societies. Dei contends that the hostility of the diaspora "influences the particular options and strategies that are open to those who are minoritized. Understanding the nature of the hostility they encounter is crucial in order not to deny the intellectual agency and power of local subjects, and the pragmatic political choices that they make" (2000: 208–209). I read Dei as a challenge to appreciate "community" as a site of resistance and affirmation with its own tensions and contradictions rather than as a homogenous collective. This understanding of community connotes the need for Africans in the diaspora to have a foundation for political consciousness/activism, economic support, and a space wherein the self is articulated and affirmed. With this in mind, community-based mothering in the African diaspora must be looked at through critical lens for a broader understanding of how it is experienced both as a political act and as an expression of a holistic self.

Historically and presently, community mothering practices were and are a central experience in the lives of many black women. Participation in mothering is a form of emotional and spiritual expression in societies that marginalize black women. Collins (2000: 11) correctly points out that insightful self-definitions nurtured in suppressed communities, enabled African black women to use African-derived conceptions of self and community to resist negative evaluations of black women. Community mothering is one of the ways in which this was done, and is a practice that is evident in the Caribbean experience with which I am familiar.

Between 1973 and 1975, extensive research was conducted with forty-five African Jamaican women to determine the dynamics of conjugal relations in the society's belief system at specific historical periods (Brodber 1986: 23). The women were born from about eighteen sixty-one to nineteen hundred. The study used the testimonies and life histories of the women to develop "a multi-dimensional and dynamic figure of the free woman as she perceived herself to be" as a way of understanding conjugal relations, extended kinship practices, and female independence. The research found that:

> ... "taking" and "growing" other people's children was normal behaviour for Afro-Jamaican women of the early twentieth century. The children who entered the units in this way were treated as blood relatives and the surrogate parents, despite what emotional attachments might have developed between themselves and their "taken children" were easily able to pass them on to other adults or back to the parents themselves. This act was looked upon as one carried out "through love." (Brodber, 1986: 26)

All of the women in the sample had reared children at some point, whether or not they had given birth to them. The researchers argue that the shifting and changing nature of the relationship between children and caregiver resulted in constant accommodation to subtraction and addition of persons. This experience, they argue, produced individuals with the ability to relate emotionally to a wide range of people in the face of their imminent departure, a characteristic referred to as "emotionally expansive" (Brodber, 1986: 25).

My own childhood unfolded under the guidance of extended family and many othermothers who took responsibility for raising children in the community. Men and women in the community saw themselves as empowered to feed, bathe, and generally care for each other's children without concern for blood-related ties. Both my mother and my aunt, who live in Canada, have shared many stories about what it meant to grow up in an extended community of other mothers and caregivers. Speaking about the childhood/adolescent years as she and her siblings experienced them, my mother told me that:

> When we were out playing, our parents didn't worry about where we were or if we were being fed. The only thing is that we all had to come home at night ... there was always someone to take care of you, to

discipline you ... my brothers got more beatings from people in the community than us girls because we were girls. The teachers in the community were also involved in our lives outside of school, sometimes too much. It was like a small village raising kids, that's how I would describe it.

In addition to the emotionality of extended mothering and its connection to the development of women-centred community bonds, motherhood/mothering is also a site for community economic survival and political expression among black women.

Inaccessibility to mainstream institutions of power means that black women exercise influence and exert power in their everyday lived realities through a series of mothering activities described as motherwork (Collins, 2000: 208–209). Motherwork facilitates the articulation of political consciousness by blood mothers and othermothers in women-centred family networks. For example, black women use their power in the home, in the church, and in other community-based institutions to foster self-reliance and self-confidence in children.

Motherwork as the impetus for child and community development is evident in the everyday lives of Caribbean women. Caribbean women define themselves primarily through their mothering roles, the development of their identities on the ability to be good mothers, and putting the spiritual well-being of their children above all else (Barriteau, 196: 145). Thus, when children suffer, women experience the worst state of material and psychological stress. Women employ a number of survival strategies to sustain family and community in the face of harsh economic measures in Caribbean societies (Barriteau, 1996; Barrow, 1986; Bolles, 1983; McAfee, 1991). Barriteau (1996, 146–147) refers to the Red Thread Collective of Guyana, whereby community members produced textbooks for children during a period of socio-economic hardship in that country. Moreover, the author describes how middle-class families, although also affected by economic upheaval, continue to support less well-off family members in exchange for child care services. Women-centred strategies stem from the reality that women and children are hardest hit by economic crisis since women are the primary providers and caregivers in most Caribbean households.

The resilience strategies that women use to sustain their children and communities have prompted Barriteau to call for a critical examination of the household as a site of important economic activity with national implications. This approach, Barriteau argues, would "not only move economic modeling closer to socioeconomic reality—that is, to the lived experiences of Caribbean people—but disrupt the hierarchical relation between households and the market behaviour" (1996: 150). Indeed, there are lessons to be learned from the ways in which black women, through motherwork blood-related or not, continue to support extended family networks and community sustainability.

Conclusion

Despite historical and contemporary depictions of the bad black mother to sustain the illusion of normalcy in Euro-American family life, mothering in the African diaspora is a complex and meaningful experience for many Black women. As such, mothering has to be examined and understood on its own terms and under the circumstances that give rise to how it occurs. Such an approach is a valuable opportunity to look at how mothering results in empowerment and transformation for black women and their communities.

Notes

1. Surgically injected into the arm, Norplant consists of six silicone capsules each about the size of a matchstick. Norplant prevents pregnancy for up to five years, but the drug causes serious side effects and complications for many women. Once implanted into poor black women, the laws prevent the removal of Norplant.
2. The *Fugitive Slave Law,* passed by the United States Congress in 1850 permitted the re-capture and return of runaway slaves to their owners.

Chapter Thirteen

COMMUNITY MOTHERING

THE RELATIONSHIP BETWEEN MOTHERING AND

THE COMMUNITY WORK OF BLACK WOMEN

Arlene E. Edwards

The role of black women in American society is said to be unique (Grant, 1989; Collins, 1993; Omolade, 1994), in that the institution of slavery rendered the gender of black women almost null and void. Though women, they were treated in the same manner as black male slaves, and different from white women. They were expected to bear the burdens, the lash, and children for their respective masters (Omolade, 1994). The ability to perform these feats left the black woman at a disadvantage for the protection of her virtue as a woman (Gilkes, 1985; Collins 1991a, 1991b), while also continuing her historical role in her community as keeper of culture and preserver of traditions (Payne, 1989; Reagon, 1990).

The historical role played by women in African communities has had the concept of mothering as central to its practice (Collins, 1987). Motherhood in this setting was different from the norm, which was defined by dependence on men, and on separation from the community through functioning in the home. Greene states that "the role of mother itself is an important one for many black women and is accompanied by tasks not required of their white counterparts" (1990: 208). According to Orleck, the accepted, though inaccurate, definition of motherhood is one of women who are "apolitical, isolated with their children in a world of pure emotion, far removed from the welter of politics and social struggle" (1997: 3). Reagon defines mothering as "the holding of life before birth, the caring for and feeding of the young until they assume independence" (1990: 177). Collins (1987) in her reference the reassessment of Afro-American motherhood cites the work of Dill (1980), who in her study of black domestics, made note of the strategies they used to ensure that their children would succeed. Gilkes (1980) is also cited, based on what Collins termed "the power of Black motherhood." Gilkes observed that many of the black female political activists had become involved in politics as a result of their earlier agitation on behalf of the children of their community. Effective black mothers were said to be the ones who are "sophisticated mediators between the competing offerings of an oppressive dominant culture and a nurturing Black value-structure" (Hall, 1980).

Reagon relates that the practice of this type of mothering is a clear choice: "a woman must come to terms with herself, her life, her sanity, and her health as well as with the health of life around her" (1987: 178). She asserts that this type of mothering is not based solely on biological reproduction, and meshes with scholarly and other professions. Clark-Hine (1986) supports this assertion in her work documenting the roles black women played in the struggles for freedom, woman's suffrage, and education for girls, among other things. The teaching profession was seen not only as laudable for black women during the late 1800s and early 1900s (Harley, 1982), but also substantiates the professional, scholarly mode of mothering presented by Reagon. The roles community and church mothers played may be due to: (1) recognition of familial influences on social functioning; (2) the tradition of female leadership in Black society; and (3) the fact that these women served as bridges between the worlds of men and women (Gilkes, 1986). The title of "mother" was often conferred on these older women who were seen to possess wisdom and experience tailored to their communities' needs in particular, and to the needs of the race in general.

Black women's mothering experiences: Othermothers

James (1993) defines othermothering as acceptance of responsibility for a child not one's own, in an arrangement that may or may not be formal. She states that this practice stemmed from the West African practice of communal lifestyles and the interdependence of communities. The experience of slavery saw the translation of othermothering to new settings, since the care of children was an expected task of enslaved black women in addition to the field or house duties. James states that the familial instability of slavery engendered the adaptation of communality in the form of fostering children whose parents, particularly mothers, had been sold. This tradition of communality, gave rise to the practice of othermothering. The survival of the concept is inherent to the survival of black people as a whole (Jones, 1984), since it allowed for the provision of care to extended family and nonblood relations. James also views the concept as forming a link toward developing new social transformation models that are black and feminist.

Community mothers

The role of community mothers often evolved from that of being an othermother (Gilkes, 1983; Collins, 1993; Reagon, 1990). In reporting on black community workers, Gilkes found that these women often "viewed the black community as a group of relatives and other friends whose interest should be advanced, and promoted at all times, under all conditions, and by almost any means" (1983: 117). Her subjects were all middle class professional women who possessed a sense of "nation consciousness." The term describes a group of middle class people who, in its political and social agitation, seeks social change by allowing the needs of the black community to influence their individual orientation in educational and employment activities. Gilkes refers to the term "going up for the oppressed" to describe the activities of this group. She defines going up for the oppressed as "a type of economic and career mobility that comprises a set of activities aimed at social change and the empowerment of the powerless" (1983: 119).

Black Clubwomen

Another example of community mothering came in the form of the Club movement by black women. The Club movement stemmed from the arrival of a black middle class—the first collective crop of formally educated black people living in black communities. Education and the social privileges it brought placed this group in positions to appreciate and to achieve the American dream. They were also in the best position, literally and figuratively, to uplift the race.

Formal inception of the Club movement is dated as occurring on July 21, 1896, in Washington, D.C., at the Nineteenth Street Baptist Church (Kendrick, 1954). At this time, the National Association of Colored Women (NACW) came into being as the representation of the collective body of colored women's clubs. Impetus for the formation of the Clubs was also provided by the horrors visited upon the black community through lynching. The protection of white female virtue as a reason for lynching was also attacked, as well as the sexual abuse perpetrated on black women by white men. According to Lerner (1974), this expression provided ideological direction for black women organizing to defend black womanhood as an integral part of defending the race from terror and abuse.

Black Clubwomen were professionals themselves, or married to professional men. In either case, given their status in the community, they possessed access to economic, political, and legal resources necessary to address many community needs. Community mothering was now done in the form of Clubs designed by prominent community women desiring to address the needs most prevalent in their communities. They formed these Clubs and charged themselves dues that were used in turn to implement their programs. Their middle class status was seen as a means to racial uplift and, in line with the motto of the NACW, of "lifting as we climb."

Church mothers and civil rights women

The black church has been described as the only autonomous organization functioning specifically to address the needs of African-Americans (Lincoln and Mamiya, 1990; Morrison, 1991; Marshall, 1970). Women have been the majority of congregants and, consequently, church supporters (Levin and Taylor, 1993). These black church women have contributed their efforts toward community development and maintenance, often without the rewards afforded to men who have done the same (Gilkes, 1975; Grant, 1989). Despite the lack of acknowledgment, they continued in their determination to "uplift the race" through different community-based interventions.

The concept of othermothering giving rise to community mothering also is exemplified in the work of church mothers. These are a particular type of community mothers in that they conducted their work primarily through the church. Use of the church as an organ of intervention was based on their vision of the need for moral mothering of the community (Gilkes, 1985). Club membership was by invitation only, and said invitation was only proffered to professionally trained women (or women married to professionals); therefore, in some regions, the church provided an almost professional means of mothering that could be recognized by the community. Work conducted by church mothers centered on teaching Sunday school, conducting home visits, caring for the sick and missionary work. Often the mission field was their community:

> these women took up membership in church women's groups, female auxiliaries to fraternal orders, and benevolent societies, which often required less affluent lifestyles, less active public roles, and had more practical benefits for their members than did predominantly middle-class reform associations. (Harley, 1982: 260)

Though the women were not perceived as leaders, they nevertheless formulated strategies and tactics to mobilize community resources for their collective actions (Barnett, 1993). In examining the experience of power wielded by church women in the African Methodist Episcopol (AME) church, Dodson (1988) suggested the concept of surrogate leadership. Women of this church possessed the numbers, organizing talents, and resources that are prerequisites for participation in power relationships. As a result they were able to exercise influence on church policy to a certain degree.

The civil rights movement is said to have been precipitated by the expansion of the community roles of Black church women in responding to needs in their community (Burks, 1990). Prominent women in this movement, such as Ella Baker, Fannie Lou Hamer, and Rosa Parks, relate the influence of older female family members whose Club or church work served as examples that they followed in their own work. Ella Baker is said to have reported seeing her mother caring for the sick and needy in her community, and being someone to whom people went to for advice (Payne, 1989). These were women who came up in the church, were schooled on their role of racial uplift, being "race women," and who also believed in the strength of their religious faith to pull them through their trials.

Work for community improvements was a continuation of black women's work as leaders in the struggle for freedom, education, and self improvement (Cantarow, 1980). Payne (1989), in his tribute to Ella Baker, states that she worked for social change by building organizations while encouraging the growth and empowerment of individuals. Baker was the first full time director of the Southern Leadership Christian Conference (SLCC) and was considered the mother of its activist phase. She was instrumental in the formation of the Student Non-violent Co-ordinating Committee (SNCC) as a separate organization, and an advisor to Martin Luther King, Jr.

Church women who participated in the movement were sometimes influenced by other women who worked primarily in the community. Annie Bell, Robinson Devine, and Unita Blackwell both indicate having a spiritual purpose in persevering through their work as civil rights workers. Crawford (1993) traces resistance strategies used by these women activists to three factors. First, their inherited spirituality and early church upbringing, which assisted them in facing the rigors of activism; second, exposure to older community women who served as role models; and third, a level of individual autonomy which allowed them to be willing to challenge the status quo.

The examples presented indicate the roles played by the black church and community women. The expected courtesy based on their contributions should have been acceptance into leadership positions, since their support has been intrinsic to the survival and functioning of the black community. Black women working for their communities have beliefs such as going up for the oppressed (Gilkes, 1983), lifting as we climb (Peebles-Wilkins, 1989; Shaw, 1991), the knowledge that ignorance of needs observed could affect the survival of the community (Reagon, 1990), and an inborn heritage of mothering and nurturing the community (James, 1993). According to Clark-Hine,

> The creation of educational, health care, and recreational institutions spearheaded by diverse black women's clubs and voluntary organizations followed no standard pattern. Rather, women launched new projects or worked to transform existing institutions into structures more adequately designed to address the needs of their respective constituencies. Recurring concerns were for education for the young, food, shelter, and clothing for the aged, medical and nursing care for the sick. (1986: 238)

Method

Reagon (1990) suggests that mothering may be used as a source for data categorization, and as a method of data analysis in acquiring a historical picture of the black community's method of evolving and surviving. Of this she states,

> using mothering as a data category affords the researcher the potential of examining mothering in its ideal from, where each generation is born into a situation that is very healthy and affirming for them ....When applied to the examination and analysis of cultural data, it can reveal much within the historical picture of how a culture evolves and how and why changes occur in order to maintain the existence of a people. (1990: 177)

James (1993) provides three reasons for the usefulness of an understanding of the roles of othermothers that gives shape to rationale and to the purpose of this study. First, understanding the roles will address feelings of importance by indicating historical ways in which Black women empowered themselves. Second, understanding allows for reconceptualization of power as a means toward action rather than a commodity. Third, the talents exhibited in analyzing and critiquing situations and developing workable strategies may be viewed as possible resources for addressing contemporary community needs. Given these premises, the study investigated the concept of mothering as it relates to the community work experience of black women, through use of phenomenological research methods.

Qualitative research methods such as interviews and observation were used to collect and analyze the data. It is a useful method in this instance because it is inductive, and aims to gain valid knowledge and understanding by representing and illuminating the how and the why of people's experiences. Aspects of qualitative research, such as unstructured interviewing and observation, were used to produce data supportive of the mothering experiences of the women. Nine women who work in black communities and churches participated in the study. Both groups of women were chosen based on their involvement in community work, and because they were at least at the ages at which the title of "mother" is conferred. They ranged in age from forty-three to eighty-four years old. Except for those used to gather demographic information, questions asked were open ended. A total of twenty-one questions were used to investigate the concept of mothering in the community work of the women who were chosen. Constant comparison (Glaser and Strauss, 1967) was used to analyze the findings.

Results

Eight themes and subthemes emerged for the data. For this paper, mothering (theme) and work, choice and need (subthemes), are discussed. Though the theme of mothering was later allowed to emerge, its presence was assumed prior to the beginning of the study. The others emerged in true qualitative style. The women participating in the study are presented (using their initials) along with excerpts of their statements as they relate to the themes being discussed.

Community women reported holding positions on the Parent Teacher's Association (PTA), designing and implementing programs, volunteering in community organizations, and sitting on local community boards. Settings in which the church women worked often included different church organizations and community boards designed to assist church members or to provide services to the community.

Few differences were found between the two groups of women in this study and the work they did, or the methods they used. Church women tended to work primarily with older adults in the community through visitations, and providing comfort and counsel. Community women, on the other hand, worked primarily with children, and to a lesser extent, with adults. There were church women who also worked with children, and there were community women who worked with adults. All the church women provided assistance in the community as well as the church. One community woman reported working in the church in addition to community work, while the other three did not report church activity.

Another small difference was means of involvement. While church women more readily reported being asked, or being chosen to do community work, community women usually reported responding to needs they observed. This difference seems to be in keeping with the settings in which the women function most intimately. Church mothers, for example, are in more of a position to be approached by someone in the church or surrounding community because of familiarity and consistent contact. A community woman on the other hand would be more likely to respond to a need she observed in her child's school or community rather than being asked to do so, partly because of a lack of this type of familiarity.

Both groups of women reported using innovative means to conduct their work. For example, one church woman reported her work in the Progressive Committee, raising funds for scholarships, or for the purchase of a sign for the front of the church. The money is raised through whatever means are deemed best, and that will result in the most funds. Community women reported determining the existence of needs through observation, but then meeting them through coalition building and protest or support of each other.

The following excerpts are some of the ways these women express their community mothering. NJ and LM responded to being asked to define community mothers, and whether they believed the description could apply to them, the other excerpts occurred spontaneously:

NJ: I consider myself to be a neighborhood mother, because whatever neighborhood I live in I automatically get to know all the children around, and my house becomes the Kool-Aid house. *I immediately adopt all the children in the neighborhood.*

LM: Um, a community mother would make sure that if you see a child walking up and down the street and the child does not look like he or she belongs on the street they would at least say: *"Baby where you going," not that it could be any of my business.*

KW: Um, I don't know why they do that, you know some people I didn't know they, um, I mentioned this the other day, *they will mention things to me that they won't mention to somebody else.* You know like a member could come and say "hi sister so and so how you doing today," and they may say "I'm all right" "you need anything" "no". But then I could call, I don't know why its like that and they'd like say "I do need so and so and so, if you don't mind, or if you have time." But I don't know why. You know I don't know why. But that happens.

HR: So I'm very close to the *family and you know they consider me more or less as their mother.* And its quite interesting that my neighbor on this side often says, "I want to be just like you when I grow up." And my other neighbor that owns the house on the other side she's moved out and she uses that same term, terminology.

TA: Because these are children who walk up to me and hug me, *and I fuss at them, I yell at them, I scream at them "why are you doing that, don't you know better, why did you say that word."*

TA: *But on Mother's day all of them chipped in and got me the film* Sankofa. And they got me a card saying if we had a mother to choose it would be you. And so to me that was much more prestigious than any award anyone could give me, or recognize.

This type of behavior resembles mothering because it is spontaneous, nurturing, supportive, and it is accomplished in a familiar way. For example, church mothers are older, respected members of the congregation, who are also familiar with church members. These women could enquire as to the whereabouts of absent members without seeming intrusive. Based on the response to their inquiry, a plan could be developed to meet any needs arising from the reason for the absence.

In both groups, the spontaneous choice and subsequent helping behavior is reminiscent of mothering. Though this may resemble the simple act of volunteering, it is not, since once the need was recognized, the woman usually had to devise a way in which to meet the need (Collins, 1991a). Statements describing this subtheme include:

HR: She has a roomer but the roomer works all the time. *And so that's my individual project in the neighborhood to take care of that one.*

TA: And some people may say it's selfish but I think everyone must listen to what their calling is and I don't think that my purpose is to sit in meetings. *My purpose is to talk and tell the story and uh, and get as many people to listen, both white and black.*

SG: *Because there are lots of young people in our community as well as our church that needs some activities as well as things to do.*

LM: *I started out as a tutor because there was a definite need.*

HR: *And also during the period of time that I worked there I had to apply for a notary seal. So I would be able to notarize different documents* and my notary is still active and *I have community members that often calls upon me to notarize different things for them.*

UR: I was interested in what they were doing *and I just decided that whatever I could do to help.*

KW: I feel a lot of times our service means a lot more to people than money, than going in to give them a donation of flowers.

SG: And I'm the type of person would work anywhere I'm needed not just no special place.

These excerpts are similar to the points made by Gilkes (1975, 1983, 1985), Reagon (1990), and James (1993) regarding the types of behaviors community mothers and othermothers engage in as they perform mothering activities. Reagon's (1990) reference to othermothers as culture keepers, and James' reference to them as being central to the community is signified in the behavior of these women in responding to recognized needs without being asked, or being asked with the confidence that the request would be honored. Based on the way the church women reported being chosen, it seems there is an expectation of being mothered or handled in a motherly manner on the part of the recipient. For example, congregants in the experiences related by KW (members bypassing other women and seeking her out to ask for assistance) and HR (members telling her they just felt she could help them). In these instances, the recipient believes that the women are capable of providing the service before they make the request. TA and LM, who are community women, report mothering behavior in their administration of community work. As the following excerpts indicate, the women have particular methods of doing community work, and often their community work in method and implementation includes motherly behavior, or a motherly frame of reference. This behavior and the accompanying expectation may be seen as an example of how these women use strategies that are not only innovative but also motherly when doing community work. For example,

> LM: *I think that's a role they see me in.* Because they know that if they do something wrong and I catch them *I will get on the phone and call their mother. And I think the children understand that it's not snitching on them, it's caring.* If I see a child crying in the hallway for no reason, I will come home that night and call the mother *and I'll say "you know I saw so and so crying in the hall and I couldn't find out why, and it was just too early in the morning, and no one could find out why and I just want to let you know so you can find out what happened."*
>
> And our children don't feel protected. *And they see me outside the school building and I'll break up a fight. And I'm not scared of them.* And that's another thing, it's too many of us adults are scared of children. The children know I'm not scared of them, and I think they appreciate that. So, um ... I think they see me as more than just my daughter's mother. I think my daughter gets jealous sometimes, *but I think they see me as more than just my daughter's mother. By how they respond to me.*
>
> SG: And so anyway after they all went back in and I went upstairs and I come back down she said ... and she was standing there laughing. And I said ... "what are you laughing about?" And she said "I'm laughing because of what the kids [said] when they saw you come out they said 'here come the principal'". I said "the principal? I'm not the principal." I said "that's bad." She said "no, no, no, no it's good." She said "they respect you enough to know that when you come out you want them to go back in, you know you don't have to say anything they know if you want them, in other words they're not supposed to be out here congregating in the hall."

Discussion

Mothering emerged in review of the literature and provided a framework to investigate the underlying, motivating factor for black women doing community work. Therefore mothering was studied as a phenomenon intrinsic to the work. As suggested by Gilkes (1983) and Omolade (1994), open-ended questions were used to allow the uniqueness of these black women and their community work experiences to be reported accurately. Dickson (1987) and Murray (1987) also suggest caution in researching predominantly ignored populations such as women.

Mothering was an expected theme in doing this study. Statements were made that both directly and indirectly described the concept. Direct mothering may be seen when the community or church woman attempted to influence another, for example; scolding a child, providing some type of service that is nurturing, or satisfying a need. Indirect mothering may be seen through the responses of others to the presence of the woman, or her assumed presence, or expectations tied to her presence without her direct input. Examples include others changing their behavior due to the woman's presence or knowledge that she is approaching, and continuing behaviors she had suggested without the woman being present to reinforce the behavior.

Mothering is present in the reasons given for choosing to do community work. Reagon (1990) and Collins (1987) report on othermothers who wielded influence by the knowledge of their presence as well as their actual work. These women served as role models for young black women by behaving in a manner that was often entirely different from what society prescribed for women in general, and black women in particular. One participant (TA) stated that her role in providing an "unconventional" example for her daughters and their friends. Gilkes (1985) provides examples of the legacy of community work done by mothers of the Sanctified church, and Grant (1989) supports this indirect work through her statement about women being the literal and figurative "backbone" of the Black church. According to the literature and statements made by the women in this study, the work was accomplished without expectation of an expression of gratitude.

Though the discovery of mothering was not a goal of this study, it served as a framework to investigate the community work of black women. Its presence in the review of the literature and its influence on the choices of early church, community, and othermothers raised the question of whether mothering continues to influence the community work of contemporary black women. Additionally, its presence in the language of the women in the study solidifies its intrinsic presence as a motivating factor and possible reason for doing community work for contemporary black women.

Chapter Fourteen

"You'll Become a Lioness"

African-American Women Talk About Mothering

Trudelle Thomas

Being a woman is about … having positive, reciprocal relationships with your lover, your husband, your friends, your family. In other words, if you give, you want to get back. I don't believe in unconditional love.
— Camilla Cosby, quoted in interview in
O: The Oprah magazine (May 2000: 307)

Not long ago, I found myself interviewing a young African-American mother. "I wish I could tell young girls that when they have a baby, they will change …. You'll become a lioness. You'll protect this baby!" Kennedy went on to describe with calm conviction the ways her ambitions and confidence and resolve had grown stronger since her son's birth five years earlier.

Indeed, Kennedy's comments were typical of the African-American mothers that I interviewed. These women articulated a model of contemporary motherhood that is pro-active, pragmatic, and multi-faceted. This "lioness" model undercuts the mainstream "Giving Tree" approach to motherhood which dominates Euro-American thinking. I believe the insights of these African-American women can help all mothers—Euro-American and African-American alike—who are searching for new metaphors for motherhood in this post-industrial age. Because of its theological/pastoral slant, the following essay will be of special interest to those in positions of leadership in Christian churches and other institutions whose membership includes mothers. Those working with mothers in the settings of social agencies or the medical world will find valuable insights.

This essay summarizes a series of interviews carried out in 1999. The interviewees quoted in this essay are all African-American mothers who are currently raising young children. To interpret the interviews, I draw upon theories of African-American feminists (notably Collins, 1990; Cole, 1993) and also upon Euro-American scholars, including theologians.

In the course of my interviews four themes emerged, which I will examine in greater detail below, quoting from the interviewees themselves: (1) these women speak candidly of the complexity of mothering—the joys as well as the fears, struggles, and injustices; (2) these mothers are determined to set an example for their children which combines both the virtues of achievement and the virtues of nurturing (they assume that they will work outside the home, and that they will strive for upward mobility, as a way to promote their children's well-being); (3) for these women, motherhood has fostered an expanded sense of self and a deeper spirituality, even when such spirituality is not well supported by organized religion; and (4) these women shed light on the practical and spiritual needs of mothers, needs that could (and should) be addressed by Christian churches and other religious institutions.

The interviews

This essay focuses upon six interviews with African-American women. These six interviews were part of a larger study that included open-ended interviews with twenty-five individual women (all living in the U.S., of various ethnic backgrounds but predominantly Euro-American), during which each woman talked about her experiences as a mother in relation to her own spiritual development.

Of this smaller group (i.e., the African-Americans), all were mothers of one or two children ranging in age from two to twelve. The women's ages ranged from twenty-three to forty-seven. All were relatively well-educated; one was working on a B.A., while all the others had completed college degrees, and two had masters' degrees as well. Two of the women were married, one was divorced, and three had never married. All came from married, two-parent homes. Finally, all were affiliated with different Protestant (Christian) denominations ranging from Pentecostal to Baptist to Episcopal.

The six African-American voices provided a striking counterpoint to the Euro-American mothers I interviewed. What distinguished them was the dramatic way they diverged from the conventional rhetoric of self-sacrifice that ran through the other interviews. Most of the Euro-American women accepted a line of thinking that ran something like this: "When I became a mother, I learned how to sacrifice so that I could become a good mother. I learned to put myself on hold for the good of my children." Another spiritualized this sacrificial ideal: "As a mother, you just keep giving and giving—even when you think you have nothing left to give .... It's like Jesus says—'Unless a seed falls into the ground and dies, it cannot create new life.' As a mother, I must 'die to myself.'"

I was surprised that despite many decades of consciousness-raising in the United States, many mothers, even those who are sophisticated, progressive, and feminist in other ways, do not challenge the assumption that motherhood is founded on endless self-sacrifice. Others (such as Miller-McLemore) have referred to this as the "Giving Tree" approach to maternity (1994: 185).

The term "Giving Tree" refers to a very popular children's book by Shel Silverstein (1964) that portrays the generosity of an apple tree (not surprisingly portrayed as female) toward a little boy who grows into a self-seeking and exploitative man. Early on, the boy and tree have an intimate and joyful mutual relationship, but as the boy grows up he takes the tree's apples, then her branches, and finally her trunk (which he makes into a boat). When the tree has nothing else to give, the boy returns as a tired old man and sits on her stump, and "the tree was happy," having given everything with no thought of return. This heinous little tale is widely read as an example of altruistic love.

In contrast, Kennedy and the other African-American women I interviewed endorsed a model of motherhood that is like a Lioness rather than a Giving Tree (or stump). My interview sample is small (six interviews) so it is, of course, impossible to generalize about all African-American mothers based upon them. Still, the interviewees' positive self-definitions provide insight into contemporary American experiences of motherhood. Because religious faith has been an important source and strength and hope for many African-Americans, I give special attention to the things my interviewees say about what they need from their churches and other religious institutions.

Speaking candidly of the complexity of mothering

The women I interviewed all spoke with passion about the joyful aspects of motherhood. Compared to the Euro-American women I interviewed, these African-American were much more ebullient in describing the joy their children had brought them. For all of them, new motherhood had occurred in less than ideal circumstances, and it had brought unexpected challenges. Yet they all spoke with great vigor of their love for their children and the pleasure their children had brought them. For example, Anita was twenty-four and engaged to be married when she became pregnant. For several months, she wrestled with whether to continue the pregnancy. In the face of her misgivings, a difficult pregnancy, and a complicated birth, Anita was surprised by the pleasure she experienced once her son was born.

> When I finally held my baby and nursed him, I was in tears—I was so relieved and happy! I was so glad I made that decision! I was *so happy!* John [my fiancé] said, "I told you so. I told you [that] you would be happy." And my baby [now age five] has been my *sunshine* since birth. [emphasis hers]

Another woman, Gail, was thirty-five when she adopted an infant after many years of infertility treatment. Like Anita, she is surprised by joy:

> I was *thrilled*. I was so ready for a baby. All of a sudden, all the anguish and tears of not being able to conceive, wanting a child—it was all gone. I lost about fifteen pounds because I dropped all that weight of depression. I'd been carrying that burden of grief for seven years! [Bonding with my daughter] was a *magical process*. She put a new level of joy in my life that I did not know existed.

Certainly, women have been speaking of the joys of motherhood throughout time, but still I was surprised by how strongly these women emphasized this aspect. Their comments seem to reinforce Patricia Hill Collins' assertions that motherhood is a source of growth and hope in the African-American community, as well as a source of status and power (1990: 115). Compared to the Euro-American women I interviewed, these African-American women spoke more freely, perhaps because they are part of a community that assigns a greater value to motherhood.

Nonetheless, these mothers took a very pragmatic view of motherhood, speaking candidly of the sorrows and costs brought about by raising children. They are very aware of the physical challenges of pregnancy and birth, and also of the enormity of their task of raising children in a hostile environment.

Anthropologist Kathryn March makes an important point when she observes that, in mainstream U.S. culture, we promote an unbalanced view of maternity. "[W]e surround ourselves with a discourse of joy, ... deceived by our shared faith that chosen childbearing is always happy" (1994: 148). March studied women in Nepal who "publicly bewail infertility, repeat miscarriages, hard births, and deaths in [i.e., during] and near birth" (1994: 150). She found that Nepalese women "talk about loss and fear in mothering frankly and openly ... they are part of mothers' talk" (1994: 152–153).

Similarly, the African-American women I interviewed spoke frankly about fear and difficulty, even as they spoke about maternal pleasures. They all struck me as remarkably pragmatic and tough-minded in their ready assumption that the world is a foreboding and dangerous place for children and mothers. Like the Nepalese women, they were blunt regarding the difficulties of pregnancy and birth, and they were candid about the long-term challenges of childrearing. Anita puts it this way:

> I'm raising a 1990s child. Things are happening with black males now— to children now—that didn't happen when I was growing up. I have to worry about things my mother didn't worry about—I worry about my

son being molested. The black community has to work together to raise our children. We can't expect anyone else to look out for them.

On a similar note, Marcia is trying to teach her eighteen-month-old daughter to toughen up:

When she's doing something wrong and she gets hurt, I don't come running. She needs to learn how to behave …. I want to be a "hands-off mother"— to stand back—lay down the law. As a single parent, I have to lay down the rules. I've seen doting ruin children, so I'm not going to dote.

Another woman, Nina, prepares her children for challenges by strengthening their moral characters:

We've tried to bring [our children] up the right way—morally—and teach them what's right—even though it's not what they will experience or what peer pressure is. We tried very very hard [to prepare ourselves] before becoming parents. I thought to myself, "I'm gonna make sure my child does this and this and this and this, and this is the way I'm gonna build this child up."

Anita is trying to instill a deep religious faith in her son, to help him in the face of injustices or dangers:

I'm trying to teach him that you have to believe that God is going to bring you through any situation, through all the storms. Your faith *will be tested*. There will be obstacles put in your way. You have to rely on God to bring you through the storm. [emphasis hers]

While some of the women were more explicit than others in talking about racial injustice, all were sure that there would be "storms" in their children's futures, and that their task as mothers included "building [their children] up."

Moreover, the women I interviewed saw childrearing from the outset as solitary and difficult. Kennedy, for example, talks about the loneliness of early motherhood:

No one told me how difficult it would be …. I was by myself. [My first day home from the hospital] my husband had a houseful of people wanting to see the baby. They weren't any help. I remember nursing [my son] in my room and crying and wondering when all those people would leave.

Why couldn't they bring a covered dish or [greeting] card and *leave*? They didn't help at all.

Another woman, originally from Africa (Sierra Leone), comments on how lonely she finds childrearing in the U.S.:

[Our isolation] hits me whenever I have to fill out any forms for my kids—who should we contact in case of emergency? That particular line is always blank for us, because [my husband and I] have nobody here. It's a big struggle for us.

She poignantly compares her own experience with the treatment of mothers and children "back home" in Africa:

[Back home] when you become a new mother, you don't even cook for a long time. You just sit and take care of the baby—you don't even have to get up …. Everyone is at your beck and call. You don't even have to ask. People just stream to your house and do everything for the baby. They send food. [An older woman] will take charge of your baby and come every morning and wash the baby's hair, bathe the baby, do everything for you …. At home the family is very important, but here [U.S.] people don't tolerate the kids. They invite you but they don't want the kids …. *Some people don't even want kids in their houses.* They will have an animal and *prefer that animal* in their house to having a child …. [emphasis hers]

All the women had received practical support in early motherhood from their own mothers; two said that their mothers came to stay for several weeks post-partum, and another (the only one who lived in the same city as her own mother) reported that her mother helped with child care while she worked.

Still, of all the women I interviewed, only one (the oldest of the group at age forty-seven) described a dense network of family and friends. All the others felt that the task of childrearing rested upon her shoulders alone, or upon hers and her husband's. This sense of isolation challenges Collins' 1990 assertion that black mothers mother within a context of women-centered networks that support biological mothers. In fact, all the women I interviewed expressed a strong commitment to their extended families, especially their parents. Yet, often family loyalty meant more responsibility, not necessarily more support. Kennedy repeats a common theme:

When [my son] was about three, I went home to take care of my mother [who was dying of cancer]. I'd take her to chemo, talk to the doctor ….

Taking care of my mother ruined my marriage—my husband felt so neglected that he had an affair.

Several of the women were aware that daughterly caregiving had caused them to neglect other relationships, including spouse and children. Career advancement had also been affected. Some of the women mentioned that such caregiving was distributed unevenly within families. Sons, even much-favored sons, did not exhibit the same filial devotion as daughters. Marcia comments on gender roles within her family:

In my family, the brothers were cherished but not the girls. Myself, I wasn't mothered well. Most black women will tell you that their brothers got better treatment, and so do their brothers' kids .... And not much is expected from them.

It is only fair to point out that even though these women experienced limited practical support, most reported a strong sense of emotional support from their families. In the face of practical needs (including financial, child-care, health care, housing, etc.), most women felt they were on their own. Still, all said they felt very emotionally connected to family and friends. Anita, for example, lived at a distance from her family during her pregnancy, yet she reported that her mother and several sisters each traveled 600 miles to spend time with her. Marcia said that she had several friends who were away at school yet kept in touch with her, and Nina [the woman originally from Sierra Leone] maintained ties with extended family throughout the U.S. and overseas by means of letters and family reunions.

For most of these women, a loss of practical support was a trade-off caused by upward mobility. All had moved geographically once or more for college or employment. Most would envy the situation described by the woman from Africa, who recalls, "Back home, there are always lots of relatives around. There is family right through your life. If you have problems in your marriage or with your kids, there is help. There is always someone to watch your child. You are never all alone." Perhaps the sense of isolation was a factor of age; most of the women were still completing their education or launching careers. Perhaps as they get older they will be able to tap into a network of support such as Collins described. It is unfortunate that for these women, as for most mothers in the U.S., the intense demands of early parenting coincide in time with the geographic mobility often required to advance their education and careers.

In summary, the women I interviewed expressed a thoughtful and complex view of mothering. While they were in touch with the profound joys of motherhood, they were also aware of racial injustice, fears for their children, inequities within their extended families, and social isolation. The word that came up over and over again was responsibility. All these African-American women were emphatic about the colossal sense of responsibility that came with children, much more emphatic than the Euro-American women I interviewed. I found myself wondering if this were a response against the internalized image of the Welfare Mother that Collins wrote about as a false and destructive stereotype. All were determined never to become dependent in such a way; rather, they had definite ideas about creating a better life for themselves and their children.

Setting an example for their children

The women I interviewed all speak of motherhood in terms that challenge the mainstream United States culture. Theologian Teresa E. Snorton points out that the "cult of true womanhood" has shaped how we think of family life in the U.S., yet that "cult" is Euro-centric, in direct contrast to the African-American understanding of womanhood. "The [so-called] true woman is self-contained within her nuclear family, with specific and separate roles for men and women, and with an economic dependence on men, in such a way that motherhood is one's true occupation" (1996: 57). Psychoanalyst Roszika Parker describes the ideology surrounding motherhood in slightly different terms,

> Despite changing beliefs about babies' capacities and thus childcare priorities, the representation of ideal motherhood is still almost exclusively made up of self-abnegation, unstinting love, intuitive knowledge of nurturance, and unalloyed pleasure in children. (1995: 22)

Such narrow views of motherhood may have little to do with contemporary reality, especially for the vast majority of African-American women. Snorton observes, "Flexible sex roles, outside-the-home employment, and a responsibility to and for one's extended family are certainties and necessities for most African-American women" (1996: 57). Hence motherhood as one's "true [and only] occupation" is a view that few African-American women have wanted to adopt. In prizing motherhood, rather, they have adopted healthy attributes that include self-sufficiency, independence, personal accomplishment, alongside the capacity for nurturing and caring (Cole, 1993: 71).

The women that I interviewed spoke with pride of their capacities to bring such a range of attributes to their mothering. Specifically, they spoke of being an example to their children, providing a strong foundation, and passing on a deep religious faith. Kennedy, for example, speaks of her new self-confidence:

> It used to be, my self-esteem was flat line …. Now I take a stand. I'm involved with my son's school—I have to protect him! … My [six-year-old] son sees me study. He'll lay on the bed beside me when I'm studying,

and I'll say, "When it's your time to go [to college], maybe you'll appreciate it .... My being in school is gonna do you a world of good!" I can't let myself feel guilty. I'm making a better life for us! ... I wish I could tell young girls that when they have a baby, they will change. You may be a passive wimp, but you'll become a lioness. You'll protect this baby!

On a similar note, Marcia felt that her first pregnancy helped her develop virtues that lay the groundwork for the coming years:

> The process of carrying [my child in the womb] was a spiritual experience. You have to reach in *every* day and find the strength to move forward. You gotta find a spiritual force to *get up* .... Through my pregnancy, I learned to lean on God, because I [as an unmarried mother with little support] was the one with complete responsibility .... To me, God is a force, a spirit that helps you in hard times. I'm learning to be independent, self-sufficient—you have to!

While some might think that "leaning on God" is incompatible with being "independent, self-sufficient," Marcia's experience suggests otherwise. Anita also links personal strength and determination with religious faith, and she sees all these as important traits to impress on her five-year-old son:

> After I finish my master's [degree], I really want to get a PhD. I want [my son] to see that learning is cool, that great things happen to people who go to college. But it's not enough for him to see "My mother goes to work and she brings home a paycheck and she goes to school and she's really smart"—he also needs to see my relationship with God. I am driven to be closer to God because I need to be an example to my son. He needs that spiritual foundation too! I want him to know that *if you believe in God and have faith, good things will happen.* That's what my life has been based upon. [emphasis hers]

According to Snorton, surrender to God is an essential way of coping for African-American women: "The womanist shifts her focus from the finitude of life to the transcendent nature of the human experience. This is not a 'pie in the sky,' [or] 'otherworldly' attitude but rather a survivalist stance" (1996: 57).

The women I interviewed embody a wide range of healthy attributes. On the one hand, they carry out the traditionally feminine tasks of nurturing, protecting, and training children, but they bring to those tasks many traits often considered masculine, including strength, determination, self-sufficiency, courage, and industry.[1] Other abilities that the women spoke of were the ability to juggle competing responsibilities, to cultivate serenity in the midst of difficulty, and to play and enjoy life. Many expressed appreciation toward their children for teaching them these latter traits.

Cole points out that strong African-American women have often unfairly been made to feel defensive or guilty for their strength (1993: 71). A more appropriate description comes from spiritual writer Edith Stein (1891–1942). A Carmelite nun writing in the 1940s, Stein is an unlikely spokesperson for contemporary African-American mothers, yet her comments fit the African-American women I interviewed:

> Christ embodies the ideal of human perfection: in Him all bias and defects are removed, and the masculine and feminine virtues are united and their weaknesses redeemed. That is why we see in holy men a womanly tenderness .... while in holy women there is a manly boldness, proficiency, and determination. (Stein, 1996: 84)

An expanded sense of self and a deeper spirituality

The strong emphasis on spirituality surprised me, in light of the fact that my interviewees all reported strained or disappointing relationships with organized religion. All were affiliated with Protestant Christian churches, yet none expressed satisfaction with them, and most felt that becoming a mother had alienated them from their churches. For example, Anita, the daughter of a minister, felt hurt by her church:

> My church said, "You're a disgrace for having a child outside wedlock ...." I say, "You don't pay my bills—*I don't need you* —what right do you have to judge me?" But deep down it hurt me. I couldn't bring myself to go to church or read the Bible for four years.

All had experienced difficulty finding a church where they felt at home. One felt uncomfortable with the formality of her husband's Episcopal church, others found their churches to be unfriendly or too large, and some felt their churches did not provide enough attention to their children.

Yet, in spite of this alienation from religious institutions, all the women expressed belief in God as a source of comfort, guidance, and strength. One woman asked to be baptized during her first pregnancy, and all felt it was important to raise their children as part of a religious tradition. And all the women I interviewed spoke of a deepening spirituality. Anita, for example, speaks vividly about her prayer life:

> With a newborn son, I prayed more than I had ever prayed before. My labor had slowed down, so on the delivery table I prayed and cried and

prayed—"God please let me push this baby through the birth canal!" God helped me give birth. Once I had [my son], I was so scared! I had never held a baby before. I said, "God, you have got to walk me through this process. Give me the knowledge and strength to take care of my son." He helped me. When he cried, I would sing, "Yes, Jesus loves me." That would soothe him and soothe me too—because I knew Jesus does love me.

Gail also spoke about praying in an unconventional way:

I love walking in the morning when it's quiet—that's my serenity. I don't need organized religion .... I have this keen sense of another world. I'm raising a child, and I recently helped my mother die [by caring for her during her last months] and then my father .... All these things have made me grow spiritually .... Some new things are opening up in my life [and] when it's time, that door will open and I'll go through it .... I'll be ready for it, and that's what I want to teach my daughter. *To be ready.* To be ready. [emphasis hers]

As the women spoke of spirituality, I was struck by the absence of an emphasis on self-sacrifice. According to theologian Brita Gill-Austern, Christians have historically been shaped by a theological tradition that views self-denial and self-sacrifice as the defining attributes of Christian love (1996: 308). Gill-Austern observes that for most women "the unholy trinity of self-abnegation, self-doubt, and false guilt [are] always knocking at the door" causing them to feel they are less important, less valuable, and less essential than men (1996: 307). If self-sacrifice is held up as an ideal for Euro-American Christians, it is held up all the more highly for those within such traditions who are mothers.

The women I interviewed were aware of the ideal of self-sacrifice with its attendant false guilt and self-doubt, yet they do not embrace that "unholy trinity"; it is as if self-abnegation, self-doubt, and false guilt are intruders they cannot afford to admit. Several expressed ambivalence about having to leave a young child in child-care, for example, or sorrow about having to work or study long hours, but they did not speak in terms of feeling guilty. Gail was typical:

When I went back to work, I missed her terribly—it was physically painful. I hated it. Then you know you adjust and that was just reality. I come from a household where my mother always worked. That's a reality. Black women are used to two income households because financially most households needed two incomes in order to survive.

Moreover, although all the interviewees were making personal sacrifices to ensure a better life for themselves and their children, no one sentimentalized or idealized sacrifice as a desirable ideal. Rather than saying "I will imitate Christ by suffering and sacrificing," these women seem to say, "I want my kids to have a better life. I will do what it takes to make that happen, and God will give me strength" (Gill-Austern, 1996: 309). Gill-Austern sees the Christian ideal of love as self-sacrifice as inherently misguided. She writes,

> Jesus' teaching was simply not disinterested or devoid of all self-concern. He wanted to show others how their life might be enhanced if they followed in his way. His way entailed suffering and required sacrifice but its promise, its ultimate destination, was abundant life and joy. (1996: 309)

Gill-Austern's emphasis on "abundant life and joy" resonated throughout all my interviews with African-American mothers, much more strongly than those with Euro-American mothers. They had their eyes set on the goal of a better, more abundant life, and were willing to endure what it took to realize that life; they had no need to seek out or idealize self-sacrifice.

Shedding light on the practical and spiritual needs of mothers

Since historically many African-Americans have looked to the church as an important source of community and guidance, I asked each woman what they would like to receive from their churches. In some cases, I prodded them to think about needs that have not been traditionally addressed by churches. Six areas of need emerged that will be of interest to those in leadership in Euro-American churches as well as in African-American churches. Social agencies seeking to support mothers and children would also do well to listen to these themes.

(a) *Practical support and knowledge.* All the women felt a need, especially in very early motherhood (i.e., the first few months), for practical support in the form of child-care, household help, and meals. During this intense period of adjustment, many women felt "spiritual help means practical help." In addition, women commented on the need for information on topics such as breastfeeding, child immunizations, CPR (cardio-pulmonary resuscitation), nutrition, childhood illnesses, and maternal health. Virtually no one felt they had received adequate information about these issues from the medical world, and many expressed the belief that these basic concerns went hand in hand with their desire for spiritual growth; spiritual needs could not be separated from practical health and household-related needs.

(b) *Guidance in prayer*. Women expressed a need to "move to a new level" in terms of their spirituality. Personal prayer and communal prayer both become more important to a woman who is adjusting to new and ongoing motherhood. Anita's example of asking God to help her deliver her baby, and of singing "Jesus Loves Me" to her newborn suggest a few forms such prayer might take. Many women felt that motherhood forced them to grow spiritually, and that personal prayer was an important avenue for such growth. To my surprise, few expressed concern for feminine images of God.

(c) *Intergenerational support for childrearing*. Women expressed a longing for a church as a source of community, especially for their children. My interviewees felt the need and desire for people of a range of ages to help them to "build up" their children spiritually—by loving their children, advising them as mothers, and being role models for children. One woman said that single mothers were often not adequately included in church-communities. Another observed that African-American churches had a huge reserve of competent, wise older women and grandmothers who could be a tremendous resource for young mothers. One woman commented, "Churches could offer parenting classes. There's a wealth of resources in a lot of churches, a wealth of professions—people whose kids are grown, who have raised successful children—they could offer classes out of their experience."

(d) *Good religious education for their children*. These women desire churches where their children are welcomed and receive good instruction. Some expressed impatience with "long, dull religious services" or with "enforced passivity" for children. Some mentioned children's church, a good nursery, and Vacation Bible School as desirable ministries in a church, and said that these were less common now than when they themselves were children.

(e) *Preaching and teaching that reflect their own life experience as growing adults*. These women desire sermons and teaching that focus on growth and hope and "abundant life" rather than on death and self-sacrifice. They would like to hear from the pulpit their experiences as mothers and as people seeking to grow into full personhood. Both strength and vulnerability should be valued for both men and women. Especially, women desire a place where they can express vulnerability and need and yet feel safe and cherished. All the women felt they were growing, and that the church was a place that could help women grow into full personhood.

(f) *An outlet for their talents*. These women were eager to give to a church community as well as receive from it. Many women felt they had untapped gifts. Anita, for example, said, "I would love to teach parenting classes—I would love to take that on. My friends [with new babies] come to me for leadership [because my son is doing so well]." Women want to contribute to their church without emulating "the giving tree model of spirituality," that is, endless self-giving without mutuality (Miller-McLemore, 1994: 185).

Note

1. Philosopher Sara Ruddick (1995) offers a helpful definition by focusing on their work as mothers:

> Mothers are not identified by fixed biological or legal relationships to children but by the work they set out to do .... [M]others are people who see children as "demanding" protection, nurturance, and training; they attempt to respond to children's demands with care and respect rather than indifference or assault. (xi)

Writing fifty years earlier, Stein speaks of mothers' inclination to "cherish, guard, and preserve" (73).

Chapter Fifteen

Reflections on the Mutuality of Mothering

Women, Children, and Othermothering

Njoki Nathani Wane

Your books and pens are the tools of your trade; master them, put them
to good use. They will assist you ... until you find your destiny—a destiny
different from mine. I do not know whether it will be better than mine.
Look at you, you cannot even hold a hoe properly. I do not blame you;
it is rough on hands. Look at my hands; see what years of struggle and
hard work have done to my hands. Touch them! Rough, eee!

> —Recollection of my mother's repeated counsel,
> 1970 (Nathani 1996: 116)

When I was growing up in Kenya, my mother was always the first to rise and the
last to go to bed. By the time the rest of the household was awake, she had been
to the river and back, collected elephant grass from the riverbed for the cows; fed
and milked them; swept the floors; and prepared a breakfast for the family. I
normalized these acts of mother-work and gave little thought to what they meant
to me, my mother, my siblings, and to the community at large. I now look back
and realize that her sacrifices, hard work, and commitment to change enabled
me to be where I am today. It was her advice and refusal to treat girls differently
than boys that instilled an intolerance of sexism in me. My mother's exemplary
mothering practices, passed down to her by her own mother, must be passed
down to my children. In "Passing the torch: A mother and daughter reflect on
their experience across generations," Bernard and Bernard examine how "Black
mothers have historically been charged with the responsibility of providing
education, social and political awareness" (47). As they eloquently state, black
mothers are expected to pass on the torch to "their daughters, who are expected
to become the next generation of mothers, grandmothers, or othermothers, to

guard future generations" (47). As I discuss later in this chapter, othermothers look after children to whom they have no blood relations or legal obligation. There is usually a mutual agreement between mothers, aunts, uncles, or fathers who play the role of othermothers in a given community. A woman elder who mothers both adult and children assumes community mothering on the other hand. She assumes leadership roles and she becomes a consultant for her community.[1]

This chapter is a reflection on mothering. It is based on my Canadian mothering experiences, and on the mothering experiences of the Embu women who participated in my research on the role of women in indigenous forms of food processing technologies. I do not want to essentialize or idealize African motherhood or motherwork. I certainly do acknowledge the difficulties in mothering, especially when practised in the midst of other work, such as school activities, household chores, or farm work. My intention is to illustrate and underscore how women interweave motherhood and other aspects of their lives.

In 1991, after a one-year separation, my three-year-old daughter came to live with me in Toronto. I would have brought her with me at the time of my admission, but there was no vacancy at the university's family housing. Although enrolled as a full-time student at the Ontario Institute for Studies in Education at the University of Toronto, the decision to bring my daughter to Canada as soon as I got an apartment was an easy one. I knew I could organize for babysitting with other mothers in the family residence. Coming from Kenya, a neo-colonial country that was experiencing the effects of structural adjustment policies (SAPs), including substantial cutbacks in the social services, I was more than prepared to mother my child here on a limited student budget. At no time did I imagine that her presence might interfere with my studies. Feminist writers, including Gloria T. Emeagwali (1985), Patricia Stamp (1992), and Vandana Shiva (1990), assert that SAPs[2] reflect patriarchal guidelines and depend on patriarchal social relations at the household, community, national, and global levels to support the entire structural adjustment process. The reduction of government and donor support for social services has increased the work done by women in the home and community; strengthened the gender division of labour in the household economy; and reduced women's access to formal employment. Lower household incomes have forced women and girls to engage in difficult and unpaid household work. Not surprisingly, the implementation of SAPs has brought increased suffering to the poor, particularly to women and children who have had to bear the heaviest burden of the current economic crisis in Kenya. Many women have had to resort to traditional methods of social organizing that rely upon pooling resources. Their communal activities include helping each other with farm work, and raising funds for school projects or tuition through *Harambee* (the Swahili word for "let us pull together").

Although women have formed mutual groups as a way to deal with the current cutbacks, the social formation of mutual groups reflects the principles of African collectivism. In other words, they form in response to the needs of a community, a village, or a group of women. The mutual groups hold no set rules or written mandates to organize their collective efforts. By natural inclination, the group members know their obligations. There are different types of mutual groups seeking different goals, but all are governed by communal needs. For instance, some groups meet to help a mother who has given birth. Others meet to work collectively on members' farms and share the plowing, planting, weeding, and harvesting of crops. The only form of remuneration is reciprocity, cohesiveness, and strengthened community ties. In some instances, mutual groups meet once a month. The purpose for the meeting is to contribute money to a common fund, and each member receives the money on a rotational basis. Women's collective efforts have given them voice and confidence, and enabled many African women to own property, send their children to school, and raise their families' standard of living. When my daughter arrived in Canada, I did not hesitate to find out whether or not similar principles of mutuality would work in Toronto.

Harambee spirit in Toronto

Within a few weeks of my daughter's arrival, I talked to four other mothers in my apartment building. We agreed to take turns picking up our girls from daycare and babysitting for each other. This schedule was organized on a weekly basis, so each mother would pick up the children only twice or three times each semester (thirteen weeks in one semester). In addition, our arrangement involved feeding, bathing, and assisting the five children with their homework. As a result, the five of us, who were graduate students at the University of Toronto, were able to schedule our classes, study routines, and work, without worrying about babysitting arrangements. The communal childcare arrangements I made upon my daughter's arrival in Canada were not new to me. I had come from a community where a child is not the sole responsibility of the biological mother, but the responsibility of the larger community.[3]

When I first came to Canada, my niece, who was still breastfeeding her own daughter, did not hesitate to mother my daughter during my absence. Therefore, it was quite natural for me to talk to other women who had children of my daughter's age and arrange for community mothering. We had very little in common except for the fact that we were all graduate students. We came from different cultural backgrounds and different parts of the world. Three mothers were from Africa, one from Europe, and one from Lebanon. But we trusted each other, despite the fact that we barely knew one another. This chapter explores the roots of my mothering experiences in Canada as a single parent, graduate student, and Kenyan woman.

Roots of African motherhood

A brief survey of pre-colonial and colonial societies is useful in understanding the structure upon which African motherhood is based. Most of pre-colonial Africa was founded upon and sustained by collectivism. Social systems sought to achieve a balance between the physical and metaphysical world by being in tune with, rather than in opposition to, nature (Nathani, 1996). Communal and cooperative values were privileged over individualism and accumulation. Labour was organized along parallel rather than hierarchical lines, thus giving equal value to male and female labour. Social organization was based on the principle of patrilineal or matrilineal descent, or a combination of both. Mothering practices were organized as a collective activity (Nathani, 1996).

During the colonial and neo-colonial period, my mothers and grandmothers still employed the mothering practices that had been passed down to them. They still prepared foods, bananas, yams, arrowroot, green vegetables, and fruits, using the traditional methods. They would roast, boil, or fry foods, then mash them using a pestle and mortar to make them soft for their children. My mother breastfed us until our milk teeth starting falling out. I still recall that when something would get into my eye, my mother would open the eye wide and either blow on it or use her tongue to remove the object. Our mothers, aunties, sisters, and community mothers carried us on their backs until some of us were ready for second *Mambura*.[4] Boys and girls learnt to take care of young ones, to balance them on our backs, and to feed them. Seven-year-old children were taught how to carry newborn babies on their backs, and taught how to comfort them if they cried. Women like my mother played an integral role in ensuring that such community mothering practices survived. These women practised what they preached.

However, during the colonial period, schooling interfered with mothering practices. Initially, only boys were sent to school.[5] As a result, girls had to carry out the boys' work, which included looking after the herds and running errands, in addition to their own work. It also meant the mothers and the grandmothers had to adjust their mothering practices. The mothers were conscious of the fact that caring for young siblings, a duty that had previously been shared by boys and girls, had now become the girls' responsibility. It was not long, however, before various communities realized there was a benefit to sending all children to school regardless of their gender. Unfortunately, in addition to attending school, girls were still expected to carry out their household chores.

By the time Kenya achieved independence in 1963, most people believed that a Western education was beneficial. Unfortunately, the cutbacks introduced by the International Monetary Fund (IMF) and the World Bank eroded educational opportunities in Kenya, particularly for women. The cutbacks that marked independence forced many women to adjust their lives to accommodate all the mothering responsibilities bestowed upon them. During my research, it was evident that mothering responsibilities had tripled. Due to the social cutbacks, the government has reduced funding for preschool institutions, hospitals, and higher education. Women are expected to care for children who are unable to attend preschool, prepare traditional herbs for the sick, and engage in fundraising to send their children to university. As previously discussed, women have had to rely on their collectivism in order to cope with the impact of SAPs. Women have had to compensate for the loss of government services due to SAPs in the areas of health, education, and economics. Despite the cutbacks, Embu women have not relinquished their responsibility of educating, socializing, and "passing on the torch" to the next generation.

To situate motherwork in African contexts requires one to examine how African women in their local, everyday lived realities negotiate the meanings of mothering. During my research in Kenya, I could not help but admire women's commitment to their children and community. For example, Wangeci, a single mother with a grade-seven education told me she had made a commitment to her ten-year-old daughter when she was born:

> I will sacrifice my life for this baby. I will do what it takes to make sure that she does not end up like me: no education, no money, and no land. At present I am not sure how I will do it. But all I know is her life will be different and better than mine. I let my mother down by dropping out of school, I have to do something that will make her know that her efforts, her sacrifices were not in vain ... it appears pretty hopeless now, but I know things will change. (interview, 1994)

In her late twenties, Wangeci spoke with determination and dignity. I was not surprised when I visited her two years later to find that she had managed to send her daughter to a private boarding school. When I asked her how that was possible, she pointed to her head, then spread out her hands to show me the palms and almost in a whisper she said:

> Hard work. I work in peoples' homes, on farms and in coffee plantations or factories. At the end of the day, people offer me grains, beans, cash, or space to cultivate my own food. Once I have accumulated enough grains/beans, I sell them and save the money. I get very little for the work I do, but as the saying goes "kidogo, kidogo ndio kina jascha kipapa" (bits and pieces fill the pocket or a penny earned is a penny saved). (interview, 1996)

Wangeci's main goal is to educate her daughter. Among African people, there is a saying that when you educate a girl, you educate a whole clan. Wangeci might not be an orator, or a renowned feminist; nonetheless her commitment to make a difference in her daughter's life speaks volumes. Wangeci is an activist who is very aware of the struggles and sacrifices she must make as a mother to provide her children with the opportunity for better lives.

Nyawira, a woman in her mid-sixties, was another participant in my research. She has five children who have all completed their secondary education. She spoke of her children with passion:

> Although all my children are grown and live in the city, I still prepare large amounts of foods. I recall many times, I would prepare homemade cookies to go and sell to raise school fees. Sometimes I did not sell even one, and some other times I sold everything. I sacrificed everything I had to put my children through school. My husband had to sell part of our land to raise school fee. But here I am alone. All my children have moved to the city. I am lonely, but I am happy for them. (interview, 1994)

Situating these women's narratives in pre-colonial, colonial, and neo-colonial knowledges on mothering enables us to understand the dilemma mothers face in contemporary Africa. However, I would like to state that although there are commonalities in mothering practices across African communities, I do not wish to generalize about these practices because African communities are not homogeneous. Nevertheless, I believe that there is a shared African philosophy that views parenting, especially mothering, as an integral component in the survival of African traditions and cultures.

The practice of mothering is not universal, and the way it is conceived, celebrated, and practiced differs across cultures. In some instances, mothering as a practice is portrayed as oppressive and problem-laden both socially and culturally. For example, in Western feminist legal theory, motherhood has often been seen as problematic for women because mothers are seen to embody dependency while simultaneously being trapped by the dependency of others (Fineman, 1995: xi). Thus, motherhood, based on Western ideologies, tends to be conceptualized as a dutiful obligation. Often women's economic and social problems are presented as partially or primarily linked to motherhood (Fineman, 1995: xi). Western feminists often promote the notion of "shared parenting" as one possible solution to the social problems that have come to be linked to mothering. Typically, they envision fathers as "equal" parents with corresponding rights and obligations within the context of an egalitarian family. As a result, Western feminist theorists often continue to privilege patriarchal family structures, and subsequently continue to formulate social and legal policies that position the nuclear family as the paradigmatic core social institution (Fineman, 1995: xi).

The notion of "ideal" or "good" mothering, and the culturally specific assumption that a woman must be a mother before she is considered a mature, balanced, and fulfilled adult, promotes compulsory motherhood. In other words, it promotes the belief that becoming pregnant, giving birth, and exhibiting nurturing behavior are integral to fulfilling one's gendered destiny (Kline, 1995: 118). According to Wearing:

> A "good" mother is always available to her children, she spends time with them, guides, supports, encourages, and corrects as well as [loves] and [cares] for them physically. She is also responsible for the cleanliness of their home environment. A "good" mother is unselfish; she puts her children's need before her own. (Wearing, quoted in Kline, 1995: 118–120)

Kline explains that motherhood has been ideologically constructed as compulsory only for those women considered "fit," and not for women who have been judged "unfit" on the bases of their social location. During the last century, this has held true for disabled women, Black women, First Nations women, immigrant women, Jewish women, lesbian women, women who are the sole-support of parents, poor women, unmarried women, young women, and others (1995: 120–121).

The social construction of the good or ideal mother demonstrates the extent to which mothering remains a site of struggle. Slaughter argues that, "The forces of social power are always at war. [Our] task [as women] is to resist and unmask the power behind the institutions and discourses that name" (1995: 77). The ideology of motherhood, therefore, speaks not only to gender roles and behavior, but also privileges specific locations within the social relations of race, class, gender, sexuality, and ability. Historically, White, middle-class, and able-bodied women have been most likely to be viewed as "appropriate" mothers as Kline notes:

> Thus, motherhood is better conceptualized as a privilege than a right, a privilege that can be withheld, both ideologically and in more material ways, from women who are not members of the dominant groups in society or who are otherwise considered unfit. Within this framework, so-called unfit women who want to have children are often confronted with serious barriers and difficulties. The bad mother, by corollary, is constructed as the "photographic negative" of the good mother. (Kline, 1995: 122)

It is my belief that assumptions about which women can and cannot be mothers or good mothers are a form of social control embedded in the capitalist mode of production and rooted in patriarchal systems. Ideally, assumptions about who constitutes a good mother would not be based on one model of mothering, but would be determined in culturally and community specific contexts. In Toronto, where people from various cultures often live together in the same building or in close proximity, individual mothers should be free to make choices about how to mother across cultural differences. This is what I have had to do in mothering my daughter. Understanding who I am as a person and the cultural contexts that have had an impact on my life have been the best preparations for being a parent. With a grounded understanding of "self," I have been able to better understand the different cultural environments in which I find myself, and to begin choosing which aspects of these cultures to embrace as I mother my daughter away from my culture. Recognizing myself as a diasporic subject has also enabled me to more effectively address the challenges mothers face when mothering away from their familiar communities. When attempting to understand differences in mothering practices, I have discovered that we tend to resort to the most readily available reference points—our own cultural frameworks. The use of a different cultural context as a basis for understanding mothering is inevitably challenging. However, having a strong cultural reference point is essential as women's mothering practices are often judged in relation to the institutionalized mothering practices carried out in schools and daycares, and represented by the media.

Mothering among African communities

Within African communities, mothering is not necessarily based on biological ties. Established African philosophy suggests that children do not solely belong to their biological parents, but to the community at large. This philosophy and tradition inform what we refer to as "othermothering" and "community mothering." Significantly, even in the face of Western conceptions of mothering, which often view community-mothering practice as deviant and negligent, African understandings of mothering continue to thrive. Throughout the African diaspora, black women care for one another and one another's children regardless of their cultural backgrounds. Stanlie James clearly states that mothers among African-American communities incorporate nurturing responsibilities for children other than their immediate offspring (1997: 45). Evidence indicating that this practice is still prevalent in African communities with polygynous relationships suggests that shared parenting or othermothering is part of the value system inherent to pre-colonial Africa.

Othermothering in black communities involves the same hard work, self-sacrifice, mentoring, and love that black women give their own children. The bonds that are created between those who mother and those who are mothered are passed down through a "lineage of mothering" (Wane and Adefarakan, forthcoming). Although I focus on black women who mother children and one another, such practices exist beyond gender and racial boundaries. It is not unusual to find young boys mothering their younger siblings, and uncles and fathers mothering their nieces and/or nephews. My mothering experiences in Toronto have also shown that women from different racial backgrounds may step in as othermothers or community othermothers. Othermothers usually care for children. Community mothers take care of the community. These women are typically past their childbearing years. They are usually charismatic and embrace a communal spirit. According to James: "Based upon her knowledge and her respected position, a community othermother is also in a position to provide analyses and/or critiques of conditions or situations that may affect the well being of her community" (1997: 48). This is not to suggest, however, that community othermothering does not differ from culture to culture.

"Othermothers" may also be defined as mothers who assist blood mothers in the responsibility of child care for short or long-term periods, in informal or formal arrangements. They can be, but are not confined to, such blood relatives as grandmothers, sisters, aunts, cousins, or supportive fictive kin (James, 1997: 45). They not only serve to relieve some of the stress that can develop between children and parents but also provide multiple role models for children. As othermothers and community othermothers, black women keep the traditional African value systems of communal sharing and ownership alive. James argues that the entire community benefits from black women's motherwork, and suggest that it serves as "an important Black feminist link to the development of new models for social transformation" (1997: 45). In short, whether we are mothers, othermothers, or community othermothers, African traditional notions of community are functional strategies that sustain the survival of African peoples all over the world.

As an African woman, I am gravely concerned about the way in which racist and colonial discourses have constructed black female-headed households. While the dominant society denigrates black single motherhood, and often dismisses these women as welfare queens, black female-headed households have been the core of survival for African peoples in Africa, the Caribbean, the Americas, and Europe. When black men were absent from home due to migratory labour, family abandonment, or other reasons, black women were left with the difficult and challenging task of caring for themselves, their children, and other community members.

Mothering within African communities can be understood as a form of cultural work or as one way communities organize to nurture both themselves and future generations (James, 1997: 44). Among Embu women, mothering is a cultural phenomenon. Women without children prepare meals as if they are expecting a number of children for both the midday and evening meals. If no child drops by, the women pack the food and take it to a home where there are children. The actions of such women stand as evidence of the extent to which mothering is not limited to females with biological offspring, but is a community practice (James, 1997: 44). For example, women in traditionally polygynous relationships, who are compatible with each other, often share the care of all the children in the household so they can more easily and efficiently carry out their daily responsibilities (James, 1997: 44). As James (1997) explains:

> In addition to patterns of shared childcare in polygynous households, childcare responsibilities were also diffused through the common African practice of fostering children. African communal societies were characterized by high degrees of interdependence and the belief that individual self-development and personal fulfillment were dependent upon the well being of all members of the community. Fostering children was one means of promoting these communal values and ensuring the likelihood of co-operative interaction. (46)

Thus, women in an African context do not foster children simply because they are orphaned. Othermothering is a way of extending children's primary relationships to a larger number of people within the extended family and the community at large. It is also a way to relieve mothers from some of the responsibilities associated with nurturing young children. Similarly, community othermothering, a role usually preserved for "elders," recognizes the value of communal mothering practices.

Conclusion

Mothering is a very complex institution. It is only by documenting our mothering experiences and by telling our stories that we can begin to understand and appreciate its complexity. Every time I visited my grandmothers as a child, they always had a story for me. Looking back, these stories did not always make sense to me at the time, but have now become my source of reference for mothering. Each story illustrated some aspect of our culture. From them, I learned about our culture, clan lineage, and rites of passage. Here in Toronto, I have tried to follow in my mothers' and grandmothers' footsteps. When my busy schedule permits, I sit with my daughter and tell her stories. I tell her stories about Kenya, and stories about the Embu people, my mothers, and grandmothers in particular. I do this with the hope that she will pass on these stories to her children, my grandchildren, and in so doing, pass on the torch to the next generation.

Notes

1. For a more detailed discussion of the notion of community mothering in Africa, see James (1997).
2. For further reading, see Emeagwali (1995).
3. Coming from Kenya, subsidized day care services for children were quite new to me. My experiences with children's services were interesting and informative. I was pleasantly relieved to learn that I would only pay a dollar a day for my daughter's daycare services.
4. In traditional societies, the significant stages in one's life were marked by a special ceremony referred to as *Mambura*. The most celebrated stages were the birth of a child, ear piercing, circumcision for both girls and boys, and marriage rites. The ceremonies were marked by community gatherings. During these ceremonies there would be drinking, eating, dancing, rejoicing, and teaching. Unfortunately, by the time I initiated my own research on Kenyan community practices, most of these rites were no longer being practised. The practices had been outlawed, been rendered too lavish under the current economic conditions, or lost their significance.
5. For further reading on the cultural barriers, see Mwagiru and Ouko (1989).

Section Four

MOTHERS AND DAUGHTERS

Chapter Sixteen

Across the Divide
CONTEMPORARY ANGLO-AMERICAN FEMINIST THEORY
ON THE MOTHER-DAUGHTER RELATIONSHIP

Andrea O'Reilly

Sometimes it seemed as if we were engaged in an Olympic competition to decide whose mother was absolutely the worst. We ground them up in our long conversations and spit them out.
—Anne Rophie, *Fruitful: A real mother in the modern world*

I cannot forget my mother. Though not as sturdy as others, she is my bridge. When I needed to get across, she steadied herself long enough for me to run across safely.
—Renita Weems, "Hush mama's gotta go bye-bye"

"The cathexis between mother and daughter, essential, distorted, misused," wrote Adrienne Rich in 1976, "is the great unwritten story."[1] I am a daughter and I am a mother of daughters. My feminism as it is lived and as it is practised in my scholarship and teaching is decidedly mother-centred; its aim is to recover, narrate and theorize the unwritten stories of mothers and daughters. What I discovered close to ten years ago, when I began my work on motherhood and the mother–daughter relationship, was that our stories as mothers and daughters had in fact *already* been written—narrated by the larger patriarchal culture that scripted the roles mothers and daughters were expected to play. The received view of mothers and daughters, or what author Toni Morrison calls in another context, the master narrative, is that this relationship, particularly in the daughter's adolescent years, is one of antagonism and animosity. The daughter must distance and differentiate herself from the mother if she is to assume an autonomous identity as an adult. The mother, in turn, is perceived and understood only in terms of her maternal role, viewed either as devouring shrew or devoted madonna, bitch or victim; her own subjectivity as woman is eclipsed by her maternal identity. The mother represents for the daughter, according to the received narrative, the epitome of patriarchal oppression that she seeks to transcend as she comes to womanhood, and yet the daughter's failings, as interpreted by herself and the culture at large, are said to be the fault of the mother. This is the patriarchal narrative of the mother–daughter relationship.

The lives of mothers and daughters as they are lived are shaped by these larger cultural narratives even as mothers and daughters live lives different from, and in resistance to, these assigned roles. The aim of my research and teaching is to deconstruct this patriarchal narrative by first exposing this narration as precisely that: a narrative, an ideology, that, by definition, is a construction not a reflection of the actual lived reality of mothers and daughters, hence neither natural nor inevitable. Second, my work is concerned with how daughters and mothers may unravel the patriarchal script to write their own stories of motherhood and daughterhood. As part of this larger project, I designed a first year course on mothers and daughters that I have taught at York University for the last four years.[2] The objective of this course, entitled "Mothers and daughters: From estrangement to empowerment," is to situate the mother–daughter relationship as a *cultural* construction. Students are taught to think critically and consciously about the cultural meanings assigned to the mother–daughter relationship; they are taught to explore how their own experiences of being mothered, and their perceptions of motherhood in general and of their own mothers in particular, are shaped by the larger patriarchal narrative of motherhood and daughterhood. The course aims to identify, challenge, and dismantle the patriarchal narrative of mother–daughter estrangement; in particular, it asks students to uncover the historical/psychological origins of this narrative. Students track the manifestations of patriarchal narrative in various cultural practices as diverse as media, education, government policy, and psychological theory; analyze its workings in their own personal relationships; imagine ways it may be deconstructed; and finally construct an alternative mother–daughter narrative scripted for empowerment as opposed to estrangement.

An in-class writing assignment at the beginning of the course asks students to reflect upon their relationship with their mother. They are asked to describe this relationship at three points in their lives and are given a series of instructions and questions to help them do this: Describe your mother both inside and outside her role as mother. What do you want/need from your mother? What does she want/need from you? Are you like your mother? Do you want to be like your mother? Describe how your mother has helped or hindered you in achieving your life goals. This assignment serves as the first entry in the students' course journals: weekly written reflections on course readings, discussions and so forth. One student, reflecting upon this assignment at the close of the course, commented:

When I look back to the beginning of the course only eight months ago I realize how different I was—how naive I was. To gain some perspective as to how my attitudes have changed concerning my own mother, I reread my first journal entry. I still agree with most of what I wrote, however after looking at the questions you asked us to answer, I realized that I had overlooked the most crucial of all the questions posed. I neglected the questions, "Do you know your mother as a person other than your mother? Who is your mother?" I think at the time I didn't really understand the significance of these questions nor could I have answered them for I didn't know my mother as a person. I didn't even know that I didn't know.[3]

This student's reflections, and in particular her comment "I didn't even know that I didn't know," serve as an appropriate epigraph for our positioning as daughters in the patriarchal narrative of mother–daughter estrangement. So thoroughly do we identify with this script that its cultural staging has been rendered invisible to us and we see it as merely "the way things are"—hence natural and inevitable. African-American essayist and poet Audre Lorde once said we must "name the nameless so that it can be thought."[4] The aim of this course, for daughters and mothers alike, is to render visible the "invisible hand of patriarchy" so as to see how thoroughly our lives are produced and shaped by patriarchal ideologies that are not of our own making.

Matrophobia, mother-blame and daughter-centricity

I begin the course with Nancy Chodorow's classic essay "Family structure and feminine personality,"[5] and a lecture on her "reproduction of mothering" thesis as it is developed in her book of the same name.[6] Nancy Chodorow, as Penelope Dixon noted in her feminist annotated bibliography on mothers and mothering, "was one of the first to write on the subject [of mothering] and subsequently has authored more books and articles on this subject than any other feminist writer."[7] Indeed, Chodorow's writings, particularly her now classic *The reproduction of mothering*, have influenced the way in which a whole generation of scholars view motherhood. What is less acknowledged, however, is how this influential writer, who is identified as a feminist, reinscribes the patriarchal narrative of mother–daughter estrangement even as she seeks to dismantle it.

Chodorow contends that female mothering constructs gendered identities that are both differentiated and hierarchical. The pre-Oedipal mother–daughter attachment, she argues, is more prolonged and intense than the mother–son relationship. Because the daughter and the mother are the same gender, the mother perceives and treats her daughter as identical to and continuous with her self. The sameness and continuity of the pre-Oedipal mother–daughter symbiosis engenders a feminine psychic structure that is less individuated and differentiated. The daughter's sense of self is relational; she experiences herself as connected to others. The relational sense of self that women inherit from their mothers and bring to their own mothering, Chodorow goes on to argue, exacerbates female self-effacement and frustrates women's achievement of an authentic autonomous identity. Relationality, Chodorow concludes, is problematic for women because it hinders autonomy, psychological and otherwise, and since daughter–mother identification is the cause of this relationality in women, it is, in her words, "bad for mother and [daughter] alike."[8]

Chodorow has been criticized heavily in the twenty years since the publication of The reproduction of mothering. What concerns critics most is Chodorow's bracketing of the "real" world in her psychoanalytic abstractions of family patterns and gender formations. Critics have pointed out that Chodorow's mother-involved, father-absent family is quite specifically a white, urban, middle-class family structure of the first world. The gendered personalities that this specific family structure might create should not be used, as Chodorow does, to account for universal male dominance and gender difference. Moreover, Chodorow's theory of mother–daughter mutual psychological over-identification, used to explain women's subordination, far too readily glosses over women's lived powerlessness in a patriarchal world. While I argue wholeheartedly with the above criticisms, I am nonetheless disturbed by the fact that among the hundreds of articles written about Chodorow's theory only a handful assume as their focus of critique what I find to be the most troubling premise of Chodorow's reproduction thesis; namely, the pathologizing of mother–daughter identification/intimacy, particularly in positioning it as the cause of women's inadequacy, psychological, and otherwise. One early critic of Chodorow, Marcia Westkott faulted Chodorow for failing to understand that women's relationality and dependency result not from psychology but from culture: "The need of mothers to remain close to their daughters arises because mothers are given few other choices, not just because of an infantile personality structure."[9] Here, as with Chodorow, mother–daughter identification is construed as a liability.

In Don't blame mother, Paula Caplan writes, "women love connection. But in a society that is phobic about intimacy and extols the virtues of independence, we mistakenly regard connection and closeness as dependency, fusion, and merging."[10] The aim of the introductory section is to expose the pervasiveness of the pathology of mother–daughter intimacy and identification in contemporary culture. As one student commented, "It greatly disturbs me when women, such as Chodorow, write powerful stuff which influences a lot of people. I expect it from Freud but not from someone who calls herself a feminist." The sanction against mother–daughter intimacy observed in Chodorow is one of the many cultural practices that render mother–daughter estrangement natural and inevitable. It also originates from and reinscribes another central tenet of mother–daughter estrangement—mother-blame and the devaluation of motherhood.

In *Of woman born*, Adrienne Rich distinguishes between two meanings of motherhood: "the *potential relationship* of any woman to her powers of reproduction and to children; and the *institution*, which aims at ensuring that that potential—and all women—shall remain under male control."[11] I use the term motherhood to refer to the institution of motherhood, which is male-defined and controlled, and mothering to refer to experiences of mothering, which are female-defined and centred. According to Rich, the reality of patriarchal motherhood contradicts the possibility of gynocentric mothering. Across cultures and throughout history most women mother in the institution of motherhood; that is, women's mothering is defined and controlled by the larger patriarchal society in which they live. Mothers do not make the rules, Rich emphasizes— they simply enforce them. Whether it is in the form of parenting books, a physician's advice, or the father's rules, a mother raises her children in accordance with the values and expectations of the dominant patriarchal culture. Mothers are policed by what theorist Sara Ruddick calls the "gaze of others." Under the gaze of others, mothers "relinquish authority to others, [and] lose confidence in their own values." Ruddick calls this an abdication of maternal authority. "Fear of the gaze of the others," she continues, "can be expressed intellectually as inauthenticity, a repudiation of one's own perceptions and values."[12] The institution of motherhood is predicated upon inauthentic mothering and the abdication of maternal authority.

A daughter, Ruddick emphasizes, perceives this inauthenticity and understands the powerlessness that underpins her mother's compliance and complicity. In *Of woman born*, Rich speaks of the rage and resentment daughters feel toward this powerlessness of their mothers. However, at the same time, the daughter feels rage toward her mother: she is expected to identify with her because the daughter is also a woman who, it is assumed, will some day become a mother/ wife as her mother did. The daughter resists this identification because she does not want a life like her mother, nor does she wish to be aligned with someone who is oppressed and whose work is so devalued. "Thousands of daughters," writes Rich, "see their mothers as having taught a compromise and self-hatred they are struggling to win free of, the one through whom the restrictions and degradations of a female existence were ... transmitted."[13] Rich calls this distancing between mothers and daughters matrophobia: "the fear not of one's mother or of motherhood but of *becoming one's mother*."[14] Matrophobia, she writes,

> can be seen as a womanly splitting of the self in the desire to become purged once and for all of our mothers' bondage, to become individuated

and free. The mother stands for the victim in ourselves, the unfree woman, the martyr. Our personalities seem dangerously to blur and overlap with our mothers, and in a desperate attempt to know where mother ends and daughter begins, we perform radical surgery.[15]

When daughters perform this radical surgery they sever themselves from their attachment with their mother.

The institution of motherhood and the cultural devaluation/subordination of mothers, and the practice of inauthentic mothering on which it is predicated, gives rise to mother-blame. Paula Caplan argues that mother-blame is rampant in contemporary culture, among both professionals and the population at large. "The biggest reason daughters are upset and angry with their mothers," writes Caplan, "is that they have been *taught* to do so."[16] Similar to the feeling of matrophobia identified by Rich, mother-blame distances daughters from mothers because mothers come to be seen not as sources of empowerment but as the cause of all and any problems that may ail the daughter.

Marianne Hirsch, in her highly acclaimed book *The mother/daughter plot: Narrative, psychoanalysis, feminism*, argues that the feminist theory written in the 1970s is characterized by a daughterly perspective or subjectivity that Maureen Reddy and Brenda Daly call "daughter-centricity."[17] "It is the woman as daughter," Hirsch writes, "who occupies the center of the global reconstruction of subjectivity and subject-object relation. The woman as mother remains in the position of other, and the emergence of feminine daughterly subjectivity rests and depends on that continued and repeated process of othering the mother."[18] She goes on to say, "The adult woman who is mother continues to exist only in relation to her child, never as a subject in her own right. And in her maternal function, she remains an object, always distanced, always idealized or denigrated, always mystified, always represented through the small child's point of view."[19] Hirsch argues that such ambivalence expresses itself in the rhetoric and the politics of the 1970s movement:

Throughout the 1970s, the metaphor of sisterhood, of friendship or of surrogate motherhood has been the dominant model for female and feminist relationships. To say that "sisterhood is powerful," however, is to isolate feminist discourse within one generation and to banish feminists who are mothers to the "mother-closet." In the 1970s, the prototypical feminist voice was, to a large degree, the voice of the daughter attempting to separate from an overly connected or rejecting mother, in order to bond with her sisters in a relationship of mutual nurturance and support among women. With its possibilities of mutuality and its desire to avoid power, the paradigm of sisterhood has the advantage of freeing women from the biological function of giving birth, even while offering a specifically feminine relational model. "Sisters" can be "maternal" to one another without allowing their bodies to be invaded by men and the physical acts of pregnancy, birth, and lactation. In this feminist family romance, sisters are better mothers, providing more nurturance and greater encouragement of autonomy. In functioning as mutual surrogate mothers, sisters can replace mothers.[20]

Thus, while mothering as nurturance was celebrated amongst 1970s feminists, real mothers and the biological processes of mothering were displaced and disparaged.

Hirsch identifies four reasons for the 1970s "avoidance and discomfort" with the maternal. First, for daughters motherhood represented a compliance with patriarchy of which they wanted no part. Second, feminists feared the lack of control associated with motherhood. Third, feminists suffered from what critic Elizabeth Spelman has identified as "somatophophia"—fear and discomfort with the body.[21] And nothing, as Hirsch has observed, "entangles women more firmly in their bodies than pregnancy, birth, lactation, miscarriage, or the inability to conceive."[22] Fourth, and characteristic of much feminist theorizing in the 1970s, was an ambivalence about power, authority, and anger—all of which are part of mothering and associated with the maternal. "Feminist theoretical writing in the U.S.," writes Hirsch, "is permeated with fears of maternal power and with anger at maternal powerlessness."[23] Caplan argues that men fear maternal power. It would seem that women, too, fear it. The sisterhood metaphor of the 1970s thus may be read as a gesture of displacement or containment. The maternal power that is feared is rendered safe by transforming it into mothering between sisters—no power imbalance—and by objectifying and "otherizing" the person who seems to wield this power, the mother.

To a young child, the powers of the mother appear limitless. Our own individual flesh-and-blood mother is also connected to the primordial Great Mother, who held very real life and death powers over mortal men. In our individual and collective unconscious we remember that time when we lived under the mother's power in the pre-Oedipal and pre-patriarchal world. In *The mermaid and the minotaur*, Dorothy Dinnerstein argues that the fear of maternal power and the hatred of women generally originate from infant experiences which, in turn, come to structure adult consciousness.[24] The mother, Dinnerstein reasons, cannot satisfy all of the child's needs and desires. The inevitable dissatisfaction, discomfort, frustration, and anger felt by the child directs itself at the person whose responsibility it was to meet those needs. In contrast to Dinnerstein's view, I would suggest that the experiences of infancy, given that they include both pain and pleasure, engender not misogyny but a deep ambivalence that becomes organized around polarized constructions of the mother. The Good Mother and the Bad Mother are created; all that we find desirable about mothers is signified by the former, and all that we fear and hate is marked by the latter. This delineation is, I would suggest, mapped along an already established historical topography of separation and specialization. I refer here to what we speculate occurred at the dawn of patriarchy when the many diverse qualities of the original Great Goddess were separated and used to create several distinct goddesses. That which mortal men feared in the original Goddess—particularly her powers over life and death—was displaced upon a terrible mother goddess, like the Hinud goddess Kali, who represented death and destruction while that which was desired was retained and assigned to a beneficent power. In Catholicism, for example, Mary, the mother of Jesus, is such a woman. The polarization and specialization of the maternal self continue to structure our ambivalence.

The fear of maternal power is at the heart of such disparagement and idealization. However, as Ruddick reminds us: "All power lies at least partly in the eye of the beholder. To a child, a mother is huge—a judge, trainer, audience, and provider whose will must be placated .... A mother, in contrast to the perception her children have of her, will mostly experience herself as relatively powerless."[25] However, as we speak to and about the very real powerlessness of mothers, we must not forget the power a mother does possess. Ruddick writes:

> There are many external constraints on [a mother's] capacity to name, feel, and act. But in the daily conflict of wills, at least with her children, a mother has the upper hand. Even the most powerless woman knows that she is physically stronger than her young children. This along with undeniable psychological power gives her the resources to control her children's behavior and influence their perceptions. If a mother didn't have this control, her life would be unbearable.[26]

Mothering is a profound experience of both powerlessness and power; it is this paradox of motherhood that helps explain women's ambivalence about motherhood. This ambivalence about maternal power—along with fear of the maternal, mother-blame, cultural devaluation of motherhood, and matrophophia—distance daughters from their mothers and scripts the relationship of mother and daughters as one of disconnection and estrangement.

Mother–daughter connection and empowerment: Theories and narrative

Once students have identified these cultural practices that distance daughters from the mothers, they explore ways in which these practices can be resisted.

The sanction against mother–daughter identification, with which I began this chapter, is challenged by Elizabeth Debold, Marie Wilson, and Idelisse Malavé, in their important work, *Mother daughter revolution*. They argue that psychological theories of development are organized around the assumption that adolescence is a "time of separation when daughters are struggling to be independent, particularly from their mothers; and daughters in adolescence don't want to listen to their mothers or be like them in any way."[27] Separation from parents is mandated in developmental theory to enable the emerging adult to achieve an autonomous sense of self. *Mother daughter revolution* calls into question this "sacred cow" of developmental theory—the equivalency of separation and autonomy—and argues that it constitutes a betrayal of both mothers and daughters:

> Separation and autonomy are not equivalent: a person need not separate from mothers emotionally to be autonomous. Under the dominion of experts, mothers are urged to create a separation and disconnection from daughters that their daughters do not want. Early childhood and adolescence are the two stages of life where separation has been decreed as imperative to the independence and autonomy of children. To mother "right," women disconnect from their daughters and begin to see them as society will. Rather than strengthen girls this breach of trust leaves girls weakened and adrift.[28]

Mothers want to "do right" by their daughters so, as dictated by developmental theory, they distance themselves from their daughters when the daughters reach adolescence. At the same time, they propel the daughters out of the maternal space of childhood and into the heterosexual realm of adulthood.

What is most disturbing about this pattern of separation and betrayal is its timing. "In childhood, girls have confidence in what they know, think, and feel."[29] With the onset of adolescence, girls between the ages of nine and twelve come up against what Debold, Wilson, and Malavé call "the wall." "The wall is our patriarchal culture that values women less than men ... To get through the wall, girls have to give up parts of themselves to be safe and accepted within society."[30] Before adolescence, girls are, in their words, "fully themselves," but at the crossroads between childhood and adolescence,

> girls come to label their vitality, desires, and thoughts as "selfish," "bad," or "wrong." They lose the ability to hold on to the truth of their experience .... They begin to see themselves as others see them, and they orient their thinking and themselves towards others .... [They] have to give up their relationship with the world of girls and women, the

world that they have lived and loved in, and also give up relationship with parts of themselves that are too dangerous to keep in the adult world of male desire. Girls give up these relationships for the sake of the relationships that have been prescribed for them in male-led societies. The wall of patriarchy expects girls to separate from what they know, from each other, and from the women who care for them.[31]

Central to *Mother daughter revolution* is the belief that mothers can help their daughters resist being influenced by the wall. With her mother beside her, the daughter is empowered and can learn to compromise less of herself. The key to the mother's ability to do this is the reclamation of her own girl self. The authors write:

> If mothers decide to join with daughters who are coming of age as women, mothers must first reclaim what they themselves have lost. Reclaiming is the first step in women's joining girls' resistance to their own dis-integration. Reclaiming is simply the process of discovering, describing, and reappropriating the memories and feelings of our preadolescent selves .... The goal is not to become a preadolescent girl. That wouldn't be desirable even if it were possible .... But women can reclaim and, thus, reintegrate the vital parts of themselves that they discarded or drove underground.[32]

This reclamation empowers the mother and enables her to help her daughter in her resistance. As *Mother daughter revolution* suggests, if mothers reclaim their driven-underground pre-patriarchal selves, their reclaimed selves can join their daughters, and empower them to withstand the loss or compromise of their own female selfhood. Mothers and daughters together "can claim the power of connection, community, and choice. And this power just might bring down the wall."[33]

Another contemporary theorist read in my course champions mother–daughter connectedness as a mode of resistance. Miriam Johnson, the author of *Strong mothers, weak wives*, emphasizes how daughters may connect with their mothers to withstand what may be called the heterosexualizing behaviour of the father. In Chodorow's psychoanalytical account, the differential treatment of sons and daughters by their mothers is said to be the cause of both gender difference and male dominance. Johnson challenges this argument. She writes: "It is the wife role and not the mother role that organizes women's secondary status."[34] Women's secondary status, she maintains, originates not from the maternal core of women's subjectivity (Chodorow's relational self) but from their heterosexual identity as wives of men. In contrast to Chodorow, Johnson maintains that male dominance originates not from the mother–child attachment, but from the father–daughter relationship.

The relationship of father and daughter, Johnson asserts, "trains daughters to be wives who are expected to be secondary to their husbands."[35] She argues that fathers often romanticize the father–daughter relationship and interact with their daughters as a lover would. Fathers feminize their daughters: daddies teach their girls to be passive, pleasing, and pretty for men. In Johnson's words, the father–daughter relationship "reproduce[s] in daughters a disposition to please men in a relationship in which the male dominates." In other words, "daddy's girls are in training to be wives."[36] Because daddy's girls are trained and rewarded for pleasing and playing up to men, they grow up to be male-defined and male-orientated women. In most so-called normal (male-dominant) families what is experienced is psychological incest. "The incest ... is psychological, not overtly sexual. The father takes his daughter over. She looks up to him because he is her father. He is the king and she is the princess. It is all OK because the male is dominant in 'normal' adult heterosexual relations."[37]

Johnson argues that these princesses are in need of rescue, and that the rescuer is the mother: "If daddy's girls are to gain their independence they need to construct an identity as the daughters of strong mothers as well."[38] In *The reproduction of mothering*, Chodorow attributes women's lack of autonomy to the feminine-related sense of self which the mother–daughter relationship engendered. In contrast, Johnson argues that women's lack of autonomy originates from the daughter's psychological dependency on her father as a male-orientated daddy's girl. According to Johnson, a daughter's identification with her mother, far from prohibiting authentic female autonomy, produces and promotes that authenticity and autonomy. Chodorow suggested in her earlier sociological work that daughters are empowered by identification with their mothers in matrifocal cultures. Johnson believes that an empowering mother–daughter identification is also possible under patriarchy if the daughter relates to her mother as a mother and friend, not as the father's wife. Johnson contends that the mother–daughter relationship is the key to overcoming women's psychological inauthenticity as daddy's girl and, by implication, women's social oppression in patriarchy. Thus the daughter achieves authentic autonomy not through greater involvement with the father, but through a heightened identification with the mother.

For Johnson, the daughter must identify with the maternal part of her mother's identity rather than the heterosexual one. This identification empowers the daughter in two ways: first it allows her to step outside her oppressive daddy's girl role; and second, it allows her to identify with an adult woman's strength rather than her weakness. In Johnson's view, women are strong as mothers but made weak as wives. In identifying with her mother as mother, the daughter may construct a strong female identity outside of the passive heterosexual one patterned for her by her father and by society at large. In *Mother daughter revolution*, the emphasis is on the mother joining the daughter, while the focus of *Strong mother, weak wives* is the daughter connecting to the mother. Though different, both positions are mapped along what feminist writer Naomi Ruth Lowinsky calls "the motherline."

In *Stories from the motherline: Reclaiming the mother–daughter bond, finding our souls*, Naomi Ruth Lowinsky explores "a worldview that is as old as humankind, a wisdom we have forgotten that we know: the ancient lore of women—the Motherline." She goes on to say:

> Whenever women gather in circles or in pairs, in olden times around the village well, or at the quilting bee, in modern times in support groups, over lunch, or at the children's party, they tell one another stories from the Motherline. These are stories of female experience: physical, psychological, and historical. They are stories about the dramatic changes of woman's body: developing breasts and pubic hair, bleeding, being sexual, giving birth, suckling, menopause, and of growing old. They are stories of the life cycles that link generations of women: Mothers who are also daughters, daughters who have become mothers; grandmothers who also remain granddaughters.[39]

Most women today, Lowinsky contends, are cut off from their motherline; they suffer from what she calls "the feminist ambivalence about the feminine."[40] "Women," she writes, "seemed to want to live their father's lives. Mother was rejected, looked down upon ... In the headlong race to liberate those aspects of ourselves that had been so long denied, we left behind all that women had been ... Many of us," she continues, "who joyfully accepted the challenge of new opportunities discovered in retrospect that we had cut ourselves off from much of what was meaningful to us as women: our mothers, our collective past, our passion for affiliation and for richness in our personal lives. We felt split between our past and our future."[41] Lowinsky asks that women integrate their feminine and feminist selves: women "must connect the historical self that was freed by feminism to live in the 'real' world, with the feminine self that binds us to our mothers and grandmothers."[42]

Daughters of the so-called baby boom are the first generation of women, at least among the middle classes, whose lives are radically different from those of their mothers. These daughters, Lowinsky argues, have "paid a terrible price for cutting [them]selves off from [their] feminine roots."[43] By disconnecting themselves from their motherline, these daughters have lost the authenticity and authority of their womanhood. Women may reclaim that authority and authenticity by reconnecting to the motherline:

> When a woman today comes to understand her life story as a story from the Motherline, she gains female authority in a number of ways. First, her Motherline grounds her in her feminine nature as she struggles with the many options now open to women. Second, she reclaims carnal knowledge of her own body, its blood mysteries and their power. Third, as she makes the journey back to her female roots, she will encounter ancestors who struggled with similar difficulties in different historical times. This provides her with a life-cycle perspective that softens her immediate situation .... Fourth, she uncovers her connection to the archetypal mother and to the wisdom of the ancient worldview, which holds that body and soul are open and all life is interconnected. And, finally, she reclaims her female perspective, from which to consider how men are similar and how they are different.[44]

Virginia Woolf wrote in *A room of one's own*: "[W]e think back through our mothers if we are women."[45] Writing about Lowinsky's motherline in her book *Motherless daughters: The legacy of loss*, Hope Edelman emphasizes that "motherline stories ground a ... daughter in a gender, a family, and a feminine history. They transform the experience of her female ancestors into maps she can refer to for warning or encouragement."[46]

These stories are made available to daughters through the female oral tradition, or what we call gossip and old wives' tales. These feminine discourses, however, have been trivialized, marginalized and discredited; they are, to borrow French theorist Michel Foucault's term, "subjugated knowledge[s]" that circulate outside the master narrative. Moreover, the language of the motherline is rendered in a specifically feminine discourse or dialect that has been discursively and culturally marginalized by patriarchal culture.

In *Motherless daughters*, Edelman studies daughters who lost their mothers between infancy and their early thirties, and considers the impact this loss had on the daughters' lives.[47] The daughters' narratives speak of feelings of incompleteness and fragmentation. "Our mothers," Edelman explains, "are our most direct connection to our history and our gender. Regardless of how well we think they did their job, the void their absence creates in our lives is never completely filled again."[48] When the mother dies daughters lose their connection to the motherline. "Without a mother or mother-figure to guide her," writes Edelman, "a daughter has to piece together a female self-image on her own."[49] A girl who loses her mother has little readily available, concrete evidence of the adult feminine to draw from. She has neither a direct guide for sex-typed behavior nor an immediate connection to her own gender. Left to piece together her own feminine identity, she looks to other females for signs that she's developing along an appropriate gendered path.[50]

Motherless daughters long to know and to be connected to, what Lowinsky calls, the deep feminine, or in Edelman's words: "that subtle unconscious source of feminine authority and power we mistakenly believe is expressed in scarf knots and thank-you notes but instead originates from a more abstract gendered core."[51] "Without knowledge of her own experiences, and the relationship to her mother's," Edelman continues, "a daughter is snipped from the female cord that connects the generations of women in her family, the feminine line of descent ... the motherline."[52]

Adrienne Rich writes in *Of woman born*, "The loss of the daughter to the mother, the mother to the daughter, is the essential female tragedy."[53] In Edelman's work, this loss refers to the daughter losing her mother through death, abandonment, or neglect. In these instances, separation occurs as a result of the mother's leaving the daughter. More frequent, in patriarchal culture, is the loss of the daughter to the mother: daughters become disconnected from their motherline through specific cultural practices, notably the devaluation of motherhood and the reinforcement of maternal powerlessness, fear of the maternal, mother-blame and matrophobia, discussed earlier.

Journalist Marni Jackson calls maternal space "the mother zone; [the] hole in culture where mothers [go]."[54] Motherhood, she writes, "is an unexplored frontier of thought and emotion that we've tried to tame with rules, myth, and knowledge. But the geography remains unmapped."[55] She emphasizes that "[m]otherhood may have become an issue but it's not yet a narrative."[56] Maternal stories are forgotten and lost before they are spoken because "[m]others in the thick of it have not the time or brain cells to write it down, to give it life. [When they] have the time, amnesia moves in ... all the raw extremes of emotion are smoothed over and left behind .... Culture," she continues, "encourages this amnesia, by excluding mothers from its most conspicuous rewards—money, power, social status."[57] Because our mothers' stories remain unspoken, she argues, "the true drama of mother and child is replaced by the idealization of motherhood."[58] Julia Kristeva identifies the maternal with the unspeakable. The maternal is found outside and beyond language, "spoken" only in the extralinguistic, nonverbal discourse of the semiotic.[59] Perhaps, the maternal is, as Hirsch speculates in *The Mother/Daughter Plot*, "unnarratable."[60] Or, as Ruddick writes, maternal voices have been drowned by professional theory, ideologies of motherhood, sexist arrogance, and childhood fantasy. Voices that have been distorted and censored can only be developing voices. Alternatively silenced and edging toward speech, mothers' voices are not voices of mothers as they are, but as they are becoming.[61]

Much of current feminist writing and activism is concerned with the recovery of the maternal voice. While recognizing how difficult it is to speak that which has been silenced, disguised, and marginalized, writers today seek to make the maternal story narratable. In earlier times the ancient lore of the motherline was told around the village well or at the quilting bee; today, the oral tradition of old wives' tales is shared through written narratives.

In *Writing a woman's life*, Carolyn Heilbrun observes, "Lives do not serve as models, only stories do that. And it is a hard thing to make up stories to live by. We can only retell and live by stories we have heard .... Stories have formed us all: they are what we must use to make new fictions and new narratives."[62] Recent writings on the mother–daughter relationship call upon the mother to speak and the daughter to listen. Debold, Wilson, and Malavé argue in *Mother daughter revolution* that the compromise of the female self in adolescence may be resisted or, at the very least, negotiated, when the mother connects with the daughter through stories. The mother, in recalling and sharing with her daughter her own narrative of adolescence, gives the daughter strategies of resistance and, hence, an alternative script for coming into womanhood. Caplan, in *Don't blame mother*, emphasizes that only by speaking and hearing the mother's story can women move beyond mother-blame.[63] In turn, Lowinsky and Edelman argue that a daughter's very identity as a woman is acquired through connection to, and knowledge of, her mother and the motherline of which she is a part. Rich writes, "mothers and daughters have always exchanged with each other—beyond the verbally transmitted lore of female survival—a knowledge that is subliminal, subversive, pre-verbal: the knowledge flowing between two alike bodies, one of which has spent nine months inside the other."[64] The lore Rich refers to here is, of course, the lore of the motherline that constructs female experience outside the patriarchal narrative.

Conclusion

The theories and narratives read by the students in this course expose the cultural practices that underpin the patriarchal narrative of mother–daughter estrangement—sanction against mother–daughter intimacy, mother-blame, daughter-centricity, matrophopia, and fear of maternal power—and offer various strategies by which mothers and daughters may deconstruct the patriarchal narrative so as to write their own stories of motherhood and daughterhood, ones scripted from relations of empowerment as opposed to estrangement. As another student remarked in her journal at the conclusion of the course:

I want to tell you how much your course has meant to me and how much my life has changed because of it. I feel almost as if I am a different person now. You helped me break the cycle instilled in me by a patriarchal society that I was doomed to repeat. Most significantly, you provided me with the means to eliminate mother–blame from my life, and for that I am eternally grateful.

Through this course, I hope to create a dialogue between mothers and daughters that in turn will help them build a bridge over which they can cross the patriarchal divide that separates them. By doing so, mothers and daughters can construct a truly lasting politics of empowerment.

Notes

1. Adrienne Rich, *Of woman born: Motherhood as experience and institution* (New York: W.W. Norton, 1986), 225.
2. The course described in this chapter was designed and taught from 1993 to 1997 at York University as part of the college course programme. In the first two years, the course examined the mother–daughter relationship from a cross-cultural perspective: students read selected novels and poetry by Anglo-American, Anglo-Canadian, Caribbean, African, Native, Chinese, Jewish, African-American, and African-Canadian women writers. In 1995, the focus of the course became an in-depth and detailed study of the representation of the mother–daughter relationship in the dominant Anglo-American feminist tradition. In the second term of the course, students were introduced to theory and literature on mothers and daughters by African-American and Caribbean women writers, in order to problematize the received feminist tradition. This chapter explores only the first part of the course. My research on the mother–daughter in African-American women's theory and literature may be found in "'Ain't that love?': Anti-racism and racial constructions of motherhood," in Maureen Reddy, ed., *Everyday acts against racism: Raising children in a multiracial world* (Washington: Seal Press, 1996); "'In search of my mother's garden, I found my own': Motherlove, healing and identity in Toni Morrison's *Jazz*," *African-American Review* 30, 3 (1996); "Talking back in mother tongue: A feminist course on mothering and motherhood," in Paula Bourne et al., eds., *Feminism and education* (Toronto: CWSE Press, 1994). This topic is also explored in my article "'I come from a long line of uppity irate black women': African-American feminist theory on motherhood, the motherline and the mother–daughter relation," in Andrea O'Reilly and Sharon Abbey, eds., *Mothers and daughters: Connection, empowerment and transformation* (Rowman and Littlefield, 2000). See also my *Toni Morrison and motherhood: Politics of the heart* (SUNY, 2004). Also see Nina Lyon Jenkins in "Black women and the meaning of motherhood," and by Sylvia Hamilton in "African Nova Scotian women: Mothering across the generations," in Sharon Abbey and Andrea O'Reilly, eds., *Redefining motherhood: Patterns and identities* (Toronto: Second Story Press, 1998).

Regrettably, in 1996, York administration made the decision to cancel the College Course Programme as part of its cost-cutting and restructuring initiative and practice. This was a great loss to the students and faculty at York.

3. Journal entry from a student in my "Mothers and daughters" class, York University, April 1995. All other student writings used in this chapter are taken from journal entries in this class.

4. Audre Lorde, "Poetry is not a luxury," *Sister outsider* (New York: Quality Paper Back Club, Triangle Classics, 1993), 37.

5. In Nancy Chodorow, *Feminism and psychoanalytic theory* (New Haven: Yale University Press, 1989), 44–65.

6. Nancy Chodorow, *The reproduction of mothering: Psychoanalysis and the sociology of gender* (Berkeley: University of California Press, 1978).

7. Penelope Dixon, *Mothers and mothering: An annotated bibliography* (New York: Garland Publishing, 1991), 4.

8. Chodorow, *The reproduction of mothering*, 217.

9. Marcia Westkott, "Mothers and daughters in the world of the father," *Frontiers* 3, 2 (1978), 9.

10. Paula Caplan, *Don't blame mother: Mending the mother–daughter relationship* (New York: Harper and Row, 1989).

11. Rich, *Of woman born*, 13. Emphasis in original. Adrienne Rich emphasizes that motherhood is a cultural construction that varies with time and place. Ann Dally, in *Inventing motherhood: The consequences of an ideal* (London: The Hutchinson Publishing Group, 1982), argues that there have always been mothers but that motherhood was invented. Her book convincingly shows how the ideology/occupation of motherhood as woman's natural calling was constructed in response to the socioeconomical transformation in the late eighteenth century from an agricultural to an industrialized based economy. With the rise of industrialization, middle-class women lost their jobs as active producers/contributors in the agriculturally based family economy, so a new profession was designed for them—motherhood. The 1950s witnessed a similar occurrence. After World War Two, women were expected to give up their wartime jobs for the returning soldiers. To facilitate this change a new ideology/occupation of motherhood emerged, that of the full-time mother and housewife. For further information on the historical constructions of motherhood, see Elizabeth Badinter, *Mother love: Myth and reality* (New York: MacMillan Publishing Co., Inc., 1980), and Shari L. Thurer, *The myths of motherhood: How culture reinvents the good mother* (New York: Penguin Books, 1994). For an interesting comparative reading of Rich's and Badinter's works, see Liesbeth Woertman, "Mothering in context: Female subjectives and intervening practices," in Janneke van Mens-Verhulst, Karlein Schreurs, and Liesbeth Woertman, eds., *Daughtering and mothering* (New York: Routledge, 1993), 57–61.

12. "Teachers, grandparents, mates, friends, employers, even an anonymous passerby," writes Ruddick, "can judge a mother by her child's behavior and find her wanting." Sara Ruddick, *Maternal thinking: Toward a politic of peace* (New York: Ballantine Books, 1989), 111–112.

13. Rich, *Of woman born*, 235.

14. Ibid., 236. Emphasis in original.

15. Ibid.

16. Caplan, *Don't blame mother*, 2. Emphasis in original.

17. Brenda Daly and Maureen Reddy, *Narrating mothers: Theorizing maternal subjectivities* (Knoxville: University of Tennessee Press, 1991), 2. "In psychoanalytic studies," write Daly and Reddy, "we frequently learn less about what it is like to mother than what it is like to be mothered, even when the author has both experiences" (1991: 2).

18. Marianne Hirsch, *The mother/daughter plot: Narrative, psychoanalysis, feminism* (Bloomington: Indiana University Press, 1989), 136.

19. Ibid., 167.

20. Ibid., 164.

21. As quoted in Hirsch, *The mother/daughter plot*, 166.

22. Hirsch, *The mother/daughter plot*, 166.

23. Ibid., 167.

24. Dorothy Dinnerstein, *The mermaid and the minotaur: Sexual arrangements and the human malaise* (New York: Harper Colophon, 1976).

25. Ruddick, *Maternal thinking*, 34. Many, many works have examined women's feelings of powerlessness in the institution of motherhood. See, for example, Meg Luxton, *More than a labour of love* (Toronto: Women's Press, 1980).

26. Ruddick, *Maternal thinking*, 35.

27. Elizabeth Debold, Marie Wilson, and Idelisse Malavé, *Mother daughter revolution: From good girls to great women* (New York: Bantam Books, 1994), 36.

28. Ibid., 22.

29. Ibid., 11.

30. Ibid., 12. Several feminist scholars have written on the loss of the female self in adolescence. See, for example, Lyn Mikel Brown and Carol Gilligan, *Meeting at the crossroads: Women's psychology and girls' development* (Cambridge, MA: Harvard University Press, 1992); Shere Hite, *The Hite Report on the family* (New York: Grove Press, 1994); Judy Mann, *The difference: Growing up female in America* (New York: Time Warner, 1994); Mary Pipher, *Reviving Ophelia: Saving the selves of adolescent girls* (New York: Grosset/Putnam, 1994); Mieke de Waal, "Teenage daughters on their mothers," in van Mens-Verhulst, Schreurs, and Woertman, eds., *Daughtering and mothering*, 35–43.

31. Debold, Wilson, and Malavé, *Mother daughter revolution*, 15.

32. Ibid., 101.

33. Ibid., 38.

34. Miriam Johnson, *Strong mothers, weak wives: The search for gender equality* (Berkeley: University of California Press, 1989), 6.

35. Ibid., 8.

36. Ibid., 184.

37. Ibid., 173.

38. Ibid., 184.

39. Naomi Ruth Lowinsky, *Stories From the motherline: Reclaiming the mother–daughter bond, finding our female souls* (Los Angeles: Jeremy P. Tarcher, 1992), 1–2.

40. Ibid., 30.

41. Ibid., 29.

42. Ibid., 32. It is important to emphasize that Lowinsky does not advocate "turning back the clock" and pushing women once again out of historical time.

43. Ibid., 31.

44. Ibid., 13.

45. Virginia Woolf, *A room of one's own* (1929; reprint, New York: Granada, 1977), 72.

46. Hope Edelman, *Motherless daughters: The legacy of loss* (New York: Delta, 1994), 201.

47. In Edelman's work, motherless includes several types of absences—"premature death, physical separation, mental illness, emotional abandonment, and neglect" (Ibid., xxv).

48. Ibid., 61.

49. Ibid., xxv. One woman, whose mother died when she was eight, spoke about the longing for guidance of a mature, experienced woman who would teach her "how to be."

50. Ibid., 178.

51. Ibid., 179.

52. Ibid., 200.

53. Rich, *Of woman born*, 237.

54. Marni Jackson, *The mother zone: Love, sex, and laundry in the modern family* (Toronto: Macfarlane Walter and Ross, 1992), 13.

55. Ibid., 9.

56. Ibid., 3.

57. Ibid., 4, 9.

58. Ibid.

59. Julia Kristeva, *Revolution in poetic language*, Margaret Walker, trans. (New York: Columbia University Press, 1984).

60. Hirsch, *The mother/daughter plot*, 179.

61. Ruddick, *Maternal thinking*, 40. Emphasis in original.

62. Carolyn Heilbrun, *Writing a woman's life* (New York: Ballantine, 1988), 32.

63. Caplan writes: "[Women] must humanize [their] image of [their] mother ... [in order] to see the real woman behind the mother-myths" (Caplan, 147). Significantly, Caplan argues that such may be achieved through listening to the mother's story and writing a biography of her life.

64. Rich, *Of woman born*, 220.

Chapter Seventeen

THE GLOBAL SELF-ESTEEM OF AN AFRICAN-AMERICAN ADOLESCENT FEMALE AND HER RELATIONSHIP WITH HER MOTHER

Barbara Turnage

Like all children, the developing African-American girl needs a secure and consistent environment to form the foundation for a positive global self-esteem.[1] Self-esteem consists of two components: feeling that one is lovable and feeling that one is competent.[2] Self-esteem can be viewed as an individual's attitude about herself, as well as her estimate of how capable, worthwhile, and successful she feels she is as a person.[3] Self-esteem exists on a continuum, and a person's self-esteem level can appear anywhere along this continuum, from high to low self-esteem.[4] An individual with high self-esteem, as defined by Rosenberg, "feels that [she/he] is a person of worth; [she/he] respects [her-/himself] for what [she/he] is, but [she/he] does not stand in awe of [her-/himself] nor does [she/he] expect others to stand in awe of [her/him]."[5] This individual communicates to the world an attitude of being "good enough."[6] Joseph identified high self-esteem, for adolescents, as protective armor.[7]

At the opposite end of high self-esteem is low self-esteem. An individual with low self-esteem is viewed to exhibit behaviors that reflect "self-rejection, self-dissatisfaction, [and] self-contempt."[8] Unlike an individual with high self-esteem, this individual does not respect nor enjoy her current self. Although she may wish otherwise, she finds her self-picture to be disagreeable.[9]

A variety of factors influence a person's overall or global self-esteem level.[10] In reference to adolescents' self-esteem, Wade and his colleagues, based on a review of the literature, identified five factors. They are "physical and sexual development, sexual activity, physical and sexual attractiveness, interpersonal relationships, and competency."[11] These authors concluded, using a data set of 1,153 adolescents who were tested at age eleven and again at age seventeen (336, or 29 percent, of these adolescents were African-American), that "predictors of self-esteem for Black respondents do not resemble those of White respondents."[12] The authors further noted that, based on gender, the factors also differed for the African-American respondents.[13] As Wade and his colleagues demonstrated, knowing the factors that influence European-American males' (and/or females') and African-American males' self-esteem will not help predict the factors that influence African-American females' level of self-esteem.[14] For example, physical attractiveness influenced the self-esteem of both African-American and European-American females in Wade and his associates'[15] study; however, the standards of beauty differed. The European-American females were more influenced by media-imposed standards of beauty than the African-American females. Of particular importance to an African-American female's global self-esteem level are the levels of her ethnic identity,[16] appearance evaluation,[17] and trust of mother (attachment).[18]

The purpose of this investigation is to add another dimension to the scholarly discussion of the African-American mother–daughter relationship. Specifically, this research will investigate interrelationships between the daughter's global self-esteem, her ethnic identity, appearance evaluation, and the daughter's trust of her mother (secure attachment).

Factor one: Ethnic identity

The first of the three factors, ethnic identity, is derived from membership in a social group.[19] Historically in the United States, African-oriented features (darker skin-tones, thick lips, broad noses, kinky hair, etc.) have been devalued and ridiculed.[20] Unfortunately, this practice continues. However, today's African-American female who possesses African-oriented features has at her disposal a variety of self-esteem enhancing materials.[21] The most significant is her mother.[22]

Many African-American mothers have been charged with the task of providing an environment in which their daughters can become emotionally and spiritually sound, happy, healthy, and productive African-American women.[23] This enormous task is made more difficult because of America's racist and sexist history. African-American mothers who choose to play this role must be willing to prepare their daughters to live as black women.[24]

There is no room for many African-American mothers to forget what it means to confront racial and sexist barriers. Also, in the day-to-day lives of black women, racism and sexism can lead to various forms of prejudice and discrimination.[25] Grier and Cobbs contend that "a parent's essential and fundamental purpose, beyond assuring the child's survival, is to provide an interpretation of the society to the child."[26] Thus, an African-American mother may work to communicate to her daughter how these experiences and their consequences may affect her psychological well-being.[27] Through information she receives from her mother, and through personal experiences, the daughter learns of life's pitfalls on a daily basis. Sadly, through each experience, she learns to prepare herself for the next. On occasions, lessons learned through experience (personal or example) are not enough protection. Her mother, along with her father and significant family and non-family members, teaches her that life isn't fair, and sometimes it just is that way.

Under these circumstances, ethnic group identification, "together with the value and emotional significance attached to membership,"[28] can have either a positive or negative impact on the African-American girl's global self-esteem. During adolescence and into adulthood, "concerns about ethnicity shift from learning one's ethnic label to understanding the significance of one's group membership."[29]

Factor two: Appearance evaluation

While learning what it means to be an African-American female, the adolescent further exposes her unfolding self-esteem to public scrutiny. As a result, by identifying herself as a black woman, she will most likely incur all of the negative (and positive) connotations associated with both her ethnic identification and her gender identification.[30] For example, an adolescent may, inside her home, be told that her hair is attractive and versatile, while outside her home she experiences ridicule from non-African-American peers based on her hairstyles.[31] The conflicting nature of the messages may lead her to question the relevance of the information received from either inside or outside of her home. Depending on how she evaluates her appearance, she may discontinue her expression of her ethnic identity through the wearing of ethnic-oriented hairstyles—that is, if she chooses conformity. The ridicule invoked by her peers may weaken her global self-esteem level and spur her to seek solace in their acceptance (to conform). However, if her global self-esteem level includes an appearance evaluation that was established based on her ethnic heritage, she may choose to continue expressing her African-American pride through her hairstyles.

Concerning the significance of peer-related conformity, Makkar and Strube report that black women who possessed high self-esteem, and high African self-consciousness, were more likely to judge their physical appearance in accordance with members of their own ethnic group.[32] The women in Makkar and Strube's study, ages seventeen to twenty-two years, consistently chose other black women as reference points when asked questions about their appearance evaluation (body image). Many of these reference points were inside of their immediate family.[33]

Based on her personal experiences, one would expect an African-American mother to encourage her daughter to develop an appearance evaluation based on African-American beauty standards.[34] A person's appearance evaluation (body image) is her opinion of her body, and is impacted by her shape, age, size, gender, self-esteem level, culture, ethnicity, and historical time. According to Singh, "the female body shape is determined by both the amount of fat and its distribution."[35] Both body-fat distribution (body shape) and overall weight (body size) may jointly determine the perception of ideal female body shape. Thus, it is not necessarily the amount of fat (how much the person weighs) that determines how one looks, but the fat combined with the elements mentioned here (shape, age, size, etc.). Rucker and Cash add the element of culture as another determining factor.[36] They state that "cultures purvey gender-specific standards for physical attractiveness, body weight, and body shape."[37] From their point of view, "cultural standards shape the individual's body-image experiences and his/her adjustment behaviors."[38]

Factor three: Trust of mother

Many African-American women during adolescence struggled with the task of filtering out non-obtainable images of womanhood.[39] Based on these firsthand experiences, these women may possess the ability to identify and dismantle inappropriate images of womanhood that are directed at their daughters. An African-American mother may present obtainable images of womanhood into her parenting practices.[40]

Based on the emotional bond that developed between the mother and daughter during the daughter's early years of life, a level of trust was established.[41] That is, the daughter develops a level of trust in regard to her mother's ability/ willingness to soothe and protect her. In her role as mediator,[42] an African-American mother signals to her daughter that she is willing to serve as a secure base from which her daughter can explore and experience the world.[43] As her daughter's mediator, an African-American mother also signals to her daughter that she wishes to take an active role in her daughter's life. She teaches her daughter to "stay the course" when times get hard, that she is worthy of love and respect, that she has the right to dream and accomplish her dreams, and that others' opinions of her should be secondary (if at all) to her opinion of herself. For her daughter to achieve a positive global self-esteem, an African-American mother must not only verbally encourage her daughter, she must model the image of womanhood she wishes her daughter to obtain.

To ensure her daughter's global self-esteem survives the onslaught of negative stimuli directed at African-American females, an African-American mother must be prepared to mediate the harm attached to these stimuli.[44] Regardless of the situation, an African-American female needs to sure that her mother will either assist her efforts to alleviate the problem or take care of the problem herself. Knowing that her mother is willing and able to assist her efforts to develop renews the trust that was developed early in the daughter's life. This trust helps the daughter tackle the most insidious stress. Without her mother, an African-American adolescent female may be left unprotected.

By instilling a positive global self-esteem in her daughter, an African-American mother works to mediate the dangerous societal forces identified earlier. This can occur through an African-American mother encouraging her daughter to develop an African-American ethnic identity, providing her daughter with an appearance evaluation that is reflective of her daughter's ethnic heritage; the enhancement of a trusting mother–daughter relationship; and teaching her daughter effective coping strategies. For the reasons already stated, the global self-esteem of an African-American girl is "the armor that protects [her] from the dragons of life."[45] These dragons may be early withdrawal from high school, early pregnancy, drug usage, and/or crime.

Methodology

This section will present the two research hypotheses, information about study participants, study procedures, and study instruments. The sampling method used in this exploratory, cross-sectional study was convenience. For the sake of clarity the term *predictor variable* will be used when addressing the three independent variables—Ethnic Identity Achievement, Appearance Evaluation, and Trust of Mother.

Hypotheses

Hypothesis 1 addresses the relationship between global self-esteem and the predictor variables. That is, self-esteem will be positively correlated with ethnic identity achievement, appearance evaluation, and trust of mother.

The second hypothesis addresses the amount of variance that could be explained by the predictor variables. That is, an African-American adolescent female's global self-esteem level can be predicted by levels of ethnic identity achievement, appearance evaluation, and trust of mother.

Subjects

Data for this study were collected from 105 African-American females recruited from a Catholic, all-girls high school in an urban area. The participants were twelfth graders between the ages of sixteen and eighteen (mean age: 16.83). Of the 105 participants, twenty-four (twenty-three percent) were sixteen, seventy-five (seventy-one percent) were seventeen, and six (six percent) were eighteen (see Table 17.1).

Table 17.1: Participant's Parent's Education and Employment

Participant's Age in Years

Parents' Level of Education	16		17		18		Sum
	Mother	Father	Mother	Father	Mother	Father	
High School and Below	7% (7)	7% (7)	11% (11)	19% (19)	4% (4)	3% (3)	25% (51)
Some College and Associate	7% (7)	8% (8)	30% (31)	30% (30)	1% (1)	2% (2)	39% (79)
College Degree and Above	10% (10)	8% (8)	30% (31)	21% (21)	1% (1)	1% (1)	36% (72)
Total	23% (24)	23% (23)	71% (73)	71% (70)	6% (6)	6% (6)	100%
Work Outside of Home	21	23	67	59	4	5	

Overall, half (fifty-one percent) of these young women lived with both of their biological parents, while thirty-nine percent of them lived with their biological mother only. Of the remaining ten percent, seven percent lived with their mother and a stepfather, two percent lived with their grandmother, and one percent lived with another family member.

There were 103 participants who responded to the question concerning their mother's education (see Table 17.1). Forty-eight percent of the participants reported their mothers receiving some type of college degree. Of this forty-eight percent, seven percent were reported to have obtained an associate degree, twenty-nine percent had obtained a bachelor's degree, and twelve percent had obtained a graduate or professional degree. Only three percent of the mothers had obtained less than a high school education (one mother had less than nine years of schooling). There was a significant correlation ($r = .338$, $p = .000$) between mothers' education and fathers' education.

Procedures

Data was collected on two separate days. Participants were surveyed in their religion class on either Monday or Tuesday. The research packet consisted of four instruments—one self-esteem (HARE Self-Esteem Scale), one ethnic identity achievement (My Ethnicity), one appearance evaluation (My Body), one attachment to mother (My Mother). Research instruments were counterbalanced to protect the data from order effects by reducing the possibility of missing data and nonrandom error. The counterbalance procedure consisted of arranging the odd-numbered packets with the self-esteem instrument first (the format presented earlier), while the even-numbered packets had the attachment to mother instrument first.

Instruments

The participants completed four instruments. The HARE General and Area-Specific (School, Peer, and Home) Self-Esteem Scale (HARE)[46] was used to measure participants' global self-esteem. The HARE is a thirty-item self-administered instrument. The seven-item Ethnic Identity Achievement subscale of Phinney's[47] Multigroup Ethnic Identity Measure was used to measure participants' ethnic identity. To measure participants' appearance evaluation, the seven-item Appearance Evaluation subscale of Cash's Multidimensional Body-Self Relations Questionnaire[48] was used. Trust of mother was measured by the ten-item Trust subscale of the Parent Inventory of the Inventory of Parent and Peer Attachment.[49] Chronbach alphas for this study's instruments study ranged from 0.81 to 0.95.

Results

This section will discuss the results of a stepwise multiple regression and a test of correlation (Pearson Product Moment). The stepwise multiple regression was run to test Hypothesis 1: An African-American adolescent female's global self-esteem level can be predicted by levels of ethnic identity achievement, appearance evaluation, trust of mother, and coping. This hypothesis was supported. Ethnic identity achievement, appearance evaluation, and trust of mother together explained forty-three percent of the variance in global self-esteem (see Table 17.2).

The correlation analysis was used to test Hypothesis two: Self-esteem will be positively correlated with ethnic identity achievement, appearance evaluation, and trust of mother. This hypothesis was also supported. The results of a test of correlation revealed that ethnic identity achievement, appearance evaluation, and trust of mother were significantly ($p = .000$) correlated to self-esteem (see Table 17.3).

Discussion

The results of the statistical tests performed revealed that, of the three predictor variables, the trust of mother variable was key when predicting global self-esteem. The strength of the relationship between trust of mother and global self-esteem truly reflected non-shared variance ($r = .52$, $p = .000$). This variable, trust of mother, was the first predictor variable to be entered in the stepwise regression analysis where it alone explained twenty-seven percent of the variance in global self-esteem. Adding ethnic identity achievement and appearance evaluation only increased the explained variance by sixteen percent (three percent and thirteen percent, respectively).

The second variable to be entered in the stepwise regression analysis was appearance evaluation. The strength of the beta weight for appearance evaluation, combined with the amount of variance it explains, is boosted by the presence of ethnic identity achievement. The significance of these two variables clearly illustrates the critical role attributed to the evaluation of one's appearance from an ethnic position. Without a doubt, possessing an ethnic- (African-American-) oriented appearance evaluation contributed to how these young women felt about themselves. In particular, a positive African-oriented body image (appearance evaluation) for this sample had a direct bearing on their global self-esteem (correlation between appearance evaluation and global self-esteem: $r = .46$, $p = .000$).

Table 17.2: Results of stepwise regression with predictor variables on self-esteem

	Global Self-Esteem	
Variable	Beta	Alpha
Ethnic Identity Achievement	.19	.021
Appearance Evaluation	.32	.000
Trust of Mother	.40	.000

Table 17.3: Results of correlation analysis between global self-esteem and the predictor variables

Variables	Global Self-Esteem	Ethnic Identity Achievement	Appearance Evaluation	Trust of Mother
Global Self-Esteem	—			
Ethnic Identity Achievement	.40[a]	—		
Appearance Evaluation	.46[a]	.31[b]	—	
Trust of Mother	.52[a]	.26[c]	.19[d]	—

[a]Significant at the 0.000 level (2-tailed).
[b]Significant at the 0.001 level (2-tailed).
[c]Significant at the 0.01 level (2-tailed).
[d]Significant at the 0.05 level (2-tailed).

Conclusion

As this study suggests, the major contributors to its participants' global self-esteem, in relation to this study's predictor variables, were (1) trust of their African-American mothers, and (2) their acceptance of their appearance based on an understanding and an embracing of their African-American heritage.

This study demonstrates that African-American mothers play an important role in their daughters' self-esteem development. That is, the young women in this study who had high self-esteem also trusted their mothers to be there for them. A second important finding was the acknowledgment of an African ancestry. This theme resounded throughout all of the statistical tests that were performed. For the young women in this study, ethnic identity achievement was the only predictor variable that was significantly correlated with all of the study variables (see Table 17.2).

African-American mothers have been charged with the task of providing an environment in which their daughters can become emotionally and spiritually sound, happy, healthy, and productive African-American women. To accomplish this task, during their daughters' developmental years, many African-American mothers mediate their daughters' exposure to external environments.[50] These African-American mothers, in raising their daughters to respect their ethnicity, have experienced America's disgust for difference. For an adolescent African-American female, knowledge of her African heritage helps her define her body image and structures her expectations.

The information provided by these young women, although not generalizable, delivers a clear message in reference to their mothers. The significance of this message cannot be overstated. The relationship between these African-American young women and their mothers instilled in them the knowledge that they are competent and lovable. Based on their trust in their mothers, these young women believed, when confronted with difficult situations, that they could rely on their mother's assistance. Thus, as they grow into black womanhood, they grow with the knowledge that they can accomplish their goals, and that they are worthy of love and respect.

Notes

1. Beverly A. Greene, "What has gone before: The legacy of racism and sexism in the lives of black mothers and daughters," *Women and Therapy* 9, nos. 1 & 2 (1990): 207–30; Beverly A. Greene, "Sturdy bridges: The role of African-American mothers in the socialization of African-American children," *Women and Therapy* 10, nos. 1 & 2 (1990): 205–25.
2. W.B. Swann, *Self-traps* (New York: Freemand, 1996).
3. Jeffrey Bogan, "The assessment of self-esteem: A cautionary note," *Australian Psychologist* 23, no. 3 (1988): 383–89.
4. Earle Silber and Jean S. Tippett, "Self-esteem: Clinical assessment and measurement validation," *Psychological Reports* 16 (1965): 1017–71.
5. Morris Rosenberg, *Society and the adolescent self-image* (Princeton, N.J.: Princeton University Press, 1965), 31.
6. Rosenberg, *Society and the adolescent self-image*, 31.
7. Joanne M. Joseph, *The resilient child: Preparing today's youth for tomorrow's world* (New York: Plenum, 1994).
8. Rosenberg, *Society and the adolescent self-image*, 31.
9. Rosenberg, *Society and the adolescent self-image*, 31.
10. Bruce R. Hare. "Self-perception and academic achievement: Variations in a desegregated setting," *American Journal of Psychiatry* 137, no. 6 (1980): 683–89; C. Mruk, *Self-esteem research, theory, and practice* (New York: Springer, 1995).

11. T.J. Wade, V. Thompson, A. Tashakkori, and E. Valente, "A longitudinal analysis of sex by race differences in predictors of adolescent self-esteem," *Personality Individual Differences* 10, no. 7 (1989): 717, 727.

12. Wade et al., "A longitudinal analysis of sex," 717, 727.

13. Ibid.

14. T.J. Wade, "Race and sex differences in adolescent self-perceptions of physical attractiveness and level of self-ssteem during early and late adolescence," *Personality Individual Differences* 12, no. 12 (1991): 1319–24.

15. Wade et al., "A longitudinal analysis of sex," 717, 727.

16. Jean S. Phinney, "The multigroup ethnic identity measure: A new scale for use with diverse groups," *Journal of Adolescent Research* 7, no. 2 (1992): 156–76.

17. Jalmeen K. Makkar and Michael J. Strube, "Black women's self-perceptions of attractiveness following exposure to white versus black beauty standards: The moderating role of racial identity and self-esteem," *Journal of Applied Social Psychology* 25, no. 17 (1995): 1547–66.

18. Howard C. Stevenson, Jr., "Validation of the scale of racial socialization for African-American adolescents: Steps toward multidimensionality," *Journal of Black Psychology* 20, no. 4 (1994): 445–68.

19. Phinney, "The multigroup ethnic identity measure," 156–76.

20. Selena Bond and Thomas F. Cash, "Black beauty: Skin color and body images among African-American college women," *Journal of Applied Social Psychology* 22, no. 11 (1992): 874–88.

21. Vivian Church, *Colors around me* (Chicago: Afro-American, 1971/1993); Deborah Easton, *Color me proud* (Milwaukee: Identity Toys, 1994).

22. S. Hammer, *Daughters and mothers: Mothers and daughters* (New York: Quadrangle/New York Times, 1976); Deborah Plummer, "Patterns of racial identity development of African-American adolescent males and females," *Journal of Black Psychology* 21, no. 2 (1995): 168–80.

23. Greene, "What has gone before," 207–30; Greene, "Sturdy bridges," 205–25.

24. Patricia Hill Collins, *Black feminist thought: Knowledge, consciousness and the politics of empowerment* (New York: Routledge, 1991).

25. Carlton T. Pyant and Barbara J. Yanico, "Relationship of racial identity and gender-role attitudes of black women's psychological well-being," *Journal of Counseling Psychology* 38, no. 3 (1991): 315–22.

26. W.H. Grier and P.M. Cobbs, *Black rage*, 2nd ed. (New York: Basic Books, 1992).

27. Pyant et al., "Relationship of racial dentity and gender-role attitudes," 315–22.

28. Phinney, "The multigroup ethnic identity measure," 156–76.

29. Ibid.

30. Althea Smith and Abigail J. Stewart, "Approaches to studying racism and sexism in black women's lives," *Journal of Social Issues* 39, no. 3 (1983): 1–15.

31. Makkar et al., "Black women's self-perceptions of attractiveness," 1547–66.

32. M.B. Lykes, "Discrimination and coping in the lives of black women: Analyses of oral history data," *Journal of Social Issues* 39, no. 3 (1983): 79–100.

33. Lykes, "Discrimination and coping in the lives of black women," 79–100.

34. Greene, "What has gone before," 207–30; Greene, "Sturdy bridges," 205–25.

35. Devendra Singh, "Body fat distribution and perception of desirable female body shape by young black men and women," *International Journal of Eating Disorders* 16, no. 3 (1994): 289–94.

36. Clifford E. Rucker and Thomas F. Cash, "Body images, body size-perceptions, and eating behaviors among African-American and white college women," *International Journal of Eating Disorders* 12, no. 3 (1992): 292.

37. Rucker et al., "Body images, body size-perceptions," 292.

38. Ibid.

39. Daisy L. Bates, "I did not really understand what it meant to be a negro," in *Black women in white America: A documentary history*, G. Lerner, ed. (New York: Vintage Books, 1973), 306–8.

40. Greene, "What has gone before," 207–30; Greene, "Sturdy bridges," 205–25.

41. John Bowlby, "Attachment and loss: Retrospect and prospect," *American Journal of Orthopsychiatry* 52, no. 4 (1982): 664–78; V.L. Colin, *Human attachment* (Philadelphia: Temple University Press, 1996); Robert Karen, "Becoming attached," *Atlantic Monthly* (February 1990): 35–70.

42. Vetta L. Sanders Thompson, "Socialization to race and its relationship to racial identification among African-Americans," *Journal of Black Psychology* 20, no. 2 (1994): 175–88.

43. Bowlby, "Attachment and loss," 635–70.

44. Greene, "What has gone before," 207–30; Greene, "Sturdy bridges," 205–25.

45. Judith McKay, "Building self-esteem in children," in *Self-esteem*, Matthew McKay and Patrick Fanning, ed. (Oakland, Calif.: New Harbinger, 1987), 327–73.

46. Hare, "Self-perception and academic achievement," 683–89.

47. Phinney, "The multigroup ethnic identity measure," 156–76.

48. Thomas F. Cash, *The multidimensional body-self relations questionnaire manual* (Norfolk, Va.: Old Dominion University, 1994).

49. Gay C. Armsden and Mark T. Greenberg, "The inventory of parent and peer attachment individual differences and their relationship to psychological well-being in adolescence," *Journal of Youth and Adolescence* 16, no. 5 (1987): 427–54.

50. Greene, "What has gone before," 207–30; Greene, "Sturdy bridges," 205–25.

Chapter Eighteen

Don't Blame Mother

THEN AND NOW

Paula Caplan

This chapter is about the practice of mother blame, from the time leading up to my writing *Don't blame mother: Mending the mother–daughter relationship*[1] to the present. First I shall explain what motivated me to write the book beginning in the mid-1980s, then I shall discuss how much of what was relevant then remains relevant today, and finally I shall describe the way I have attempted to put some themes about mother blame into theatrical form.

I became interested in mother blaming when I was working in a clinic where we were evaluating families. I noticed that no matter what was wrong, no matter what the reason for the family's coming to the clinic, it turned out that the mother was always assumed to be responsible for the problem. And if, in the assessment interview, she sat right next to the child, my colleagues would say afterward, "Did you see how she sat right next to the child? She is smothering and overcontrolling and too close and enmeshed and symbiotically fused with the child." But if she did not sit right next to the child, she was called cold and rejecting—and, if the child was a boy, castrating.

So my interest in mother blaming began because it seemed that there was nothing that a mother could do that was right, and it was particularly interesting and painful to me because I myself was a mother.

In 1986, when I received tenure and considered what I most wanted to teach, one of the two courses I created was about mothers. I wasn't aware at the time of any other course about mothers, so I started trying to design the course and talking to people about it. Often, both men and women would laugh and say, "What are you going to talk about for a whole semester?" or just, "Hah! A course about mothers?" You may remember a similar reaction people had ten years earlier to "Oh! You're going to have a course about women?"

Teaching that course to graduate students at the University of Toronto's Ontario Institute for Studies in Education led to my writing *Don't blame mother*. In the book, I describe aspects of girls' and women's socialization that create or exacerbate problems between mothers and daughters, as well as methods that mothers and daughters have found helpful in repairing rifts between them. (I did not believe and still do not believe that the mother–daughter relationship is more fraught with problems than the mother–son relationship, or the relationships between fathers and their children of either sex. However, as a feminist I was primarily concerned with the kinds of socially created—and, therefore, hopefully surmountable—barriers between women.) In addressing the question "To what extent is the content of *Don't blame mother* applicable today?" I find it depressing that most of the basic principles that concerned me as I wrote the book still apply today. I shall return to this point later.

After my experience in the clinical setting described earlier, I did some research with Ian Hall-McCorquodale,[2] looking at articles in clinical journals written by psychoanalysts, psychiatrists, social workers, psychologists, behavior therapists, and clinicians of all stripes. We found that mothers were blamed for virtually every kind of psychological or emotional problem that ever brought any patient to see a therapist. We were also disappointed to find that the sex of the person who was writing the paper did not determine the presence or absence of mother blaming, and, even more depressingly, that it didn't get better as the years passed after the resurgence of the women's movement during the 1970s. With respect to mother blame, so many therapists still seemed to be buried under their rocks.

When I began to bring up this subject of mother blame I pointed out that there are myths about mothers that allow us to take anything a mother might do and turn it into evidence of something "bad" about her. Important work that a mother does goes largely unnoticed, except when she doesn't do it, as when she is sick and can't make dinner. I would point out that nobody I knew of was likely to say to their mother, "That was a great week's work of dusting you did," or "That was a week of delicious and nourishing meals that you prepared." When I would say this, people would laugh—and still do, in fact.

So we have to ask, "Why does this make us laugh? Would you laugh if I said, 'Dad, the lawn looks great now that you have mowed it?'" Nobody laughs at that. Why? Because we laugh at the unexpected. It is so unimaginable to us that anyone would express appreciation for, or a sense of valuing of, the work that mothers do as mothers and housekeepers and cooks and chauffeurs. So I used to talk about that.

As observed in a review of *The time bind: When work becomes home and home becomes work*,[3] Arlie Hochschild points out that women increasingly spend time at paid work because they feel appreciated there. She says that even for relatively uninteresting work, such as factory work, women find work to be a greater source of self-esteem than home life. This was something that had concerned me years ago, because it seemed to me that, as in that story about no one thanking you for dusting, even if you work at a really boring, miserable job, every week or two somebody hands you a paycheque. The cheque might not be much, but it communicates the notion that somebody puts some value on the work that you do. And it's still no better in terms of mothering.

At the heart of *Don't blame mother* are mother myths I call the "Good Mother Myths" and mother myths I call the "Bad Mother Myths." The Good Mother Myths set standards that no human being could ever match, such as that mothers are always, naturally, one hundred percent nurturant. We have a double standard. We don't have that kind of expectation of fathers. So, when, one percent of the time, mothers don't do what we wish they would do, we feel betrayed, because the myth is that they naturally are able to and, in fact, are desperate to be nurturant all the time. But when our fathers do anything nurturant, we feel that it is wonderful that Daddy did something like that. (Naturally, the answer is not to stop appreciating what fathers do but rather to be ready to give mothers equal credit when they are nurturant.)

The Bad Mother Myths allow us to take mothers' neutral or bad behavior— because mothers are human, so we do some bad things—or even mothers' good behavior, and transform it into further proof that mothers are bad. One example that disturbs me the most is the myth that mother–daughter closeness is sick, that it is a form of psychopathology. When *Don't blame mother* was first published, and I was doing media interviews, every woman interviewer would confess, with the microphone turned off, that she talked to her mother every day. I would ask her, "How do you feel afterward?" and the woman would reply, "Oh, great. My mother has a great sense of humor, and we are great friends, and we give each other advice." I would then ask her, "Do you have a partner?" "Yes." "Do you talk to them every day?" "Yes." "Does that embarrass you?" "No." And I would ask, "Well, then, why did you confess that you talk to your mother every day?" These women would reply that they worried that the daily talks with their mothers were signs that they hadn't "individuated" or "achieved autonomy" from their mothers, and if they had been in therapy they would say, "I know it means we're enmeshed or symbiotically fused." My point here is that anything associated with mothers becomes devalued and pathologized.

If you look at the myths about mothers, you find that some of them are mutually exclusive.[4] One of the Bad Mother Myths is that mothers are an endless drain on our energy: just on the basis of strict physics principles alone, you cannot be constantly putting out force (nurturance), while constantly taking in force and energy as you are draining it from others. Another set of mutually exclusive myths involves the Good Mother Myth, according to which mothers naturally, perhaps for hormonal reasons, know everything they need to know about mothering, and the Bad Mother Myth, according to which mothers cannot raise emotionally healthy children without the advice of lots of experts.

I believe that these mutually exclusive myths continue to coexist because every society needs scapegoated groups if the people in power want to maintain their power. What happens if I'm in the powerful group and some member of the scapegoated group does something good? Somebody might get the idea that the scapegoated people are not as bad as I portray them to be, and if that's the case, maybe I don't deserve to have all of the power I have. So I have to make sure there is a myth for every occasion, so that no matter what the members of that scapegoated group might do, I can transform it into further proof that they are wrong, bad, or pathological, and deserve to continue to have no power and be scapegoated.[5] That is the powerful function that these myths serve, and that is why we need to keep questioning them.

This power hierarchy still exists, and the women's movement hasn't been able to change it yet. I think it hasn't changed partly because we often substitute the word *mother* for *woman*. For instance, people at a party may stop you when you tell a "joke" that is woman-hating, but if you change the word *woman* to *mother*, you can still get away with the comment. You are much less likely to have someone interrupt you to say, "I don't think that's funny, and I don't want you to go on like that."

What the women's movement can do is to make the repeated exposure of mother myths—the placing of them front and center—a priority. Anti-feminist backlash makes all feminist efforts more difficult, of course. But until we recognize the need for what we might call "the Norma Rae-ing of mothers' struggles," the need to reveal mothers' oppression and its systemic nature, few women of any ethnic or racialized group or class or sexual orientation (and certainly not women with disabilities or women who don't weigh the "right" amount) will be free. Why? Because we all had mothers, and so we're connected with what is done to, what is said about mothers. Because we have all been subjected as women to strong pressure to prove we are unlike our mothers. You'll often hear women say, "My greatest fear is that I will be like my mother." What I find that these women usually mean if you explore that statement is, "I don't want to be treated the way she has been treated. I don't want to be demeaned and undervalued the way she is." At the same time as we are taught to not want to be like our mothers, we are taught—sometimes subliminally—that we should want to be like our mothers, when they are passive, pliable, and ashamed of themselves. And no one is free until the truths about mothers are highlighted, because all women, and especially as we age,[6] are expected to be motherly, motherlike, as in being self-denying and serving others.

No, it's not getting any better—not socially and not in the research arena. A recent issue of the *American Journal of Orthopsychiatry* includes a longitudinal report on "Preschool antecedents of adolescent assaultive behavior."[7] The researchers studied children from preschool through adolescence in an attempt to discern the determinants of adolescents' assaultive behavior. How did they look at the alleged determinants? Among other things, they observed what they call early in their article "parental interactions" with the young children. That really meant "mothers' interactions," even though eighty-six percent of the children in their study had both a male and a female parent in the home. When they looked at how mothers interact with children, and then later on looked at which children become assaultive, it is not surprising that they concluded that it was the children's negative interactions with their mothers that led to their assaultive behavior.

The methodology you choose can go far to determine the results that you get. I believe that there are at least two major methodological problems evident in this study. One problem is not looking at the fathers or the society in which the children live, and what the determinants of their assaultive behavior might be. The second is a cause-effect problem. People who are assaultive when they are teenagers, for reasons that may have had nothing to do with their mothers, might have been difficult to handle as children, and thus their mothers' interactions with them would have been observed to be relatively "negative." For example, their mothers might have had to do more of the disciplining of them, more of the saying "no." That is just one example of the persistence of the practice of mother blame in "scholarly" journals.

Mother blame also persists on a grand scale in the arena of the diagnosis of mental illness. My book *They say you're crazy: How the world's most powerful psychiatrists decide who's normal*[8] is an exposé of the *Diagnostic and statistical manual of mental disorders*[9] (also called the DSM). The DSM is the "Bible" of mental health professionals that lists 374 supposedly different mental disorders. It is marketed as "science," but the way it is put together is far from scientific, and pieces of relevant scientific research are often ignored or distorted. I became involved in learning about the DSM in 1985 because I was concerned about a new category the American Psychiatric Association was proposing to include in the DSM called "Self-Defeating Personality Disorder." This new category might be described as "the Good Wife, or Good Mother Syndrome." It included criteria such as not putting other people's needs ahead of one's own, feeling unappreciated, and choosing less desirable options for their lives when clearly better ones are available. But this is what society still thinks we are supposed to do as a mother and as a "good" woman. Once involved, I was horrified when I learned about the way that the DSM's authors decide who is "normal." I ended up calling their process "Diagnosisgate" because of the similarities to Watergate in terms of lies, cover-ups, and distortions of what the research literature shows.[10]

This "Self-Defeating Personality Disorder" is a real catch-22 for women. If women act in those ways, they supposedly have this mental disorder, but if they do not act in those ways, they are rejected and pathologized for not being real women, not being "good" women.[11] Because there was a virtual blackout of *They say you're crazy* by the major media, and I wanted people to know about the Diagnosisgate issues, I decided to write a play on the theme of who decides who is normal. The play is called *Call me crazy*,[12] and I shall include here a couple of excerpts from it. It is a dramatic comedy, with scenes alternating between relatively serious ones in a mental hospital case-conference room, and comedic-grotesque, "campy" ones like a quiz show called "What's My Diagnosis?" Most of the second act takes place in the conference room where the psychology intern is making it possible for patients to tell their stories. I chose the stories for the two women and two men patients because they are typical of what happens in the traditional mental health system. For the two women's stories, this includes the therapists' disbelieving what women tell them, and their pathologizing of women in general. Here is the story told by Patient 3:

Patient Three: I was a cheerleader in high school—and homecoming queen. During my second year in college, I married Eugene, my high school sweetheart. Then I got pregnant, and as soon as my tummy started to swell, he started getting drunk and beating up on me, calling me a fat pig, saying it made him sick to have sex with me. He left me the night our daughter Tammy was born. It was hard ... being a single mother, working in a ribbon factory, trying to get my pre-pregnancy body shape back. At the factory, I met Sam. He's a truck driver, and he's gone a lot, but when he's home, he's wonderful—funny, gentle, a wonderful father to Tammy. I feel so lucky to have him, and I'm scared to death of losing him. He says he loves me, not how I look but who I am. I hope that's true, but I get so frightened of putting on weight. It's weird. Sometimes the only thing that makes me feel better when I get scared of getting fat and losing him ... is eating ... like a whole chocolate cake or a whole pot of macaroni and cheese at once. And as soon as I do that, 'course I get scared again right away ... so ... I make myself throw up. My stomach hurts, and my throat gets raw. I went to a psychologist, and she said I made myself throw up because I enjoyed that pain! I told her I didn't, but she didn't pay any attention. She said now that I didn't have Eugene around to hit me and call me names, I had to make the suffering myself! I told her I hate feeling bad, but thinking about losing Sam was even worse than throwing up to try to stay thin so he wouldn't go. She wouldn't listen. And I didn't know it then, but she wrote in my chart that I enjoyed suffering, that I had a mental illness called "Self-Defeating Personality Disorder." I found out because, when Tammy was four, Eugene suddenly showed up and went to court to take her from me. I'd stayed friends with his sister, so Eugene found out that I'd been seeing a psychologist. And they made her bring my chart to court. The judge sent Tammy to live with Eugene because I was mentally ill. I get to see her two hours every second Sunday.

This scenario is typical of what happens to women, often because of the kinds of women and mothers they are trying to be, and because of the way such efforts are interpreted by the mental health system.

Here is one more excerpt from *Call me crazy*. No one has ever heard from Freud's mother, and I thought it was time. How many people even know her name? I went to the library, thinking that I wanted her to be a character in my play but that if I could find no interesting information about her, I would make something up. But as I began to read little fragments about her life in the biographies of her son, I found myself gasping, because it seemed pretty clear to me what she probably would have felt about the various things that happened to her. She wrestles with the question of what is good and normal mothering. In the play, she steps out of history to speak to the audience. The people who are in the case conference are behind her and have been talking about the DSM.

Amalia: Thank you for coming. I'm Amalia Freud. Amalia Nathanson Freud. I lived to be ninety-five years old. For decades, I wanted people I met to know my son was the great psychoanalyst, winner of the Goethe Prize for literature. But behind their polite smiles I saw the thought, "This is the mother whose son discovered that all little boys want to have sex with their mothers." Discovered. Hah! Guessed. Claimed. Wrote a story.

A man says with aplomb, "This is what happens," and already it's a discovery. A woman says, "This is what happens," and she's exaggerating or manipulating.

And about girls and their mothers what did he "discover"? That our daughters resent us for not having had the courtesy to provide them a penis. That they look down on us because we don't have penises. I had five daughters. How do you think his words made me feel? I love my Sigmund, but this is too much ....

Sigmund was a bright boy, brilliant probably. But maybe he had too much.

He told people he felt all his life like a conqueror because he was my "indisputable favorite." Hah! So he thought. The truth is I adored all of my children. How could I not? My husband, he valued me for my son. His first wife had two sons. Sigmund was my first-born, when I was twenty-one and his father was forty-one. I loved my daughters but kept having to have more—five in all—until Jacob got one more son ten years after Sigmund was born. Most of the time Sigmund was growing up, his father and all the other children and I shared three bedrooms, but he had his own. He needed to study. Often, he took his meals alone in there and received his friends there. He was the oldest child, so maybe it was right to give him his own room. He complained that his sister Anna's piano lessons were noisy when he was trying to study. We got rid of the piano. Anna and I were sad but not angry. We understood. Maybe he had too much. And he decided who was normal.

You know, he threw up his hands in despair and said, "What do women want?" He said women were a dark continent to him. (Shakes her head.) What's not to understand? Is it healthy to take a mother's love or a wife's love and make it seem so complicated?

(Shrugs her shoulders.) Normal, shmormal. Oh, I realize some people have to be put away—they can hurt themselves, or someone else. But it's a tough problem. You start putting people away, and somebody's going to decide who gets put away, somebody's going to choose the rules. Is what these guys (indicating the giant DSM) decide any better than what my son decided? Thinking about it makes my head hurt.

But I'll tell you what I have noticed. Who decides is who has the power. And somehow, they seem to decide the people most like them are the normal ones, the good, the healthy, the deserving. It's the others who are derided, called dangerous ... sent away. My five daughters— one went to New York, three were gassed in Auschwitz, and the last one starved to death in the camp at Theresienstadt.

Thank you for listening.

(Amalia leaves the stage.)

I want to close with what Patient Three says about classifying people on the basis of the forms of their emotional anguish. What she says applies to seeing mothers and all women through the prism of the myths about mothers.

Patient Three: When you look up at the night sky, there are lots of stars. There are no real constellations, but people decide how to divide up the stars into groups and give those groups names. And forever afterward they think they see the Big Dipper and Orion. It makes it hard to see, really see, one unique star as itself.

I hope that this sampling of the recent history of mother blame makes it clear that, despite some gains that feminists have made, there are still miles to go before we can relax in the knowledge that mother blame has been eradicated.

For this reason, I suggest that we join together in declaring that women don't speak enough and don't speak up enough, certainly not in defense of mothers. Let us vow that at every possible opportunity we will protest, we will educate, even interrupt—as we would a sexist or a racist "joke"—when anyone in any setting utters or implies any of the dangerous myths about mothers.

Notes

This chapter is the slightly edited text of an address I gave on September 27, 1997, at York University, for their International Conference on Mothers and Daughters.

1. Paula Caplan, *Don't blame mother: Mending the mother–daughter relationship* (New York: Routledge, 2000)
2. Paula Caplan and Ian Hall-McCorquodale, "Mother-blaming in major clinical journals," *American Journal of Orthopsychiatry* 55 (1985): 345–53; Paula Caplan and Ian Hall-McCorquodale, "The scapegoating of mothers: A call for change," *American Journal of Orthopsychiatry* 55 (1985): 610–13.
3. Arlie Hochschild, "A review of sex role research," in *Changing women in a changing society*, ed. Joan Huber (Chicago: University of Chicago Press, 1973), 249–67.
4. Caplan, *Don't blame mother*.
5. Ibid.
6. Rachel Josefowitz Siegel, "Old women as mother figures," in *Woman-defined motherhood*, Jane Price and Ellen Cole, ed. (New York: Harrington Park, 1990), 89–97.
7. Roy C. Herrenkohl, Brenda P. Egolf, and Ellen C. Herrenkohl, "Preschool antecedents of adolescent assaultive behavior: A longitudinal study," *American Journal of Orthopsychiatry* 67 (1997): 422–32.
8. Paula Caplan, *They say you're crazy: How the world's most powerful psychiatrists decide who's normal* (Reading, Mass.: Addison-Wesley, 1995).
9. American Psychiatric Association, *Diagnostic and statistical manual of mental disorders IV* (Washington, D.C.: American Psychiatric Association, 1994).
10. Caplan. *They say you're crazy*.
11. For apparently political reasons, Self-Defeating Personality Disorder was removed from the most recent edition of the DSM, but that has not kept it from being used.
12. Paula Caplan, *Call me crazy* (1996), script copyrighted by and available from author.

Chapter Nineteen

MOTHER OF MOTHERS, DAUGHTER OF DAUGHTERS

REFLECTIONS ON THE MOTHERLINE

Naomi Lowinsky

Touching what her hand made
eight hundred years ago
a woman
like my mother, like myself
I feel her sitting
in my bones ...[1]

There is a worldview that is as old as humankind, a wisdom we have forgotten that we know: the ancient lore of women—the motherline. Whenever women gather in circles or in pairs, in olden times around the village well, or at the quilting bee, in modern times in support groups, over lunch, or at the children's park, they tell one another stories from the motherline. These are stories of female experience: physical, psychological, and historical. They are stories about the dramatic changes of a woman's body: developing breasts and pubic hair, bleeding, being sexual, giving birth, suckling, menopause, and growing old. They are stories of the life cycles that link generations of women: mothers who are also daughters; daughters who have become mothers; grandmothers who always remain granddaughters. They are stories that evoke the dead: mother who died while her child was very young; a child who never made it to adulthood. They are stories that show how times have changed, and that show that nothing much changes at all. We all know these stories. The voices of our mothers and grandmothers telling stories from the motherline are among our earliest memories. They flesh out what we know about what it means to be human. Yet little of this worldview surfaces into print, or into our collective understanding of history. Women lament the lack of narratives of women's lives, yet women's stories are all around us. We don't hear them because out perception is shaped by a culture that trivializes "women's talk" and devalues the passing down of female lore and wisdom.

Carnal self-knowledge

It was my fate, unlike that of many of my generation, to become a mother at a very young age. I have been wondering about our cultural attitudes toward the mother ever since. I remember myself as an earnest young woman, newly married; full of longings to write great poetry, to make a contribution, to be somebody. I remember how my whole life changed with the missing of a period.

The physical experience of giving birth changed my universe. I had a dream, during the pregnancy, of facing a gate through which I had to pass. There was no choice about it. On the other side of the gate lay darkness. I was afraid. I didn't know whether it was the darkness of birth or of death I was facing. I learned that it was both. Huge waves of energy, outside of my control, passed through me and opened me up to push an unknown being out of the darkness of my body into the light of his first day. This brought me carnal knowledge of my own animal body, my instinctive nature, my connection to all things.

My then very young first husband, present at the birth, was impressed and moved. This lifted the shame off my naked labor and my blood. My bodily experience initiated us both into the sacred connection of all human life to the female body. The universe had moved through me and he was a witness. We were both a part of everything that was alive. I felt at once whole and broken, fulfilled and empty, vibrant with life and sorely wounded. He held his baby son in his arms. It was as if one part of me, as newly born as my firstborn son, or the daughter that came a few years later, blinked in the light of a new consciousness: the consciousness of the primal experience of giving birth. I knew in my own body the story of where I came from, where my mother came from, where my grandmother came from. How they were born and how they bore; how all the women all over the world and throughout human time have born and been born; how their waters have broken; how their bellies have tightened and their focus been drawn into the absolute power of the contraction; how they have labored and pushed and breathed and cried out and sweated and bled and opened up their most vulnerable private secret selves to bring the new life out.

I had been initiated into a great mystery. I had participated in the origin of human life. I was in love with my baby boy. When he woke from his nap, I raced to see his beautiful face, to smell his body, to touch his warm sweet skin.

Another part of me felt totally lost, disoriented, my body given over to the needs of another, my consciousness devoured by crying and feeding and diapering. My husband returned to his studies. But where was the one I used to be? The one who wanted to write poetry? In a daze of exhaustion, a rapture of pleasure, an annihilation of old self and confusion of new selves, I felt utterly lost. I had grown up in an academic family. I had been taught to look for books to read when in struggle and turmoil. I could not find books or poems by women about this overwhelming experience I was in; this was the early 1960s. I didn't know that my struggle was the beginning of the thread that would tie me into the pattern of the Motherline, and tug at me until I began to understand it, until I wrote my own book. I did not know I was part of a generation of women that would be finding our own voices, telling our own stories.

Cycles, the moon, and the womb

But what do I mean by the term *motherline?* Let me give you some images from my own life to illuminate it. I am walking down a long stretch of beach with my mother and my two daughters. I walk between them, linking generations. It is one of those cool, clear, winter days that bless the northern coast of California. Sea and sky are a vivid blue. There is a light wind, and someone thinks she sees whales out there. I can't remember what we are talking about. But I do remember a surge of feeling that goes beyond words, of overarching connections, of the present moment holding within it the seeds of both past and future, and all of it held in the bodies of these four women of three generations. Walking between my daughters' younger bodies and my mother's older body evokes the feeling of another walk in another time. This time I am the daughter, nine or ten years old. My mother and grandmother walk with me around a lake sparkling in the morning sun. My grandmother's walk is slower. She is older than my mother is now. I am younger than my daughters are now. Time swirls. My grandmother has been dead for many years. How will it feel to become the age she was when I was nine? How will it feel when I am the grandmother, the mother of mothers, as she was, as my mother has become?

Back on the beach, my daughters are giggling, looking at me, then at each other. I realize I must have sunk into that deep place about which they love to tease me. "Oh, oh. Mommy's having one of her archetypal Motherline experiences. Watch out, Grandma—she's going to be talking about cycles, the moon, and the womb!"

The bridge between generations

The Motherline is an idea that crept up on me during my years of being a mother and having a mother. I was profoundly moved to see my younger self in my children's development, and to see my older self in my mother's maturation. But I did not fully see the pattern I was in until I did a research project on mothers.

I was interested in how women described their own experience as mothers. A woman, whom I'll call Carolyn, told me a story that illuminated the Motherline. She was talking about her daughter's first menstruation:

> I can remember the date, February 14, Valentine's Day! She came in and showed me her underpants and she said, "Have I started menstruating?" And I said yes, and I started to cry. I could just feel, it was an incredible experience, that connection, that sense of being in the middle between my mother and my daughter, and that I was the bridge between generations. She said, "Oh, Mom, what are you crying for?" But I was so moved by it. It confirmed my womanhood, the woman in me. I was seeing the continuum of the women in the family, the pride of being a woman. I think I had a sense both of my mortality and my immortality.

Carolyn was granted a vision of what I came to call the motherline: the sacred experience of the embodied feminine mysteries. Her daughter begins to menstruate: she has within her the potential to bear a child. Mother and daughter stand outside ordinary time in this moment of recognition: the birth-giving goddess is revealed in a stain on the daughter's underpants.

For women, the motherline is the living knowledge of ourselves as life vessel. For men it is the connection to woman as life vessel. Women are the carriers of the species, the entry way to life. Although a woman may choose not to have children or be unable to do so, every woman is born of woman. Every woman alive is connected to all the women before her through the roots of her particular family and culture. The motherline is body knowledge and birth story and family story and myth.

Those of us who have children, and those of us who do not, are tied by blood to the physical source of our lives, tied by powerful emotions to the woman in whose body our life began. The motherline ties us to our mortal bodies, our bloody beginnings and endings, our experience of the blood mysteries. Every woman who wishes to be her full, female self needs to know the stories of her motherline. We all participate in the human drama; our personal motherlines connect us to universal myths.

The motherline is not a straight line, for it is not about abstract genealogical diagrams; it is about bodies being born out of bodies. Envision the word *line* as a cord, a thread, as the yarn emerging from the fingers of a woman at the spinning wheel. Imagine cords of connection tied over generations. Like weaving or knitting, each thread is tied to others to create a complex, richly textured cloth connecting the past to the future.

Adult children of terrible mothers

To tell the human story from the experience of mothers, to honor the carnal, to speak of how the past becomes the future, is to commit a heresy against twentieth-century psychological thought. To include our mothers' stories in telling our stories undercuts a collective fantasy we hold about the perfectibility of childhood. We mothers are seen as all-powerful in psychology, but are personally disempowered. Our subjective experience is unknown and devalued. Yet we suffer the collective wound of being seen as the perpetrators of all suffering.

In my work as a Jungian analyst, I sit with the adult children of terrible mothers day after day. Angry, intrusive mothers who appear as birds of prey in their daughters' dreams, or profoundly depressed mothers who appear half-dead in the psychological landscapes their offspring describe. The woman I've called Carolyn told me a story of the working through of a terrible mother–daughter relationship. All through her childhood and early adulthood she lived at the edge of a bitter chasm that severed her from her mother. In her story, the nature of a birth, the first days of life, create a Motherline rift that takes most of two lifetimes to untangle. This is what she told me:

> I was born prematurely, two months early. I weighed three pounds. My mother had to leave me in the hospital for six weeks. During that whole time she never touched me. In those days they wouldn't let you. I never understood this until recently: I must have bonded to someone else, a nurse in the hospital. And so when I came home there was this stranger, pretending to be my mother. I think our whole life together has been trying to bridge that gap.

How did they bridge that gap? Many things helped, beginning with the birth of Carolyn's first child. Carolyn said:

> I remember my mother calling me up after Tommy's birth and saying, "Oh, my baby has had a baby!" I can still see her face the first time she saw him. He had just awakened from a nap and was standing up in his crib. Her whole demeanor was so loving. She gave him some sugar on her finger. Put her finger in his mouth. You have to understand that my mother is a very restrained woman, not warm, not physically affectionate. When I saw her do this, put her finger in Tommy's mouth, it was so sensual. I had never seen that side of her before. It warmed me, touched me deeply.

Carolyn remembered having told a male analyst that she had a memory of being in an incubator. He laughed. She dropped it. She told me that recently, working in therapy with a woman, she was able to understand that the distance between her mother and herself had much to do with her premature birth and lack of bonding. Her mother was her father's second wife. There were children from the first marriage whose mother had died. So she was a stepmother. Carolyn did not begin to understand the complexity of this until she herself became a stepmother. Then she could identify with her mother and appreciate how hard she had worked to hold the family together. And her mother, at age seventy-eight, went into therapy and began to see her own life more psychologically and her daughter less judgmentally.

Wrestling with the mother

These two women engaged in a long process of what I call mother–daughter wrestling, the struggle at once to identify and differentiate from one another. Mothers and daughters wrestle with bodily, temperamental, stylistic, generational, and usually very emotional differences between them. They also have to wrestle with the power of the feminine mysteries and how little they are honored in our culture.

From the mother's point of view the process of differentiation tugs at the most primal places in her nature. She remembers the child she bore in the very cells of her body. What mother is not wildly subjective about her offspring, driven by a passionate core connection that is the psychological ghost of her pregnancy, her birth-giving, her breastmilk letting down when her baby cried? What mother does not remember being a daughter and the fierce fight to establish her separateness from her mother?

What I learned from Carolyn and other women I interviewed was that looking at stories from the middle of a woman's life, when she can identify both as mother and as daughter and loop back and forth in the generations, gives a rich and complex view of the psychology of women and of the Motherline as an organizing principle. Motherline stories weave pregnancies, births, miscarriages, abortions, deaths, and psychological development into one fabric, not separating body and psyche.

These subjective experiences are not usually recognized in our official version of the world; they are too fearful. Woman as mother is a part of nature. Caught in the awesome jaws of fate in the birth-giving process, her stories clash with our cultural fantasy about mastering the natural world. When she comes to visit we fear the news she brings. We want to believe we can do things better than she did.

The ballad of my grandmother

For many, the grandmother is an easier link to the Motherline than is the mother. Less familiar, less everyday, a grandmother is a woman of another time, telling stories out of long ago; standing closer to death she remembers the dead. She is often the first to tell us the stories of our origins.

I had just one living grandparent when I was growing up. This was my mother's mother, whom my brothers and I called Oma. She was especially important to me when I was a new mother. Once a month, as regularly as the waning moon, we visited my Oma on Sundays, my first husband, my baby, and I. I was taking classes at the university; my husband was in medical school. Life was arranged around midterms and finals. I was disoriented, as chaotic on the inside as was my living room, with its heaps of unfolded laundry on the couch and Virginia Woolf's *Mrs. Dalloway* lost somewhere under a pile of baby pants.

It was a chorus in my life, a monthly refrain that took us to a sanatorium in the northern California wine country, where Oma lived. Little happened on our visits. We walked around the grounds. We ate a meal together. She held the baby. She told me again and again the central stories of her life. They were the myths of my development. How her mother had died in childbirth when she was very young, and how she had been raised by a cruel stepmother. How she had gone to Italy as a young woman to study painting. How she had suffered so loudly at the birth of her first child that her husband, who had been pacing the hours of her pain in an adjoining room, came to her after the birth and said. "I'll never put you through that again." There were five more children. Three of them were to die young. Ruth, for whom I was named, died of diabetes when she was ten. Oma told me about the death of her sons. They were young men in their early twenties. They had gone to Austria to ski. There was an avalanche. They never returned. Oma was in her menopause. She told me she went crazy with grief. The only comfort she found was in painting portraits of those she loved. She was a fine painter, and these portraits live with me and my brothers and my mother to this day.

Seeing Hitler

Motherline stories have a terrible side, giving us a glimpse of life's horror our "self-help" culture would like to deny. The death of Oma's sons, through an unbearable irony, was the avenue of our family's survival. This part of the story opens simply in a restaurant in Berlin. When Oma told this part she spoke in a voice of such horror that even now, remembered years after her death, I can feel the fear at the bottom of my spine. For in that restaurant, in Berlin, she saw Hitler, just a few feet away from her. He looked straight at her and it pierced her being. She knew that he knew she was Jewish. I can see him, looking though her to me—old terror. She felt that terror and went home and told my grandfather that they had to get out of the country, that this man Hitler would destroy them all.

My grandfather was a successful businessman. Being Jewish was not an important part of his identity. He was an engineer, the manager of a company. He always had been treated with respect. He thought my grandmother was being hysterical. Hitler would pass, just like other difficult political phases passed. After the death of his sons, however, he agreed to listen to his wife and to leave Germany. That was 1932.

Always, telling this story, Oma would shake her head in wonder at the workings of fate. "We might all have died in concentration camps. He would never have agreed to leave with one boy in medical school and the other studying engineering. If they had not died we might all have been dead."

That I am here today would not have been possible without my grandmother's terrible losses. I am now about the age she was when she left Germany. I can't imagine facing the journey she had to make, leaving behind all her familiar world and the graves of three of her children.

Ghost stories

Motherline stories are haunted by ghosts. The unredeemed grief and suffering of generations of women haunt us. Those who were stillborn and those who died in childbirth, those who were orphaned, abandoned, murdered, and abused live on past their lives in the nightmares of their descendants. Women whose ties to life and family were disrupted by the wild tides of history—natural disasters, human cruelty—cast shadows on our souls.

Nobody can choose her motherline or her fate. We are all born into a lineage, a family, a historical time filled with difficulties over which we have no control. But we can honor our stories, attend to our ghosts, remember our ancestors, tell their stories to our children and grandchildren.

Motherline stories evoke a worldview in which all beings and times are interconnected, and in which the feminine mysteries are honored. They are as common as the repetitive loops made in weaving, crocheting, and knitting. They are as powerful as the memory of touching a grandmother's face, or seeing a daughter suckle her newborn child.

Note

1.   Naomi Ruth Lowinsky, "Anasazi woman," *Psychological Perspectives* 19, no. 1 (Spring–Summer 1988).

Chapter Twenty

A DAUGHTER'S PRAISE POEM FOR HER MOTHER
HISTORICIZING COMMUNITY ACTIVISM
AND RACIAL UPLIFT AMONG SOUTH AFRICAN WOMEN

Dolana Mogadime

My parents became exiles of the South African apartheid military regime in 1963 (the year I was born). We lived in Botswana, Zambia, (Lusaka, Chipata, Livingston) and various other then-recently independent African countries before migrating to Canada in 1970. My parents' original decision to flee from South Africa was based on their defiance of the Bantu[1] Education Act of 1953, an oppressive law that legitimized and enforced the mass under-education of black people for the purpose of maintaining white military dictatorship (Hartshorne, 1992; Troup, 1976).

My parents' act of protestation, and their privileged professional locations—one a teacher and the other a medical doctor—mobilized their exile from South Africa. The research I engage with in this chapter arises out of the process of coming to terms with my educational biography from the interconnected axes of protestation, privilege, and exile.

Though a privileged educational background aided our departure, for my brother, sisters, and myself, migrancy entailed loss in the form of the dispossession of an indigenous language, extended family, and the communities within which South African cultural identities are nurtured and sustained. This sense of loss fuelled my endeavour to study the stories my mother tells me that are based on South African cultural and social matrices of influences. The inquiry into her life history provides a means to remembering, mending, and reconnecting with a South African family history and cultural identity, which would otherwise become lost as an outcome of my parents' protestation to European hegemony and their exertion of agency through exile.

Challenging the silencing around middle-class South African black women's community activism

Shula Marks' (1986) analysis of the "black intelligentsia" in Durban, South Africa, during the early 1900s, has assisted me (with some limitations) in locating the economic, religious, and political contexts of my mother's family history as a Msimang. Marks analyzes several key black political figures such as John Dube, as well as families such as the Msimangs in the region of Natal and their material transition to the colonial political economy (1986: 46). The Msimangs were a part of a small group of African landowners in Natal.[2]

At heart is the crucial issue of choice. That is, learning how and why black women in my family, specifically my mother, Goodie, and grandmother, Dudu, chose to use their position in the political economy as middle-class and "privileged" to become community leaders who worked toward empowering and liberating other black women and their communities from oppression.

Until recently (Ravell-Pinto, 1995), the counter hegemonic work of black women across classes had been censored because of the lack of black self-representation within the research. Goldberg refers to this issue in relation to social research when he makes the following statement:

> In short, as in South African society at large at the time, all meaningful forms of black self-representation are stripped away. The black majority is never properly represented, never allowed so speak for itself but always authoritatively spoken for and to. Far from being considered autonomous agents, black South Africans are treated as little more than problematic objects of research. (179)

The problematic "missing" black self-representation is also due to the systematic denial of education to blacks under apartheid. In "Curriculum as a political phenomenon: Historical reflections on black education," Jensen (1990a) outlines apartheid governmental political manoeuvres which were imposed in order to restrict black educational advancement. The racially differentiated curricula, lack of basic facilities, inequitable distribution of school equipment, and deliberate inadequate government expenditure augmented the deterioration of black schools.

As I mentioned before, my parents left South Africa in order to escape the restrictions of the Bantu Education Act on my own educational opportunities as a black South African. Therefore, when I weigh the privileged education I gained through exile against the legislated separate education for the black majority in South Africa under the Bantu Education Act, the disparities has had implications for me in terms of the choices I feel I have to make in my academic work. As a feminist researcher committed to social justice in education I feel directly accountable to other black South African women through my work.

Russell, Lipman, and Goodwin, have each made known the fact that research about black women's social activism and leadership has been marginalized by racial politics in South Africa. Therefore, I feel it is imperative for me to engage in the much-needed task of recording and reinterpreting the activist/leadership traditions and work of black South African women. My focus on the life and work of my mother and grandmother allows for the academic exploration of this history of activism.

Recording our mothers' communities of resistance

Wilentz and hooks identify the woman-centred genre of storytelling as a site within the "homeplace" for the politicalization of "a community of resistance" (hooks, 1990: 42). Wilentz (1992) informs us that it is the black mother-and-daughter dyad relationship, and black women-to-women community supportive relations, which have provided the social context for both telling and hearing these stories. It is these supportive female relations that black women writers in the diaspora have turned to and recorded (Childress, 1982; Shange, 1975; Walker, 1983; Marshall, 1983).

For black women writers the idea of thinking back through our mothers is rooted in the notion of revisiting and learning about maternal knowledge and female-centred networks as expressions of African continuities in contemporary society. For Wilentz, rather than an attempt to return to a stagnant glorified past, identification with the matrilineal knowledge basis of storytelling is conceptualized in terms of reconnection and re-memory with a "reusable past" (117). The purpose being to "create an atmosphere of liberation" (Ibid.) for our children through the stories that we tell, which negates inscribed racism and sexism.

African-American women writers (Childress, Shange, Walker, Marshall), and many others quoted by McLaughlin (1990), have committed their work to celebrating the lives of black women who have resisted oppression. This celebration is reflected in McLaughlin's statement: "The literary upsurge by black women in the second half of the twentieth century unveils a renaissance of the spirit inspired by those who have refused to surrender" (xxxi).

I locate my work recording my family's matrilineage knowledge within this celebratory framework. In a sense, my mother and I are both keepers of a matrilineage knowledge that is expressed through our "praise poems" about our mothers. In our praise poems, we both offer our telling of our mother's life history and honour the merits and achievements of our mothers' work in relation to the community. Praise poems reaffirm an ethic of group connectedness and cultural accountability.

In this context, this chapter shows how the oral cultural tradition of praise poetry assisted in the development of women who refused to surrender to the effects of racial oppression on their communities. Indeed such counter narratives have been reshaped in the contemporary era and have acted as guide posts for the liberation of South African people.[3]

My grandmother Dudu was educated in domestic science during the 1920s, at Endaleni College, an institution with similar educational aims as those described by Cocks (1990) for Lovedale College:

> Their education was aimed largely at socialising the girls into domestic roles both in the girls' own homes and, as servants, in those of other [white] people. This education for domesticity fitted in with the ideology of subordination which the colonists saw as appropriate to all blacks, males as well as females. (89)

Far from preparing her for a life of "domesticity" working as a servant for white people, Dudu used her training to resist this prescribed societal division of labour. Her domestic science skills were applied in creative ways to generate an income that eventually financed the building of several local businesses. Her cafe, grocery store, and deli were businesses that contributed toward financially supporting her family as well as people from the community and the church.

The significance of Dudu's businesses and the leadership they represented becomes recognizable in relation to knowledge of how the following pieces of government legislation, "closely linked with the removal of Africans' civil rights in South Africa as a whole," influenced the personal lives of black people—the Native Land Act of 1913 (Rogers, 1972: 11) and legislation under Native Education initiated in 1910 requiring separate education according to race (Jensen, 1990a).

Rogers points out that "the idea of territorial segregation" was the impetus for the Natives Land Act of 1913. This legislation "scheduled certain of the areas already in African occupation, and prohibited Africans from acquiring land in any other parts of the country" (11). The Native Land Act appointed thirteen percent of the land area for the majority black population, leaving the remaining eighty-seven percent for whites (Nkomo, 1984: 48). After that point in time, Africans were not able to buy land (or titled deed) in South Africa except in two restricted areas (Edendale and Claremont). This legislation was successful in halting agricultural development and prosperity among black people.

The dwindling possibility of subsistence from farming the land, coupled with the mandated hut tax, had the affect of siphoning the flow of migration to the mines where African men would seek paid labour. With "the discovery of South Africa's enormous mineral wealth," migrant labour for the mines became an "essential item in the white economy" (Rogers, 1972: 3). With the removal of their husbands, women seeking work for the subsistence of their families migrated to central urban areas set aside for blacks (Edendale and Claremont), and then commuted to the cities to work.

In a manner similar to other small numbers of land owners in Edendale and Claremont, Dudu, my grandmother, built rooming houses on the land she inherited in order to accommodate the exploding population. Although Marks highlights the antagonisms between the tenants and the owners and the "greed" among the mostly male landowners for more profit, my mother, Goodie, provides a story that is strikingly different, one that suggests that gender might have influenced how this position of power unfolded differently from men:

> We lived in one crisis after another, that was typical of South African life of a black growing during apartheid time, as far as I can remember, there was always a crisis. You had to develop the courage and determination to survive in those situations. It makes you do that .... So when there was a crisis, my mother wanted to see what she could do. She initiated different projects throughout her life with that passion in mind. So, for instance, when she heard that there were students in Claremont at the University of Durban who couldn't go back to their own homes and that they needed a place to sleep she made a boarding house for them. She built rooms and rooms. And then they would eat in her cafe. She served them meals at a reduced rate—to all these students.

In 1949, the University of Durban, a government designated university set aside exclusively for those classified as Coloureds and Indians under racial laws, first admitted blacks to its medical school (Marks, 1987). Black medical students were admitted from all over the country. Some, whose homes were too far away from the university, were without accommodation or food during school breaks and holidays. In response to their needs, Dudu built a boarding house for the students and provided what my mother referred to as "a subsidized meal plan" where as customers of her cafe, they would pay a minimal amount or according to what they could afford. For most, that meant nothing:

> So they all came to my home, and they accepted her as their mother.[4] So even when there was a graduation, she was there. She was invited because they knew that she had helped them. You know when they came there, they didn't have much money, so she gave them all these things for nothing. That's just the type of woman she was. She just had open hands and she just accepted everybody and she helped everybody. That's why she was never rich. She accumulated all these things, these businesses and properties but she was never rich because she got the

money but then she took it out [she gave it back to the community], it never stayed. (Goodie)

Goodie's story about my grandmother Dudu is about an individual who, in the spirit of a community worker as an "othermother," used her material resources to respond in times of crisis in order to ensure the survival and well-being of the young. Dudu's position is reflected in Collins' discussion of meaning of community othermother: "Community othermothers work on behalf of the black community by expressing ethics of caring and personal accountability which embrace conceptions of transformative power and mutuality" (Kuykendall, quoted in Collins, 1991: 132).

Such power is transformative in that black women's relationships with children and other vulnerable community members is not intended to dominate or control. Rather, its purpose is to bring people along, to—in the words of late-nineteenth-century black feminists—"uplift the race" so that vulnerable members of the community will be able to attain the self-reliance and independence essential for resistance. (Collins, 1991: 132)

Dudu's actions empowering the community occurred through her financial support of the community as a businesswoman, her participation in women-centred religious self-help organizations like the *manyanos* (independent Methodist prayer groups led by women), and her leadership as president of the Methodist Church. My mother witnessed her mother's participation and leadership within "black female spheres of influence" (Collins, 1991: 141). Her activist role in the community therefore served as a role model for Goodie's own gender socialization.

Collins takes up the notion of "black female spheres of influence" in her conceptualization of black women's traditional activism. She describes this activism through two interdependent dimensions. The first is characterized as "the struggle for group survival" within existing structures of oppression. According to Collins:

Women in this dimension do not directly challenge oppressive structures because, in many cases, direct confrontation is neither preferred nor possible. Instead, women engaged in creating black female spheres of influence indirectly resist oppressive structures by undermining them. (141)

Dudu's role in sustaining the well-being of young aspiring students is an example of this process of undermining oppression.

Collins describes the second dimension as "the struggle for institutional transformation" (142). Here the efforts to actually change existing structures of oppression are fully articulated through group action to challenge black women's subordination.[5] Collins insists that black women's activist traditions and political activity within the first dimension occur in the context of everyday life but that they have been overlooked.

An example of Dudu's activism within the first sphere is her participation in women-centred organizations. Dudu belonged to the "Zulu of Natal" *manyano* prayer "union." The *manyano* "union" of prayer groups was a religious self-help network comprised of women who took an active role in supporting each other and their families when there was no support from elsewhere. As Gaitskell (1990) points out, "by 1940, there were at least 45,149 women in the Methodist *manyano* throughout South Africa" (269). Gaitskell clearly demonstrates the impact of the *manyano* organization:

> Those interested in exploring the history of African women's lives, or indeed social change and religious and political mobilisation of different African communities, cannot afford to ignore what was happening in the supposedly "closed" world of the manyano. (271)

The absence of male migrant workers (which I discussed earlier) resulted in the upheaval of the family structure under apartheid. The *manyano* women's prayer groups were thus fundamental for the emotional and psychological well-being of women in female headed households.

Gaitskell shows how emotional revivalism played a key role in the prayer meetings. "The emotional, participatory expressive culture of the manyano was the choice and creation of the women themselves" (271). She describes the *manyano* as a vehicle for female spiritual leadership across social classes. Gaitskell notes that literacy was not required among those taking the leadership in prayer and preaching because women memorized hymns and spoke at length about biblical passages introduced by someone else, and then led the prayer. This form of worship was particularly appealing in light of

> ... the vitality of indigenous traditions of oral expression in which women shared—oratory, folk tales and praise poems vigorously performed to a convivially responding group. (267)

They not only cried, sang, and read the bible together, the *manyano* was also about women assisting women to solve their problems (often related to the effects of living in poverty). They had the opportunity to tell their stories during testimonials and have the members pray spontaneously about immediate and personal needs. They also addressed these needs by organizing and raising funds for the community and for each other. Goodie recalled her mother's role as president of a *manyano* prayer group and as president of the Methodist Church: "My home was just buzzing with activity. We just cooked big pots, because people always just walked in for various things, for various problems."

By organizing themselves into *manyanos*, women were able to play a pivotal role in sustaining their families and the community. Through women-to-women supportive relations, *manyano* women found a way to survive the repressive limitations enforced on the family structure.

What I am suggesting is that as a member of the *manyano* prayer group, as well as through her work in the community, Dudu provided Goodie with the techniques for survival that actually prepared her daughter to be able to affect change through "the struggle for institutional transformation." In the *Canadian Women's Studies* issue on "Women in Education," I look at how the mother and daughter female sphere of influence shaped Goodie's involvement with black women's activism. Goodie's pioneering leadership in spearheading the opening of Pietermaritzburg Community College in South Africa during the late 1980s represented black women's struggle for institutional transformation (Mogadime, 1998). The opening of Pietermaritzburg community college to the local black community represented the changing winds in "the New South Africa" where the educational "upliftment" of the previously racially excluded has become the prime concern of educational development initiatives during the 1990s.

By socializing and preparing Goodie to conceptualize black women as self-determined and self-reliant, Dudu assisted her daughter in acquiring the inner resources to affect change in the community. That is, Dudu's struggle against oppression, and her sense of self-determination, represents the "patterns conscious and self expressions," or the "something within" that shapes the culture of resistance in the life of the daughter (Collins, 1991: 142).

Dudu's relationship with my mother urged Goodie to define herself not only in relation to her family, but also to community struggles. These teachings converge with what black feminists refer to as the "utility of black women's relationships with one another in providing a community for black women's activism and self-determination" (Collins, 1991: 4). A notion of self-determination allows us to place both our individual and our collective concern for the community at the centre of our agenda. Within this context, the mother and daughter dyad relationship, and black women's connection with each other as community workers, nurtures and sustains the community struggle for social justice and racial upliftment.

Notes

1. Writing in 1972, Troup explained "Bantu" as the official government term for African.
2. Although researchers (Marks, 1986; Meintjes, 1990) emphasize the materialist gains derived by the *kholwa* ("Christian intelligentsia") to explain historical aspects of the polarities between the small material-based middle class and the poor black majority during apartheid (Gaitskell, 1984), investigating the lives and subjectivities of black women assists in the process of understanding how middle-class subjectivities might have been used alternatively, as a site for community transformative rather than for merely personal and individualistic ends.
3. Gunner identifies praise poetry as a fluid indigenous language system that assisted in counter hegemonic teachings. She provides an illustration of the political resistance among the popular praises performed by protesters at trade unions rallies in South Africa.
4. My father, Dr. Henry Mogadime (1931–1998), became one of the medical students Grandma assisted in her capacity as "othermother."
5. Collins describes African-American women's leadership role in the church, their role as othermother in the community and their participation in community organizations as locations where black women acquire and exert the first sphere of influence known as "the struggle for group survival" (1991: 95). Whereas in the second dimension or in the "struggle for institutional transformation," Collins refers to women's participation in unions and political organizations that has worked toward the actual legislation of social change.

MOTHERS AND SONS

Chapter Twenty-One

IN BLACK AND WHITE

AFRICAN-AMERICAN AND ANGLO-AMERICAN FEMINIST PERSPECTIVES

ON MOTHERS AND SONS

Andrea O'Reilly

In "Man child: A black lesbian feminist's response," African-American poet and essayist Audre Lorde (1995) asks us to "consider the two western classic myth/ models of mother/son relationships: Jocasta/Oedipus, the son who fucks his mother, and Clytemnestra/Orestes, the son who kills his mother" (76). These ancient myths are continually retold and reenacted in Western culture and function, in Louis Althusser's terms, as ideological apparatuses that interpolate mothers and sons into specific relationship positions that are most fully dramatized in the narratives of Clytemnestra and Jocasta. The sanction against mother–son closeness and connection is signified and achieved by the incest taboo, while the enforcement of mother–son separation is represented and enforced by the murder of Clytemnestra. Both patriarchal narratives are enacted through the denial and displacement of the maternal presence.

I open this chapter referencing the above narratives because it is my contention that maternal erasure and disconnection are central not only to patriarchal thinking on mothers and sons but also to Anglo-American *feminist* thought on mothers and sons as well. This chapter will, through a close reading of three early, classic, Anglo-American, feminist texts on mothers and sons, examine how the early Anglo-American perspective on mothers and sons scripted mother–son attachment in terms of these hegemonic narratives of maternal erasure and disavowal. Next, the chapter will consider how recent Anglo-American feminist writings on mothers and sons call into question this patriarchal and early feminist view of maternal displacement to emphasize mother–son connection. Finally, the chapter will review recent African-American feminist theory on mothers and sons to explore both its emphasis on maternal presence (as opposed to maternal erasure) and its specific, racially determined, mode of rearing sons.

Patriarchal narratives

The story of Oedipus and his mother Jocasta was first told by the playwright
Sophocles, but is known to us today through Freud's psychological theory of the
Oedipal complex. The son's first love object, according to Freud, is the mother,
but the son renounces this love upon the realization that this desire is forbidden
and will result in his castration by the father. In the story of Clytemnestra and her
son Orestes, the mother, as most accounts tell it, kills her husband Agamemnon
upon his return from Troy to avenge his sacrificial killing of their daughter, Iphigenia,
and because he has brought home with him a concubine. In retaliation against
his father's death, Orestes kills his mother, which he defends as just vengeance
for the death of his father. The Furies, the female chorus who are judge and jury,
excuse the mother's crime because "the man she killed was not of her own
blood." The son retorts: "Am I of my mother's blood?" To which they respond:
"She nourished you in the womb ... do you disown your mother's blood?" Apollo,
called in to settle the dispute, states that: "the mother is not the parent of the
child which is called hers. She is the nurse who tends the growth of the young
seed planted by its true parent, the male." Finally, Athena, a female goddess
born from the head of Zeus, is asked to decide the verdict and rules: "No mother
gave me birth. Therefore, the father's claim and male supremacy in all things
wins my whole heart's loyalty." With her vote the son is pardoned, and the
Furies, the last representatives of the mother right of ancient goddess times, are
banished. These myths narrate the consolidation of patriarchal power through
the son's identification with the patrilineal line, and script mother–son separation
as the precondition of manhood.

These ancient myths, functioning as ideological apparatuses, are continually
reenacted and retold in our contemporary culture. A cursory review of twentieth-
century popular culture reveals many and diverse manifestations of the ancient
patriarchal narratives of forbidden Jocasta/emasculated Oedipus, and of
triumphant Orestes/defeated Clytemnestra. Philip Wylie in his immensely popular
Generation of vipers (1942) coined the term "momism": "Our land," writes
Wylie, "subjectively mapped, would have more silver cords and apron strings
crisscrossing it than railroads and telephone wires. She is everywhere and
everything .... Disguised as good old mom, dear old mom, sweet old mom ... she
is the bride at every funeral and the corpse at every wedding" (185). In the 1960s,
the Moynihan report advanced the now infamous black matriarchy thesis that
described the black family as dysfunctional and argued that mothers were to
blame for the pathologies of the race. "In essence," wrote Moynihan, "the Negro
community has ... a matriarchal structure which ... seriously retards the progress
of the group as a whole" (1965: 75). Or, as African-American writer/critic Michelle
Wallace puts it "The Moynihan Report said that the black man was not so much

a victim of white institutional racism as he was of an abnormal family structure, its main feature being an employed black woman" (12). The 1980s gave us Robert Bly, the father of the men's mytho-poetic movement and author of the best-selling *Iron John*, the notorious thesis which suggests the American man has grown up with too much mothering and not enough fathering; they suffer from what Bly diagnosed as "father hunger." "[The modern man] is not happy," laments Bly, "he is life-preserving but not life-giving, he is full of anguish and grief" (1990: 2–4). Men have discovered their "feminine side," but have left unexplored their true essential masculine identity. For Bly, healing occurs only when the son "cut[s] his soul away from his mother-bound soul" and moves, again in Bly's words, "from the mother's realm to the father's realm" (1990: ix).

Feminism has long critiqued Wylie's momism, Moynihan's black matriarchy, and Bly's father hunger for their blatant misogyny and virulent mother blame. From a sociohistorical perspective, they are clearly backlash texts. *Vipers*, popular after World War II when women were being reprogrammed from workers back into mothers, articulates the culture's uneasiness with what Miriam Johnson has called the white, middle-class matrifocality of the 1950s. The minimal involvement of fathers in those postwar years meant that the home was a maternal dominion where sons grew to manhood under the mother's influence, with little or no involvement from the father. The matrifocality of the home in the 1950s is what is said to have caused, according to many social commentators, the "feminine" men of the 1960s—how Alan Alda came to replace John Wayne as the ideal identity of manhood. The Moynihan report was written in the 1960s, the decade that witnessed the civil rights movement and the beginnings of the feminist movement. *Iron John* takes as its cultural context the 1980s, that witnessed increased economic independence for women, skyrocketing divorce rates, and, significantly, the beginning of the father's rights movement.[1]

Early Anglo-American feminist theory on the mother–son relationship

The purpose of this chapter is not to detail the patriarchal script of maternal displacement and denial. Rather, I am interested in exploring how this displacement and denial are represented, recast, and resisted in *feminist* theory on mothers and sons. The first and longest section of this chapter offers a close and detailed reading of three classic Anglo-American texts on the mother–son relation: Judith Arcana's *Every mother's son: The role of mothers in the making of men* (1983), Linda Forcey's *Mothers of sons: Toward an understanding of responsibility* (1987), and Babette Smith's *Mothers and sons: The truth about mother-son relationships* (1995),[2] in order to examine how this literature mimicked, albeit unintentionally, the patriarchal dictate of maternal displacement and denial. The three books, though spanning fifteen years, can be grouped together as a representative writing of the earlier Anglo-American feminist perspective on mothers and sons.

Judith Arcana's *Every mother's son* (1983)

In the prologue to *Every mother's son*, Arcana asserts that: "mothers need to understand that we are creating and nurturing the agents of our own oppression; once we make them, their education as men in this misogynist society will pull them from our arms, set them above us, and make them the source of our degradation" (3). She goes on to argue that: "we would prevent this if we could, and to do so we must enter into conscious struggle with our sons, actively seeking to change what is currently defined as male and female behavior" (34). This book, developed from sixty interviews with mothers and with sons, and from Arcana's own personal reflections on raising her son Daniel during his first ten years, explores how current practices of masculine socialization give rise to expectations of entitlement as boys grow into men, and how they result in the disavowal of all things feminine in the adult male psyche.

Over the course of her interviews with mothers and sons, Arcana discovered that most mothers reject traditional definitions of masculinity. However, the sons of these same women had assumed, for the most part, a conventional gender identity, or were aware that such was expected of them. What accounts for this disparity between intent and consequence? A small number of sons in Arcana's study reported that their mothers consciously and enthusiastically socialized them to be masculine, while another small group said that while their mothers did not engage in overt gender socialization, it was done unconsciously and indirectly. However, the majority of sons in Arcana's study stated that they could not recall any incident in which their mother had explicitly or implicitly directed them to be "men." The disparity, Arcana argues, may be attributed to three factors of masculine socialization.

The first is that mothers, for the most part, are lesser agents in the socialization of sons. Many of the sons identified "culture" or "the father" as where they learned patriarchal masculinity. "Basic sex-role conditioning," as Arcana observes, "is not in mothers' hands, but in the hands of men who've made this culture" (120). Second, mothers raise children but they do not determine the material or ideological conditions of their mothering. Women, as Adrienne Rich (1986) reminds us, mother in motherhood, the latter being a patriarchal institution which is male-defined and -controlled. Mothers raise boys but they don't make men, because, as Arcana explains, mothers are "contractors rather than architects, following specifications not of our design" (115). Women, Arcana continues, "are relatively powerless in this culture, and though we raise the children we bear, almost none of us are free to bear and raise them *if or when we choose*, much less *as we choose*" (115).

Finally, while mothers may not initiate or enforce the gender socialization of their sons, they do accommodate it. A central and constitutive demand of mothering, as Sara Ruddick explains in *Maternal thinking*, is "training children in the behavior acceptable to their social and cultural group" (1989: 110). Thus, while mothers may reject patriarchy and its constructions of masculinity, they realize, consciously or otherwise, that their sons must take their place in that world. "The fear of alienating a male child from 'his' culture," writes Adrienne Rich, "seems to go deep, even among women who reject that culture for themselves every day of their lives" (1986: 205). Rich goes on to ask: "What do we fear? That our sons will accuse us of making them into misfits and outsiders? That they will suffer as we have suffered from patriarchal reprisals? Do we fear they will somehow lose their male status and privilege, even as we are seeking to abolish that inequality?" (Ibid.). "As mothers in this time," Arcana writes, "we are faced with a dilemma: we see that the old ways are not good; we wish to raise our children differently—but we fear they'll suffer ostracism, alienation, and loneliness in a society that has by no means given up its old definitions and restrictions" (1983: 1).

Another explanation Arcana offers to account for this discrepancy between aim and consequence centers on maternal practice itself. Mothering is about caring for and catering to the needs of children, and about nurturing self-esteem so that children see themselves as special and deserving; what Ruddick defines as the second demand of maternal practice, "to foster growth ... sponsor or nurture a child's unfolding, expanding material spirit" (1989: 83). However, with sons this nurturance may be, according to Arcana, interpreted as privilege and entitlement: "Though children of both sexes put their mothers in the positions of servants ... mothers of sons are, whether we feel it in the moment or not, inadvertently reinforcing the sexist premise that women exist to serve men .... Men learn from infancy to expect and solicit selfishness and cherishing care at the hands of women" (1983: 101, 102). While "[d]aughters learn from our mothers to *be mothers*, to give in that disastrously self-destructive way that has been honored by men as true motherhood; sons learn *to expect such treatment from women*" (1983: 102). Women in patriarchal culture are expected to devote their time and attention to children and men; sons thus, as Arcana identifies, derive double benefits from these patriarchal imperatives as both men and children. Given that women's secondary status is enforced in both the gender arena (service to men) and in the maternal realm (service to children), mothers must, if they hope to raise non-sexist men who reject traditional masculinity, challenge both patriarchal imperatives. Women, Arcana writes, "need to live out of ourselves. We wrong ourselves and our children if we subordinate our lives to theirs" (1983:

235). Mothers must, Arcana continues, "reject [the] traditional mother role [and] ... accept ... our sons into our daily lives" (1983: 247). In so doing, the mother will enable her boy child to see her outside and beyond her maternal identity that positions her as secondary to, and in service to, children and men. Coming to know their mothers outside motherhood, sons learn to view and appreciate their mothers as, in Arcana's words, "whole people."

According to Arcana, mothers must, therefore, reject traditional motherhood if they hope to raise non-traditional sons; that is, men who have renounced patriarchal masculinity and the entitlement and privilege that such accords. No longer can mothers be, or be seen as, "the primary source of praise, encouragement, and selfless service" (1983: 280). However, as mothers reject this role of selfless service to sons, traditional male socialization, as Arcana explains, teaches boys "that they are to be the beneficiaries of a male culture: they will grow up to power, status, and the admiration and support of women .... When [a mother] moves to change that pattern with her son, he understands that she wants him to give up power .... [A] boy has to begin by *losing*" (Ibid.). In other words to become more human, he must become less male. This, then, is the second paradox of feminist male child rearing: sons gain by losing, and mothers are better mothers by "being less of a mother." This, in Arcana's view, is both the challenge and contradiction of feminist mothering of sons.

Arcana maintains that the patriarchal institution of motherhood oppresses women, impedes mother–son equality, and fosters both sexism and patriarchal masculinity. Women thus must reject traditional motherhood and become, in Rich's words, "outlaws from the institution of motherhood" in order to effect the gender transformations they wish for themselves and their sons, for women and men. Arcana perceptively identifies the many ways traditional motherhood oppresses women and perpetuates traditional masculinity. However, less clear in this critique is a distinction between motherhood and mothering. In *Of woman born*, Rich distinguishes between two meanings of motherhood: "the *potential relationship* of any woman to her powers of reproduction and to children; and the *institution*, which aims at ensuring that that potential—and all women— shall remain under male control" (1986: 15). Motherhood refers to the institution of motherhood, which is male-defined and male-controlled, and mothering refers to experiences of mothers which are female-defined and female-centered. Across cultures and throughout history most women mother in the institution of motherhood. Patriarchal motherhood, however, does not negate the possibility and potentiality of gynocentric mothering. Mothers have always mothered against, beyond, and outside patriarchal motherhood. In dismissing motherhood, Arcana, I would suggest, loses sight of the radical potentiality of mothering; if you will, she throws the baby out with the bathwater.

Arcana also finds problematic the way mothering places mothers in service to children and in particular to sons. However, I would argue that maternal practice, as Ruddick argues, is by necessity concerned with meeting the physical, psychological, and social needs of children. "These three demands—for preservation, growth, and social acceptance," writes Ruddick, "constitute maternal work; to be a mother is to be committed to meeting these demands by works of preservative love, nurturance and training" (1989: 17). Service, the word Arcana uses to describe such work, is what one (a woman or man) must do when one engages in maternal practice; however "service" does not necessarily require the subordination and enslavement of the mother. Moreover, care of children does not preclude care of self, nor does service equal servitude or require self-erasure. However, because service becomes confused in Arcana with servitude, as does the distinction between mothering and motherhood, motherhood is represented as an essentially oppressive state and hence rejected. This in turn results in the displacement and disparagement of the maternal.

Linda Forcey's *Mothers of sons: Toward an understanding of responsibility* (1987)

The teaching of antisexism and the undermining of masculine socialization are, according to Arcana, the explicit goals of feminist mothering of sons. This is to be achieved by challenging both traditional practices of male socialization *and* traditional ways of mothering. Linda Forcey's *Mothers of sons: Toward an understanding of responsibility*, the second book-length feminist work on mothers and sons, considers, as the title suggests, the issue of responsibility. The position advanced in her 1987 book differs significantly from Forcey's current thinking on mothers and sons. Thus the following exposé and critique of Forcey's responsibility thesis is pertinent only to this early work—as it laid the foundation for contemporary thinking about motherhood—and not to Forcey's subsequent research.

Mothers of sons, based on the oral histories of one hundred women from various socioeconomic backgrounds, examines, in Forcey's words, "how mothers perceive their relationships with their sons. That is, what do they have to tell us about the relationship, and their responsibility to and for it?" (3). Her book opens with a review of early feminist thought on motherhood—the writings of de Beauvoir, Friedan, Bernard—and argues that these early feminist texts question "the sagacity of the assignment of solitary responsibility for 'mothering' to mothers [and] find it harmful to children of both sexes but especially sons" (32). Forcey recognizes that children must be nurtured; this is, in her words, "beyond dispute." However, Forcey goes on to argue that "what is not beyond dispute ... is who should be responsible for seeing that the requisite nurturing gets done, and precisely what constitutes effective nurturing in order to promote this preservation and growth" (42). Traditional "malestream" mother-blaming thought, as feminists have rightly argued, is preoccupied with the so-called failures of mothers to fulfill their maternal responsibilities. However, Forcey maintains that this perspective informs *feminist* thinking on mothering as well; it too operates as a regulatory discourse, reinscribing mothers in the traditional ideological matrix of responsibility and blame:

> The differences between the traditional and the recently revised feminist approach to the mother–son relationship center on the reasons why mothers mother the way they do, and what it means to be a "good" mother. For these feminists, the "good" mother is she who, in spite of her oppression, assumes the responsibility for raising sons who are physically, emotionally, and socially well-adjusted and who do not separate from her, do not identify with their fathers, and do not assume the traditional masculine values .... As with the conventional wisdom on mothers of sons, this recent feminist scholarship implicitly assumes that mothers are all powerful. It calls on women to assume their rightful responsibility for their children's welfare in order to affect a nonpatriarchal society. (1987: 46, 47)

Feminists, in Forcey's view, have merely redefined the meaning of "good mothering" and have left unquestioned the "wisdom of the responsibility assignment itself" (46). As well they have failed to challenge the patriarchal premise that assumes "[that women] are more relational than men [and thus] should be assigned the primary responsibility for the care of children" (59).

Recent feminist writings, notably Nancy Chodorow's feminine relationality argument and the different voice theory advanced by Carol Gilligan, work to reconstitute women, Forcey maintains, as natural mothers, while in the feminist instance it is psychology and not wombs that predispose women to nurturance. The challenge of feminism should not be to determine how women may fulfill their responsibility as feminist mothers, Forcey argues, but rather to question the responsibility assignment itself. "No person," Forcey writes, "can successfully be responsible for the meaning of another's being. Not even mothers of sons" (59). Such a view, Forcey continues, "is personally and politically damaging for both mothers and sons, women and men" (59).

Most of the women in Forcey's study "perceived themselves to have the primary responsibility for the well-being of their sons, a responsibility they find to be enormous and never-ending" (47). Nevertheless, women experience their identity and work as mothers as "responsibility" because such a role accords women a purpose and power not otherwise available to them in a patriarchal culture. Forcey explains: "Many women, particularly those in mid-life, do express their satisfaction in life in terms of how they view the results of their years as mothers as measured by the happiness of their sons. For many women being the 'essential' one in the family is a hard role to give up" (59). However, mothers must, Forcey argues, for the good of their sons *and* themselves, reject this maternal self-definition, and come to define themselves outside and beyond their maternal identity, as well as learn to share the work of child rearing with others.

In her final chapter, appropriately entitled "Jocasta unbound," Forcey argues, in a manner similar to Arcana, that women must develop identities outside their maternal role; the three locations she identifies are school, work, and women's friendship. When women balance "caring and selfhood" they are less likely to define their identity and worth in the context of the responsibility assignment that, Forcey argues, is damaging to both mothers and sons. It is important to note that Forcey calls for the "unboundness" from motherhood in order to free *mothers* from the matrix of blame and responsibility, while Arcana champions unboundness, or in her words, rejection of traditional motherhood, so that *sons* do not see women exclusively in service to children and secondary to men. However, both agree that mothering must be shared; as Forcey concludes her book: "When the sons of tomorrow are the responsibility of the many instead of the one they will grow freer, stronger, and more caring, as will their mothers" (151). Thus both Arcana and Forcey advocate "less mothering" in order to effect the desired transformations in gender relations/roles for both men (Arcana) and women (Forcey).

Forcey maintains, as examined above, that the traditional and revised feminist view of the responsibility of mothers for sons "is personally and politically damaging to mothers and sons, women and men" (59). She exhorts mothers to renounce the exclusive and essentialist responsibility role through the formation of self-identities other than that of mother, and by sharing the task of childrearing. The task of responsibility is, no doubt, "enormous" and "never-ending," as Forcey argues. However, I would suggest that the problem rests not so much with responsibility as with the way motherhood becomes defined in the dominant Anglo-American culture. A therapist interviewed by Forcey, and who worked with poor and "struggling" mothers, observed that "[such mothers] are just too busy. Their whole lives cannot be wrapped up in their sons .... If you are very, very busy, she argues, you don't put quite the same emotional burden on the child." (67). "The major difference between middle-class and working-class mothers of sons," she speculates, "was that in the case of the latter the mother was not the central person in the son's life and sons were not the central people in the mothers' lives" (67).

It would seem that the problem is not responsibility per se but rather that motherhood, as it is defined in Anglo-American culture, assigns this responsibility exclusively to mothers. Furthermore, the work of mothering is assumed to preclude or take precedence over any other work, and is defined solely as nurturance; paid employment is not seen as an aspect of mothering but rather as something that prevents women from mothering. Forcey apparently recognizes this, as suggested by her insistence upon the need for both shared childrearing and non-maternal work and identities. Nonetheless her book, as its subtitle suggests, focuses on the responsibility assignment rather than on the way motherhood is organized in Anglo-American culture. Moreover, in Anglo-American culture mothers are assigned the responsibility but given no power—and accorded no real status—for the maternal work they do. Mothers do not make the rules, they simply enforce them. Again, it would seem that motherhood becomes oppressive to women not because of the responsibility assignment, as Forcey would argue, but rather because this responsibility comes with little or no power and prestige and because maternal responsibility—defined exclusively as care rather than work in Anglo-American culture—confines mothering and mothers to the home. Finally, as discussed earlier, mothering does, and must, mean being responsible for the children in your care; those who engage in maternal practice assume this task upon the arrival of the child, by birth or adoption. However, because Forcey, in her early work, identifies the responsibility assignment as the problem, her argument, as does Arcana's, advances "less mothering" as the solution and partakes in the displacement and disparagement of the maternal.

Babette Smith's *Mothers and sons: The truth about mother-son relationships* (1995)

The final book on the mother–son relationship under consideration is Babette Smith's *Mothers and sons: The truth about mother-son relationships*. Smith's research, developed from a comparative study of postwar and post-1960s mothers and sons, explores how mothers' and sons' perceptions of one another and of their relationship have changed over the last fifty years. This study focuses on two interrelated questions: How do mothers perceive masculinity? And how do sons, in turn, perceive their mothers and their mothering? Of interest to us here in the discussion of the way motherhood is represented in feminist thought on the mother–son relation is Smith's second concern: sons' perceptions of maternal practice.

The postwar sons' reflections on their mothers and mothering were both startling and sad. These sons, Smith writes, "were struggling to love where they had little respect, to believe they *were* loved when they remembered no affection, to justify their love by saying their mother was *not typical*" (33). While the ideology of "the Good Mother," particularly as it was represented in the 1950s, demanded that mothers be selfless, moral, pleasing, passive, and subservient to their husbands, and led mothers to believe that they would be honored and appreciated for this, the views expressed by the now middle-aged sons interviewed by Smith reveal the contrary: the mothers were neither admired nor respected for their maternal devotion. As one son commented: "The worst thing I think was the way she made herself a martyr to what everyone else wanted" (34). The few sons who spoke or wrote favorably about their relationship with their mothers remembered their mothers as "female people rather than [just] 'mothers'" (50). The memories of these sons "reveal that these women had also developed wide-ranging interests beyond the home, 'artistic and intellectual curiosity,' 'stories from work,' 'has published a book'" (50). They felt their mothers were "adaptable," or they had "broadness of outlook and knowledge," qualities that their sons celebrated (Ibid.).

In contrast, the post-1960s sons genuinely liked their mothers and enjoyed being in their company. Smith writes:

> The male experience of the mother–son relationship changed substantially. The consensus which emerged from these younger sons' opinions was a reversal of the past. The percentage which once ran 70:30 negatively about a man's mother, had turned right around to run approximately 70:30 positively. Most sons of this age group spoke enthusiastically about their mothers, the percentage as well as the tone of the assessment, holding good among those who explored the subject in some depth and those who answered a briefer questionnaire. These sons loved their mothers, as their fathers had loved theirs, but the younger generation also liked them. (175)

The reasons, the interviews would suggest, are: (a) the mothers of these sons were less invested in the ideology of the Good Mother; (b) as a result of increased education, work, and travel opportunities for women, these mothers had more in common with their sons; and (c) the familial, economic, and cultural changes occasioned by feminism gave women more confidence and clout. As well, and of particular significance to the discussion at hand, according to Smith, for the post-1960s son "it was noticeably easier for [him] to agree that he admired or respected his mother when he did not have to pass judgement on her parenting at the same time … [in contrast], [1950s] sons had no choice but to evaluate their mothers in her maternal role" (182). Smith elaborates:

> [When they could,] sons of all ages nominated their mothers' achievements outside the home. Younger men who had this option more often were more readily admiring. They could avoid the ambivalence caused by passing judgement on the women's parental success in their own lives and external yardsticks, such as occupation, income, or title,

were concrete evidence that society endorsed their personal opinion. This was the benefit which a woman's outside work could bring to the mother–son relationship—not as a role model, as it was for daughters (although these young sons did not automatically exclude their mothers as a role model), but by providing the boys with something about their mother which was understood and valued in their male world. (182)

Mothers who exhibited attributes valued in male culture, and/or achieved what was deemed success from the masculine standpoint, were more readily respected and admired by their sons. As one schoolteacher observed of the sons in the class: "Boys identify with mothers who are independent, freethinking, nice people, not only for security and emotional reasons, but also because they happen to like their mothers as people. These are mothers who actually present themselves to their sons as people *without overt[ly] 'being Mother'*" (185, italics added). And while Smith argues that the variable is not so much paid employment as self-confidence, she nonetheless concludes that women's work outside the home benefited the mother–son relationship because it, as noted above, "[provided] the boys with something about their mother which was understood and valued in their male world" (182). Male respect and admiration for mothers, Smith goes on to argue, is essential "because, without those elements, there is no basis for equality between them" (185).

Though not always explicitly acknowledged or addressed, the "beyond motherhood" thesis, if you will, of Arcana, Forcey, and Smith begins with the recognition that motherhood in patriarchal culture is neither valued nor respected, and that mothers do not acquire any real or substantive power, status, or agency—economic, cultural, or otherwise—for the work they do as mothers. Thus, as a mother, the woman is not able to secure the respect of her son. Though this is a concern for all three, it is of particular importance for Smith because her theoretical platform for improving gender relations hinges upon sons respecting and admiring their mothers.

The problem, according to Smith, is "[how do] sons ... hold their own mothers dear in a society which has little regard for mothers" (180). Smith argues, as we saw earlier, that this problem may be remedied through mothers fashioning an identity and role "beyond motherhood" in the public, male realm of work so as to, in Smith's words "provid[e] [their sons] with something about their mother which [is] understood and valued in their male world" (182). Smith's argument here resonates with earlier liberal feminist thinking on motherhood. Smith recognizes that motherhood is devalued in our culture, but instead of addressing this larger problem, she exhorts women, as did much of earlier liberal feminist theory, to abandon the private realm of motherhood and obtain personhood, power, and prestige by entering the public arena of (paid) work. Smith's argument thus reinscribes, as did much of 1970s liberal feminism, the hierarchal gender opposition that privileges masculine values over those that are associated with the feminine, and in so doing both mimics and perpetuates the patriarchal disparagement and displacement of the maternal.

As Smith's argument seeks to distance mothers from motherhood and downplay their maternal role and identity, it also calls for the abdication of maternal authority and power. Smith argues that post-1960s mother–son relationships are more successful because they are based on equality, and that this equality is what makes possible the respect Smith deems essential for a successful mother–son relationship. While equality in relationships is generally understood to be a good and desired thing, in the mother–child relationship such equality is problematic because it denies the mother the power and authority that is rightly hers as the mother of the child. "There are," as Sara Ruddick observes, "many external constraints on [a mother's] capacity to name, feel, and act. But in the daily conflict of wills, at least with her children, a mother has the upper hand .... *If a mother didn't have this control, her life would be unbearable*" (1989: 55, italics added). The mode of mothering advocated by Smith is what Valerie Walkerdine and Helen Lucey define in their book, *Democracy in the kitchen*, as "sensitive mothering": "[A defining characteristic] of the sensitive mother is the way she regulates her children. Essentially there should be no overt regulation; regulation should go underground; no power battles, no insensitive sanctions as these would interfere with the child's illusion that she is the source of her wishes, that she had 'free will'" (1989: 25, 24). Sensitive mothering is child-centered, characterized by flexibility, spontaneity, affection, nurturance, playfulness, and most importantly democracy, and is contrasted to the stern, rigid, authoritative, "child should be seen and not heard" variety of parenting. While sensitive mothering may make possible the mother–son equality so valued by Smith, it centers on and depends upon the abdication of maternal power and authority.[3]

Smith argues, as did Forcey and Arcana ten years earlier, that the less a mother relates to her son as "mother," the greater the chances will be of raising non-sexist, non-masculine (as it is traditionally defined) boys and improving relations between mothers and sons and men and women generally. This will allow sons to see their mothers as other than secondary persons subservient to men and children, according to Arcana; will undercut the responsibility assignment; according to Forcey; and will enable boys to respect and admire their mothers, according to Smith. Each downplays, denies, and in some instances, disparages, the responsibility, authority, and power of mothers as mothers of sons, while according the same to women as women. In so doing Smith, Arcana, and Forcey script the mother-relation, albeit subtly and no doubt inadvertently, in terms of the patriarchal imperatives of maternal erasure and displacement, as enacted in the narratives of Clytemnestra and Jocasta.

New Anglo-American feminist perspectives on the mother–son relationship

Feminist theory on mothers and sons has been informed by and has developed in the context of feminist thinking on mothering and motherhood over the last thirty years. More specifically, Anglo-American feminist theory on mothers and sons mirrors and reenacts the theoretical trajectory of Anglo-American feminist thought on the mother–daughter relationship. In the 1970s, the received view—or what Toni Morrison calls, in another context, the master narrative—of mothers and daughters was that this relationship, particularly in the daughter's adolescent years, was one of antagonism and animosity. The daughter must differentiate herself from the mother if she is to assume an autonomous identity as an adult. The mother, in turn, is perceived and understood only in terms of her maternal identity. The mother represents for the daughter, according to the received narrative, the epitome of the patriarchal oppression that she seeks to transcend as she comes to womanhood; the daughter's failings, as interpreted by herself and by the culture at large, are said to be the fault of the mother. This is the patriarchal narrative of the mother–daughter relationship. The lives of mothers and daughters are shaped by these cultural narratives even as mothers and daughters live lives different from, and in resistance to, these assigned roles. Feminist Anglo-American writers, most notably Nancy Chodorow, author of the influential *The reproduction of mothering*, and Nancy Friday, author of the best-selling *My mother/my self*, argue that mother–daughter identification is ultimately detrimental to the daughter's attainment of autonomy. For Chodorow, writing from a psychoanalytic perspective, this is because mother–daughter identification results in the daughter having weak "ego-boundaries"; with Friday, separation is required to enable the daughter to assume an adult sexual identity as a woman.

The 1970s feminist view that problematizes if not pathologizes mother–daughter identification has now fallen out of favor among Anglo-American feminist theorists. Indeed most Anglo-American feminists, since at least the mid-1980s, regard mother–daughter connection and closeness as essential for female empowerment. From the early 1980s, feminists, both lay and academic, have increasingly linked female power to mother–daughter connection. Today, Anglo-American feminist writers challenge the normative view of mother–daughter attachment that scripts estrangement as both natural and inevitable; they argue that identification empowers mothers and daughters alike, giving rise to the transformation of patriarchal culture. Drawing upon the ancient Elyeusis rites of Demeter and Persephone, recent feminist writings on the mother–daughter relation celebrate mother–daughter connection, and explore how such is achieved and sustained through maternal narratives, the motherline, feminist socialization of daughters, and gynocentric mothering. To this end, feminist theorists identify and challenge the various cultural practices and assumptions that divide mothers and daughters, and seek an alternative mother–daughter narrative scripted for empowerment as opposed to estrangement.[4]

A similar trajectory may be observed in Anglo-American feminist writing on the mother–son relation, with an approximate ten-year time lag. The texts examined above tend to downplay women's maternal role and identity. In contrast, the contemporary Anglo-American feminist view emphasizes mother–son connection, and positions it as central to the reconfiguration of traditional masculinity. Similar to the new Anglo-American feminist literature on mothers and daughters that recasts connection as empowerment by referencing the mythic mother–daughter dyad Demeter and Persephone, the contemporary Anglo-American feminist emphasis on the mother–son connection is also frequently conveyed through a mythic mother–son relation, that of Thetis and Achilles.

"Thetis, according to the myth, dipped her son Achilles into the river Styx to render him immortal. However, fearing that he might be lost to the river, she held onto him by his ankle. Achilles, as the story goes, remains mortal and vulnerable to harm. Thetis would be forever blamed for her son's fatal flaw, his Achilles heel." However, contemporary feminist theorists reinterpret the traditional reading of this narrative to argue, as Nikki Fedele and Cate Dooley do in their chapter in this book, that "the holding place of vulnerability was not, as the myth would have us believe, a fatal liability to Achilles. It was the thing that kept him *human and real*. In fact, we consider it *Thetis' finest gift* to her son" (page 357, this volume). Fedele and Dooley's research with mothers and sons, as discussed later in this volume, reveals that "boys with a secure maternal connection develop stronger interpersonal skills and enjoy healthier relationships as adults" (page xxx, this volume). Mother–son connection, they conclude, is what makes possible the new masculinity we desire for our sons and men in general.

The Thetis and Achilles model of mother–son attachment advanced by Dooley and Fedele is examined fully in Olga Silverstein and Beth Rashbaum's 1994 book, *The courage to raise good men*. The book opens with a poem about Thetis and Achilles that Silverstein wrote many years ago for her now-middle aged son upon his birth. Presenting herself as Thetis, Silverstein worries that her love, like that of Thetis, might damage her son's manhood:

> Even Thetis, dipping her mortal boy
> In Styx, dreaming of armouring him
> Against both worlds, gripping her joy
> In fatal fingers, allowed the dim
> Danger of her handhold on his heel [...]
> If immortal mothers are to such folly prone,

How am I to guard against the thumbprints
On my own? (Silverstein and Rashbaum, 1994: 1)

As a young mother whose views on childrearing were very much shaped by the larger patriarchal culture of 1940s America, Silverstein believed, as do many mothers, that she, like Thetis, "might fail to let [her son] go, and the love [she] felt for him might in some way damage the armour of his manhood, rendering him as vulnerable as Achilles—who of course died of a wound to that very heel by which his mother had once clung to him" (1). "Hands (and thumbs off) is the warning to mothers of son," Silverstein notes, so that to mother a son is to engage in a continuous "process of pulling back" (1–2).

Silverstein challenges this received view of mother–son relation and argues that the mandate of disconnection and the taboo against mother–son intimacy is the root cause of sons' difficulties as adults. The assumption is that boys, as scripted by the Freudian Oedipal scenario, gradually withdraw and distance themselves from their mothers as they grow into manhood. A close and caring relationship between a mother and a son is pathologized as aberrant, while a relationship structured upon separation is naturalized as the real and normal way to experience mother–son attachment. Silverstein explains: "[Our culture believes] that a male child must be removed from his mother's influence in order to escape the contamination of a close relationship with her. The love of a mother—both the son's love for her, and hers for him—is believed to 'feminize' a boy, to make him soft, weak, dependent, homebound .... [O]nly through renunciation of the loving mother, and identification with the aggressor father, does the ... boy become a man" (11). In other words, the majority of us in Western culture see mother–son separation as both inevitable and desirable.

Silverstein challenges the central, organizing premise of patriarchally mandated mother–son separation, namely that this process is both natural, hence inevitable, and "good" for our sons. She emphasizes that what we interpret as a normal process is, in fact, a culturally scripted and orchestrated act. Moreover, she argues that it is mothers and not boys who both initiate and direct the separation. "By expecting our sons to cut off from us," she writes, "we make sure that they do" (159). The mother, aware that mother–son connection and closeness is disparaged and pathologized in our culture, is ever-vigilant that she not be "overclose" with her son. While her son nurses in her arms, she may worry about the intimacy and stiffen, pull back, or look away; so too when her eight-year-old scrambles onto her lap she will laugh proudly and nudge him off, saying that he is now a big boy and cannot fit in her lap; and when she is kissed by her teenage son, she will turn her cheek, tense her body, and mumble to hurry and not be late. The gestures of distancing are often subtle yet cumulative. A boy, Silverstein argues, "absorb[s] at an unconscious level that his mother is somehow uncomfortable with him, that she is pulling back from him, that their closeness is problematic" (31). "Soon," Silverstein continues, "he responds in kind, so that his mother, who wasn't aware that she herself was the original actor in this scenario of withdrawal, eventually assumes that the withdrawal was his not hers" (31). Once the son reaches adolescence, the mother, increasingly concerned about mother–son closeness and the damage such may inflict on her son's incipient manhood, may abruptly withdraw from her son; an act that the son may experience as abandonment. Confused and hurt by his mother's rejection of him, the son decisively breaks from his mother and forges an identity separate from her modeled upon the masculine values of self-sufficiency and autonomy, particularly as they pertain to emotional identity. Whether the son is fully aware of the mother's distancing, he nonetheless, Silverstein argues, experiences a deep and inexplicable loss that is seldom understood or articulated, a loss that profoundly scars the boy and causes him to grow into a psychologically wounded man. William Pollack, in *Real boys: Rescuing our sons from the myths of boyhood*, maintains that the force of such separation is "so hurtful to boys that it can only be called a trauma—an emotional blow of damaging proportions ... [A] relational rapture [that] profoundly affects the psychology of most boys—and of most men—forever" (1998: 12, 27).

Demanding that young boys distance and differentiate themselves from their mothers, we require them to deny or repress the so-called feminine dimensions of their personalities. Silverstein argues that sons are deeply betrayed by their mothers' rejection of them and deeply wounded by the loss of the feminine in themselves occasioned by this separation. The result of this, she says, is: "lost boys, lonely men, lousy marriages, and midlife crises," or, as Pollack describes it, "a deep wellspring of grief and sadness that may last throughout [men's] lives" (1998: 12). Over the last decade, and particularly in the last few years, our culture has identified a crisis in masculinity. Though varied and diverse, the majority of commentators on this "crisis in masculinity"—from Robert Bly to feminist journalist Susan Faludi in her recent best-selling book *Stiffed: The betrayal of the American man*—agree that masculinity must be redefined, and that such is to be achieved through a reconnection of father and son. In contrast, Silverstein counters this received narrative to argue that: "the real pain in men's lives stems from their estrangement from women" (1994: 225). Similarly, Pollack emphasizes that boys and men: "[are] forever longing to return to [the mother], and to the 'holding' connection she once provided him, a connection he now feels he can never regain. If a boy had been allowed to separate at his own pace, that longing and sadness would not be there" (1998: 27). "As a culture we have to," as Silverstein concludes, "face up to the longing [of sons for mothers]—its power, its persistence throughout a man's life, its potential for destruction when unacknowledged" (1994: 225).

Early Anglo-American feminist theorists on mothers and sons believed that motherhood oppressed women, impeded mother–son equality, and fostered both sexism and patriarchal masculinity. This literature consequently downplayed, denied, and at times, disparaged women's maternal identity, viewing as problematic women's responsibility and authority as mothers. A mother must rear her son outside/beyond motherhood, they argued, in order to raise a non-sexist, non-masculine (as it is traditionally defined) boy, and to improve relations between mothers and sons, and men and women generally.

In contrast, the "new" Anglo-American feminist theory argues that too little mothering, and, in particular, the absence of mother-son connection, is what engenders both sexism and traditional masculinity in men. Thus a mother must foreground her presence in the life of her son; she must establish and maintain a close and caring connection with her son throughout his life. The mother is, accordingly, afforded agency as a mother, and her maternal responsibility and authority are emphasized and affirmed. This perspective positions mothering as central to feminist politics in its insistence that true and lasting gender equality will occur only when boys are raised as the sons of mothers. As the early feminist script of mother–son connection required the denial of the mother's power and the displacement of her identity as mother, the new perspective affirms the maternal and celebrates mother–son connection. In this, it rewrites the patriarchal and early feminist narrative to give Jocasta and Clytemnestra presence, voice, and a central and definitive role in the lives of their sons.

African-American feminist theory on the mother and son relationship

Most of the writing by African-American women has tended to focus on the mother-daughter relationship; little has been written on the mother-son relationship.[5] The notable exceptions are Joyce Elaine King's and Carolyn Ann Mitchell's *Black mothers to sons: Juxtaposing African American literature with social practice* (1995) and *Saving our sons: Raising black children in a turbulent world* (1995) by novelist Marita Golden.[6] In the introduction to their book King and Mitchell, explaining their research interest in mothers and sons, write: "Considering the particular vulnerability of black males in this society and the role that mothers typically play as primary nurturers, this focus on black mother-to-son parenting is long overdue" (2). The initial question King and Mitchell explored in selected African-American fiction and asked of their research participants was: "What have you done to protect your son(s) from society's hostile forces?" (6). In their study of African-American literature they found that protection was the primary aim of black mothering and manifested itself in two diametrically opposed modes of mothering: "mothers who whip their sons brutally 'for their own good' and mothers who love their sons to destruction through self-sacrifice and overindulgence" (9). The first strategy is sustained by the belief that "a black man-child duly 'chastened' or broken at home will pose less of a threat to a society already primed to destroy him" (10), while the latter seeks to shield the child from all that is deemed harsh and upsetting. Each position, they argue, psychologically maims the son; the first by breaking the child's spirit, the latter by thwarting the child's maturation to true selfhood. The conflicting demands of protection and nurturance first identified by Ruddick in *Maternal Thinking* become, in the instance of rearing black sons, an impasse, an irreconcilable contradiction. The women interviewed by King and Mitchell all spoke of this paradox in the mothering of black sons: while sons must go into the world to mature socially, psychologically, and otherwise, this same world threatens their very physical survival. The question black mothers ask in the raising of their sons is, in the authors' words: "How [can they] help sons develop the character, personality, and integrity a black man-child needs to transcend these forces?" (19).

Golden's book also assumes as its central theme the survival of black men, and is dedicated to the black men who have died violently in Washington, D.C., since 1988. Golden wrote this book, as she explains in her epilogue, "because at this moment there is no subject more necessary to confront, more imperative to imagine. Until I wrote about our sons, I could not speak or think or dream of anything else" (1995: 185). Homicide, Golden tells us, is the leading cause of death for young black men in America. The violence, drugs, crime, joblessness, and killing of black male youth mark, according to Golden, a new kind of Middle Passage. Her book narrates this crossing as it tells the story of her own son's journey into manhood; in this telling and testifying Golden lists possible causes, drafts solutions, and seeks to imagine what, in her words "we will look like, how will we sound, once we are spewed forth from the terrible hold of THIS ship" (9). As in King's and Mitchell's literary and sociological study, Golden recognizes that for blacks who have the financial means, retreat has become the strategy of choice. In the instance of her own life, Golden withdrew her son from public school in Washington, D.C., and enrolled him in a private boarding school, as she and her husband had purchased a house in the suburbs. However, in saving your son this way, you remove him from the black community, the "sites of resistance"—family, community, history—that have traditionally nurtured and empowered African-Americans by creating black-defined narratives and identities. The women of King and Mitchell's study spoke of the "liberating, healing power of family lore, bloodlines, and family secrets" (1995: 37). "Knowing about ancestors," King and Mitchell write, "strengthens identification with family values that can help a son overcome anger and hopelessness. Such family lore can also develop a son's confidence in himself ... it frees black males from the diminished definitions of their humanity and self-worth that society offers them" (38). Golden, too, recognizes that the double consciousness Du Bois eloquently wrote of more than a hundred years ago is, in her words, "draining and sometimes killing our spirits" (14). With integration came the loss of communities, traditions, beliefs, legends, narratives, and rituals, the "sites of resistance" that have long sustained and enriched black American culture. While suburbs and boarding schools may save black sons from the killing fields of the so-called American inner cities, they also result in the further disintegration of black communities, the very thing that holds the promise of salvation for African-Americans.

This again is the impasse of black mothers; one that is etched on the very bodies of black men. As Golden remarks of her own son: "The unscathed openness of Michael's demeanor was proof that he had been a protected, loved child. But this same quality was also suddenly a liability, ones that he has to mask" (95). Nurturing sons to be confident and proud, mothers recognize that these same traits—because they may be misconstrued as insolence, obstinacy, and arrogance by other black youth, police, or whites—put their sons at risk. Golden realizes, as do King and Mitchell, that this paradox of mothering black sons necessitates a new mode of mothering, one fashioned specifically for black male children. And while King, Mitchell, the women of their research group, and Golden have not designed a blueprint for such mothering, they all agree that sons must be taught, in Golden's words, "that the first line of defense against racism is to mold themselves into disciplined, self-respecting refutations of its ability to destroy our souls or ourselves" (186). Or, as James Baldwin wrote in 1971: "It evolves upon the mother to invest the child, her man child, with some kind of interior dignity which will protect him against something he really can't be protected against, unless he has some kind of interior thing within him to meet it" (as quoted by King and Mitchell, 39). Audre Lorde wrote in "Man child: A black lesbian feminist's response" that: "for survival, Black children in America must be raised to be warriors. For survival they must also be raised to recognize the enemy's many faces" (Lorde, 1995: 75). She goes on to say:

> The strongest lesson I can teach my son is the same lesson I teach my daughter: how to be who he wishes to be for himself. And the best way I can do this is to be who I am and hope that he will learn from this not how to be me, which is not possible, but how to be himself. And this means how to move to that voice from within himself, rather than to those raucous, persuasive, or threatening voices from outside, pressuring him to be what the world wants him to be. (77)

The aim of black mothering is thus to nurture and sustain the "singular soul," "the voice from within," and the "interior thing" of black sons, so that they are able to transcend the maiming of racism and grow into manhood whole and complete. Mothers of black sons, according to these writers, must negotiate between the need to keep their sons physically safe while simultaneously promoting their psychological maturation: this pull between nurturance and protection is at the heart of raising the black male child. This may be contrasted to the challenge and contradiction of feminist mothering according to early Anglo-American feminist thought, which is to redefine loss as gain; boys must learn that in renouncing patriarchal masculinity they achieve humanity. Thus the mothering of sons, according to Anglo-American thought, centers on the taking away of power from sons, while for mothers of black men, it means bringing their sons *to* power; to nurture and sustain that "soul," "voice from within," and "interior thing." For mothers of black sons this is achieved by grounding sons in their culture of origin, the black community. Anglo-American feminist mothering, in contrast, necessitates a challenge to the son's community of identification, the male peer group, or more generally patriarchal culture.

African-American feminist theory, as with the new Anglo-American feminist perspective, emphasizes women's agency, responsibility, and authority as mothers. The presence and involvement of the mother are recognized as crucial and essential to the son's maturation. African-American mothering of sons, however, is specifically racially determined in its emphasis on survival. "The major challenge ... to a black mother raising sons today," as Claudette Lee and Ethel Williams explain, "[is] survival ....[:] Racism, discrimination, and oppression define the childhood of an African-American male. Mothering for an African-American woman is defined by fear for her male child. Therefore her approach and relationship with her son must be different" (2001: 56–7). In its focus on survival— what Ruddick defines "as the central constitutive, invariant aim of maternal practice" (1989: 19)—African-American mothering foregrounds, even more than the new Anglo-American perspective, the importance and centrality of the mother in the sons's life, for it is she who both provides protection and teaches her son how to protect himself, physically and otherwise. African-American feminist thought on mothers and sons, in its emphasis on maternal agency, responsibility, and authority, particularly as they pertain to ensuring the son's survival, recasts Jocasta and Clytemnestra as pivotal characters in the mother–son drama.

Conclusion

Early Anglo-American feminist thought tended to downplay, devalue, and at times disparage motherhood. Arcana asked mothers to abandon traditional motherhood to allow sons to see their mothers in roles other than ones of service and subservience; Forcey championed the "unbinding" of motherhood to free women from the oppressiveness of the responsibility assignment; and Smith argued that only by relating to her son outside of motherhood could a mother hope to secure his respect so as to achieve a relationship based on equality. Sexism and patriarchal masculinity, they contended, are perpetuated and reinforced through maternal practice, by placing women in service to boys (Arcana), by making women responsible for sons (Forcey), and by preventing sons from respecting women (Smith). Maternal responsibility is censored by Forcey and, to a lesser degree, Arcana; maternal authority, in turn, is criticized by Smith. In each, the woman, as *mother* in both definition and act, becomes absent and silent. In contrast, recent Anglo-American feminist thought focuses on maternal presence, arguing that mother–son connection is what makes possible the new non-patriarchal masculinity we desire for our sons, and for all men. The stress on maternal presence and involvement is underscored by an insistence on the significance of maternal responsibility, agency, and authority. Maternal presence and involvement are further emphasized in African-American feminist theory—as is the affirmation of the importance of maternal responsibility, agency, and authority. Presence and participation in the sons' lives are stressed in African-American feminist theory because black boys' lives are at risk. Black mothers must protect their sons to ensure their survival, both physically and psychologically, and teach them how to do the same for themselves.

The above developments in Anglo-American feminist thought on mothers and sons, along with the emergence of a distinct African-American feminist perspective, have recast the roles of mothers and sons. They have rewritten the patriarchal script of mother–son separation/maternal absence as they are enacted in the narratives of Jocasta and Oedipus, Clytemnestra and Orestes. In so doing, they give both voice and presence to the mother and make mother-son connection central to the redesign of both traditional masculinity and the larger patriarchal culture. This new perspective, I want to suggest, allows for real and lasting social change. Feminist positions that depend upon the marginalization of motherhood and a mitigation of maternal authority and agency, I argue, cannot effect change, because they reinscribe, albeit inadvertently, the valorization of the masculine and the degradation of all that is deemed feminine in our culture. The denial and disparagement of the maternal bespeaks a larger unease with, and aversion to, the feminine. The new feminist perspectives—Anglo-American and African-American—in highlighting maternal voice and presence, affirming maternal agency, authority, and responsibility, and foregrounding mother–son connection, have imagined and made possible a truly feminist narrative of mothers and sons.

Notes

1.   The disparagement and erasure of the mother that these texts enact may also, as many feminist theorists have argued, be interpreted psychoanalytically as bespeaking both male

fear of maternal power, and the need to deny and repress the feminine in order to construct a masculine identity. Nancy Chodorow, in *The reproduction of mothering*, argues that the father's absence from the home in the sons' early years necessitates the son defining his masculinity by negation; that which his mother is, he is not. As well, for the infant son, the powers of the mother appear limitless. Our individual flesh-and-blood mother is also identified archetypally with the primordial Great Mother, who held very real life-and-death powers over mortal men. In our individual and collective unconsciousness we remember that time when we lived under the mother's power in the pre-Oedipal and prepatriarchal world. Dorothy Dinnerstein, in *The mermaid and the minotaur*, maintains that fear and hatred of women, and of mothers in particular, originate from the infant's experiences of dependency and helplessness, which in turn come to structure adult consciousness.

2. *Mothers and sons*, though written by the Australian writer Babette Smith, advances an Anglo-American view on feminism in general and the mother-son relation in particular.

3. For a detailed discussion of sensitive mothering, please see my article, "'Ain't that love?': Antiracism and racial constructions of motherhood" in Maureen Reddy, ed., *Everyday acts against racism* (Seattle: Seal Press, 1996), 88–98.

4. This is examined at length in my two recent articles on Anglo-American feminist theory and the mother–daughter relation: "Across the divide: Contemporary Anglo-American feminist theory on the mother–daughter relationship" in Sharon Abbey and Andrea O'Reilly, eds., *Redefining motherhood: Changing identities and patterns*, (Toronto: Second Story Press, 1998), 69–91, reprinted in this volume; and "Mothers, daughters and feminism today: Empowerment, agency, narrative," *Canadian Women's Studies* 18:2 & 3 (Summer/Fall 1998): 16–21. See also the introduction to Andrea O'Reilly and Sharon Abbey, *Mothers and daughters: Connection, empowerment, transformation* (New York: Rowman and Littlefield, 2000).

5. African-American motherhood has been examined in recent African-American feminist theory. See in particular Patricia Hill Collins, *Black feminist thought: Knowledge, consciousness and the politics of empowerment* (New York: Unwin Hyman/Routledge, 1990); "The meaning of motherhood in black culture and black mother–daughter relationships" in Patricia Bell-Scott and Beverly Guy-Sheftall, eds., *Double stitch: Black women write about mothers and daughters* (New York: HarperPerennial, 1993), 42–60; "Shifting the center: Race, class, and feminist theorizing about motherhood" in Evelyn Nakano Glenn, Grace Chang, and Linda Rennie Forcey, eds., *Mothering: Ideology, experience, and agency*, (New York: Routledge, 1994), 45–65. See also my article, "'I come from a long line of uppity irate black women': African-American feminist thought on motherhood, the motherline, and the mother–daughter relationship" in Andrea O'Reilly and Sharon Abbey, ed., *Mothers and daughters: Connection, empowerment, and transformation* (New York: Rowman and Littlefield, 2000), 143–159. See also the *Journal of the Association for Research on Mothering* 2:2, on "Mothering in the African diaspora."

6. This chapter will examine book-length studies of African-American mothers and sons as it did with Anglo-American feminist theory. Audre Lorde wrote the classic article, "Man child: A black lesbian feminist's response" in *Sister outsider* (Freedom, CA: The Crossing Press, 1993).

Chapter Twenty-Two

Bringing Our Boyz to Men
Black men's reflections on their mothers' childrearing influences

Wanda Thomas Bernard

Introduction

This paper will critically examine the role of African mothers in the diaspora, who are raising sons, from the perspective of sons. Using a reflective analysis of data gathered in a cross-national research project that explored survival strategies used by black men in Halifax, Nova Scotia, and Sheffield, England, this paper will specifically focus on their discourse about mothers and black women who fulfill *mothering* roles in their lives, as grandmothers, sisters, aunts, and *othermothers*. The findings in this research challenge some of the social science literature that pathologizes the role of black women, who are described by Symonds (1989) as "loving their sons" and "raising their daughters."

My interest in this topic is both personal and professional. The professional interests emerged through the conduct of the research with black men. However, this was also deeply embedded in my personal connection to the topic. I have spent considerable time analyzing the different relationships I observed between my mother and her sons, as compared to her daughters. I have also looked at these relationships across generations and over time. I am a step-mother to a young black man, and I have been an othermother to my brothers, nephews, and community sons and daughters. I want to develop richer understandings of the multi-generational motherlines between mothers and sons. This is a beginning journey, a work in progress, which examines black men's views of their mothers, grandmothers, and othermothers contributions to their successful negotiation to manhood. This chapter explores the three themes that emerged in this study: black mothers and othermothers are seen as superwomen and are key to black men's survival; grandmothers are guardians of the generations, particularly the maternal line; and othermothers lessen the negative impact of mother absence. I begin with a review of the literature on black motherhood.

Naming contradictions: The experiences of black motherhood

It has been argued in the literature that the black woman, as matriarch, is largely responsible for the social castration of black men (Moynihan, 1965 [qtd. in Rainwater and Yancey, 1967; Staples, 1978]). The relative lack of involvement of black men in the parenting role (regardless of the reasons for this phenomena), has frequently meant the over involvement of black women in the lives of their sons (Bernard, 1996). Some suggest that the institution of black motherhood has helped to exonerate men from authentic fathering and shared parenting roles and responsibilities (Franklin, 1984).

Collins (1990) provides a useful critique of the literature and the various perspectives on black motherhood. She challenges white male scholars' claim that black mothers, as matriarchs, have contributed to the deterioration of the family structure as we once knew it. Collins (1990) also asserts that whilst white feminists have challenged white male perspectives on motherhood in general, they have not significantly challenged the matriarch image of black motherhood. Finally, Collins (1990) challenges the black male scholars who tend to glorify black motherhood and have helped to fuel the superwoman image.

In examining the politics of black motherhood, Bernard and Bernard (1998) state that black motherhood may be the site of oppression, or an opportunity for creativity, empowerment, and social action. Acknowledging the contradictory nature of black motherhood, they go on to suggest that black mothers' ability to cope with race, class, and gender oppression should not be confused with transcending those conditions. Placing black women on a pedestal, as the strength of black families and communities (Bernard, 1996), also sets them up for failure in the role, particularly in relation to the mother/son relationship. Collins (1990) advances our analysis of black motherhood with her position that self-definition is essential, as externally defined definitions of black motherhood are always problematic, both those that are positive and affirmative, and the more visible negative and controlling images. Externally imposed definitions of black motherhood help to reinforce the marginalization and oppression faced by black women, children, and families (Bernard and Bernard, 1998). Collins (1990) argues that when black women self-define black motherhood, they expose the contradictions that are inherent in the role, the tensions between the oppression that is reinforced through the controlling images of black mothers, and the potential empowerment and independence that the site of black motherhood offers.

Black women have been described as the "strength" of black families, the matriarch, the superwoman. McCray (1980) says:

> the Black woman has either been depicted as the dominating, castrating female under whose hand the Black family and the Black community are falling apart, or as the romanticised, strong, self-sufficient female responsible for the survival of the Black family and of Black people. (67)

These dichotomized views of black women permeate the social science literature, and the popular media. Collins (1990) identified four controlling images of black women: mammy, matriarch, welfare mother, and jezebel (the sexually aggressive woman). She argues that these images, designed as tools of domination, are used to make poverty, racism, and sexism appear to be a natural part of everyday life. These images are transmitted through institutional sites such as the media, schools, and other external sites; and through internal sites within African communities such as the family and the Church.

The "matriarch" image that has dominated the social science literature allows black women to be blamed for the success or failure of black children (Collins, 1990: 74), and for the perceived social castration of black men (Moynihan, 1965 [qtd. in Rainwater and Yancey, 1967]). Collins argues that these views divert attention away from the systematic inequalities that black women face socially, politically, and economically. It also serves to create divisions between black women and men, diverting attention from issues of racial and gender inequality. What is needed is a more balanced perspective that looks at the various roles performed by black women in families and communities. Given the opportunity to tell their own stories, some black men present a different view of the roles of their mothers and black women as othermothers in helping them to negotiate the rocky terrain they must navigate on the journey to manhood. In this chapter, I explore the role of black motherhood in the rearing of sons who are perceived as successful, from the voices of the sons themselves.

The research study

This participatory action research project involved two groups of black men, in Halifax, Nova Scotia, and Sheffield, England, called Research Working Groups (RWGS), in an exploratory study of the strategies they used to survive in societies where they were expected to fail. They also examined the definition and meaning of success, as defined by black men themselves. Data gathering included individual interviews with forty men, twenty in each site; two focus groups in each site, involving another twenty men; and a conference in each site, which allowed for a wide range of black men, as well as others interested in black masculinity, to be involved in the research.

The RWGs did an initial thematic analysis of the data, which was further developed by the focus group participants, and the conference participants. The conferences and focus groups enabled many more men to be involved in this research, creating member checks and inquiry audits (Lather, 1991). The research process was fluid and dynamic. The participatory model was a successful tool for a woman to use in engaging men in an exploratory study of their lived reality. However, this success was also partly due to the way in which we developed a working relationship, where people from diverse backgrounds and social positions, and shared histories, were able to build partnerships as they engaged in this collective study.

One of the survival strategies that emerged in the research was the significance of family and friends. Further analysis of this finding suggested that in naming family, many of the black men were referring to the significant roles their mothers, grandmothers, and othermothers played in their survival. Our analysis suggests that the role of black mothers in particular and othermothers or community mothers, were key to the survival of many of the men who participated in this research. What follows is a discussion about the ways in which black women, as mothers, othermothers, and community mothers, contributed to the survival and success of black sons, as told by the sons. The men's stories are organized around the following themes: black women and mothers are superwomen, and are essential to black men's survival; grandmothers are the guardians of the generations; and the impact of mother absence is lessened by the presence of othermothers.

Black men's views of their mothers' influences

Black mothers as superwomen

The majority of our Sheffield participants described their mother's influence as very positive, nurturing, and caring.

> She played a major role in my survival, but she has also performed her duties as a Mom, in terms of protection: we are all very well balanced in terms of morality .... She is supportive in terms of work, goals and achievement .... (Sheffield)

> My mother was nurturing, and I value that a lot. She would worry about my safety, and always had a great caring thing .... She would look after my needs .... She was protective and fussy .... (Sheffield)

> Most of what we [Black men] learn, we learn from Black women [mothers]. They make more contributions to our survival than the men .... (Sheffield)

The Halifax participants shared very similar descriptions about their mother's role and influence:

> My mother was a very strong, caring and dedicated woman. She was always there for her children .... She was there to cook, clean, sew, and to heal you when you got sick. Her affection was always evident and outgoing. (Halifax)

> Black women have made quite a lot of contribution to my survival, beginning with my mother who gave me protection and always shielded me from harm. (Halifax)

> Black women have given me life; they taught me how to be a strong person. My mother ... [has] been the most influential in my survival. (Halifax)

In both Halifax and Sheffield, the mothers are described as the epitome of strength, and the foundation of the family. These views are consistent with the ways in which black women have been typically viewed in the literature. Confronting both racism and sexism, black women know intimately the place of oppression. A tradition of resistance and a collective black women's consciousness does exist, yet these are consistently overlooked, or misunderstood in the movements to eradicate sexism and racism (Collins, 1990; Scott, 1992). Black women have much to offer, however, the persistence of such dichotomised views about their role leaves us divided on many levels. Yet these men tell a somewhat different story. The black men in this study stressed the significance of black mothers and othermothers in their struggle to survive, and to become men that their mothers could be proud of. One participant put it succinctly:

> I never got into trouble with the law, thanks to my mother .... I was always more afraid of disappointing her, than I was scared of the police. I had such respect for her that I would never do anything to bring her shame or distress .... (Halifax)

Another participant offers a similar perspective. He said:

> I would not have survived if it had not been for my strong and supportive family, especially my mother .... I could not have coped with all the racism in the world without them as my safety net. (Sheffield)

Whist the literature suggests that the matriarch role and the superwoman image helps with the social castration of black men, these men credit their mothers strong, supportive and stern presence as one of the most significant contributions to their survival and success. For many, their mothers have been role models and mentors that have helped them prepare for survival in a hostile and unwelcoming environment, where they are constantly devalued. In addition, despite the superwoman image that is evident in these men's stories, there is also a recognition of the struggles and suffering that black women endure. The following quotations are illustrative of their perceptions and serve as an acknowledgement of the difficulties that black women deal with as they fight for the survival of their families and communities.

> They [Black women] have taken on burdens above and beyond the call of duty .... Their strength has been passed on to their children .... They have worn our problems for too long, and now it is time for us to "give back" as Black men .... (Sheffield)

> The perseverance of Black women is admirable ... I want to emulate this ... we need to gather strength from each other .... Black women can't carry the burdens on their own .... I would like to see a better, stronger Black family in the future .... As families we must realize that we are in this struggle together so we must work together .... (Halifax)

> Brothers could take a lesson or two from a page of the Black woman's book of struggle and success ... we have a lot to learn from our sisters and it is time for us to shoulder more of those responsibilities .... (Halifax)

More than an acknowledgement of their strength and the additional burdens they have carried historically, these men called for their brothers work more collectively with black women, and to take on responsibilities for nurturing and mentoring black sons and daughters. There is also an acknowledgement of the role of mothers across generations. We heard many accolades about the strengths of black grandmothers, especially the maternal line. Similar to their views about their mothers, these men's stories reveal a reverence and respect for their grandmothers, and one gets a sense of their positive contributions to the survival of black men.

Grandmothers: Guardians of the generations

There has been little research done on the experiences of black grandparents. However, Taylor et al. (1990: 998), reviewing a study done by Cherlin and Furstenberg (1986), reveals that in comparison to whites, black grandparents take a more active part in the parenting of grandchildren. The reasons for this vary, however, cultural traditions of extended family and elasticity of roles may explain this in part, as is evidenced in some of our data. The role of grandmothers, particularly maternal grandmothers, is quite similar to that of mothers, with many of them being seen as superwomen, and as guardians of the generations.

> My grandmother gave me much insight and was a strong influence. She was always there, even when my parents were not. We had such respect for our grandparents, especially our grandmother ... I am sad that my kids don't have that in this country ... but we have found replacements ... older women in the community are like community grandmothers. They pass on the wisdom from the former generation .... (Sheffield)

However, for many of our respondents, especially in Sheffield, grandparents are generally not available and/or accessible, as they are more likely to be still living in the Caribbean. Fifty percent of our Sheffield respondents had no contact with their grandmothers who were either still living in the Caribbean (fifty percent of this group) or had died when they were young (twenty-five percent), or before they were born. For the fifty percent who had contact, seventy-five percent of these had positive, nurturing contact with their maternal grandmothers, and none with their paternal grandmothers. There appears to be more contact with the maternal lineage.

The other twenty-five percent of this sample had positive contact with both grandmothers. For those with contact, the relationships were usually described as caring, loving, supportive, and nurturing; in fact, as indicated, these are strikingly similar to the way in which their mothers are described.

> She (maternal grandmother) was like my mother. I was very special to her and she to me. (Sheffield)

> She (maternal grandmother) was always there for guidance and support. (Sheffield)

> I was influenced very early by my grandmother. She was always a constant source of strength and love for me. She always stressed that I should be all that I could be, and I always knew and believed that she wanted the best for me. (Sheffield)

Halifax participants described their grandmothers' influence in similar ways: supportive, encouraging, and caring, and a replacement Mom.

My (maternal) grandmother taught me about human emotions; that everyone can cry. I learned from her that crying was "okay" even when everyone else said it was bad .... (Halifax)

My (maternal) grandmother kept me in line. She was there for me at lunch and after school because my mother worked. (Halifax)

My grandmother was a carer and she taught me to be a caring person. She also taught me how to respect and love myself so that I could learn how to love and respect others. She handed down all sorts of stories and family traditions that I still share with my children today. (Halifax)

Once again, we see incredibly high expectations of grandmothers, particularly maternal grandmothers. Frazier (1966 [quoted in Hutchinson, 1994]) described grandmothers as the guardians of generations. McCray (1980 [quoted in Hill, 1977]) argues that grandmothers are the most significant force in the socialisation of black children. These findings support the theory that grandmothers, especially maternal grandmothers are very significant in the socialization of black men, for their positive survival. The lineage from mother—to daughter—to children appears to be the one most strongly identified by our respondents. Despite this generally positive picture that emerged about grandmothers, there was also some concern expressed about the preservation of that role given the challenges faced by families who are displaced due to immigration and migration. One participant aptly states:

I am concerned about the future of Black families and Black men because parenting is changing .... Today's parents are forgetting their cultures; they do not teach their children the things that we were taught, and they don't have contact with the grandparents who were able to fill the gaps .... What will happen to the next generation? (Sheffield)

Who will fill the role of grandmothers as guardians of the generations for the next generation? To what extent can community mothers and othermothers help in the process of bringing our *boyz* to men?

Mother absence: Othermothers and community mothers

A major gap in the literature that explores black motherhood is the lack of attention paid to the issue of mother absence. As noted previously, black women are seen as the epitome of strength, and few writers dare to examine mother absence in African communities. Collins (1990) begins a dialogue about the challenges faced by some black women who do not want to be, or are not able to be mothers to their children. The topic emerged in this research as black men talked about their mothers and those people who became replacement mothers when their birth mothers were not able to be there for them.

In most of the Halifax cases, the mothers, othermothers, and community mothers were identified as being present, and as an integral part of the lives of these men. One Halifax participant was raised by foster parents, who described his foster-mother as being very significant. However, wanting to find his biological mother was an issue that he struggled with during adolescence. For another, the death of both parents led to bonding with othermothers who filled those roles.

> After my parents died I had to have somebody that I could confide in and to console me; I had my Godmother and some aunts. I had a lot of people that were instrumental in my life .... (Halifax)

> My adopted mother is a white woman, and I love her to death, but I went to Black women in the community to really find out who I was, to find my true identity. I will be forever grateful to the Black women who helped me to understand myself and Black women .... (Halifax)

In Sheffield, two participants indicated they were not raised by their mothers:

> My mother was an absent parent; her always being away perhaps affected my relationship with women. (Sheffield)

> I still get angry sometimes when I think about my mother leaving .... Things were never the same when I joined her in this country ... the mother–son bond was broken ... and this angers me. (Sheffield)

There appears to be an undertone of anger and resentment towards these absent mothers, which was not evident in respondents' responses regarding absent fathers.[1] This may reflect a position of internalised sexism and the expectation that mothers are "supposed" to be there, and that all bloodmothers want to be mothers. However, as Collins (1990) and Bryan (1992) argue, motherhood may be burdensome and oppressive for some women.

The mothers in our sample were described as having a very important, significant influence on the survival of their sons. Even in the absence of blood mothers, the mother's influence was sought and found by these men, as noted in the examples cited above. For the most part, these women are revered and placed on a pedestal in the eyes of their sons. These stories help to fuel the stereotype of the black superwoman, which fails to reflect the diversity in the lives of black women. Higginbotham (1982) argues that although black women

are able to overcome very difficult situations, they are not superwomen who
have no needs or emotions. An assessment of black women's roles as mothers
reflects such a diversity of experience. That diversity can be seen in the way in
which these men described the significance of other women in their lives who
performed the nurturing roles. This extended family network is common amongst
African families throughout the diaspora. Migration has broken those bonds for
some Africans and African Caribbeans in Britain and Canada; however, the kin
network remains a strong stabilizing influence in black families. The separation
of blood kin was also a focus of discussion at the Sheffield Conference on Black
Masculinity that we held as part of this research. In the workshop on "Black
men and displacement," participants discussed the impact of forced migration
and immigration on black families. The resulting absence of mothers and
grandparents in the Sheffield sample is one example of this. However, for many
of our Sheffield and Halifax respondents, this void has been replaced by the
development of other family support networks, and reinforces the significance
and value of othermothers (Collins, 1990), the extended family network (Stack,
1974; McAdoo, 1980; McCray, 1980; and Neverdon-Morton, 1989), and what
Edwards (2000) calls "community mothers." The men's stories proclaim the
significance of othermothers and community mothers.

> My parent's friends became aunts and uncles because we had no other
> family here .... (Sheffield)

> My Aunt has sort of replaced my parents, who are now dead. She's like
> a grandmother to our children, so the lineage continues ... (Sheffield)

Participants identified a host of extended family and friends, in the absence
of family or in addition to, who have had a positive, supportive and encouraging
impact on their survival. Aunts, uncles, cousins, neighbours, and parent's friends
were identified as significant people in the lives of these men.

> All of my family have had a strong influence on me. We are a strong,
> close family. The extended family maintains contacts, although we are
> on several continents now. (Sheffield)

> I have no other family in England. We had family friends who were
> considered family, special aunts, uncles and cousins. (Sheffield)

> Because the communities are divided, the family, including extended
> family members, has the strongest stabilizing influence. The children
> especially have an impact on the lives of Black men. (Halifax)

... This continuation of family networking is vital to our future ... I believe
that family unit, and community support tempers everything else. The
family including the extended family, is the "buffer zone." It is a great
source of social support for Black people. (Sheffield)

It appears that in addition to being a source of support, comfort and nurturance,
the black family is also seen to have an educative role, one which imparts social,
political, and cultural education, as well as values and morals. The data here also
suggest that the women have been seen as the primary performers of these
expectations. Are these role prescriptions that black mothers, grandmothers,
othermothers, and community mothers want to take on? Is this consistent with
how black women see themselves in their families? How does this fit with the
ways in which black women are described in the literature?

Conclusion

Do black women place too high expectations on black men? Or conversely, are
their expectations too low? Do these positive perceptions of black women's
contributions to the survival and success of black men, from the voices of sons,
reflect an acceptance of the matriarchal role of women as care-takers, nurturers,
and primary child rearers? The findings in this study suggest that these black
men perceive the role of black women in a positive light. Black mothers are seen
as superwomen who are crucial to the survival of their sons. Grandmothers
share a similar role, but are more important as guardians of the generations,
passing on traditions, values, history, and legacies from one generation to the
next. Finally, when mother is not there, emotionally or physically, then
grandmothers, othermothers, and community mothers fill the nurturing roles
that have been ascribed to black mothers.

However, an issue that needs further discussion is the potential for these
perceptions to reinforce patriarchal sexist definitions of black women's
contributions to the survival of black men. There is some attention paid to the
multiple oppression of black women, and the sacrifices that black women have
made, and continue to make, in their efforts to help the family and community
survive but is this understood? How do we move forward from here? We need to
continue the dialogue that gets black men and women talking with each other
about black women's roles in bringing our *boyz to men*. We need to critically
examine these roles, strengthening that which is working, and challenging those
things that are problematic. Black men in this research project thank their mothers
and black women in general for the work they have done over the years to
preserve and protect the black family, including black boys. They also invite their
brothers to take on more of the responsibilities for helping to bring black boys to
manhood.

Note

1. Further discussion of black men's experiences with their fathers can be found in *Bernard's black men: Endangered species or success story* (Halifax: Fernwood Publishers, forthcoming).

Chapter Twenty-Three

SWIMMING AGAINST THE TIDE

FEMINISTS' ACCOUNTS OF MOTHERING SONS

Alison M. Thomas

Introduction

Most academic definitions of socialization are based on the theme of adults preparing children to take their place in the society into which they have been born. In most cases this involves children learning how to act out adult roles by modeling the behavior of those around them, especially that of their parents or those most involved in their upbringing. This applies as much to children's acquisition of gendered behavior patterns as to any other learned behavior, and psychological theories concur in identifying the modeling of parental behavior as the primary way in which children learn the gendered roles considered appropriate in their society (Maccoby, 1966).

Such a process is obviously facilitated when models of both genders are readily available to children to observe and imitate, as in societies in which production, as well as reproduction, is carried out in or close to the home. However, in most "modern" industrialized societies[1] this is no longer the case, since adult work is generally performed away from the home and therefore typically removes one or both parents from the home for large portions of each working day.

Throughout most of the twentieth century, the ideology of the family wage and the definition of the father's role as that of "family breadwinner" meant that for most men the amount of time they were able to spend in the home with their children was restricted to a couple of hours in the evenings and time together on weekends (Beail and McGuire, 1982; Parke, 1996). As Julia Brannen and Peter Moss (1987) pointed out, this necessarily limited their chances of playing an active part in their children's upbringing, at least on a day-to-day basis. Joseph

Pleck quotes a "breadwinner" father interviewed in a 1950s community study, lamenting his own lack of involvement with his family: "I'm a rotten Dad. If our children amount to anything it's their mother who'll get the credit. I'm so busy I don't see much of them and I don't know how to chum up with them when I do" (Pleck, 1987: 89). With "homemaker" mothers thus taking on primary responsibility for child rearing and fathers routinely absent from everyday activities in the home, Mirra Komarovsky (1953) was the first of many to observe that men often risked becoming marginal figures in their children's lives (see also Pleck, 1987; Parke, 1996). In contrast to this, however, children typically had far greater daily exposure to adult females and the activities they engaged in, whether this was via their mother or another woman—since throughout the twentieth century it continued to be the case that most alternative caregivers and the majority of elementary school teachers were female.

In other words, one of the important consequences of these twentieth century work/family patterns was to restrict the opportunities that children had to interact with their father and model his behavior directly, in the way that the gender socialization theories stipulated. Instead, children of both sexes were for all intents and purposes raised and socialized primarily by their mothers in an everyday world populated predominantly by women.

Theorizing "masculine" socialization

Some versions of the standard socialization theories recognized the gender implications of this asymmetry of parenting and incorporated this into their accounts of gender identity development, arguing that because boys generally lacked the direct access to adult role models of their own sex that girls enjoyed, this necessarily made the process of gender identification more difficult for them (see Hartley, 1959; Lynn, 1966; and Greenson, 1968). According to this analysis, rather than developing an understanding of their adult gender role by modeling the behavior of their same-sex parent (as girls were able to do), boys would have to do a lot of their learning about how to be "masculine" indirectly, and primarily by learning how to differentiate themselves from their mother and other women— that is, in effect, by learning how *not* to be "feminine" (Maccoby and Jacklin, 1974).

This analysis, in highlighting the greater difficulties for boys of forming a gendered identity, thereby granted a "scientific" basis to many of the concerns of popular child-rearing books of the 1940s and 1950s (such as Wylie, 1942; Spock, 1945).[2] These had focused on how boys deprived of sufficient exposure to their father (and at the same time at risk of "coddling" by their mothers) might be damaged by this: mothers were therefore exhorted to pay particular attention to ensuring that their sons did not grow up effeminate. Indeed, in the absence of the father, it was felt to be a mother's job to "interpret" him and his role in the family to her children—and especially to her sons (Farber, 1962; Blendis, 1982).[3] Even as recently as the 1980s, Jacqueline McGuire (1991) found that many mothers she interviewed reported making a deliberate effort to foster their son's relationship with his father, and justified this in terms of their belief that this father–son identification had a particular importance, even if it meant relinquishing their own closeness with their son. For according to Olga Silverstein and Beth Rashbaum, "Most women ... fear that a mother's influence will ultimately be harmful to a male child, that it will weaken him, and that only the example of a man can lead a son into manhood" (1994: 9).

Many, however, have noted the distress that this separation process often risked causing, both to mothers and to their growing sons: as both tacitly acknowledged the unwritten rule requiring them to develop a gradual distance from each other, each was liable to misinterpret the other's stance as evidence of a withdrawal of affection (Silverstein and Rashbaum, 1994). There are, moreover, other negative consequences of this process of masculine self-differentiation. Insofar as it requires a boy to distance himself from his mother and reject "femininity," in favor of identifying with the often artificial extremes of "macho" masculinity depicted by the mass media, it has potentially damaging consequences in many areas of gender relations. It can, for example, manifest itself in the expression of misogynist attitudes and sexual harassment (Wood, 1982; Thomas 1997), as well as in aggressive behaviors toward other males (Ryan, 1985) and is thus, arguably, detrimental to society.[4]

The perpetuation of this masculine socialization process thus places limits on the possibility of bringing about any significant changes in the organization of adult gender roles, since it is clearly difficult to encourage men to be more nurturant and emotionally expressive (and thereby better able to share responsibility for childrearing, for example) when such qualities are widely regarded as "feminine" ones in modern Western societies, and the essence of "masculinity" is to repudiate all such traits. It follows that raising a son to be any of these things would necessitate taking the risk of making him "deviant," and since—as Silverstein and Rashbaum have observed—"The fear of what would befall an insufficiently 'masculinized' boy in this society is enormous," the majority of mothers have refrained from taking such a risk (1994: 5).

Until quite recently, then, even though mothers may have disliked many aspects of their son's passage into manhood, it seems clear that most nevertheless collaborated in this process and sought to ensure that their son grew up with an appropriately "masculine" identity by encouraging him to grow away from their influence.

The impact of social change

However, over the last few decades we have seen significant changes in the gender-differentiated family patterns that characterized most of the twentieth century, as increasing numbers of women have entered the workforce and abandoned the full-time "homemaker" role.[5] The rapid growth of "dual-earner" families and the corresponding erosion of the former dominance of the single-earner "breadwinner" family have had a dual impact on the gender socialization process. First of all, it is now the case that the majority of children no longer have a "stay-at-home" mother to take charge of their early upbringing, thereby blurring what was previously the most salient distinction between mothers and fathers from their children's perspective. Second, given the changes to gender roles that have occurred in their own working lives, many parents are now questioning the appropriateness of continuing to bring up sons and daughters to expect to take on gender-differentiated roles in adulthood. The gender roles that were once viewed as "natural" are now problematized, and as a consequence we have become increasingly self-conscious about how we communicate the significance of gender to our children. As Ivan Illich observed, "How to choose, assume and transmit sex roles has become a major worry for many people" (1983: 82).

This concern is particularly relevant for mothers, since the changes that occurred as women moved into the workplace have exposed a notable lack of change in the home. By the mid-1980s there was growing concern that women were taking on paid work outside the home without relinquishing their "traditional" responsibility for domestic work within it—thus effectively taking on a "second shift" (Hochschild and Machung, 1989). Women had changed, but men, for the most part, had not. Over the past fifteen years, this has therefore led to a renewed interest in reappraising and redefining traditional male roles, especially in the home, and from this it has indeed become apparent that while men's attitudes toward their role in the family may well be shifting, their behavior has been generally slow to change—especially amongst older generations.[6] It is for this reason that many women are now choosing to focus their efforts on the next generation and are trying to raise both sons and daughters to resist gender-differentiated roles, rather than see them perpetuate the same gendered asymmetries and inequalities in their own adult lives.

Once again, however, this is something that is easier for them to achieve with daughters than with sons. According to Ruth Hartley's claims (1959), girls should be able to develop a flexible idea of adult female roles by simply observing and modeling their mothers' behavior, and indeed, many feminist mothers have been successfully encouraging their daughters to grow up challenging conventional expectations of "femininity" through their own example. This is of course made easier by the fact that there are also obvious and tangible rewards for young women in resisting conventionally feminine roles (especially when this entails relinquishing some of the burden of responsibility in the home), since such roles are no longer accorded much status in contemporary society.

However, the situation is rather different for sons: for a start, there has been a general lack of anti-sexist men willing and able to act as unconventional role models for their sons (at least until recently), and this has again meant that mothers are the ones who are taking responsibility for directing their sons toward resisting traditional forms of masculinity. On top of this, it is clear that for young men the "costs" of challenging conventional masculine roles are much higher—given a society that still does attach considerable prestige to "masculinity"—and when this entails (for example) sharing domestic responsibilities with women, such "costs" are not clearly compensated by tangible benefits.

All of these factors have made the task of rearing antisexist sons a formidable one, and have once more brought to the fore the concerns expressed some fifty years earlier regarding the risks to boys of being emasculated by their mothers. Many mothers indeed feel ambivalent about this, since, as Adrienne Rich (1977: 204) noted, "The fear of alienating a male child from 'his' culture seems to go deep, even among women who reject that culture for themselves every day of their lives."

Nevertheless, in recent years there have been growing numbers of women who have decided to defy traditional norms and ominous cautionary tales and who have set out to raise their sons to be different. Rather than encouraging them to follow the conventional path of gradual separation from themselves and their "feminine" influence in order to assume a "masculine" identification with their father or other adult males, these women have chosen to resist such a distancing and to encourage their sons to remain close to them. In the next section I report the experiences and insights of some of the many women who have attempted this—and who are thus "swimming against the tide."

Outline of study

In 1994, Robyn Rowland and I launched a small-scale qualitative research study aimed at collecting feminist mothers' accounts of their experiences of raising sons (Rowland and Thomas, 1996).[7] Over a period of several months we wrote to forty-two women whom we knew to have one or more sons, and invited them to reflect on and write about their particular experiences *as feminists* bringing up sons, either via responses to an open-ended questionnaire, or in the form of an independent personal account along the same thematic lines. Working in part from our own experiences as mothers of sons, we highlighted a number of themes for them to consider in their responses:

- what their initial reactions were on discovering the sex of their child(ren) (and how others had reacted, especially feminist friends);
- how they felt about their son(s) now;
- what they felt had been the particular rewards and/or difficulties of having a son or sons;
- how the experience of mothering their son(s) had altered as he/they grew older;
- how their feminism had affected their experience of mothering their son(s);
- how having a son or sons had affected their feminist politics;
- any specific moments when they had been made aware of their gender differences as a barrier between them;
- their hopes for their son(s); and
- differences between mothering their son(s) and daughter(s).

The women to whom we wrote (mostly in the United Kingdom, Australia, Canada, and the United States) came from a variety of different class and ethnic backgrounds and covered a wide age range (as did their sons). For some their son was their only child, while others had more than one son, or daughters as well as sons. Some were bringing up their son(s) alone, others with a partner; of these, we took care to include those in both lesbian and heterosexual relationships.

In all, we received personal accounts from thirteen women, while a further seventeen women completed the questionnaire.[8] The sons of these thirty women ranged in age from five and one-half months to thirty-two years old. For eleven of the women, their son was their only child; eight had more than one son; and the remainder had one or more daughters as well as the son they wrote about. Seven of the women were (or had been) bringing up their son single-handedly; one had joint custody of her son with his father, from whom she was separated; one had raised her now-adult son in a collective household; four had raised sons with their woman partner, and the remaining seventeen with the boy's father or stepfather.

Findings

Elsewhere Robyn Rowland and I have highlighted a range of themes that emerged from the accounts and questionnaire responses of these feminist mothers of sons (Rowland and Thomas, 1996). Here I wish to focus on three of these themes in more detail: these are first, their efforts to encourage an alternative and more positive style of masculinity in their sons; second, the frustrations which these women expressed with regard to the everyday difficulties of bringing up their sons to resist masculine stereotypes in the context of immense pressures from elsewhere to conform to these; and third, the ambivalence many nevertheless expressed regarding the effects of their own active attempts to sabotage a conventional masculine identification in their sons.[9]

Theme one: Envisioning a new masculinity

Most feminist mothers see themselves as aiming to bring up their sons to be different from the masculine "norm" in various ways, and the women who participated in our study were no exception. Elsie Jay wrote of her conscious commitment to "creating a new man—sensitive, expressive, nonviolent, respectful and loving of women" (Jay, 1996: 122), and this was a predominant theme, with most of the mothers describing their efforts to encourage nurturant behavior and emotional expressiveness in their sons, and to discourage aggressive behavior of all kinds:

> I actively encourage affectionate, sensitive, and emotional behaviour/conversation and deliberately never encourage "macho" or masculinist dress/behavior/language/violence. (Kate)

> I have sought to appreciate his emotional sensibilities and encouraged him to do so, even if this means not being "boyish." (Deborah)

> I've encouraged him to pursue "feminine" interests, like reading, and talking about feelings. I've discouraged macho pursuits like toy guns, etc. (Susie)

Others also mentioned more practical concerns, such as wanting their sons to be competent in the domestic sphere:

> I actively sought to "enable" him to stand on his own feet as a human being; he can cook, wash, clean, etc. and should never be a burden on another woman. (Celia)

Those with older sons referred to their often lengthy discussions with their sons about how they had tried to raise them, and to their efforts to point out to them the gender inequalities that they were liable to encounter as they grew up:

> I have been able to discuss with them how I have raised them and why, and discuss how they feel. (Connie)

Yet it was often difficult for them to feel confident of having achieved the right balance; as Arlene McLaren noted, "at one and the same time I worry about ramming feminist, anti-oppressive ideas down my son's throat and not doing it enough" (McLaren, 1996: 124). Yvonne reported that as her son got older she spent a lot of time discussing with him "the negative aspects of masculinity, violence, machismo" that they saw around them. Louise Enders felt that it was important not only to influence the way her own sons behaved but also to make them aware and critical of the negative masculine traits they might encounter in others, including their own friends. She wrote:

> My sons can recognise patriarchal patterns in their friends' behaviour. I hope that I have equipped them with the knowledge to contribute to challenging and changing other men's phallocentric behaviour. (Enders, 1996: 128)

However, several mothers with older sons acknowledged that their sons had often responded by accusing them of making it harder for them to fit in with their peers:

> They both feel that relations with girls have been affected (because girls prefer more macho men) and accuse me of making them into wimps. (Connie)

One particularly poignant theme for many mothers in this context was how they felt about the risk of "losing" their sons to patriarchy. They had seen their sons enter the world innocent of the demands and expectations to be "masculine" that would soon be directed at them, and many expressed their fears and regrets at the perceived inevitability of the erosion of this innocence. Bev Thiele wrote of the challenge of preserving her six-month-old son and his "cheerful openness" in the face of the pressures she anticipated he would later face to "be tough," "to be a man" (Thiele, 1996: 101). Yvonne wrote of the joys of having known her son (now adult) "as a child unspoiled by socialisation into masculinity"; but also admitted that she had eventually come to accept that "other institutions have a far greater influence on learned masculine behavior than my home." This became a second major theme in women's accounts—that of the struggle to "swim against the tide" in mainstream male-dominated society.

Theme two: Swimming against the tide

This was a universal theme in women's accounts—the realization that feminist mothers attempting to raise their sons to be different are always "going against the grain of the dominant culture" (Connie). Where these mothers reported the struggle to be most intense was in relation to the expectations of the school system, peer group pressures, the mass media, and, for some, the influence of their son's father and other adult role models.

Several mothers reported having found themselves in conflict with the masculine ethos of their son's school, in which traditional values of manliness were promoted, and Connie acknowledged that this had sometimes created problems for her sons, who felt caught between two different value systems. Kate noted two stages in the socialization process that her son had encountered within the school system:

> There were two difficult times—when he first went to infant school and had to learn to be more like a "boy" by hiding/controlling his feelings, then at secondary school, where he "toughened up" further, including playing rugby and all that entails. (Kate)

Yvonne also identified the pernicious influence of the dominant cultural models of masculinity emanating from the mass media and competitive sports, to which her son was drawn. These, she felt, had been instrumental in socializing her son into a particular style of macho behavior which she felt promoted an identification of masculinity with aggression and "ruthless power," which again she deplored.

Deborah, a British Afro-Caribbean woman, had experienced the added complication of having to deal with covert racism at her son's school, where she felt he had been adversely affected by "white racist perceptions of black boys." However, at the same time as helping him to resist such stereotypes and find a positive identity for himself as a young black man, she had wanted to discourage him from identifying with some of the black male role models available to him via popular culture (such as rap), because of their blatant sexism.

In many cases, in fact, mothers reported that it was the combination of popular culture and peer group pressure, rather than the school system per se, which had the most influence over their son(s). Nancy wrote of the "machismo trip" each of her sons had embarked upon while disengaging from her and "trying on" various masculine traits in the years of middle childhood. Connie was so appalled at the behavior of some of her son's friends when they visited her home that she had made active efforts to work on them also, letting them know that even if *their* mothers cleared up after them, she would not!

While most mothers whose sons had reached school age mentioned similar experiences of trying to counter the pressures toward peer-group conformity, some had also had to tackle the influence of other older (adult) role models on their sons: Yvonne reported a number of "outright confrontations" over this while her son was in his late teens. For those raising their son alone after separating from his father, this was a particular problem. Zarina, having just split up with the father of her two-year-old son, was concerned at how sharing joint custody with her ex-husband was likely to limit the control she would have over her son's upbringing from now on. Zoe, also divorced, stated quite bluntly that her main problem with her son involved repairing the psychological damage done to him by his father, who in her view had "screwed him up."

Even among those women who were in continuing relationships with the father of their son, there were some who expressed reservations about the influence he had over him. Deborah, for instance, mentioned that she had to "block" some of the sexist expectations and values that her partner conveyed to their son. Connie expressed her disappointment that her efforts to rear her sons to resist traditional masculinity had been unsupported by her husband, and that she had failed in her hope of transforming him, too, into a "New Man" in the process.

Nevertheless, several other women made reference to the active, practical support they felt they had from their son's father for their aims: Bev Thiele found it helpful for her son to be growing up with a father who did not conform to dominant stereotypes of what a "man" should be. Arlene McLaren remarked upon the significance of the fact that when her son was young he was cared for primarily by his father during a period in which she was commuting long-distance to work. Such early experience of close care from fathers was seen by many as significant in influencing how their sons formed their own expectations of the gendering (or not) of adult roles.[10]

Clearly, having some support in the bid to raise a non-sexist son in a still-sexist society was recognized as an asset by those who had benefited from it. Yet all women wrote of their feelings of "swimming against the tide" and of finding it an exhausting struggle. While some expressed the hope that their efforts to "inoculate" their son(s) against patriarchy would succeed, at least in the longer term, others were less optimistic about this. As Zoe commented regarding her nineteen-year-old son: "No matter what we have said, the pressure of peers/ friends/extended family/society generally to 'be a man' has been overwhelming."

Theme three: The risks in sabotaging "masculinity"

A particular difficulty expressed by many women in our survey was their recurrent anxiety as to whether what they were striving to do with their son was justified or whether they were—in Yvonne's words—"compromising his masculinity." Louise Enders admitted:

> I raised my son to be different to other males, often, I felt, at his expense .... In effect, my son was/is a social experiment. (Enders, 1996: 127–28)

For some of the feminist mothers in this study and in the special issue of *Feminism and Psychology* (1996), their concern was indeed related to the perceived risk of making their son *too* "different," thereby exposing him to potential ostracism from his peers. As Arlene McLaren explained:

> I want my son ... to be able to socialise with his peers, to understand them, to find a place among them, and not to be so "other-worldly" and principled that "cultural reality" is too hard to bear. (McLaren, 1996: 125)

While all wanted their sons to resist the "warrior" models of macho masculinity promoted in popular culture, they were nonetheless wary of rendering them "too" sensitive and thereby vulnerable to being picked on and bullied for being different. Susie, in common with many, expressed her ambivalence in this regard:

> It's hard to encourage him to be sensitive and caring, whilst knowing his peers might then see him as a "softie" or a wimp. (Susie)

Interestingly, amongst the mothers whose sons were now adult, several admitted to feeling relieved that their sons appeared to have emerged more or less unscathed by their own feminist influence upon their development, having achieved some kind of balance between their values and those of the dominant culture. As Judith confessed:

> Having secretly feared the impact of my feminism upon them, I think I have had an *ever* increasing sense of relief at their normality. (Judith)

While concern for their sons' ability to relate to their peers was raised by many women, others also mentioned their fear of damaging their own relationship with their son by their constant criticism of the negative aspects of traditional masculine values. Another concern expressed by several women was that this kind of criticism might risk undermining their son's self-confidence. As Zoe explained:

> It has been difficult to challenge some aspects of his masculinity without making him so vulnerable that it is counter-productive. (Zoe)

For many women this therefore meant looking for as many opportunities as possible to find compensatory ways of being positive toward their son—though without overdoing this. Susie described herself as "trying to draw a line between encouraging his personal development and stopping him developing a macho type personality." Deborah had found the same difficulty in getting the balance right with her son:

There is a constant tension between not reinforcing male expectations
of women to look after them and "save them" and responding to his
real emotional needs for nurturance, support, and a place to be vulnerable.
(Deborah)

She pointed out that given the added difficulties that sons of feminist mothers
face in having to deal with two conflicting messages about being male, she felt
that she owed it to her son to offer him extra support, while at the same time
being wary of allowing him to take that support for granted. Here, then, as in so
many other areas, we find yet more evidence of the contradictions faced by
feminist mothers of sons and the feelings of ambivalence that these contradictions
provoke in them.

Discussion: Finding a role for fathers?

A recurrent motif in all of these accounts is that of the struggle many mothers
experience when they try to help their sons grow up in ways that defy traditional
masculine stereotypes. Many women made it plain that their commitment to
doing this stemmed from their commitment to feminism and indicated that they
drew strength from their belief that it was important for their sons to learn "new
ways of being men" (Rich, 1977: 210). Indeed, as Louise Enders observed,
"Having sons is integral to my hope for the future of feminism" (1996: 129).
However, as noted earlier, many also reported feeling a lack of support for their
efforts, not merely from wider society (which was only what they expected) but
also from those around them, and this made their self-appointed task seem all
the more daunting.

Here, then, I want to focus on an aspect of their experiences that intersects
in important ways with all three of the themes outlined in the previous section:
that is, the question of men's role in supporting (or resisting) these women's
efforts to raise a feminist son. To what extent do men share women's vision of
a "new masculinity"? Are they prepared to swim against the tide of convention
in encouraging their sons to be different? And how do they appraise (and
themselves cope with) the risks of sabotaging masculinity?

As noted earlier, it has long been the case that women have carried the main
responsibility for childrearing. However, insofar as the mothers in this study are
now seeking to teach their sons that being a man can (and should) involve
participating on a more equal basis in child rearing, one might expect those of
them living with the fathers of their sons to seek greater involvement in this
project from them. Why, then, was so little mention made of them?

It is of course important to remember that in focusing specifically on women's
personal involvement with their sons' upbringing, this research did not directly

address the contribution of any co-parents. It may thus be that the absence of attention to fathers in women's responses merely reflects the absence of questions asked regarding their role. In fact, as we have seen, some women did make reference to the support received from their partners; nevertheless, the dominant impression gained from studying these accounts is that these mothers see themselves as fighting mostly single-handedly for their son's future. What can we infer from this? Are men still reluctant to participate in women's efforts to bring up their sons to resist hegemonic masculinity? Or are women wary of involving men in a cause to which they may doubt their commitment?

Although, as we have seen, fathers did not participate as much as mothers in their children's upbringing throughout most of the twentieth century, the prevalence today of dual-earner families has to a certain extent already begun to reduce the previous imbalance in parental involvement. However, there is at the same time considerable evidence to suggest that many mothers continue to feel a sense of ownership of responsibility for their children's upbringing (Thomas, 1999). As one mother in this study commented wryly, "It is mothers who raise children—whatever men may think" (Harriet). Insofar as this is a legacy of women's traditional role within the family, it may thus be hard for many to concede any part of this traditional "territory" to men (McBride and Darragh, 1995). Moreover, given what we know of the present inequitable division of labor in most households (including those of many heterosexual feminists!), some women may have quite justifiable doubts as to the extent of their partner's commitment to their own vision of gender equality for their son, and so prefer not to relinquish their own influence over him.

Deborah, for example, noted that her son was more strongly attached to her than to his father, and admitted to having mixed feelings about this: while her partner's "sexist values" made her want to keep her son under her influence, she nevertheless regretted that she was not able to feel comfortable letting him identify more closely with his father. This is something that Johnetta Cole has highlighted in questioning whether "a father can participate in raising a feminist son until the father deals with his own sense of masculinity" (Cole, 1993: 43). Harry Christian, in his research on antisexist men, claimed that many had learned to challenge and resist hegemonic masculinity not from their father, with whom they often had a rather distant relationship, but through having a close and warm relationship with their mother (Christian, 1994). Like Cole, he therefore claims that until men are able to be nurturant, nontraditional role models to their sons it is better for the sons *not* to identify with them.

This is of course welcome support for all those women who, like Zarina, Zoe, and Deborah, do not see their son's father as a desirable role model for the "New Man" they want their son to become. However, other women (such as Connie) clearly cherish hopes of making the rearing of an antisexist son a joint project with their son's father, with the idea that this might also serve to change *his* attitudes and behavior in the process; and a number of the women in this study and in the special issue of *Feminism and psychology* (such as Livingstone, McLaren, Thiele, and Thomas) indicated that their son's father was already playing an important part in this endeavor.

Although until recently it was evident that fewer men than women were making a conscious effort to raise antisexist sons, there are some signs that this may soon start to change. During the 1990s, there was a surge of interest in the father–son relationship, much of it focusing on the "father-hunger" which many men reported feeling as a consequence of growing up with a remote and emotionally distant father.[11] Recent research with younger fathers suggests that many men wish to enjoy a closer relationship with their children than they had with their own father and are, accordingly, committed to greater involvement in their children's lives and a more nurturant father role.[12]

On the evidence of the psychological theory and research reviewed earlier, this would mark an important change in boys' gender socialization. As Hartley (1959) and Lynn (1966) observed, boys have frequently had to learn what it means to be male indirectly (whether from their mothers or from the mass media) rather than directly, from their own fathers, and this has been seen to have a number of undesirable consequences (Thomas, 1997). However, the same theories indicate that the most straightforward way for boys to develop a healthy, flexible, and less artificial identification with their gender should be for them to have the opportunity to model themselves directly on a nurturant and fully involved father figure, just as girls have benefited from being able to observe and model the increasing flexibility in their mothers' adult roles as these have evolved over the past quarter century.

Research on families in which fathers are participating in "shared parenting" does indeed show that boys gain from having before them a positive model of nurturant fathering, which enables them to see practical alternatives to conventional masculine role models (Coltrane, 1996). Coltrane, moreover, argues that his research indicates that there may in fact be benefits for all family members when shared parenting is practiced. For although the theories emphasize the developmental benefits for boys in particular, children of both sexes appear to prosper from increased contact with their fathers. Another obvious benefit that shared parenting offers is to women, as they are able to shed some of the burden of responsibility for child rearing. However, possibly the most significant outcome for the families in Coltrane's study was that the fathers' increased hands-on involvement in child care had the effect of making them more competent at parenting, more sensitive to the children's needs, and more nurturant. This was rewarding not only to the men themselves, but also to their partners; as Coltrane notes: "When fathers and mothers both perform routine child care and housework, it can promote mutual understanding and enhance marital solidarity" (1996: 78).

While studies such as Coltrane's thus provide strong support for the benefits of this kind of shared parenting, it is of course important to remind ourselves that—as seen here in the cases of Zoe and Zarina—there are many women who for good reasons may not wish to involve their son's father (or any other man) in his upbringing. However, for any woman who is raising her sons within a stable, non-abusive, heterosexual relationship, sharing childrearing with a partner who is, like her, committed to a new vision of a less gender-differentiated society must surely be the best way forward, benefiting mother, son, and father alike. As others have observed before me, if men are the problem, then they can also (and indeed should) be part of the solution.

Conclusion

In this chapter I have discussed the experiences of mothers who are raising their sons to resist traditional forms of masculine behavior, and I have reviewed evidence that suggests the potential benefits of encouraging more men to share in this endeavor. As we start to see signs that increasing numbers of men *are* choosing to become more actively involved in their children's daily lives—and with positive consequences—we can begin to hope that the tide may at last be starting to turn in our favor, and that as feminist mothers we will no longer have to swim against it.

Notes

1. In this chapter I am confining myself to discussing the gender socialization of boys in modern industrialized societies, since it is there primarily—in societies such as those of North America, Western Europe, and Australia—that twentieth-century changes in gender roles have led to the problematizing of masculinity in the last quarter century.
2. Silverstein and Rashbaum (1994: 22) cite various other such books, including *Their mothers' sons* by Edward Strecker and David Levy's ominously titled *Maternal overprotection*, both first published in 1945 and sufficiently popular to warrant reissue in the 1950s.
3. Farber (1962), for example, noted that mothers often referred to the values and expectations of the father in dealing with their children in his absence (e.g., "What would Daddy think/ say?"), and by these means contrived to present him as a role model for their children.
4. According to Ryan, "Masculinity, then, can be viewed as a defensive construction, developed … out of a need to emphasise a difference, a separateness from the mother. In the extreme this is manifested by machismo behavior with its emphasis on competitiveness, strength, aggressiveness, contempt for women and emotional shallowness, all serving to keep the male secure in his separate identity" (Ryan, 1985: 26).

5. For a detailed historical account of the ways in which parental roles have been influenced by social and economic changes, see Demos (1982) and Pleck (1987).

6. See, for example, Charlie Lewis and Margaret O'Brien (1987) and Lynne Segal (1990).

7. No claims are made for the representativeness of this sample: our purpose in conducting this research was simply to explore some of the issues that had been faced by these self-identified feminist mothers in their efforts to bring their sons up to resist traditional forms of masculinity. While some of the concerns of these mothers may not apply to others, it is evident that many of the problems they reported facing are common to all parents as they contemplate their sons' futures in a changing world.

8. Thirteen of these individual accounts were published in the special feature on mothering sons, "Mothering sons: A crucial feminist challenge," in *Feminism and psychology* (Robyn Rowland and Alison M. Thomas, 1996), in which they are discussed along with responses from twelve women who completed questionnaires; a further five questionnaires were received after the publication of this feature but are included for discussion here.

9. In this section those women whose personal accounts were published in the special feature are cited by name with references to the page number in *Feminism and psychology* (see note 8); those whose questionnaire responses are quoted here are identified by a pseudonym.

10. In my own case I remember being thrilled to hear my son, then aged six, declare that both mummies and daddies were "someone who looks after you." He too, was speaking from his own experience of being cared for as much by his father as his mother.

11. See for example Robert Bly (1990) and Steve Biddulph (1994).

12. See for example Charlie Lewis (1986), Kerry Daly (1994), and Scott Coltrane (1996).

Chapter Twenty-Four

Raising Relational Boys

Cate Dooley and Nikki Fedele

Introduction

Achilles, mightiest of the Greeks, hero of the *Iliad*, was nearly immortal. According to myth, his mother, Thetis, dipped him into the river Styx. The sacred waters of this river that led to Hades, the world of the dead, rendered whomever they touched impervious to harm. But Thetis, good mother that she was, worried about the dangers of the river; and so she held onto Achilles by his heel. As the story goes, because of that one holding spot, Achilles remained mortal and vulnerable to harm. Thetis would be blamed forever after for her son's so-called fatal flaw, his Achilles heel.

However, the holding place of vulnerability was not, as the myth would have us believe, a fatal liability to Achilles. It was instead the thing that kept him *human and real*. In fact, we consider it *Thetis' finest gift* to her son. Every mother of a son hopes to prepare him for life's "battles" while also preserving his emotional/relational side. Because mothers value connection, they want to "hold on," to keep open that place of vulnerability. But, faced with cultural pressures that suggest restraint and withdrawal, rather than comfort and nurture, many mothers feel conflicted about their desire to stay connected to their sons. Traditional wisdom cautions that "holding on" will be damaging and create psychological problems for sons. Faced with this dilemma, mothers often give into cultural pressures and disconnect from their young sons because they think it is the right thing to do.

This chapter describes the application of relational theory to a model of parenting-in-connection. We describe the natural ebb and flow of parent–child relationships through a cycle of connection, disconnection, and new connection, while detailing issues and conflicts specific to boys' development at four distinct stages. The mother–son relationship is, we argue, the most important context within which boys can learn how to move from disconnection to even better connection. Highlighting the dominant cultural model for boys' development—which we believe affects all mother–son relationships despite variations based on race, class, and other factors—we use specific examples drawn from our workshops and clinical work to demonstrate the potential of the alternative parenting-in-connection approach.

Our work with mothers of sons is based on relational/cultural theory, a view of development for women and men, which grew out of Jean Baker Miller's 1976 book, *Toward a new psychology of women*. In her book, Miller introduces a new view of women and their development. After many years of listening to and studying women, she concludes that relationship and affiliation are essential to their healthy development. She notes the attitudes about women and their roles embedded in the fabric of Western culture. She further states that this cultural view diminishes women's self-worth.

We highlight the mother–son relationship because we feel that this same devalued view of women affects mother–son interaction. The culture tells mothers to disconnect from their sons. Closeness with mom has often been misunderstood and pathologized. The mother-son connection is ridiculed ("go run to mama"; "crybaby"), cautioned against ("you better let him go"; "push him out to the world"), prohibited ("don't coddle him"; "no more hugs and kisses"), and maligned ("she's turned him into a mama's boy"; "he's tied to her apron strings"). We feel that this disparaging attitude and the early call for separation from their mother isolates boys "from relationship"—first with their mother and consequently with others.

In this chapter we are referring to the dominant cultural model for boys in the United States. We recognize that there are many variations of this model dependent upon race, ethnicity, religion, sexual orientation, family structure, socioeconomic class, as well as other factors. We focus on the mainstream model supported by media images and messages, because of the strong negative influence it has on boys' development. We feel that all mothers, regardless of diverse circumstances, are impacted in their relationship with sons by this culturally prescribed paradigm of disconnection.

Infant studies show that physical and psychological development is dependent upon a good mother–infant connection. Without such a connection we see a developmental "failure to thrive" in babies. Ed Tronick of the Brazelton Touchpoint Project (1998), notes that infant development occurs only within relationship. This is also Miller's belief about our lifelong experience. In *Toward a new psychology of women* she states that "all growth and learning takes place within the *context* of relationship." While the relational presence of mother is essential for babies to thrive early on, it continues to be essential for boys' emotional and relational growth.

Jean Baker Miller and Irene Stiver speak of the need for relationship and connection as a *human need* in *The healing connection* (1997). They see this as a universal need, best met through the development of mutually empathic and mutually empowering relationships. But young boys, if deprived of sufficient opportunities to learn how to make real connections, try to meet these needs in superficial and manipulative ways. They are taught in "boy culture" to fulfil their desires and get ahead, even at the expense of others. In acting this way, boys and men are simply following established rules of the culture for males. A false bravado model not only deprives boys early on of parental empathy, but also infuses them with a sense of esteem and power devoid of internal resonance. As a result, mutually satisfying connection with others becomes impossible. In our clinical practice, men tell stories of "working the room" in executive meetings, assured that they will, ultimately, sway others and (right or wrong) get what they want. These men complain, however, that they feel no internal gratification in these interactions. All this attention and power fail to gratify and, in fact, leave them feeling empty and even more alone. We see in their experience how learned behaviors make it impossible for many men to connect authentically, leaving them with a debilitating sense of internal isolation.

This problematic developmental course may account for what appears to be a predominance of men who are self-absorbed and cut off from relationships. Perhaps if we understand more deeply the impact of culture on boys' and men's development, we can bring a compassionate and understanding perspective to our male children, partners, friends, and clients as they sort through these difficult, deeply embedded relational patterns. Perhaps if we create more empathic possibilities, these new experiences can prevent in boys, and heal in men, the wounds of this early disconnection.

A mother's prospective view

We have found in our work with more than three thousand mothers of sons that in spite of the cultural message, many mothers follow their inclination and stay in relationship with their sons. Tentatively questioning established norms, these mothers keep a place of emotionality open in their sons through continued connection. Yet at the same time, they worry that they will affect their son's development in negative ways. Mothers who resist the cultural call to disconnection are in need of validation and support. These courageous mothers are potentially the real experts in boys' development. Keeping a strong connection is the way to teach sons how to navigate the many and complex nuances of relationship. We believe it is within the mother–son context that relational learning occurs and that the groundwork is established for future relationships. Olga Silverstein and Beth Rashbaum, in their book *The courage to raise good men* (1994), demonstrated that the root of sons' difficulties as adults is linked to distance and disconnection in the mother–son relationship. Our workshops with mothers and adult sons, as well as our clinical work with men and couples, tell us that boys with a secure maternal connection develop stronger interpersonal skills and enjoy healthier relationships as adults.

Although relational theory originally developed as a way to understand women's psychology, the capacity to create and sustain growth-fostering relationships is equally crucial for boys and men. Traditional views of boys' and men's development are embedded in men's experiences and men's fears. Men who have grown up in this culture often feel that the old model is best for their sons. Even men who want to change things may worry about these new directions for boys. Fathers can be pulled unwittingly into a retrospective analysis of present-day issues because of old fears based on their own experience. Because becoming a man is closely linked with traditional ideas about being one's own man (individuation), being dominant, and not being a "girl," evolving their thinking into the realm of emotional and relational development about boys can create worry for some men. They can have much fear about turning boys into girls. Women, on the other hand, not having grown up in boy culture, may have a clearer lens in viewing the currently evolving possibilities for boys and men. Most mothers today *do* keep connection with sons, and sons *are* more aware of the benefits and possibilities open to them in relationship. These newly evolved attitudes and behaviors are actually already much more a part of everyday life for boys than is reflected in the media. Just as Jean Baker Miller (1976) insisted, we must listen to women in order to hear about their experiences; we must listen to mothers of sons to formulate a *prospective view* of the possibility of relationship for boys. It is our opinion that listening to mothers of sons will inform us about current realities and possibilities for boys.

At a recent lecture about middle-school children, a mother asked the speaker how to talk to her twelve-year-old son. The psychologist answered: "There's bad news and there's good news. The bad news is that you won't be able to get him to talk. The good news is that it won't last long, just a few years." Most of the mothers gathered at the back of the lecture hall disagreed with this notion. Even though it was difficult, they had managed to stay connected with their sons. As the "keepers of the connections" in our culture, women know about relationship. Mothers hold the hope for change in their son's relational growth.

New developmental attitudes and directions for boys can change development in many positive ways. Changing cultural expectations to include relational development for boys can change outcomes for both boys *and girls*. Valuing relational skills and emotional awareness in boys will increase respect for girls in our culture. In creating a new vision for boys, we modify the course of development for both genders. Both girls and boys are born with the capacity to have responsible and collaborative relationships. It is the work of parents to provide a safe context for boys, as well as girls, through the development of family, community, and social values that support relationship.

Boy culture: What is it? How does it affect boys?

Invisible forces in our culture take hold in the form of implicitly communicated expectations of boy behavior we call "boy culture" (Figure 24.1). Images of male dominance are projected by the media and modeled daily by older peers in countless ways. These expectations are not consciously taught or supported in most of our homes, schools, or communities. Rather, they are the insidious behavioral messages boys in our culture receive regarding boy behavior. These occur in the form of put-downs and intimidating threats in everyday interactions on the playground and in the halls of our schools. When we do nothing to intervene, thinking "boys will be boys," we implicitly give our approval to and help normalize behaviors that are disconnecting and domineering and that can later lead to what has become a pervasive societal problem of violence.

When we name and question the impact of boy culture, we are not critical of boys and men but rather of the gender straightjacket imposed on boys by the culture. Boy culture focuses on who is in the limelight. It says "be first," "win." It is built on a competitive, power-over model, in which there are winners and there are losers. Boy culture encourages young men and boys to take pride in expressions of noncompliance and disrespect, to act out, and to pretend not to care about their failings.

BOY CULTURE

IMPLICIT EXPECTATIONS FOR BOYS

- CLOSENESS WITH MOM IS FOR SISSIES/BABIES
- FEELINGS ARE FOR WIMPS/GIRLS (EXCEPT ANGER)
- BE FIRST, BE IN LIMELIGHT
- DON'T BACK DOWN
- POWER-OVER MODEL OF COMPETITION
  —WIN–LOSE
- PRIDE IN NON-COMPLIANCE/DISRESPECT
- DESENSITIZATION TO VIOLENCE
- CODE OF SILENCE

Figure 24.1

Teachers rate boys as problems in the classroom ninety percent over girls.[1] Research shows that as the number of *boy* siblings in a family increase, so does the incidence of acting out, school truancy, and social delinquency.[2] The fact that this is not the case with an increase in the number of girl siblings may speak to the powerful influence of boy culture within families. Behaviors such as bullying, teasing, stealing, noncompliance, swearing, teacher disrespect, and the like have become serious problems, even at the elementary-school level. Children, largely boys aged five to ten years, are imitating offensive, interpersonal behaviors portrayed by the media and observed in older peers.

Boy culture also says that if you retreat, if you shrink from competing, you risk being labelled "wimp," "chicken," "sissy," "scaredy cat," "baby," or even "girl."

A group of first-grade boys respond to a simple question posed by their teacher by rising up out of their seats and onto their toes, hands waving high, whispering "me first, pick me." They are so eager to be first, all their energy goes into this quest. When called on, they have forgotten the question and have nothing to say.

A third-grade boy creeps along a high wall, egged on by his peers. He is terrified but continues on for fear of being called a "wimp" or "scaredy cat."

A fifth-grade boy proudly boasts to his friends that he chased another boy down, took his prized art project, and made him cry.

A seventh-grader jokingly brags about not studying and takes pride in his prediction of a poor grade on a math test scheduled for that day.

One eight year old explained, "If my friends ever found out that I come home from school and go through my backpack with my mom and show her everything I did in school that day, they'd really make fun of me and call me a baby."[3]

Our culture's established standard of individuation and independence moves both girls and boys away from relationship. But for boys this push is especially difficult because it happens at a very young age and within the most intimate of relationships, their relationship with their mother. This move toward independence and away from mom occurs at a time in development for boys when they are still thinking in concrete ways (Piaget and Inhelder, 1969). Boys' concrete view of the loss of mom at age five is that they have lost a relationship and are on their own emotionally. Carol Gilligan (1996) and others link the increase in Attention Deficit Disorder (ADD) to this early separation from mother. Diagnostic ADD rates are higher than ever and occur predominantly in boys. Boys' loss creates sadness and anxiety, which may manifest as hyperactivity and inattention. Maybe the first diagnostic criteria to look for in these hyperactive boys should be symptoms of what we call CDD, or Connection Deficit Disorder!

The development of learning and behavioral problems in young boys has become alarmingly common. Boys learn that it is "cool" to be distant, inauthentic, and disconnected. They lose their *relational* voice, the voice that reflects authentic feelings and affiliative needs. What replaces real interaction is banter and bravado. Caught up in the expectations of boy culture, imitating behaviors seen in older peers and siblings, boys often become alienated from their own inner world. When boys disconnect from their mother, they lose access to the relational way of being with others that she represents. They lose the ability to be responsive and receptive (Miller, 1986).

Steve Bergman (1991) coins the phrase "relational dread" as a phenomenon in boys and men that grows out of early emotional disconnection from mothers. Boys lose their place within the relational context. Eventually, in the face of emotion and relationship, they freeze. They become immobilized. Isolated in the disconnection from mother, they do not know what to do or how to be in relationship with others. Bergman and Surrey aptly describe this experience of dread and the resulting avoidance of connection that has become an intrinsic part of traditional developmental models for boys. Girls and women do not always see this dread because men cover it up with avoidance, denial, and bravado (Stiver, 1998). Its impact, however, is great. This is what makes mutually empathic interactions with and between boys and men so difficult.

When mothers move away from young sons and push them toward independence, boys are denied empathic resonance with their emotions (Stiver, 1986). Without the safe relational context provided by his mother, a boy feels alone. He is too young to protest. He knows no alternative. He thinks that disconnection is what is supposed to happen. He still longs for connection, and quite rightly. But now he feels shame and confusion about his inner longings. To deal with his pain and confusion, he shuts down emotionally. He has not yet learned to differentiate and name feelings. Confused, he suffers alone, in silence. The cost of this break in relationship from mother is significant for boys' evolving relationships with others. They deal with this inner confusion and pain by shutting down access to their emotional world and by avoiding relationship. When this happens, relational and emotional development slows down.

From this point on, there are fewer empathic possibilities for boys than for girls. This early loss of parental empathy creates a void in the area of responsiveness to and identification of emerging feelings. Judy Jordan (1989) notes that a lack of empathic response will result in a feeling of personal shame. Boys learn early that emotional needs, longings, feelings, or dependencies are shameful, and subsequently they have a more difficult time developing a healthy sense of self-empathy. Their emotional needs and longings often become covered up by angry expressions and aggressive behaviors. Eventually, through continued exposure to boy culture put-downs and power-over behavior, boys seem to lose much of their capacity for empathy toward others.

There is a further twist. We all yearn for a sense of connection. Yet the inevitable disconnections that happen in relationships can be painful and threatening. Everyone experiences this flow of connection and disconnection in life, but often because of these repeated interpersonal disconnections, we pull back from relationship while we at the same time yearn for connection. Miller and Stiver (1997) write about this as the "paradox of relationship." Boys feel this paradox at a young age; they learn early not to represent themselves fully in relational encounters. Shamed by expressions of emotion, they begin to keep important parts of themselves hidden from others. They do this by developing a repertoire of behaviors for staying out of relationship. Miller and Stiver call these "strategies of disconnection." These strategies keep boys from experiencing the shaming and put-downs of boy culture, but at the cost of keeping them out of real connection with others. Some examples include silence, smart remarks that discourage conversation, elaborate demonstrations of disinterest, sarcastic humor, and the exchange of glances between boys that convey disrespect for the speaker. Yet beneath the bravado and banter, boys are hungry for connection and emotional expression. This is the paradox of relationship for them. Boys sacrifice authentic emotional connection with others for the sake of inclusion within boy culture. This accommodation helps them avoid being teased and shamed, gains them the approval of peers, and creates surface connection, but at the expense of real relationship.

Bullying, competitive banter, and bravado: these are the hurtful, power-over interactions that pervade boy culture. At the same time, boys learn about the code of silence built into these interactions. You cannot "tell" on another, even if you know his behavior is damaging and wrong. Boys learn early in life that to survive with peers they have to put up with harsh, mean, even hurtful verbal and physical behavior. Our culture expects boys to be tough, and shames them when they are not. They cannot let on when they have been hurt or humiliated. If they break the code of silence, they risk humiliation, peer isolation, and further harassment. Boys plead with their mothers not to intervene. They would rather submit to the bullying than be shamed by turning to someone for help.

Walking home from school, a group of nine-year-old boys stop at the ballpark to hit a few fly balls. Waiting his turn, Max stands behind the backstop, his fingers curled around the metal links. Whack! One of the boys smashes the bat against the backstop and hits Max's finger. Max screams and crumples to the ground in tears, clutching his hand. The group of boys stares at him, then one says,

"Oh c'mon. I don't see anything wrong. It's not bleeding. You're faking."

"What a wimp!" yells another.

"Poor baby hurt his finger?" chimes in Andrew, Max's best friend.

Bewildered, Max gets up, trying without much success to hold back the tears. His finger throbs.

"Maybe you should go over and play with those girls," taunts Andrew, shaking his head in disgust, as he and the others walk off together, leaving Max behind.

Max arrives home upset. His mother sees his tears and the finger swollen and black and blue now. She offers ice, but it's not the finger that hurts most. She tries to comfort Max, and asks what happened. "Nothing Mom, it's okay," insists Max as he retreats to his room in shame.

Mothering can be seen as a political act. It is a form of the political resistance that Carol Gilligan so eloquently describes for women—their need to speak their truth. In this case it is the truth about boys' "code of silence."

The experience of being shamed by the culture, by peers, or by parents because of vulnerable feelings can have a significant impact. Because of the recent episodes of violence in young adolescent boys (Jonesboro, Arkansas; Littleton, Colorado; Paducah, Kentucky; Pearl, Mississippi), we, as a nation, are examining the roots of this behavior. James Gilligan (1996) in his recent work on violence in men, cites the experience of intense shame as an important dynamic in the histories of violent men. The act of shaming around vulnerable feelings is a major contributor to acts of violence in these men. Shame becomes a precursor to the expression of the only feelings acceptable for boys and men, anger and aggression.

A liability built into boy culture is the expectation of repeated exposure to violent play, movies, and video games. Boys eventually become desensitized to violence. To avoid being teased or shamed, they stifle their natural emotional reactions of fear and vulnerability. Gradually, with daily exposure and practice, boys lose access to their real feelings and normal reactions to violence. Before long they can sit and watch violence, abuse, and horror on the screen, in video games, even in peer interactions without flinching!

The ebb and flow of relationship

Connection occurs when we experience a sense of mutual engagement, empathy, authenticity, and empowerment within the context of relationship. We have the mutual feeling of knowing and being with the other, immersed in their experience along with our own. Such connections provide a continual source of growth for the individual and the relationship. This form of connection has startlingly positive effects, which Miller (1986) calls *the five good things*: zest (vitality); a more accurate picture of oneself and others; increased sense of self-worth; increased desire and ability to act; and desire for more connection. When we are in a disconnection, the opposite happens. We feel cut off from the person, experience the pain of not being understood and not understanding the other, and feel confusion about what is happening. The five outcomes of disconnection are; decreased energy; confusion and lack of clarity; decreased self-worth; inability to act; and turning away from relationship.

Relationships are not static. Figure 24.2 illustrates the natural movement of all relationships. The cycle of connection disconnection-new connection demonstrates how working through disconnections can enhance relationships. Understanding this is the key to mutually satisfying relationships. The inevitable disconnects become the signal that work needs to be done in the relationship. When we do not acknowledge this and when we do not try to find a solution together, distance replaces closeness. The relationship suffers. The connection becomes derailed in the confusion and ambiguity of the disregarded issue. On the other hand, when addressed, disconnections can become opportunities to work together toward mutual understanding and solution (Bergman and Surrey, 1992).

Reconnection can be quick and easy, or take time, effort, and creativity. This is the strengthening work of relationship. When we find the way back, it is not just a reconnection, but a strengthened, enhanced, growthful leap for the relationship. Even when sons seem to be disinterested and uninvolved in this process, a mother's efforts are extremely important. This is how we continue to build relationship with sons.

The creative work looks different depending upon the unique characteristics of each family: family structure, values, importance of the issue at hand, temperament, culture, ethnicity, religion, and race. This work provides opportunities to widen the lens for sons. For example, in dealing with a power issue, white mothers can talk with their sons about how many different power differentials create disconnection. By raising their son's awareness of the dominant culture's racist views and how they affect relationships, we can help boys begin to see and deal with issues of privilege and power early in life. Discussions about social esteem[4] can help boys understand how their view of themselves and others is affected by (often negative) stereotypes and attitudes deeply embedded in our culture.

The mother–son relationship is a safe place for boys to learn how to work through disconnection. In this relationship they can use disconnections as cues, not to let go, but rather to find creative ways to reconnect. Mothers can then support, guide, and reassure their sons through small and large conflicts in

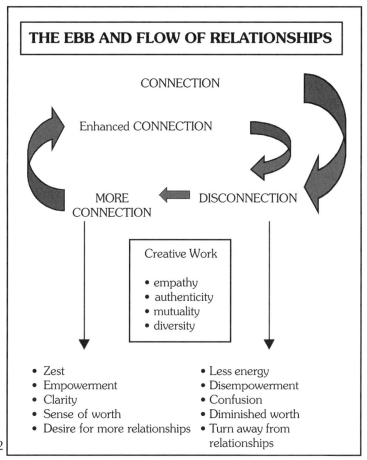

THE EBB AND FLOW OF RELATIONSHIPS

CONNECTION

Enhanced CONNECTION

MORE
CONNECTION

DISCONNECTION

Creative Work

• empathy
• authenticity
• mutuality
• diversity

• Zest
• Empowerment
• Clarity
• Sense of worth
• Desire for more relationships

• Less energy
• Disempowerment
• Confusion
• Diminished worth
• Turn away from
  relationships

Figure 24.2

relationship. These happen first with mom, then with other family members, and eventually, in peer and adult relationships outside the home. The following example illustrates how a mother's emotional connectedness to her son enhanced his relational and emotional development:

When thirteen-year-old Andy got home from school he learned that his best friend Sam's dog had been killed by a car. His own dog had died the same way just a year ago. Andy, in hearing the news, froze. His body stiffened, his face registered fear. What could he possibly say or do to help his friend at this point? He had no words. He was confused, overwhelmed, and inundated with feeling about his own dog's death. He knew the horrible loss he experienced a year ago was what Sam was feeling now but felt immobilized by his own grief and discomfort. How could he possibly approach Sam in this vulnerable state? And what about Sam? Wouldn't he be embarrassed by his own sadness?

His mom put her arm around him and said, "You know how sad Sam must be. Remember how sad we all were when Trumpet died? Sam could really use a friend right now, especially one who knows exactly how he must be feeling."

Andy panicked, "No, Mom, I can't. I don't know what to say. I'd sound really stupid."

"You know it's a really important part of a friendship to go to your friend's side when something bad happens. He needs you now," said his mother.

Andy couldn't move. He couldn't go to Sam's. He couldn't call. He was angry with his mother for her suggestion. He started walking out of the room, but his mother said, "Wait, let's do this together. We can write it out and then call him."

Andy stiffened further insisting he couldn't even think, saying, "I'm stupid. I don't know what to say."

His mother wrote it out for him, encouraging him all the way, "Look Andy, all you have to say is 'Sam, I'm sorry. I just heard about your dog. I'm so sorry. I know how you must feel. You know Trumpet died last year the same way and it crushed me. I'm really sorry.'"

Andy backed away from the phone, but his mother dialed and handed it to him. As the phone rang he mouthed "No" to his mother, dangling the receiver her way. Finally, the answering machine picked up. With a sigh of relief Andy read the message.

Later his mom was worried about how these two teenagers could make a face-to-face connection. So she offered to let Andy have a Beanie Baby she had just bought for his younger brother. "You could give this to Sam in memory of Rumpus because it looks just like him," she said. Andy was insulted.

"Wow! Step back, Mom! A *Beanie Baby*? Give me a break!" At this point his mom dropped the idea.

The next day, Sam came over to find Andy, who wasn't home yet. He repeated over and over to Andy's mom, "Tell Andy that it was so cool he called me. No one else did. Tell him I said thanks. Tell him I came over. Tell him to come over to my house when he gets home. Tell him that was really great to call."

When Andy returned, his mother told him Sam had been there. Andy stiffened in fear. But when his mother related how appreciative Sam was for the call, Andy's whole body relaxed. His eyes brightened, he had a burst of energy, and was out the door to Sam's. His mom was relieved, and then a few minutes later heard him come back into the house. As he ran up the stairs he smiled and sheepishly asked if he could give the Beanie Baby to Sam.

On his way out the door his mom gave him a quick hug and told him what a great job he'd done. He smiled as he pulled away, saying, "That's because I've got a *buena madre*."

Andy moved from alienation to emotional involvement. He moved from disconnection not only to reconnection, but even better connection with his mom and his friend. When he first heard the news, Andy disconnected and became immobilized. He exhibited all five outcomes of disconnection: lack of clarity or confusion ("I don't know what to say"), decreased desire and ability to act ("I can't"), decreased self-worth ("I'll sound stupid"), turning away from relationship (walking away), and decreased energy. With empathy, support, and mutual involvement from his mom, he was able to make the move back into relationship with his friend and with his mom. By the end of the story we see how the individuals and both relationships benefit from the move back into connection.

Andy exhibited all of the five good outcomes. He was motivated to act and did (went to his friend, came back for the Beanie Baby), he felt better about himself (smiling, joking), he had a more accurate picture of himself and others (*buena madre*), he had a desire for more connection (with his mom and Sam), and he had more energy (went to his friend, energized in his interaction with his mom). Andy learned something important about relationship and loss. His relationship with Sam will deepen because the two shared a new awareness of themselves in relation to each other's grief. And his relationship with his mother is enhanced as he more fully appreciates her efforts to help him with the difficult work of relationship.

Parenting-in-connection

Embracing the natural ebb and flow of relationship is the basis for a model of childraising we refer to as "parenting-in-connection." The goal is to enhance connection and to circumvent distance and separation. As noted above, disconnections are *opportunities* to deepen and strengthen the relationship. Thus the inevitable disconnections of parenthood become a signal that work is needed in the relationship. Mothers can teach sons by example to move toward reconnection rather than becoming derailed by disconnection. A mother's knowledge and ability can enable this learning process for boys and enrich the connection with her son. This model offers a way for mothers to stay tuned in. In a recent two-year longitudinal study of 12,000 teenagers from across the country, researchers found that a close relationship with a parent is the best predictor of a teenager's health and the strongest deterrent to high-risk behaviors. The study, published in 1997 by the *Journal of the American Medical Association*, was part of a $24 million project funded by the National Institute of

Child Health and Human Development and other agencies. A strong emotional connection with at least one parent or significant adult figure reduces the odds that an adolescent will suffer from emotional stress, have suicidal thoughts or behavior, engage in violence, or use substances (tobacco, alcohol, or marijuana). Feeling that at least one adult knew them and treated them fairly buffered the teens against every health risk except pregnancy. This finding held up regardless of family income, race, education, specific amount of time spent with a child, whether a child lives with one or two parents or in an alternative family structure, and whether one or both parents work. The evidence is overwhelming. Good relationships help create resilience against dangerous acting-out behaviors in our children.

As parents and educators, we share the painful dilemma of having important family and community values that conflict with the realities of peer culture for boys. Together, mothers and sons can develop new ways of approaching these dilemmas. We help mothers introduce the notion of repair and reparation when dealing with interpersonal violations and injuries. There is a growing need to set limits on emotionally, socially, and physically hurtful behavior toward others. But setting limits for the sake of limits does not work. Punishment without a relational context only further alienates boys. They take pride in getting busted. Acting out and noncompliance earns them points with peers. Naming the behavior that we want changed, providing alternatives to the old way, and adding interpersonal reparation making (see below), are all essential parts of limit setting with boys. They often love structure and tend to go along with a clearly outlined and defined model that they *and their friends* are expected to follow—"If you build it, they will come!" Boys need adults to point out that the behavior is hurtful, offer better alternatives, and provide concrete consequences for relational injuries.

We are suggesting a simple yet powerful change in boys' development: move the emphasis of the mother-son relationship away from separation and isolation, toward connection. When we do that, we have a chance to help sons with healthy emotional development daily in dozens of small but significant ways. We just might change the course of their lives by teaching them, through these everyday interactions, how to develop mutually empathic, mutually empowering relationships.

In reviewing boys' relational growth, we identified four stages in the development of mother–son relationships. Each developmental period has cultural expectations that influence the mother–son relationship, creating conflicts and dilemmas. We have set relational goals for each stage and defined ways mothers can counter these cultural influences and keep sons on the path of relational development. Each stage is outlined in terms of age, imposed cultural pressures, problems created, and specific methods for meeting relational goals (Figure 24.3).

I.   The early years, 3–7 years. The cultural message is the invincibility of the superhero. Little boys are besieged by superhero figures that imply that becoming a man depends on independence, strength, stoicism, total invulnerability, and the defeat of all others. The relational goal is laying the groundwork for relationship by naming, demonstrating, and validating relational abilities.

II. The middle years, 8–13 years. The cultural message involves banter, bullies, and bravado. Middle-school boys are indoctrinated with the competitive ethic of winning at all costs and exploiting power over others. The relational goal is setting limits and offering alternatives by guiding sons toward interactive, fun-filled, authentic relationships.

III. The teenage years, 14–18 years. The cultural message is shutting down to real feelings and interactions and engaging in the "locker room" culture of social, physical, and sexual dominance. The focus is on dominance, not real relationship. The relational goal is maintaining relationships as multidimensional and encouraging mutual dialogue. It also involves viewing conflict and difference as opportunities to stay in connection and learn more about each other.

IV. The adult years. The cultural message is disconnection and separation from mother. Adult sons worry about being too "attached." The expectation to disconnect can feel like disinterest and distance to their mothers. The relational goal is to encourage a mutually responsive, mutually empowering mother–son relationship.

Parenting-in-connection provides a new way of understanding and responding to disconnections. It can be teaching a two year old to share, helping a nine year old to deal with the hurt and unfairness of being bullied, empathizing with a teenager's pain in being rejected romantically, or sorting through the many decisions of adulthood together.

The early years

One mom recalls how her son, Aaron, went from being the "best boy" in preschool to becoming the "wild boy" in kindergarten. "The kids he sat with on the first day of kindergarten were rambunctious, wild boys," she recalls. He sat at the same table day after day and very soon "he became a wild boy."

Before entering a traditional school setting, Aaron was an empathic little boy who asked his preschool teacher, "Are your feelings hurt?" after another child snapped at her. He was always the first to step forward and offer a welcome when a new child entered the class. With the move to kindergarten, Aaron entered a larger, traditional setting that reflected more mainstream boy-culture

---

PARENTING-IN-CONNECTION

• STAGE I. YOUNG BOYS
AGE: 3–7 YRS.
CULTURAL MESSAGE: The Superhero years
RELATIONAL GOAL: Laying the groundwork

• STAGE II. MIDDLE YEARS
AGE: 8–13 YRS.
CULTURAL MESSAGE: Bullies, banter and bravado
RELATIONAL GOAL: Interactive, fun-filled,
authentic relationships

• STAGE III. TEENAGE YEARS
AGE: 14–18 YRS.
CULTURAL MESSAGE: The locker room culture
Physical and sexual dominance and submission
RELATIONAL GOAL: Maintaining relationships
as multidimensional

• STAGE IV. COLLEGE/ADULT
CULTURAL MESSAGE: Disconnection and
distance from mother
RELATIONAL GOAL: Reconnection as adult

Figure 24.3

expectations. His new teacher seemed to assume that all boys were rowdy, and did not really know Aaron. Feeling isolated and disconnected, he sought to establish connection by mimicking the boys at his table. He became loud and boisterous, winning acceptance by succumbing to pressures to join in with "wild boy" behavior.

In the parenting-in-connection model, the early years (Figures 24.4 and 24.5) are the time to lay the groundwork for relational mothering. Noting how essential mutual respect, honesty, empathy, and listening are to every interaction can do this. Mothers can show sons how to put these skills into action, verbally and nonverbally. Mothers often direct boys outside or into the basement to watch a video when company arrives because their aggressive energy feels too incongruent to the occasion. Why not, instead, teach boys to stop, look at, shake hands with, respond to, and initiate conversation with guests that we welcome into our homes. Keeping boys in the picture offers an opportunity for practicing interpersonal skills. Over time, these relational skills will become second nature to boys and possibly replace the high-activity behaviors they seem to use to cover their anxiety.

Boys need to be told and shown how to interact in situations that extend beyond family and friends. Mothers can be clear about expecting receptivity and responsiveness to others in the home and community. Early childhood is the

<table>
<tr><td colspan="2"> Early Childhood
Cultural issues:
Disconnect from mom; Superhero influence </td></tr>
<tr><td>

PROBLEMS
- LOSE ACCESS TO RELATIONSHIP AND EMOTIONS
- LOSS/SADNESS
- CONFUSION
- BEGIN EXPOSURE TO MEDIA AND SUPERHEROES
- LOSE ACCESS TO VULNERABILITY
- LOSE EMPATHIC RESPONSE
- AGGRESSION

</td><td>

SOLUTIONS
- SHOW AND TELL
- CHAT TIME
- FAMILY RITUALS
- TEACH RESPONSIVENESS
- MODEL & PRACTICE EMPATHY
- PRAISE RELATIONSHIP AND EXPRESSION
- REFRAME
  - STRENGTH
  - COURAGE
  - BRAVERY
- TIME OUT/IN REPAIR

</td></tr>
</table>

Figure 24.4

time to inculcate values like these. It is also the time to note the importance of being honest in communications with others and of respecting others' feelings, even though we might feel differently. These are the show-and-tell years, a time when children are open to learning and guidance that the culture does not offer and even opposes.

Our culture convinces boys early on that invincibility and imperviousness are hallmarks of strength. Little boys are fascinated by stories about Superman and they love to play superheroes. They learn that they have to be able to fix everything and protect everyone from evil forces. There is little room for expression of their vulnerable, dependent side. This inner part of boys can be quickly buried beneath shame if parents let the message of the culture take hold at this age.

Superman is powerful and invincible. But, as the story goes, his survival and strength depend upon his being apart from any trace of his "mother" planet, Krypton. Like Achilles, the underlying mythology presents the allure of invincibility and the dangers of the mother connection for sons. And the price for these illusions of strength for boys is the loss of access to feelings and authenticity in relationship.

In these early years, children are beginning to practice skills of empathy. Being responsive to family members' feelings and expressive of his own can

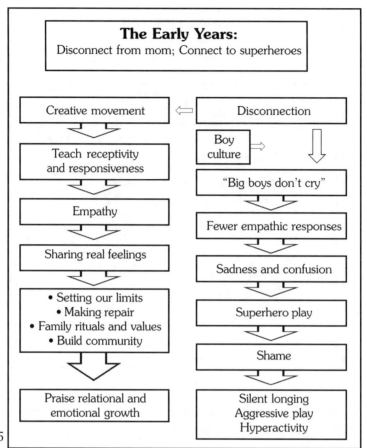

The Early Years:
Disconnect from mom; Connect to superheroes

| Creative movement | ⇐ | Disconnection |

Boy culture ⇒

"Big boys don't cry"

| Teach receptivity and responsiveness | | |

Fewer empathic responses

| Empathy | | |

Sadness and confusion

| Sharing real feelings | | |

Superhero play

- Setting our limits
- Making repair
- Family rituals and values
- Build community

Shame

| Praise relational and emotional growth | | Silent longing Aggressive play Hyperactivity |

Figure 24.5

give a little boy the opportunity to learn about mutually empathic relationships. Highlighting and validating the relational part of an activity, not just the activity itself, form another lesson for the early years.

> Maria takes her seven-year-old son cross-country skiing for the first time. When they come to a hill, John has a rough time. His mom braces him from behind, to keep him from backsliding. Resting against her, he looks up and says, "You must really hate skiing with me. I'm terrible and you're awesome."
>
> "Oh no," says Maria, "I love this. I love being with you and helping you. That's what important to me."
>
> "Really?" says John, smiling broadly.

Another simple way to create a space for relationship at this early age is to make a daily chat a part of a boy's routine. Mothers can designate a time for a private chat. This can be done in the car on the way to an activity. It can be done at bedtime as a way of wrapping up the day. It can be combined with a game or other joint activity. Mothers need not pressure their son to speak, but rather let him know that he has the opportunity. As the chat becomes ritualized, this will be a special time together. This sets a relational frame within which he can learn that it's safe to talk about *anything*.

Parenting-in-connection in the early years is a matter of teamwork. Instead of sending a little boy out to master a two-wheeler without any preparation, mother and son start by peddling a bicycle built for two. Mom is there to help her young son navigate life's inevitable bumps and twists. Working through difficult feelings and problems with Mom not only teaches the boy relational skills, but also nourishes and enriches his self-worth and their relationship. These lessons and experiences with his mother give him the confidence to remain in touch with his inner world as he ventures into the greater world beyond family.

The middle years

At this age we see the "playground" influence of teasing and bullying (Figures 24.6 and 24.7). This behavior can be both emotionally and physically hurtful. Boy culture behavior says: "I'm tough"; "It doesn't bother me"; "You can't hurt me"; "I don't care." As noted above, when we stop responding to boys from an empathic, compassionate perspective, we give them the message that they should be tough and independent both emotionally and behaviorally.

In the earlier story about Max at the ballpark, his mother went to her son's room and sat with him. Her acknowledgment of and compassion for his pain offered both validation and comfort to Max. Left on his own to deal with this experience, Max would learn to avoid the shame he felt by denying his feelings of physical and emotional pain. Mothers sometimes worry about embarrassing sons further by acknowledging and responding to their vulnerable emotions. Yet it is this very naming of and feeling compassion for hurt feelings that offers empathic response where they otherwise feel shame. This interaction teaches boys alternatives to avoiding shame by denying feelings.

We encourage mothers to jump into their son's world and react authentically to what they see and feel. Naming their emotional reaction and eliciting their son's view of the situation creates a dialogue. Mothers and sons can then further the process of sharing differences and exchanging values. While this process does not always give immediate answers, being together in a real way can create the connection necessary for them to work toward possible solutions.

A couple of years ago, a year-long, weekly values class became the setting for teaching relational skills to ten nine-year-old boys. Previous teachers warned about the impossible task of working with this group of boys, stating: "Every one of these boys meets criteria for ADHD [Attention Deficit Hyperactivity Disorder]";

MIDDLE CHILDHOOD
boy culture:
disconnect from feelings
TEASING, BULLYING

PROBLEMS	SOLUTIONS
• BOY CULTURE BRAVADO	• HUMOR
• LOSS OF RELATIONAL VOICE	• REFRAME STRENGTH AND COURAGE
• DENIAL OF FEELINGS	• EXPAND RELATIONAL EXPECTATIONS
• FEAR OF HONEST EXPRESSION AND CONNECTION	• ENCOURAGE FEELING TALK
• DISCONNECTION FROM MOTHER/FAMILY VALUES	• LEARN TO SIT WITH FEELINGS, ESP. ANGER
• DESENSITIZATION TO VIOLENCE	• ENHANCE RELATIONAL CHATS
– VIDEO GAMES	• RELATIONAL VIOLATION AND REPARATION
– MOVIES, TV	• SHARE DILEMMA BETWEEN HOME VALUES AND CULTURE
– INTERNET	
• "BAD BOY" BEHAVIOR	• FAMILY ACTIVITIES TOGETHER
• DISRESPECT	• INCLUDE FATHER'S STORY
• POOR JUDGMENT	
• DAREDEVIL TACTICS	• TALK ABOUT ALTERNATIVES
• HIGH-RISK BEHAVIOR	• ENCOURAGE BOY-GIRL FRIENDSHIPS
• POOR PERFORMANCE	

Figure 24.6

"They are impossible to work with in a classroom setting"; "Let them outside to run off their energy"; and "This group desperately needs girls to tone it down." Similarly, the boys greeted the new teacher with: "We are powerful"; "No one can control us"; "We rule"; and "You have to let us go outside and run around." The teacher of the special values class spent the first month reinforcing good relational behavior with pennies and letting the boys trade these for candy at the end of the period. She walked around the classroom dropping pennies into paper cups whenever someone was *not* participating in disruptive behavior. She was eventually able to reinforce the new relational behavior as it appeared. Slowly the boys, through the introduction of a new model of interacting, started to engage with one another in a real way. The class brainstormed ideas about old and new models of relationship for boys. As they shared their experience in the old model, they were able to share feelings of isolation and an awareness of how unfair the old model is to boys. One child likened the expectations of boy culture

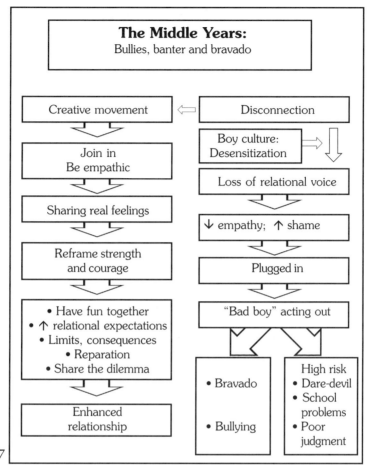

Figure 24.7

to racism: "It's like racism, you can't even have a friend who's a girl without being called her boyfriend or a wimp for hanging around with her!"

The group created its own new culture and value system for boys. Instead of running wild, they talked about relationship. They interacted honestly and respectfully with one another. They even learned to meditate to the resonance of a meditation bell!

In the same classroom Nan Stein's and Lisa Sjostrom's "Bullyproof" curriculum (1996) introduced language and concepts for participation with peers outside the group. The boys brought in examples of boy culture from their school life and talked about the dilemma of doing the right thing in the face of peer pressure to do the opposite. Stein's "web of courage" exercise renamed being honest and supportive with friends as bravery and strength. There are countless ways we can praise and build confidence in boys for going against the cultural model. One boy's brave act was calling his friend on the phone. He expressed his hurt feelings to this friend who had joined with other boys mocking him on the way home from school. The boys seemed relieved to tell their real stories and talk about feelings in a place that was relationally safe. When we create new models with new values, boys can grow in new ways.

Middle-childhood-age boys respond well to structure. Mothers can name the relational violation they see, stop the hurtful interactive behaviors, and provide meaningful concrete consequences. We teach the notion of relational repair to boys. When a behavior is hurtful to the person and the relationship, we call it a relational violation and expect that reparation be made in some concrete form of giving to the relationship to get back into connection. Boys are responsive to structured ways of coming back into connection. Making reparation to a younger brother who has been hurt can mean engaging him in his favorite game and having fun together. This can be a quick fifteen-minute interaction between siblings during which all other freedoms are on hold. The reparation piece fits with a boy's desire to fix things. The shift is important—move the focus from fixing concrete things to repairing relationship.

Mothers can draw on established family relational rituals to open and process feelings and interactions with sons. Trade the stories of your lives. Welcome all their stories and tell them yours. Children are particularly interested in their parent's stories of childhood. How did you struggle at their age? Encourage a son's daily stories. Show interest in a son's day-to-day struggles with peers and praise his creative attempts to deal with these. When mothers do this they can enhance skills that are otherwise ignored or even put down by peers and the culture at large. By joining her son in his dilemma, a mother can widen his view of new possibilities and change.

The teen years

As boys enter the teen years the cultural message is to get as far as possible from their vulnerable emotions (Figures 24.8 and 24.9). The power-over model of boyhood is transformed into a model of dominance in adolescence. Social, physical, and sexual dominance replaces authentic interactions. Because they shut down to awareness of feelings and are disconnected from parents, adolescent boys tend to act out rather than talk out their problems and conflicts. This leaves them at risk for forming insecure or abusive relationships. They may experiment with drugs, alcohol, and other risk-taking behaviors. Peer competition and pressure often motivate premature sexual intimacies. Because this type of quick intimacy is devoid of relational depth, it can often lead to a pattern of frequently shifting sexual partners.

Confusion about who they are and what they feel extends to their future and their goals. Often this translates into a state of underachievement in school and a feeling of general discontent with their lives. This path for boys leads to further

---

ADOLESCENCE

locker room bravado

PHYSICAL AND SEXUAL DOMINANCE

PROBLEMS	SOLUTIONS
• FOCUS ON PHYSICAL STRENGTH/DOMINANCE	• VALUE MUTUAL RESPONSIBILITY AND MUTUAL EMPATHY
• UNAWARE OF FEELINGS, EXCEPT ANGER	• EMPHASIZE POWER WITH OTHERS
• ACT OUT PROBLEMS AND CONFLICTS	• PARTICIPATE IN SON'S WORLD
• COMMUNICATION SHUT DOWN	– ASK QUESTIONS
• DESENSITIZED TO VIOLENCE	• CONTINUE TO DEFINE A MOTHER-SON RELATIONSHIP
– MOVIES, GAMES	• VIEW CONFLICT AS AN OPPORTUNITY FOR CONNECTION
– SPORTS	
– RELATIONSHIPS	• NAVIGATE THROUGH TRANSITIONS; PREDICT FEELINGS
• CONFUSION ABOUT SELF AND FUTURE	
• UNDERACHIEVEMENT	• NAME AND PROCESS FEELINGS; SIT WITH CONFUSION
• DISCIPLINE PROBLEM	
• PRESSURE TO DRINK, TO BE SEXUALLY ACTIVE	• TALK OUT RATHER THAN ACT OUT
• USE DRUGS/ALCOHOL TO DEAL WITH ANXIETY TO DEAL WITH	• KNOW LIMITS
	• EXPECT REPARATION
• SHIFTING SEXUAL INTIMACIES	• LEARN ABOUT MALE SEXUAL DEV.
• VULNERABILITY TO	• FRIENDSHIP PREREQUISITE TO SEX AND INTIMACY
– DATE RAPE	
– TEEN PREGNANCY	
– AIDS	

Figure 24.8

disconnection and alienation from relationship. They learn to resist influence and become relationally silent.

Mothers of teenagers often interpret their son's silence as rejection or as a desire for independence. They retreat from their son's distance. They are fearful that if they pursue connection they will be ignored or will increase the animosity they already feel from him. They are also afraid of being intrusive. They think they should respect their son's need for distance.

A group of fifteen-year-old boys responded to the question: "What are the important mother–son issues for you?" One boy went on and on saying, "She should stay out of my room, leave me alone, stop telling me to do my homework and to clean up my room." This same boy,

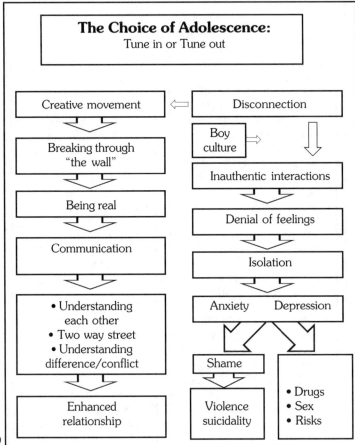

Figure 24.9

when questioned further about whether his mother ever tried to talk with him about important things, responded, "Yeah, but she gives up too easily."

In our work we encourage mothers to work hard at keeping the connection with sons. Adolescence is a time developmentally when sons need their mothers to hold onto the relationship. Even when it seems to mothers that they are "talking to a wall," these efforts mean something to boys and can become the early threads of connection. Mothers can raise issues and questions and let their son know what they think and feel. As boys mature, mothers can expect increased mutual responsibility for the work of their relationship. Mothers need to remain authentic in dealings with sons. For example, voicing frustration because she is doing all the work of the relationship and wanting more effort on his part can be the spark that wakes a son up and makes connection start to happen. Even if interactions seem to be conflicts and disagreements, the dialogue itself moves the relationship out of silence and distance into connection. Mothers need to make explicit the work of relationship so that boys learn what to do. Boys need guidance and real-life examples.

At the same time as a son's relationship with his mother becomes more balanced relationally, it can also become more balanced regarding the concrete work of family life. Mothers sometimes hold onto the role of provider and caretaker in a concrete way because that is all they have with their sons. As roles and responsibilities evolve, boys feel better about themselves and the growing mutuality with mom. They are learning how to be in relationship in a real way. Mothers can share their feelings and perspective while remaining receptive to a son's effort to communicate his viewpoint. Receptivity to a son's initiative is essential, whatever form this may take. Sometimes just being together in silence can create enough connection for sons to share a little bit more of who they are. As the relationship evolves, boys will begin to include mothers in discussions regarding dilemmas they face in the world and with peers. Learning to communicate with parental support gives boys the skills they need to deal with complex and difficult situations in life. As mentioned earlier, when there is a strong connection with at least one parent, teens do not need to turn to drugs, alcohol, or other forms of distraction and acting out.

As boys start to deal with bodily changes and emerging sexuality, mothers can provide a safe place to learn about both physical and interpersonal changes in relation to romantic and sexual partners. Mothers can keep the dialogue open, being responsive to questions, initiating concerns, and even sharing their own story. When it comes to teaching and guiding sons through the emotional, developmental topography of intimacy, mothers (as well as fathers) can be quite a good resource! Today's teens have no guidelines or structures in place to set the pace of intimacy for them. There are no rules. Teens "hook up" at parties. Dating does not exist. "Going out" and "hooking up" are loosely defined descriptions of partnering which can mean anything from talking on the phone regularly to having some form of sex together. This "no rules" situation creates problems, especially for boys. Our culture shames boys for not knowing facts or for reluctance in moving into sexual intimacy. Boys feel they should know what is going on, be in charge, and take the lead sexually. Even when sons appear to not want to talk about sexuality, it is usually out of the shame of not knowing. If mothers can voice their own feelings about these constraints, it may allow sons to come out of shame and feel safe enough to talk. Mothers need to hold this connection with their sons, creating possibilities for dialogue about relationship, intimacy, sexuality, and issues of power.

The adult years

At one of our first workshops, forty of the one hundred participants were mothers of adult sons. There was uniform concern about remaining in connection with sons in college, in marriages, and in adult life. We began the section by saying the refrain: "A daughter is a daughter for the rest of your life; a son is a son ..." and everyone in unison joined in spontaneously "... 'til he takes a wife." The cultural message of disconnection at this stage is the culmination of years of distance between mothers and sons (Figures 24.10 and 24.11). The cultural stereotypes are always of the intrusive or meddling mother or mother-in-law. There are numerous negative images in the media of close mother–son relationships. The cultural mandate of disconnection we have talked about is fiercely reinforced through exaggerated stereotypes that mockingly refer to adult men who are close to their mothers as "mama's boys."

> At age thirty-seven a young man was reflecting on the anger and distance he had felt toward his mother since adolescence. At this stage in his life he wanted to establish a better relationship with her. In answer to the question, "What was your early relationship like?" he suddenly recalled: "I remember the wonderful feeling of her sitting on my bed talking with me before I fell asleep every night. Then one night she didn't come in. I called to her, but she said she couldn't come in anymore. She never told me why and she never came in again."

A mixture of pain and shame was evident in the telling of his story. Sharing his past experience seemed to bring him greater understanding of his feelings. The clarity motivated him to discuss this incident from the past with his mother in the present. One way of connecting with adult sons is to revisit past interactions and talk about how cultural pressures affected your mother–son relationship. Mothers who disconnected did so because the culture told them to, not because they wanted distance from their sons. In opening this dialogue, both mother and son can share their perspective and their feelings about these experiences. Processing old interactions in an effort to understand each other's point of view creates connection. This can be the beginning of the mutual effort and understanding that is needed in order to heal past hurts and misunderstandings.

It is our hope to reframe the relational goal of men's adulthood as discovering renewed connection with their mothers as they enter into more mutually supportive adult-to-adult-child interactions. One mother of an adult son told us that she had been having concerns about the distance in her relationship with her grown son. When she told him that she was attending a mothers-and-sons conference, he suggested that they have lunch afterward to talk about it. It seemed that letting him know about her interest in the conference opened a door for them and had an immediate effect on their relationship.

ADULT SONS
Single, married, married with children

PROBLEMS	SOLUTIONS
• ISOLATION AND ALIENATION	• VALUE ATTEMPTS AT RECONNECTION
• NEGATIVE IMAGE OF STRONG MOTHER–SON RELATIONSHIP	• EXPECT MUTUAL RESPECT AND RESPONSIBILITY
• MEDIA DISEMPOWERS MOTHERS	• BE AUTHENTIC AND RESPONSIBLE
• SONS DISCONNECT AND DISTANCE	• HEAR HIS VOICE USE YOURS
• RIVALRY WITH DAUGHTER-IN-LAW	• ACKNOWLEDGE HIS NEEDS
• LOSS OF RELATIONSHIP	• CONNECT WiTH THE PEOPLE IN HIS LIFE
• OPPOSING NEEDS IN LIFE STAGES OF MOTHERS AND SONS	• RESPECT DIFFERENCES
	• ACKNOWLEDGE DILEMMA
	• SUPPORT NETWORK

Figure 24.10

Mothers of adult sons are represented by many different situations: mothers of single sons, married sons, sons with children, gay sons, separated or divorced sons. The variations are endless. Yet many mothers of these sons feel isolated and alienated. They feel disempowered in their efforts to maintain some connection with their son or his partner and/or family. His lack of initiative-taking and unavailability in their relationship feels like a statement from him to leave him alone.

Adulthood is composed of many developmental stages for men. The mother-son relationship faces challenges as sons move through these. Some sons live a single lifestyle; others develop intimate relationships and live with partners or marry. The introduction of a new person adds a new level of complexity to the mother–son relationship. At this point, a son's energy may be directed toward developing this intimate relationship. Others may need to invest time and energy into demanding work schedules. Some choose to have children. All of these features influence the mother–son relationship. The son is developing more interpersonal commitments and career opportunities at a time when his mother may be doing the opposite. He is less available and she is often more available. This juxtaposition can create misunderstandings and hurt feelings if not addressed by mother and son. It is important for both to talk about the impact of the situation on their relationship and about how this feels. Talking openly and

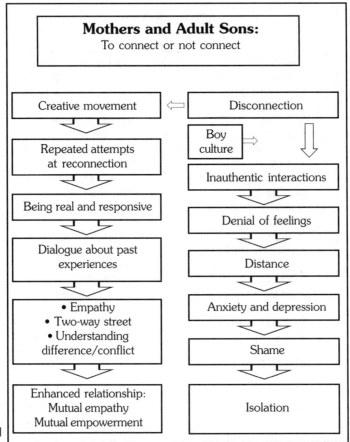

Figure 24.11

clarifying feelings created by these differences can help reestablish the connection and decrease the misinterpretation that silence can cause.

The challenge for mothers is to understand their son's expanding relationships and demands while at the same time to voice an interest in being included in some way. Both mothers and sons need to respect and embrace the other's relational efforts across these differences. Mothers can value attempts at connection by sons even when they feel as if they need more. Being authentic about one's own feelings but responsive to the other's needs and circumstances is the challenge of the adult years. At this point the relationship is the mutual responsibility of both mother and son.

Being aware of these conflicting needs and discussing the natural dilemmas they create can result in an atmosphere of acceptance. Most importantly, mothers need a strong support network of other mothers and other family members to help them deal with their evolving relational needs. Many mothers of adult sons have voiced the need to talk together about these issues. Joining with other mothers in similar life circumstances can be a healing experience for mothers of adult sons. These groups can help create the kind of connection that is often lacking in their relationships with their sons. This network of connection can empower mothers to find positive solutions to dilemmas with sons.

Conclusion

In the Greek myth, Thetis worried about what was best for her son, Achilles. In order to be a good mother, she chose to protect him from harm. In so doing, she affirmed his vulnerability. The decisions mothers face in raising boys are no less challenging today. Faced with cultural pressures that impose emotional straitjackets on boys, mothers feel unsure about how to handle their relationships with their sons. Over two thousand mothers who attended mothers-of-sons workshops intuitively knew that boys needed their emotional help but felt enormous pressure to disengage from them. In this supportive environment, they related stories of true connection and working through disconnections with sons throughout the life span. Time and time again they demonstrated that a mother's emotional connectedness to her son enhances his relational and emotional development. Good relationships are the cornerstones of psychological health and help create resilience in our sons to cultural pressures.

Notes

1. See Lewis, Lovely, Yeager et al., 1989; Boston Public Schools, 1997.
2. See, for example, Jones, Offord, and Abrams, 1980.
3. From an interview the authors conducted with a teacher discussing her experience with boys.
4. See Jenkins, 1993.

Chapter Twenty-Five

A MOM AND HER SON

THOUGHTS ON FEMINIST MOTHERING

Andrea O'Reilly

Over the past year I have been working on an edited volume tentatively entitled *Mothers and sons: Feminism, masculinity and the struggle to raise our sons* (New York: Routledge, 2001). The book is developed from the conference "Mothers and sons: Challenges and possibilities" that I coordinated on behalf of the Center for Feminist Research and the Association for Research on Mothering, in the fall of 1998, at York University. As I wrote my chapter for this collection, edited the other submissions and wrote the introduction to the volume, I found myself composing in my head, scribbling along the margins of this book, another mother and son narrative: that of my relationship with my soon-to-be sixteen-year-old son, Jesse O'Reilly-Conlin. As I sorted out the book's thematic sections and sought to clarify a particular feminist theoretical position for my own chapter, I would continuously catch myself in reverie, lost in thought, reflecting upon Jesse and my relationship, and quite oblivious to the urgent scholarly matters that awaited me on the computer screen. More often than not, the bright colours of my screensaver would awaken me from my reverie and call me back to the world of research and theory. I think this personal narrative of mine is a story both of interruption and postponement—while it is a story that demands to be told, it is a story that I have delayed telling.

Feminism, writes Babette Smith (1995) in *Mothers and sons*, "has failed the mothers of sons" (ix). As both a feminist mother of a son and an academic who teaches and researches the mother–son relation, I have often reflected upon this statement by Smith. Have we, in our academic and personal interest in the mother–daughter relationship, as I inquired in my Mothers and Sons book, wronged our sons, let them down, or simply forgotten about them? Have we in our negligence or disinterest, academic and otherwise, given our sons up to patriarchy, done to them what we have spent our lives fighting against for ourselves and for our daughters? I know that I have spent far more time this past decade thinking about mothers and daughters than mothers and sons, as I raised my own two girls, Casey (ten) and Erin (thirteen). However, as I wrote my articles, edited my books on mothers and daughters, and designed and taught a course on the topic, and as I sought to raise my girls in a feminist fashion, my son and my concerns for him as a male child in a patriarchal culture were always there; hovering, phantom-like, just beyond full consciousness or articulation. As with other mothers of sons and women who care deeply about boys today, I worried about Jesse and wondered whether he was, would be, okay in a world that seemed destined to harm and maim him emotionally, spiritually, and, increasingly, physically, as he grew into manhood. As time passed, I became more and more disturbed by the feminist silence surrounding mothers and sons, and by my own inability, or perhaps unwillingness, to theorize the mother–son relation and my relationship with Jesse as I had done for mothers and daughters in general, and my two daughters in particular. I initiated the "Mothers and Sons" conference and the book mentioned above in an attempt to make sense out of, at least from an academic point-of-view, the disturbing and puzzling silence surrounding mothers and sons. I wanted to begin a feminist dialogue on what I felt to be an urgent and timely matter. However, as I worked on the book, identifying and investigating the salient issues of this new and emerging field of inquiry, my own story as a feminist mother of a son kept intruding upon and interrupting like some postmodern ellipse, the trajectory of my theoretical ponderings. I realized then that my understanding of the mother–son relation would remain fragmentary and partial until I rememoried—remembered/recollected/relived—to paraphrase Toni Morrison's term, my own narrative. I needed to sort out for myself how feminism has shaped the mothering of my son and how being a mother of a son has redefined my feminism. I realized that in order to understand the bigger picture—feminist theory on mothers and sons—I needed to sketch my own mother and son portrait. To that I now turn.

This narrative is evidently my own; my son has his own story that I hope will be told at another time and place. I am a thirty-nine-year old woman of Irish, Scottish, and English ancestry; a professor of women's studies; and a mother of three children—a son (fifteen), two daughters (ten, thirteen)—who, along with my common-law male spouse of eighteen years, has been engaged in what I like to call radical nurturance—a feminist, socialist, anti-racist, nonheterosexist /abilist and learning/education centred parenting.[1] I was raised in a middle-class family by a working-class mother. My mother, from, what is called in my hometown Hamilton, the "wrong side of the tracks," was a divorceé with a six-year-old daughter when she met and married my father—a man from a "good," established Catholic family—in the late 1950s, and settled down in the new post-war suburbia to start a family. My class affiliation is thus middle class, though I was mothered more in accordance with working-class styles and values of childrearing; my spouse's class identity, in contrast, is decidedly and proudly working class.

I found myself pregnant with my first child, my son, in the fourth year of my Bachelor of Arts at the age of 22. Motherhood was something I had planned to do at thirty-something, only after both the career and the guy were firmly established. I was not supposed to become pregnant this way: young, poor, and in a dating relationship. Well, we decided to have the baby and three weeks later I found myself setting up house (if such is possible in student residence) with this man, obscenely happy, eagerly awaiting the birth of this child. I believed my life would go ahead as planned. I reassured my mother that with my child in daycare at six weeks my studies would resume as scheduled. I did not know then, could not have known then, how completely pregnancy and later motherhood would change, completely and forever, life as I knew it.

In the early months of pregnancy I was horribly ill with unrelenting nausea; in the later months I developed the serious condition of pre-eclampsia, which necessitated the daily monitoring of my blood pressure. I wrote a brilliant paper on the plight of "fallen women" in Victorian literature as my feet swelled and my back ached; the ironies, in retrospect, are splendid. Labour destroyed any remnants of complacency left over from my pre-pregnant self. I hemorrhaged during labour, and I never before had experienced such pain, terror, or aloneness, nor have I since. When my son was finally born, pulled from my body with forceps, my spouse held him as I watched the doctors attempt to repair my ripped and torn self.

Nothing, as any new mother will tell you, can prepare you for the numbing exhaustion and physical dislocation of new motherhood. Nor can anyone warn you about how deeply you will fall in love with your child. Motherhood, as Marni Jackson (1992) so aptly puts is, "is like Albania—you can't trust the descriptions in the books, you have to go there" (3). Motherhood radicalized and politicized me; it brought me to feminism. Though I had identified myself as a feminist for a number of years; motherhood made feminism real for me, and radically redefined it. At twenty-three I knew in my gut, though I could not yet fully articulate it, that my feminism was to be centred on motherhood. I believed as well that if feminism required of women, in either thought or deed, a repudiation of motherhood, I did not want to be a part of it. If I had to deny or downplay my maternal self (as if such were possible) to "make it," I was not interested in playing the game. Quoting Audre Lorde (1993), I believed, as I do now, that "the master's tools will never dismantle the master's house" (110). Though I now realize, some sixteen years later, that had I been willing to cleave off my maternal self and "pass" as a non-mother, my stay in academe—as a graduate student, contract faculty, and more recently as tenure track faculty—would have been a great deal easier, though far less rewarding.

I became a mother through the birth of a son. All the while pregnant, as I increasingly identified with the radical feminist celebration of sisterhood, I deeply longed for a daughter. As I marched with my girlfriends on International Women's Day, I believed I marched for and with my unborn daughter Sarah. However, as the days of my pregnancy passed, and as I caressed my swelling belly and talked to my unborn child, I knew with an uncanny certainty that she was a boy. Lesbian author and poet Jess Wells (2001), in her appropriately entitled narrative "Born on foreign soil," movingly recounts the displeasure and dismay, fear and panic, she felt upon learning through ultrasound and amniocentesis that her assumed-to-be girl was in fact a boy "I was profoundly disappointed," writes Wells, "I wept. I sobbed to my friends" (20). Wells wondered, "What did mothers and sons have in common? What could they do together?"; and worried, as a "separatist, punk dyke, a radical feminist" that she would be, in her words, "spawn[ing] a member of the oppressing class" (21). As my son was pulled from my body and I was told "it was a boy," there was a disappointment, but as I came to know and love my son, he was no longer a boy, but simply, for better or worse, Jesse.

With my first pregnancy, I lost what I refer to today as my feminist innocence. I discovered that feminism, has, at best, an ambivalent relationship to motherhood. When feminist friends and women's studies classmates learned of my unplanned pregnancy, I was greeted with sentiments of pity and concern, and when I spoke with joy and pride about my pregnancy and, later, my children, my colleagues seemed suddenly suspicious of my feminism and made me feel as if I had in some irrevocable and fundamental way failed feminism—sold out, been duped, gone over to the other side, or—in the language of current feminist discourse—fallen prey to the false consciousness of patriarchal ideology. Being a mother of a son made my motherhood identity all that much more problematic. Once at a union meeting shortly after the birth of our son, a woman with whom I had recently developed a friendship, stopped by to chat and upon learning that the baby she cooed at in the carriage was a boy, looked straight at me and said "what a shame and waste it was that a good feminist like me was now going to spend her life raising a man" and with that, turned, and walked away. In March of this year—nearly sixteen years later—as I discussed the topic of mothers and sons at the Association for Research on Mothering booth at the International Women's Day Fair in Toronto, two women dismissed both me and the topic of sons with a laugh that implied that a feminist would have to be an utter fool to spend her time worrying about boys. While views such as these are no doubt rare, I do believe they bespeak a larger feminist discomfort or disinterest in the topic of mothers and sons. Be that as it may, I can say with complete certainty, after years of teaching and researching the topic of motherhood, that feminists have been far more interested in daughters than in sons, though as of late there has been an emergent feminist interest in sons, due in part to the recent preoccupation with men and masculinity in the popular media.

The aim of this article however is not to account for the silence or to chart the emergence of this new field of feminist inquiry. Rather, I am interested in exploring, from a personal viewpoint, how my identity as a feminist influenced the mothering of my son and how, in turn, my identity as a mother of a son shaped my feminism. I turn now to the first question.

My son Jesse would be regarded as a "feminist success story." He and I enjoy a close and intimate relationship; he is as comfortable grabbing my hand or placing his arm over my shoulders as he is debating with me the finer points of feminism or competing with me at the gym. He is sensitive and kind, wise and gentle, witty and affable, empathetic and thoughtful, reliable and generous, hardworking and yet fun-loving; modeling in both his behaviour and demeanor so-called masculine and feminine attributes. He is adamantly anti-racist, anti-elitist/classist, feminist, and, in particular, anti-heterosexist in his politics. Occasionally, I am congratulated on raising such a fine feminist son; more often I am asked "How I did it?" This question, each time I am asked it, leaves me feeling baffled, anxious, and strangely off-centre. I don't believe it is possible or desirable to format a blueprint of feminist mothering; mothers don't need yet another normative discourse of the "good mother." Moreover, we know that a whole array of influences—the media, popular culture, genetics, peer groups, schools, extended family, and the like—have as much say, if not more, in how our children "turn out." At the same time, however, I realize that my son's feminine sensibilities and feminist leanings are surely no accident in a patriarchal culture that does its utmost to ensure that boys are anything but feminine and feminist.

Today, standing on my tiptoes to kiss my son good-bye, I saw a young man, wearing his long hair in a ponytail, as he has done since he was nine, sporting his normal attire of a tie-dye t-shirt and blue jeans (and not a name brand in sight), carrying in his hand his *Merchant of Venice*, which we had discussed the night before, debating whether the play is anti-Semitic, as it is often assumed. Jesse, with his straight A grades, basic decency, his love of his immediate and extended family, and so on, would do any mother proud. But what I marvel at is his determination to be himself, his refusal to give in to peer pressure, and his unwillingness to compromise his principles. Given that he has lived in a very conservative, very white, rural community since the age of eight, and attended a school that is often racist, sexist, and consistently homophopic, his conviction and courage are admirable. I remember how he was teased about his long hair, and ridiculed about his odd parents—those leftie, "shacked up," hippies "on the hill." I also recall the many times Jesse came home from school or ball practice deeply upset and troubled by the fag jokes and queer bashing he encountered on the playground. But I also remember a son who, in grade six, wrote and presented a speech about Rosa Parks and won the school speech award. In grade eight, he did a major research report on homophobia; this year he wrote for his history assignment an essay on Genital Mutilation. No doubt such views are anomalies and aberrations in our very straight (in all senses of the word), conservative "Pleasantville-like" community and no doubt we, his leftie parents, must bear/take some responsibly or credit (depending on who you are) for our son "turning out this way."

However, to return to the question asked above—the impact of my feminism on the mothering of my son—or the related question, "How did I raise him to be a feminist"—I still find myself circling, uncertain how to proceed. First, I cannot honestly say that I consciously raised him to be a feminist, nor I am not sure that my son would identify himself as a feminist. With my daughters, my feminist mothering was overt, explicit, and to the point. For example, with my middle girl, an avid reader, I would buy for her, as she began to read independently, only books by women; a justified censorship, I reasoned, given that she will be reading plenty of male-authored books in later life. Over dinner, in the car, I informed them of the injustices of patriarchy and catalogued women's achievements. No topic was taboo: a normal dinner conversation in our household, from the time they could sit up in a highchair, would shift from the witch burnings to suffrage in the time it takes to say "pass the broccoli please." Every film, music videos, song, commercial they have seen, has been analyzed "to death"—their misogyny, homophobia, or racism tracked and exposed. I used to change the endings of fairy tales when I read to the children at night, allowing the princess to "live with the prince only after she got her PhD." This year I temporarily pulled my daughter from her school in act of protest when the principal prohibited her from wearing a particular top, saying it was "distracting to the boys." The mothering of my girls has been actively and adamantly feminist and my daughters unequivocally identify themselves as feminist, though my thirteen-year-old would identify more "third wave grrrl" feminism than the feminism of my generation.

With my son, the relationship between my mothering and my feminism has been less direct and perhaps more complicated. Though Jesse has certainly been a part of thousands of conversations about women, feminism, and patriarchy, he has not been schooled and cautioned about patriarchy with the same rigour and thoroughness as my daughters have, nor has his autonomy, emotional, economical, and otherwise, been as emphasized in his upbringing as it was for his sisters. Nonetheless my son, as noted above, has feminine characteristics and feminist political leanings. How did this come to be in a patriarchal culture? The answer, despite the seeming complexity of the question, is, I think, quite simple and straightforward.

My son has a clearly defined feminine dimension to his personality because such was allowed and affirmed in his upbringing. My son, since his birth, has been an exceptionally sensitive child who has needed a great deal of attention and care, emotional, physical and, otherwise. In his first year of life he spent more times in my arms and at my breast than he did in his crib. He could not fall asleep at night without me lying in bed beside him until his early school years. Two and half years after my son was born, I would watch my newborn daughter sitting in her infant chair alone for hours on end contentedly playing with her fingers and toes: I was convinced there was something profoundly wrong with her. At the tender age of one she put herself to bed and has since. She announced to me at the ripe old age of two that "she was the boss of herself" each and every time I asked her to do something. At same age my son would not leave my side. I remember one day, I suggested to my son (age three), as we walked past the playground, that he should go in and have a play while I nursed his sister. He looked at me quite terrified and, backing away from the playground gate, proclaimed with feigned stubbornness that he would not go in there. When I, quite baffled by his behaviour, asked him why, he explained: "because children were in there." (We ended up waiting until the daycare kids left before going in for a swing and some sand play.) This image always stands in sharp contrast to the memory of my youngest daughter, also three, running through the same playground in a blur of winter hats and scarves as I waited to pick her up from daycare.

I do not recall these events to prescribe "what a good mother should do" but rather to illustrate that my son, from birth, was "always/already" a child with so-called feminine sensibilities. But it would be dishonest of me to say that raising such a child, boy or girl, was easy. I believe that with every child there is a difficult, or as the parenting books would delicately put it, "challenging" age or stage. With my son, it was, without a doubt, his first five years. He needed so much time, care, and attention that his seemingly endless demands left me exasperated and exhausted, trapped in those bad mother days that Mary Kay Blakey (2001) describes so poignantly.[2] However, despite my fatigue, irritability, and anger, I more often than not held/comforted him when he cried, cuddled him at nights, stayed close to him physically/emotionally, and honoured and protected his shy and sensitive personality—not because I was a "good mother," not even because I was a feminist mother wanting to raise a "good" man, but simply and quite honestly because it seemed to be the decent, normal, and only thing to do. When a child (boy or girl) cries, you give comfort; when a child feels lonely, you provide companionship; when a child is afraid you offer reassurance; such was my basic, but looking back now, eminently reasonable, childrearing philosophy at the age of twenty-three when I first became a mother.

On my son's first day of kindergarten when he asked if I could stay with him, I simply said yes, found a comfortable rocking chair (I had my six-week-old daughter with me), nursed my baby, and spent a morning in kindergarten as I had done a quarter century before. A few years later, when we moved and my son changed schools in December of grade three, I went with him, at his request, to his classroom on his first day and stayed with him. This time my visit was shorter; after ten or fifteen minutes, my son, with tears still falling from his eyes, told me that he would be okay now and that I could go. No doubt we were an odd sight that morning: me, a thirty-something mother, sitting in one of those straight back school chairs kindly provided by the teacher, beside my son, in his place in a row of desks, tears streaming down his face with me trying to act as if my heart was not breaking. I am sure that many people thought that, in mothering my child this way, I was spoiling him; or worse, because he was a boy, I was coddling and emasculating him, tying him to my apron strings and turning him into a Mama's boy. No doubt I worried about that, too. But what I remember most about raising my son is loving him; and that meant making sure he felt loved, protected, and good about himself. My son grew up with the knowledge that it was quite all right to be a sensitive boy and indeed quite normal to need your mother.

Today, when teachers, my friends, and other adults, describe my son, what is mentioned more often than any other aspect of his personally, is a "sense of groundedness," not necessarily self-confidence, but a self-acceptance and assurance in being who he is. I realize now that in my resistance to traditional practices of masculization I was modeling for my son the authentic, radical mothering that Judith Arcana, Adrienne Rich, and Sara Ruddick, among others, argue is necessary for a daughter's empowerment, and, I would add, makes possible a son's self assurance/acceptance in being different. More than twenty-one years ago, long before my son was born, Audre Lorde wrote about the power of such feminist mothering, in her now-classic "Man child: A black lesbian feminist's response." It seems fitting to end this section of my narrative with Lorde's words:

> The strongest lesson I can teach my son is the same lesson I can teach my daughter: how to be who he wishes to be for himself. And the best way I can do this is to be who I am and hope that he will learn from this not to be me, which is not possible, but how to be himself. And this means how to move to that voice within himself, rather than to those raucous, persuasive, or threatening voices from outside, pressuring him to be what the world wants him to be. (1993: 77)

In allowing my son to be who he was, in affirming this difference and doing so despite social demands to the contrary I raised my son "feminist" or, at the very least, I raised a son comfortable with the so-called feminine dimension of his personality. My son is also, in his political views and personal ways, very feminist. However, I do not think he would identify himself as a feminist. Rather his feminist beliefs are for him simply the normal way to see the world. Jesse and his sisters have been raised with socialist, anti racist/heterosexist, and feminist values, which seem to them to be merely sensible. All individuals and, my vegetarian daughter would add, species, are deserving of respect and equality; each entitled to a fair share of the world resources, valued for their differences across race, class, ability, sexuality, and gender, and deserving of a full life of meaningful work, good friendships and loving family. I, along with my spouse, have sought to model in my day-to-day living and to teach to my children what Carol Gilligan (1982) and others have defined as an ethic of care; or more specifically, a world view based on the values of love, respect, fairness, peace, and decency. These values have been fed to them, if you will, since they were babes in arms, served alongside their pablum and later bagels and cream cheese. Feminism for my son is not a politic or an identity but rather a lens through which he views and understands the world. When my children started to encounter sentiments of racism, homophobia, and sexism they were surprised, incredulous, and indeed quite confused. They could not understand why seemingly smart people, in the lingo of the schoolyard, could be "so stupid"; "all people are equal, good, etc." they reasoned, thus the person saying otherwise must be the fool. Of course, as they grew, they came to realize that what they understood to be the sane and sensible, normal, and natural way to be in the world—good, fair, decent to people regardless of race, class, etc.—was not seen as such by most of the children in our very conservative community. My children now understand that in their community and in the world generally, what seems to them perfectly sensible is, in fact, a particular political stance, and one that is not shared by most. Nonetheless, even today my ten-year-old daughter simply can not make sense of racism; why would someone dislike a person simply because of their skin colour, birth place, etc? To her that is just "idiotic." Likewise, my son supports feminism not because he is a feminist per se, but because for him that is what any sane and sensible person would do. I could not agree more.

In the conclusion to "Who are we this time?" Mary Kay Blakey writes:

> If I've taught [my sons] something about women and justice, my jock sons have taught me something about being a sport. In our ongoing discussions of gender politics, I've looked at the issues as urgently as ever, but through the lens of love and hope rather than anger and despair. (2001, 40)

My feminism too has been rethought, reworked, and redefined through the mothering of my son, most significantly in terms of the way I understand gender difference. Prior to my son's birth, I identified with a radical feminist theory of gender difference that positioned "the feminine" (meaning the traits normally associated with the feminine: nurturance, sensitivity, intuition, empathy, relationality, cooperation, etc.) and "the masculine" as more or less fixed and oppositional categories with the former superior to the later. Crudely put, I saw the feminine as good, the masculine as bad; and that women were, more or less, feminine and men masculine as a consequent of patriarchal gender socialization. I defined myself as "feminine" and was quite happy to do so.

However, as my son grew and he seemed far more "feminine" in his disposition than his two sisters, my complacent and simplistic understanding of gender difference was called into question. My son was both feminine and masculine; so too were his sisters. I learned through being a mother of a son that gender is not pure, essential, or stable; as post-modernism teaches us, it is fluid, shifting, and contested. As I came to appreciate the inevitable instability of gender, I continued to define myself as feminine and regarded it as superior, though I now conceded that these preferred traits was available to men as well as women.

As my son grew and I started to spend more time with him, "hanging out," I realized that the two of us were alike in many ways, and that our similarities were to be found in our so called shared masculine characteristics. This came as quite a surprise as I had never considered myself "masculine" in any sense of the word. However, with Jesse I saw myself in a different light, and came to realize that many of my personality traits are indeed masculine. I am adventurous, assertive, ambitious, more rational than emotional, carefree, usually confident, and often competitive. I pride myself on my independence, resolve, intelligence, and resourcefulness, and attribute the successes I have had in life to my drive, tenacity, stamina, resiliency, self-sufficiency, and willingness to take risks. My friends joke that I am type-A personality personified. I realize now that, while I always knew I had this type of personality, I would not self-identify as such because to do so would mean admitting to being masculine. However, over the last few years, as Jesse has grown into a man, and has begun to demonstrate many of these traits, I have named them in myself and come to see them as good and desirable as long as they are balanced with feminine characteristics. Being the mother of a "good" son I have come to realize that the masculine is not inherently evil and through this realization I have been able to discover and honour dimensions of my personality that were before unknown or shameful to me.

Eight months ago, after much urging from my son, he and I joined the local gym; we now go four to five days a week in the hour between picking him up from school and the time when my daughters' school day ends. Like many women my age, I grew up hating my body. As a teenager I was a compulsive dieter; in my twenties, as I came to both feminism and motherhood, I saw my body as an enemy—an instrument of patriarchal power and control. By my late 30s I had, more or less, forgotten about, given up on my body, and lived, as do many academics, completely in my head. By working out in the gym, I have come to trust, love, respect, challenge, and honour my body as I have my mind. I feel, in an odd way, reborn; as if I have been introduced to a new self, a self more complete and whole, strong and brave. From our time at the gym together, Jesse and I have developed a close bond based on something that is uniquely our own. No doubt many of the young men at the gym, most of whom go to Jesse's highschool, find it odd that a mom and her teenage son would hang out at the gym together. But my son and I delight in each other's company, take pride in each other's accomplishments, and have a great deal of fun doing so.

This week I started horseback riding lessons with my youngest daughter, an activity that I would not have undertaken without this new confidence and trust in my body, particularly because I was thrown from a horse when I was thirteen, never to ride again. After our first lesson, my aching hamstring muscles let me know that I would have to change my workout routine in order to strengthen these muscles. So yesterday at the gym, I tried some machines that I had not used before. At one point I dragged Jesse over to a machine and asked him to explain how it worked. The machine requires that you lie on your back and, with your legs extended, push up and down a press that has weights attached to it. There is a partial and a complete lift. On my back, with Jesse beside me, I did the partial lift and then, at my signal, he released the lever to the full lift. When the weight came down, my weak hamstrings muscles could not push the press up; so there I lay, my thighs almost pressed to my face, unable to move. Jesse and I finally managed to lift the weight and release me. I remember both of us laughing out loud, to the surprise and chagrin of the guy jocks who take working out very seriously. At that moment, as I looked at my son, I thought about this narrative and had one of those rare but profoundly wondrous moments of joy and revelation. It felt right and good to be me, the mother of this man. Reflecting upon this today, I realize that what was revealed to me in that moment was precisely the thesis of this narrative: that my son has made me a better person and hence a better feminist, and my feminism has allowed him to become the good man he was meant to be.

I would like to conclude this narrative by recalling two pivotal turning points in my intellectual travels that led me to this article. The first occurred in the summer of 1995 when I attended a session on Mothers and Sons at a women's studies/feminist conference in Scotland. Presented at the session was a preliminary report of interviews the presenters had conducted with feminist mothers of sons. Though the details of their research are evidently important, what was significant to me was their conclusion and the discussion that followed. The feminist mothers of sons interviewed for this study, the presenters concluded, while they had initially been committed to feminist childrearing, had all, more or less, given in up in their attempt to challenge and circumvent their sons' becoming sexist and traditionally masculine. They provided numerous quotations to illustrate the frustration, disillusionment, and resignation felt by these mothers. But all I can remember is the rage and despair I felt when I heard those words. In the question period, I raised my hand and struggled to vocalize the rush of emotions in my heart: "I know that it is hard to go up against patriarchy but we can't give up so quickly and easily. Our sons deserve more ... our world deserves more .... The struggle to save our daughters from patriarchy has been equally as tough but we have not given up on them ... we can't just give up on our sons." My remonstrances fell largely on deaf ears. Most in the audience agreed with the presenters, some reasoned that our time would be better spent on our daughters, others suggested that perhaps mothers, even feminist ones, secretly take pride in their sons' traditional masculinity and thus don't really want to change things. Still others cautioned that perhaps feminist mothering would turn our sons into misfits, causing them to be miserable.

I left the room shaking, and immediately went to a pay phone to call home and talk to Jesse. My spouse answered the phone and before I could get a word in edgewise he relayed the various newsworthy events of our children's final day of school before summer holidays. The most significant news was that our son, our child who proudly and publicly affirmed his difference every chance he got, had been chosen by his classmates in a year-end ceremony as "the person most liked by others." Politically I find these contests offensive, but at that moment I felt vindicated and wanted to rush back in the room—I think I would have had the session been still on—and say "told you so!" Or more reasonably, I would have tried to explain to them that my feminist mothering had not made my son a freak; in fact it had enabled him to take pride in his difference and become, through his uniqueness and his self-acceptance, the type of person people genuinely like.

The second event is more an image than a story. Last summer, my son, my mother, and I spent two weeks in Norway and then a week in London as part of my conference/research travels. My son, like myself, is an avid traveler; since the age of eight he has accompanied me on numerous research "road trips" throughout the United States. But this was his first time overseas. My mother, likewise, loves to travel, and she and I have traveled a great deal together. However, this was the first time we—a fourteen-year-old son, thirty-eight -year-old mother, and a sixty-eight year-old mother/grandmother—would be traveling together. Our trip would include a weekend jaunt to Svalbard, as close as you can get to the North Pole (a two hour flight from northern Norway), a five-day journey down the coast of Norway in a coastal steamer, four days in Tromsö (the location of the conference) and a day in Bergen and Oslo, and finally a week in busy London. (I am still paying off this trip, nearly a year later!). While I eagerly awaited the trip, I wondered whether we were up to each other's company for a full three weeks:

bunking together in the same room (on the boat our "room" would be the size of a closet), and all the time moving by boat, train, and airplane. As well, I was concerned that my son, in his youthful exuberance, would wear my mother out the first day and that he would not survive one of her shopping excursions. I need not have worried. Though there were the usual upsets as there always are when people travel together, this journey will remain one of my fondest memories of motherhood. There are hundreds of photos from this trip and even more photos in my mind, each more beautiful than the last, but I would like to conclude this narrative with just one. It is that of my son, my mother, and myself on the top deck of the steamer, as we stood by the railing of the ship, close to breathless in awe of the scenery before us. As we stood there, my son placed one of his arms around me and the other around my mother and, gesturing to the fjords across the water, said, "Isn't it beautiful?" For me the beauty of the moment was less in the fjords than in the three of us together standing arm in arm. While countless circumstances brought us to that moment, I now know, as I conclude this narrative, that what made that moment truly possible was the feminist mothering of my son. That is what I shall write beneath the photograph when it is placed in the photo album.

Notes

1. In this article I refer to "our" children as "my" children and explore raising these children largely in terms of my experience of mothering them. I do this because the article is concerned with Jesse and my relationship as son and mother. However, in practice, my spouse is as committed to the parenting described in the article as I am, and our children are as fully and completely his as they are mine.

2. "Every one of my friends," writes Blakey, "has a bad day somewhere in her history, she wishes she could forget, but can't afford it. A very bad day changes you forever" (33–34).

References

Introduction

Association for Research on Mothering and *The Journal of the Association for Research on Mothering*. www.yorku.ca/crm.

Büskens, Petra. "The impossibility of 'natural parenting' for modern mothers: On social structure and the formation of habit," *Journal of the Association for Research on Mothering* 3: 1 (Spring/Summer 2001): 75–86.

Chase, Susan, and M. Rogers. *Mothers and children: Feminist analyses and personal narratives*. New Brunswick, New Jersey: Rutgers University Press, 2001.

Crittenden, Ann. *The price of motherhood: Why the most important job in the world is still the least valued*. New York: Henry Holt, 2001.

Gordon, Tuula. *Feminist mothers*. New York: New York University Press, 1990.

Hall, Pamela Courtenay. "Mothering mythology in the late twentieth century: Science, gender lore, and celebratory narrative," *Canadian Woman Studies* 18: 1 & 2 (Summer/Fall 1998): 59–63.

Hays, Sharon. *The cultural contradictions of motherhood*. New Haven: Yale University Press, 1996.

Maushart, Susan. *The masks of motherhood: How becoming a mother changes everything and why we pretend it doesn't*. New York: The New Press, 1999.

Morrison Toni. "A conversation with Bill Moyers," in Danielle Taylor-Guthrie, ed., *Conservations with Toni Morrison*. Jackson: UP of Mississippi, 1994.

_____. *Love*. New York: Alfred A. Knopf, 2003.

O'Reilly, Andrea. *Reconceiving maternity: From sacrificial motherhood to empowered mothering*, forthcoming.

_____. *From motherhood to mothering: The legacy of Adrienne Rich's Of woman born*. Albany: SUNY, 2004.

_____. "Feminist perspectives on mothering and motherhood: Power and oppression," in Pamela Downe and Leslie Biggs, eds., *Gendered intersections: A collection of readings for women & gender studies*. Fernwood Press, forthcoming.

Reddy, Maureen, Martha Roth, and Amy Sheldon, eds. *Mother journeys: Feminists write about mothering*. Minneapolis: Spinsters Ink, 1994.

Rich, Adrienne. *Of woman born: Motherhood as experience and institution*. New York: W.W. Norton, 1986.

Ruddick, Sara. *Maternal thinking: Toward a politics of peace*. New York: Ballantine Books, 1989.

Russell, Sandi. "It's OK to say OK: An interview essay," in Nellie McKay, ed., *Critical essays on Toni Morrison*. Boston: G.K Hall, 1988.

Smith, Janna Malamud. *A potent spell: Mother love and the power of fear*. New York: Houghton Mifflin, 2003.

Thurer, Shari. *The myths of motherhood: How culture reinvents the good mother*. New York: Penguin, 1994.

Wolf, Naomi. *The beauty myth*. New York: Anchor Books, 1991.

Chapter one

Arnup, Katherine. "Lesbian mothers and child custody," in A. Tigar McLaren, ed., *Gender and society: Creating a Canadian women's sociology*. Toronto: Copp Clark Pitnam, 1988.

Collins, Patricia Hill. *Black feminist thought: Knowledge, consciousness and the politics of empowerment*. New York: Routledge, 1991.

Dally, Ann. *Inventing motherhood: The consequence of an ideal*. London: Burnett Books, 1982.

Hill, Marjorie. "Child-rearing attitudes of black lesbian mothers," in Boston Lesbian Psychologies Collective, eds., *Lesbian psychologies: Explorations and challenges*. Chicago: University of Illinois Press, 1987.

Kline, Marlee. "Complicating the ideology of motherhood: Child welfare law and First Nation women," in B. Crow and L. Gotell, eds., *Open boundaries: A Canadian women's studies reader*. Toronto: Prentice Hall and Bacon Canada, 2000.

Pollack, Sandra. "Lesbian parents: Claiming our visibility," in J. Knowles and E. Cole, eds., *Women-defined motherhood*. London: Haworth Press, 1990.

Rich, Adrienne. *Of woman born: Motherhood as experience and institution*. New York: Norton, 1976.

Richmond, Ray. *TV moms: An illustrated guide*. New York: TV Books, 2002.

Statistics Canada. Women in Canada 2000, Catalogue No. 89-503-XPE. 1990.

Thurer, Shari. *The myths of motherhood: How culture reinvents the good mother*. New York: Penguin, 1994.

Waring, Betsy. *The ideology of motherhood: A study of Sydney suburban mothers*. Sydney: George Allen and Unwin, 1984.

Chapter two

Arnup, K. *Education for motherhood*. Toronto: University of Toronto Press, 1994.

Baber, K.M., and K.R. Allen. *Women and families: Feminist reconstructions*. New York, NY: Guilford, 1992.

Bobel, C. *The paradox of natural mothering*. Philadelphia, PA: Temple University Press, 2002.

Boulton, M. *On being a mother*. New York, NY: Tavistock Publications, 1983.

Chase, S.E., and M.F. Rogers. *Mothers and children: Feminist analyses and personal narratives*. New Brunswick, NJ: Rutgers University Press, 2001.

Chodorow, N., and S. Contratto. "The fantasy of the perfect mother," in B. Thorne and M. Yalom, eds., *Rethinking the family: Some feminist questions*. Boston, MA: Northeastern University Press, 1992.

Comacchio, C.R. *The infinite bonds of family*. Toronto: University of Toronto Press, 1999.

Coontz, S. *The way we never were*. New York: Basic Books, 1992.

Croghan, R., and D. Miell. "Strategies of resistance: Bad mothers dispute the evidence," *Feminism and Psychology* 8 (1998): 445–465.

Edwards, A.E. "Community mothering: The relationship between mothering and the community work of black women," *Journal of the Association for Research on Mothering* 2 (2000): 87–100.

Eyer, D. *Motherguilt: How our culture blames mothers for what is wrong with society*. Toronto: Random House, 1996.

Forna, A. *Mother of all myths: How society molds and constrains mothers*. London: HarperCollins, 1998.

Foucault, M. *The Foucault reader*. New York: Pantheon Books, 1984.

Gordon, T. *Feminist mothers*. Basingstoke, Hampshire: Macmillan, 1990.

Hays, S. *The cultural contradictions of motherhood*. New Haven, CT: Yale University Press, 1996.

Krause, N., and H.F. Geyer-Pestello. "Depressive symptoms among women employed outside the home," *American Journal of Community Psychology* 13 (1985): 49–67.

Maushart, S. *The mask of motherhood: How becoming a mother changes our lives and why we never talk about it*. New York: Penguin Books, 2000.

Ranson, G. "Paid work, family work, and the discourse of the full time mother," *Journal of the Association for Research on Mothering* 1 (1999): 57–66.

Rich, A. *Of woman born*. New York: W.W. Norton, 1986.

Robinson, S., and L. Robinson. "Challenging the connection of mother-daughter relationships: A deconstruction of the discourse," *Canadian Women's Studies* 18 (1998).

Scott, J. "Deconstructing equality-versus-difference: Or, the uses of poststructuralist theory for feminism," in A. Hirsh, ed., *Conflicts in feminism*. New York: Routledge, 1990.

Seagram, S., and J.C. Daniluk. "It goes with the territory: The meaning and experience of maternal guilt for mothers of preadolescent children," *Women & Therapy* 25 (2002): 61–89.

Sears, W., and M. Sears, M. *The attachment parenting book*. New York: Little, Brown and Company, 2001

Stoppard, J.M. "Why new perspectives are needed for understanding depression in women," *Canadian Psychology* 40 (1999): 79–90.

Thurer, S.L. *The myths of motherhood: How culture reinvents the good mother*. New York: Penguin Book, 1994.

Chapter three

Arcana, Judith. *Every mother's son*. New York: Anchor Press/Double Day, 1983.

_____. *Our mother's daughters*. Berkeley: Shameless Hussy Press, 1981.

Blakey, Mary Kay. "Who are we this time?: An excerpt from *American mom*," in Andrea O'Reilly, ed., *Mothers and sons: Feminism, masculinity and the struggle to raise our sons*. New York: Routledge, 2001.

Caplan, Paula. *The new don't blame mother: Mending the mother–daughter relationship*. Routledge, New York, 2000.

Cooper, Baba. "The radical potential in lesbian mothering of daughters," in Sandra Pollack and Jeanne Vaughn, eds., *Politics of the heart: A lesbian anthology*. Ithaca: Firebrand Books, 1987.

DeBold, Elizabeth, Marie Wilson, and Idelisse Malavé. *Mother daughter revolution: From good girls to great women*. New York: Addison-Wesley, 1993.

Forcey, Linda. *Mothers of sons: Toward an understanding of responsibility*. New York: Praeger, 1987.

Gilligan, Carol. *In a different voice: Psychological theory and women's development*. Cambridge, Mass.: Harvard University Press, 1982.

Johnson, Miriam. *Strong mothers, weak wives: The search for gender equality*. Berkeley: University of California Press, 1989.

Kaufman, Michael. *Theorizing masculinities*. Thousand Oaks, CA: Sage, 1994.

Lorde, Audre. "Man child: A black lesbian feminist's response," in *Sister outsider: Essays and speeches*. New York: Quality Paperback Book Club, 1993.

Morgan, Robin. "Every mother's son," in Jess Wells, ed., *Lesbians raising sons*. Los Angeles: Alyson Books, 1997.

O'Reilly, Andrea. "Across the divide: Contemporary Anglo-American feminist theory on the mother–daughter relationship," in Sharon Abbey and Andrea O'Reilly, eds., *Redefining motherhood: Changing identities and patterns*. Toronto: Second Story Press, 1998.

_____. "Mothers, daughters and feminism today: Empowerment, agency, narrative," *Canadian Woman Studies* 18: 2 & 3 (Summer/Fall 1998): 16–21.

_____. "Introduction," in Andrea O'Reilly and Sharon Abbey, eds., *Mothers and daughters: Connection, empowerment, transformation*. New York: Rowman and Littlefield, 2000.

_____. "Introduction," in Andrea O'Reilly, ed., *Mothers and sons: Feminism, masculinity and the struggle to raise our sons*. New York: Routledge, 2001.

_____. "In black and white: Anglo-American and African-American perspectives on mothers and sons," in Andrea O'Reilly, ed., *Mothers and sons: Feminism, masculinity and the struggle to raise our sons*. New York: Routledge, 2001.

_____. "Feminist perspectives on mothering and motherhood: Power and oppression," in Pamela Downe and Leslie Biggs, eds., *Gendered intersections: A collection of readings for women and gender studies*. Fernwood Press, forthcoming.

_____. *Reconceiving maternity: From sacrificial motherhood to empowered mothering*. Forthcoming.

Payne, Karen, ed. *Between ourselves: Letters between mothers and daughters*. Boston: Houghton Mifflin Company, 1983.

Pipher, Mary. *Reviving Ophelia: Saving the selves of adolescent girls*. New York: G.P., 1994.

Rich, Adrienne. *Of woman born: Motherhood as experience and institution*. New York: W.W. Norton, 1986.

Ruddick, Sara. *Maternal thinking: Toward a politics of peace*. New York: Ballantine Books, 1989.

Rutter, Virginia Beane. *Celebrating girls: Nurturing and empowering our daughters*. Berkeley: Conari Press, 1996.

Silverstein, Olga, and Beth Rashbaum. *The courage to raise good men*. New York: Viking, 1994.

Thomas, Alison. "Swimming against the tide: Feminists' accounts of mothering sons," in Andrea O'Reilly, ed., *Mothers and sons: Feminism, masculinity and the struggle to raise our sons*. New York: Routledge, 2001.

Chapter four

Archives of Ontario W.C.T.U. Collection. MU 8285, Colbec, Mrs. *The Canadian Womans' Christian Temperance Union medal contest book*, No. 4

_____. *Women's journal*, October 1890.

Castle, J.B., S. Abbey, and C. Reynolds. "Sacrificing our daughters to patriarchy?" Paper presented at Canadian Societies for the Study of Education Annual Conference, Brock University, St. Catharines, Ontario, 1996.

Chodorow, N. *The reproduction of mothering*. Berkeley: University of California Press, 1978.

Cohen, S., and M.F. Katzenstein. "The war over the family is not over the family," in M. Dornbusch and M.H. Strober, *Feminism, children and the new families*. New York: Gilford Press, 1988.

Cole, J., ed. *All-American women: Lines that divide, ties that bind*. New York: Free Press, 1986.

Cole, J. "Raising sons," *Ms. Magazine* (November/December 1993): 34–50.

Commacchio, C. *Nations are built of babies: Saving Ontario's mothers and children, 1900–1940*. London, Kingston: McGill-Queen's University Press, 1997.

Connell, R.W. 1995. *Masculinities*. Berkeley: University of California Press.

Davison, K. 1998. "Manly expectations: Memories of masculinities in school," Paper presented at the annual meeting of the Canadian Societies for the Study of Education, University of Ottawa.

DeSalvo, L., and M. Leaska. *The letters of Vita Sackville-West to Virginia Woolf*. New York: William Morrow and Company, Inc, 1985.

Dinnerstein, D. *The mermaid and the minotaur*. New York: Harper and Row, 1977.

Everingham, C. *Motherhood and modernity: An investigation into the rational dimension of mothering*. Buckingham: Open University Press, 1994.

Frank, B. "Queer selves/queer in schools: Young men and sexualities," in S. Prentice, ed., *Sex in Schools: Canadian Education and Sexual Regulation*. Toronto: Our Schools/Our Selves Education Foundation, 1994.

Glendinning, V. *Vita: The life of Vita Sackville-West*. London: Weidenfeld and Nicolson, 1983.

Lamb, M.E., J.H. Pleck, and J.A. Levine. "Effects of increased paternal involvement on children in two-parent families," in R.A. Lewis and R.E. Salt, eds., *Men in families*. Beverly Hills: Sage, 1986.

Lasch, C. *Haven in a heartless world: The family besieged*. New York: Basic Books, 1977.

Lein, L. *Families without villains: American families in an era of change*. Lexington, MS: Lexington Books, 1984.

Lewis, R.A., and R.E. Salt, eds. *Men in families*. Beverly Hills: Sage, 1986

Lorde, A. *Sister outsider*. Freedom, CA: Crossing Press, 1984.

_____. "Raising sons," *Ms. Magazine* (November/December 1993): 34–50

Messner, M. "Masculinities and athletic careers," in Margaret L. Anderson and Patricia Hill Collins, eds., *Race, class, and gender*. Belmont, CA: Wadsworth Publishing Company, 1992.

Millman, M. *Warm hearts and cold cash*. New York: The Free Press, 1991.

Mischel, H.N., and R. Fuhr. "Maternal employment: Its psychological effects on children and their families," in S.M. Dornbusch and M.H. Strober, eds., *Feminism, children and the new families*. New York: Gilford Press, 1988.

Morgan, R. "Raising sons," *Ms. Magazine* (November/December 1993): 34–50

Nicolson, N. *Vita and Harold: The Letters of Vita Sackville-West and Harold Nicolson*. London: Weidenfeld and Nicolson, 1992.

_____. *Portrait of a marriage*. New York: Atheneum Press, 1973.

O'Brien, M. *The politics of reproduction*. Boston: Routledge and Kegan Paul, 1981.

Reddy, M.T. *Crossing the color line: Race, parenting and culture*. New Jersey: Rutgers University Press, 1994.

Rich, A. *Of woman born: Motherhood as experience and institution*. New York: W.W. Norton and Co, 1986

_____. 1976. *Of woman born*. Toronto: Bantam Books.

Rotundo, A.E. "Boy culture: Middle-class boyhood in nineteenth-century America," in Mark C. Carnes and Clyde Griffen, eds., *Meanings for manhood: Constructions of masculinity in Victorian America*. Chicago: University of Chicago Press, 1990.

Ruddick, S. "Preservative love and military destruction: Some reflections on mothering and peace," in Joyce Trebilcot, ed., *Mothering: Essays in feminist theory*. Totowa, NJ: Rowman and Allanheld, 1984.

_____. "Maternal thinking," *Feminist Studies* (Summer 1980): 62.

Scott, L.A. "Real chivalry, The white cross series, No. 11," Archives of Ontario, w.c.t.u. Collection.

Sebald, H. *Momism: The silent disease of America*. Chicago: Nelson Hall, 1976.

Smith, D.E. "Women, class and family," in V. Burstyn and D.E. Smith, eds., *Women, class, family and the state*. Toronto: Garamond Press, 1985.

Stafford, L., and Bayer, C.L. *Interaction between parents and children*. Newbury Park: Sage, 1993.

Thorne, B. "Feminist rethinking of the family: An overview," in B. Thorne and M. Yalom, eds., *Rethinking the family: Some feminist questions*. New York: Longman, 1982.

Thurur, S.L. *The myths of motherhood: How culture reinvents the good mother*. Boston: Houghton Mifflin Co., 1994.

Wolf, N. *Fire with fire*. Random House Audio Books, 1993.

Chapter five

Baker, Christina Looper, and Christina Baker Kline. *The conversation begins: Mothers and daughters talk about living feminism*. New York: Bantam, 1996.

Friedan, Betty. *The feminine mystique*. New York: Dell, 1963.

Olsen, Tillie. *Mother to daughter, daughter to mother*. New York: Feminist Press, 1984.

Chapter six

Australian Bureau of Statistics. *Australian social trends 2001*. Catalogue No. 4102. ABS, Canberra, 2001.

_____. *Marriages and divorces, Australia, 1999*. Catalogue. no. 3310.0, ABS, Canberra, 2000.

Australian Bureau of Statistics. "Family-living arrangements: Caring for children after parents separate," *Australian Social Trends, 1999*. Catalogue No. 4102. ABS, Canberra, 1999a.

Australian Bureau of Statistics. "Family–national summary tables," *Australian Social Trends, 1999*. Catalogue No. 4102. ABS, Canberra, 1999b.

Baxter, Janine. *Work at home· The domestic division of labour*. St Lucia: University of Queensland Press, 1993.

Bell-Scott, Patricia, et al. *Double stitch: Black women write about mothers and daughters*. New York: Harper Perennial, 1993.

Bernard, Jessie. *The future of marriage*, 2nd edition. Yale University Press: New Haven, 1982.

Bittman, Michael *Recent changes in unpaid work*. Australian Bureau of Statistics Occasional Paper. Catalogue No. 4154.0, ABS, Canberra, 1995.

Bittman, Michael, and Jocelyn Pixley. "Working for nothing," in *The double life of the family: Myth, hope and experience*. Sydney: Allen & Unwin, 1997.

Collins, Patricia Hill. *Black feminist thought: Knowledge, consciousness, and the politics of empowerment*. Boston: Unwin Hyman, 1990.

Deem, Rosemary. *All work and no play? The sociology of women and leisure*. Milton Keynes: Open University Press, 1986.

Delphy, Christine, and Diana, Leonard. *Familiar exploitation: A new analysis of marriage in contemporary western society*. Cambridge: Polity, 1992

Dempsey, Ken. "Trying to get husbands to do more work at home," *The Australian and New Zealand Journal of Sociology* 15: 3 (1997a): 216–225.

_____. *Inequalities in marriage: Australia and beyond*. Melbourne: Oxford University Press, 1997b.

Dinnerstein, Dorothy. *The mermaid and the minatour: Sexual arrangements and human malaise*. New York: Harper & Row, 1976.

DiQuinzio, Patrice. *The impossibility of motherhood: Feminism, individualism and the problem of mothering*. New York: Routledge, 1999

Dunne, Gillian, ed. *Living "difference"?: Lesbian perspectives on work and family life*. New York: Haworth, 1998.

Friedan, Betty. *The feminine mystique*. New York: W. W. Norton, 1963.

Gilroy, Sarah. "Intra-household power relations and their impact on women's leisure," in Linda McKie, Sophie Bowlby, and Susan Gregory, eds., *Gender, power and the household*. London: Macmillan Press, 1999.

Gramsci, Antonio. *Selections from the prison notebooks*. Ed. and trans. Quentin Hoare and G. Nowell-Smith. London: Lawrence & Wishart, 1971.

Green, Eileen, Sandra Hebron, and Diana Woodward. *Women's leisure, what leisure?* London: Macmillan, 1990.

Grief, Geoffry. "Working with noncustodial mothers," *Families in Society: The Journal of Contemporary Human Services* 78: 1 (1997), 46–53.

Grief, Geoffry, and Margaret Pabst. *Mothers without custody*. Massachusetts: Lexicon Books, 1988.

Harding, Sandra. "Introduction: Is there a feminist method?" in Sandra Harding, ed., *Feminism and methodology*. Bloomington: Indiana University Press, 1987.

Hartstock, Nancy. *The feminist standpoint revisited and other essays*. Colorado: Westview Press, 1998.

Hays, Sharon. *The cultural contradictions of motherhood*. New Haven: New York University Press, 1996.

Hochschild, Arlie. *The second shift: Working parents and the revolution at home*. New York: Viking, 1989.

_____. *The time bind: when work becomes home and home becomes work*. New York: Owl Books, 1998.

Hollway, Wendy, and Brid Featherstone, eds. *Mothering and ambivalence*. New York: Routledge, 1997.

Jackson, Rosie. *Mothers who leave: Behind the myth of women without their children*. London: Pandora, 1994.

Johnson, Miriam. *Strong mothers, weak wives*. Berkeley: University of California Press, 1988.

Komter, Aafke. "Hidden power in marriage," *Gender & Society* 3: 2 (1989): 187–216.

Ladd-Yaylor, Molly, and Lauri Umansky, ed., *"Bad" mothers: The politics of blame in twentieth-century America*. New York: New York University Press, 1998.

Lazarre, Jane. *The mother knot*. New York: McGraw-Hill Book Company, 1976.

LeBlanc, Wendy. *Naked motherhood: Shattering illusions and sharing truths*. Sydney: Random House, 1999

McDonald, Peter. *Families in Australia: A socio-demographic perspective*. Melbourne: Australian Institute of Family Studies, 1995.

Morris, Lydia. *The workings of the household*. Cambridge: Polity Press, 1990.

Maushart, Susan. *Wifework: What marriage really means for women*. Melbourne: Text Publishing, 2001.

_____. *The mask of motherhood: How mothering changes everything and why we pretend it doesn't*. Sydney: Random House, 1999.

Nicholson, Joyce. *The heartache of motherhood*. Melbourne: Penguin, 1983.

Pleck, Joseph. *Working wives, working husbands*. Beverly Hills, California: Sage, 1985.

Probert, Belinda, and Fiona Macdonald. *Young women: Poles of experience in work and parenting*. Fitzroy, Vic.: Brotherhood of St Laurence, 1999a.

Probert, Belinda. "Mothers in the labour force," *Family Matters* 54 (Spring/Summer 1999b): 60–65. Australian Institute of Family Studies.

Probert, Belinda, and Bruce Wilson, eds. *Pink collar blues: Work, gender and technology*. Melbourne: Melbourne University Press, 1993.

Rich, Adrienne. *Of woman born: Motherhood as experience and institution*. London: Virago, 1977.

Sanchez, L. "Material resources, family structure resources and husbands' housework participation: A cross-national comparison," *Journal of Family Issues* 15: 3 (1994): 379–402.

Shelton, B. "The distribution of household tasks: Does wife's employment status make a difference?" *Journal of Family Issues* 11: 2 (1990): 115–35.

Smith, Dorothy. *The conceptual practices of power*. Boston: Northeastern University Press, 1990.

Smith, Dorothy. *The everyday world as problematic: A feminist sociology*. Boston: Northeastern University Press, 1987.

Steil, Janice. *Marital equality: Its relationship to the well-being of husbands and wives*. Thousand Oaks, California: Sage, 1997.

Warner, Marina. *Alone of all her sex: The myth and cult of the Virgin Mary*. London: Vintage, 2000 [1976].

Wearing, Betsy. "Beyond the ideology of motherhood: Leisure as resistance," *The Australian and New Zealand Journal of Sociology* 26: 1 (1990a): 36–58.

_____. "Leisure and the crisis of motherhood: A study of leisure and health amongst mothers of first babies in Sydney, Australia," in S. Quah and J. Trost, eds., *Marriage, parenthood and social policy*. Singapore: Times Publishing, 1990b.

_____. *The ideology of motherhood*. Sydney: Allen and Unwin, 1984.

Wimbush, E. *Women, leisure and well-being*. Edinburgh: Centre for Leisure Research, 1986.

Woolf, Virginia. *A room of one's own*. London: Gratin, 1977 [1929].

Zhang, C., and J. Farley. "Gender and the distribution of household work," *Journal of Comparative Family Studies* 26: 2 (1995): 195–205.

Chapter seven

Arnup, Katherine, ed. *Lesbian parenting: Living with pride and prejudice*. Charlottetown: Gynergy Books, 1985.

Ashburn, Elizabeth. "Lovely mothers' posters," *Lesbian art: An encounter with power.* New South Wales: Craftsman House, 1996.

Beck, Ulrich, and Elizabeth Beck-Gernsheim. *The normal chaos of love*. Cambridge: Polity Press, 1995.

Bernstein, Jane, and Laura Stephenson, "Dykes, donors & dry ice: Alternative insemination," in Katherine Arnup, ed., *Lesbian pride. Living with pride and prejudice*, Charlottetown: Gynergy Books, 1995.

Boffin, Tessa, and Jean Fraser, eds. *Stolen glances: Lesbians take photographs*. London: Pandora Press, 1991.

Bright, Susie, and Jill Posener, eds. *Nothing but the girl: The blatant lesbian image*. New York: Freedom Editions, 1996.

Brosnan, Julia. *Lesbians talk: Detonating the nuclear family*. London: Scarlet Press, 1996.

Butler, Judith. *Gender trouble: Feminism and the subversion of identity*. New York: Routledge, 1990.

Cade, Cathy. "Lesbian Family Album Photography," in Tessa Boffin and Jean Fraser Jean, eds., *Stolen glances. Lesbians take photographs,* London: Pandora Press, 1991.

Cooper, Emmanuel. "Queer spectacles," in Peter Horne and Reina Lewis, eds., *Outlooks: Lesbian and gay sexualities and visual culture*. London: Routledge, 1996.

Dunne, Gillian A. "A passion for sameness? Sexuality and gender accountability," in Elizabeth Silva and Carol Smart, eds., *The new family?* London: Sage, 1999.

_____. *Balancing acts: Lesbian experience of work and family life*. Report in the ESRC, 1998. Unpublished.

Fineman, Martha Alberston. *The neutered mother, the sexual family and other twentieth century tragedies*. New York: Routledge, 1995.

Gabb, Jacqui. *Making babies: Reflections on the paradox of "sexuality" and "the family,"* IASSCS Bi-Annual Conference, Manchester Metropolitan University, 1999. Unpublished.

Heaphy, Brian, et al. *Sex, money and the kitchen sink: Power in same sex couple relationships*. BSA Annual Conference, University of York, 1997.

Kirkpatrick, et al., "Lesbian mothers and their children: A comparative study," in *American Journal of Orthopsychiatry* 51:3 (1981): 545–51.

Lewin, Ellen. *Lesbian mothers: Accounts of gender in American culture*. Ithaca: Cornell University Press, 1993.

Oerton, Sarah. "Queer housewives?: Some problems of theorising the division of domestic labour in lesbian and gay households," in *Women's Studies International Forum* 20: 3 (1997): 421–430.

Patterson, Charlotte J. "Children of lesbian and gay parents," in *Advances in Clinical Child Psychology* 19 (1997): 235–282.

Rights of Women (Lesbian Custody Group). *Lesbian mothers' legal handbook*. London: Women's Press, 1986.

Seyda, Barbara, and Diana Herrera. *Women in love: Portraits of lesbian mothers and their families*. Boston: Bullfinch Press, 1998.

Smith, Anne Marie. "Resisting the erasure of lesbian sexuality: A challenge for queer activism," in Ken Plummer, ed., *Modern homosexualities: Fragments of lesbian and gay experience*. London: Routledge, 1991.

Spence, Jo. *Cultural sniping: The art of transgression*. London: Routledge, 1995.

Tasker, Fiona, and Susan Golombok. *Growing up in a lesbian family: Effects on child development*. New York: Guilford Press, 1997.

Turner, Guinivere. *Ellen's coming out party*. Channel Four Television, 1998.

Van Every, Jo. *Heterosexual women changing the family: Refusing to be a "Wife"!* London: Taylor Francis, 1995.

Weston, Kath. *Families we choose: Lesbians, gays, kinship*. New York: Columbia University Press, 1991.

Williams Val. *Who's looking at the family?* London: Barbican Art Gallery, 1994

Chapter eight

Campey, J., T. McCaskell, J. Miller, and V. Russell. "Opening the classroom closet: Dealing with sexual orientation at the Toronto Board of Education," in S. Prentice, ed., *Sex in schools: Canadian education and sexual regulation*. Toronto: Our Schools/Our Selves, 1994.

Casper, V., S. Schultz, and E. Wickens. "Breaking the silences: Lesbian and gay parents and the schools," *Teachers College Record* 94: 1 (1992).

Epstein, D., ed. *Challenging lesbian and gay inequalities in education*. Buckingham, Philadelphia: Open University Press, 1994.

Epstein, D., and R. Johnson. "On the straight and the narrow: The heterosexual presumption, homophobias and schools," in D. Epstein, ed., *Challenging lesbian and gay inequalities in education*. Buckingham, Philadelphia: Open University Press, 1994.

Epstein, R. "Parent night will never be the same: Lesbian families challenge the public school system," *Our Schools/Our Selves* 9: 1 (1998).

_____. "Lesbian families," in M. Lynn, ed., *Voices: Essays on Canadian families*. Toronto: Nelson Canada, 1996.

_____. "Lesbian parenting: Cracking the shell of the nuclear family," in M. Oikawa, D. Falconer, and A. Decter, eds., *Resist: Essays against a homophobic culture*. Toronto: Women's Press, 1994.

Griffin, P. "From hiding out to coming out: Empowering lesbian and gay educators," in K.M. Harbeck, ed., *Coming out of the classroom closet: Gay and lesbian students, teachers, and curricula*. New York: Harrington Park Press, 1992.

Khayatt, M.D. *Lesbian teachers: An invisible presence*. Albany: SUNY, 1992.

Kirkpatrick, M. "Clinical implications of lesbian mother studies," *Journal of Homosexuality* 13 (1987).

Kirkpatrick, M., C. Smith, and R. Roy. "Lesbian mothers and their children: A comparative study," *American Journal of Orthopsychiatry* 51 (1981).

Kissen, R.M. *Last closet: The real lives of lesbian and gay teachers*. Portsmouth: Heinemann, 1996.

Lather, P. "Staying dumb? Feminist research and pedagogy with/in the postmodern," in H. Simons and M. Billis, *After postmodernism: Reconstructing ideology critique*. London: Sage, 1997.

Mac An Ghaill, M. "(In)visibility: Sexuality, race and masculinity in the school context," in D. Epstein, ed., *Challenging lesbian and gay inequalities in education*. Buckingham, Philadelphia: Open University Press, 1994.

Patterson, C. "Children of lesbian and gay parents," *Child Development* 63 (1992)

Redman, P. "Shifting ground: Rethinking sexuality education," in D. Epstein, *Challenging lesbian and gay inequalities in education*. Buckingham, Philadelphia: Open University Press, 1994

Sears, J. "Challenges for educators: Lesbian, gay, and bisexual families," *The High School Journal* (Oct/Nov 1993, Dec/Jan 1994).

_____. ed. *Sexuality and the curriculum*. New York: Teachers College Press, 1992.

_____. *Growing up gay in the south: Race, gender and journeys of the spirit*. New York: The Haworth Press, 1991.

_____. "Problems and possibilities in 'homophobia' education," *Empathy* 2: 2 (1990).

Snider, K. "Race and sexual orientation: The (im)possibility of these intersections in educational policy," *Harvard Educational Review* 66: 2 (1996).

Sullivan, C. "Oppression: The experiences of a lesbian teacher in an inner-city comprehensive school in the United Kingdom," *Gender and Education* 5: 1 (1993).

Walkderdine, V., and H. Lucey. *Democracy in the kitchen: Regulating mothers and socializing daughters*. London: Virago, 1989.

Walkerdine, V. "Poststructuralist theory and everyday social practices: The family and the school," in S. Wilkinson., ed., *Feminist social psychology: Developing theory and practice*. Milton Keynes, Philadelphia: Open University Press, 1986.

Warren, H. *Talking about school*. London: Gay Teenagers' Group, 1994.

Chapter nine

Arnup, K. "'We are family': Lesbian mothers in Canada," *RFR/DRF* 20: 3/4 (1991): 101–107.

Arnup, K. and S. Boyd. "Familial disputes? Sperm donors, lesbian mothers and legal parenthood," in D. Herman and C. Stychin, eds., *Legal inversions: Lesbians, gay men and the politics of law*. Philadelphia: Temple University Press, 1995.

Boyd, Susan. "Lesbian (and gay) custody claims: What difference does difference make?" *Can. J. Fam. L.* 15 (1998): 131.

Bozett, F.W., ed. *Gay and lesbian parents*. Westport: Praeger , 1987.

Gavigan, S. "A parent(ly) knot: Can Heather have two mommies?" in Herman and Stychin, eds. *Legal inversions: Lesbians, gay men and the politics of law*. Philadelphia: Temple University Press, 1995.

Golombok, S., and F. Tasker. "Children in lesbian and gay families: Theories and evidence," in Jess Wells, ed., *Lesbians raising sons*. Los Angeles: Alyson Books, 1997.

Gonsiorek, J.C., and J.D. Weinrich, eds. *Homosexuality: Research implications for public policy*. Newbury Park: Sage Publications, 1991.

Green, R., J.B. Mandel, M.E. Hotvedt, J. Gray, and L. Smith. "Lesbian mothers and their children: A comparison with solo parent heterosexual mothers and their children," *Archives of Sexual Behaviour* 15 (1986): 167–184.

Lahey, K.A. *Are we "persons" yet? Law and sexuality in Canada*. Toronto: University of Toronto Press, 1999.

O'Brien, C., and L. Weir. "Lesbians and gay men inside and outside families," in N. Mandell and A. Duffy, eds., *Canadian families: Diversity, conflict and change*. Toronto: Harcourt Brace, 1995.

Patterson, C.J. "Children of lesbian and gay parents," *Child Development* 63 (1992): 1025–1042.

_____. "Children of the lesbian baby boom: Behavioural adjustment, self concepts and sex role identity," in B. Greene and G.M. Herek, eds., *Lesbian and gay psychology: Theory research and clinical applications*. Newbury Park, California: Sage, 1994.

Slater, S. *The lesbian family life cycle*. New York: The Free Press, 1995.

Chapter ten

Bernstein, Jane, and Laura Stephenson. "Dykes, donors & dry ice: Alternative insemination," in Katherine Arnup, ed., *Lesbian parenting: Living with pride and prejudice*. Charlottetown: Gynergy books, 1997.

Crawford, Sally. "Lesbian families: Psychosocial stress and the family-building process," in Boston Lesbian Psychologies Collective, *Lesbian psychologies*. Chicago: University of Illinois Press, 1987.

Evans, Beverly K. "Mothering as a lesbian issue," in Dolores J. Maggiore, ed., *Lesbians and child custody: A casebook*. New York: Garland Publishing, 1992.

Falk, Patricia J. "Lesbian mothers: Psychosocial assumptions in family law," in Dolores J. Maggiore, ed., *Lesbians and child custody: A casebook*. New York: Garland Publishing, 1992.

Gil de Lamadrid, Maria. "Lesbians choosing motherhood: Legal implications of co-parenting," in Dolores J. Maggiore, ed., *Lesbians and child custody: A casebook*. New York: Garland Publishing, 1992.

Gray, Pamela. "The other mother: A lesbian co-mother's journal," in Sandra Pollack and Jeanne Vaughn, *Politics of the heart: A lesbian parenting anthology*. Ithaca: Firebrand Books, 1987.

Martin, April. *The lesbian and gay parenting handbook: Creating and raising our families*. New York: HarperPerennial, 1993.

Martin, Del, and Phyllis Lyon. *Lesbian/Woman*. New York: Bantam Books, 1972.

McCandlish, Barbara M. "Against all odds: Lesbian other family dynamics," in Dolores J. Maggiore, ed., *Lesbians and child custody: A casebook*. New York: Garland Publishing, 1992.

Muzio, Cheryl. "Lesbian co-parenting: On being/being with the invisible m(other)," *Smith Studies in Social Work, Special Issue, Lesbians and Lesbian Families: Multiple Reflections* 63 (June 1993): 209–213.

Nelson, Fiona. *Lesbian motherhood: An exploration of Canadian lesbian families.* Toronto: University of Toronto Press, 1996.

Pies, Cheri. *Considering parenthood.* Minneapolis: Spinsters Ink, 1988.

Slater, Suzanne. *The lesbian family life cycle.* New York: The Free Press, 1995.

Tortorilla, Toni. "On a creative edge," in Sandra Pollack and Jeanne Vaughn, eds., *Politics of the heart: A lesbian parenting anthology.* Ithaca: Firebrand Books, 1987.

Weston, Kath. *Families we choose: Lesbians, gays, kinship.* New York: Columbia University Press, 1991.

Chapter eleven

Abbey, Sharon, and Andrea O'Reilly. *Redefining motherhood: Changing identities and patterns.* Toronto: Second Story Press, 1998.

Arden, Jann. "Good Mother," *Living under June,* CD 31454 0789 2 (1994, A & M Records, a division of PolyGramGroup Canada, Inc.).

Ballingsley, Andrew. *Black families in white America.* Englewood, Cliffs, New Jersey: Prentice Hall, 1968.

_____, ed. *Climbing Jacob's ladder: The enduring legacy of African American families.* New York: Simon & Schuster, 1992.

Bell-Scott, Patricia, et al., eds. *Double stitch: Black women write about mothers and daughters.* Boston: Beacon, 1991.

Bernard, Wanda Thomas, and Candace Bernard. "Passing the torch: A mother and daughter reflect on their experiences across generations," *Canadian Woman Studies* 18: 2 & 3 (Summer/Fall 1998).

Collins, Patricia Hill. "Shifting the center: Race, class, and feminist theorizing about motherhood," in Evelyn Nakano Glenn, Grace Chang, and Linda Rennie Forcey, eds., *Mothering: Ideology, experience, and agency.* New York: Routledge, 1994.

_____. "The meaning of motherhood in black culture and black mother–daughter relationships," in Patricia Bell-Scott, et al., eds., *Double stitch: Black women write about mothers and daughters.* New York: HarperPerennial, 1993.

_____. *Black feminist thought: Knowledge, consciousness and the politics of empowerment.* New York: Routledge, 1991.

Edelman, Hope. *Motherless daughters: The legacy of loss.* New York: Delta, 1994.

Edwards, Arlene. "Community mothering: The relationship between mothering and the community work of black women," *Journal of the Association for Research on Mothering* 2: 2 (Fall/Winter 2000): 66–84.

Gibson, Priscilla. "Developmental mothering in an African American community: From grandmothers to new mothers again" *Journal of the Association for Research on Mothering* 2: 2 (Fall/Winter 2000): 31–41.

Golden, Marita. *Saving our sons: Raising black children in a turbulent world.* New York: Doubleday, 1995.

Gutman, Herbert. *The black family in slavery and freedom: 1750–1925.* New York: Vintage, 1976.

Hamilton, Sylvia. *Black mother, black daughter*. Video recording. National Film Board of Canada, 1989.

Hirsch, Marianne. *The mother/daughter plot: Narrative, psychoanalysis, feminism*. Bloomington: Indiana University Press, 1989.

Holloway, Karla, and Stephanie Demetrakopoulos. *New dimensions in spirituality: A biracial and bicultural reading of the novels of Toni Morrison*. New York: Greenwood, 1987.

hooks, bell. "Homeplace: A site of resistance," in *Yearning: Race, gender, and cultural politics*. Boston: South End, 1990

_____. "Revolutionary parenting," in *Feminist theory: From margin to center*. Boston: South End, 1984.

James, Stanlie M. "Mothering: A possible black feminist link to social transformation," in Stanlie James and A.P. Busia, eds., *Theorizing black feminism: The visionary pragmatism of black women*. New York: Routledge, 1999.

Jenkins, Nina. "Black women and the meaning of motherhood," in Sharon Abbey and Andrea O'Reilly, eds., *Redefining motherhood: Changing identities and patterns*. Toronto: Second Story Press, 1998.

Johnson, Miriam. *Strong mothers, weak wives: The search for gender equality*. Berkeley: University of California Press, 1988.

Joseph, Gloria I., and Jill Lewis, Eds. *Common differences: Conflicts in black and white feminist perspectives*. Boston: South End, 1981.

Kaplan, Elaine Bell. *Not our kind of girl: Unraveling the myths of black teenage motherhood*. Berkeley: University of California Press, 1997.

King, Joyce Elaine, and Carol Ann Mitchell. *Black mothers to sons: Juxtaposing African American literature with social practice*. New York: Peter Lang, 1995.

Kuwabong, Dannabang. "Reading the Gospel of Bakes: Daughters' representations of mothers in the poetry of Claire Harris and Lorna Goodison," *Canadian Women's Studies* 19: 2 & 3 (Summer/Fall 1998).

Ladner, Joyce. *Tomorrow's tomorrow: The black woman*. New York: Doubleday, 1971.

Lawson, Erica. "Black women's mothering in a historical and contemporary perspective: Understanding the past, forging the future," *Journal of the Association for Research on Mothering* 2: 2 (Fall/Winter 2000): 21–30.

Lee, Claudette and Ethel Wilson. "Masculinity, matriarchy and myth: A black feminist perspective," in Andrea O'Reilly, ed., *Mothers and sons: Feminism, masculinity and the struggle to raise our sons*. New York: Routledge, 2001.

Lorde, Audre. *Sister outsider*. Trumansburg, New York: Crossing Press, 1984.

Lowinsky, Naomi Ruth. *The motherline: Every woman's journey to find her female roots*. Los Angeles: Jeremy P. Tarcher, 1992. [Formerly titled *Stories from the motherline: Reclaiming the mother–daughter bond, finding our feminine Souls*.]

McAdoo, Harriette Pipes. *Family ethnicity: Strength in diversity*. Beverly Hills, C A.: Sage Publications, 1993.

_____. ed. *Black families*. Beverly Hills, C.A.: Sage, 1981.

Morton, Patricia. *Disfigured images: The historical assault on Afro-American women*. Westport, Connecticut: Greenwood Press, 1991.

O'Reilly, Andrea, ed. *Mothers and sons: Feminism, masculinity and the struggle to raise our sons*. New York: Routledge, 2001.

O'Reilly, Andrea, and Sharon Abbey, eds. *Mothers and daughters: Connection, empowerment and transformation*. Rowman and Littlefield, 2000.

Perry, Ruth, and Martine Watson Brownley, eds. *Mothering the mind: Twelve studies of writers and their silent partners*. New York: Holmes and Meier, 1984.

Rainwater, Lee, and William L. Yancey, eds. *The Moynihan report and the politics of controversy*. Cambridge: M.I.T., 1967.

Rich, Adrienne. *Of woman born: Motherhood as experience and institution*. New York: W.W. Norton, 1976.

Ruddick, Sara. *Maternal thinking: Toward a politics of peace*. New York: Ballantine Books, 1989.

Stack, Carol B. *All our kin: Strategies for survival in a black community*. New York: Harper & Row, 1974.

Staples, Robert, and Leanor Boulin. *Black families at the crossroads: Challenges and prospects*. San Francisco: Jossey-Bass, 1993.

Steele, Cassie Premo. "Drawing strengths from our other mothers: Tapping the roots of black history: *Journal of the Association for Research on Mothering* 2: 2 (Fall/Winter 2000): 7–17.

Turnage, Barbara. "The global self-esteem of an African-American adolescent female and her relationship with her mother," in Andrea O'Reilly and Sharon Abbey, eds., *Mothers and daughters: Connection, empowerment and transformation*. Rowman and Littlefield, 2000.

Wade-Gayles, Gloria. *Pushed back to strength: A black woman's journey home*. Boston: Beacon, 1993.

Walker, Alice. "In search of our mothers' gardens," in Alice Walker, *In search of our mothers' gardens*. San Diego: Harcourt Brace Jovanovich, 1983.

Wallace, Michele. *Black macho and the myth of the superwoman*. New York: Dial Press, 1979.

Wane, Njoki Nathani. "Reflections on the mutuality of mothering: Women, children and othermothering," *Journal of the Association for Research on Mothering* 2: 2 (Fall/Winter 2000): 105–116.

Washington, Mary Helen. "I sign my mother's name: Alice Walker, Dorothy West, Paule Marshall," in Ruth Perry and Martine Watson Brownley, eds., *Mothering the mind: Twelve studies of writers and their silent partners*. New York: Holmes and Meier, 1984.

Chapter twelve

Augustine, N.A. "Learnfare and black motherhood: The social construction of deviance," in Adrien Katherine Wing, *Critical race feminism: A reader*. New York: New York University, 1997.

Barriteau, E. "Structural adjustment policies in the Caribbean: A feminist perspective," *NWSA Journal* 8 (1996): 142–156.

Barrow, C. "Finding the support: A study of strategies for survival," *Social and Economic Studies* 35 (1986): 131–76.

Beckles, H. "Sex and gender in the historiography of Caribbean slavery," in V. Shepherd, B. Brereton, and B. Bailey, eds., *Engendering history: Caribbean women in historical perspective.* Kingston: Ian Randle, 1995.

Bolles, L. "Kitchen hit by priorities: Employed working class women Jamaican women confront the IMF," in J. Nash and M. Fernandez Kelly, eds., *Women and men and the international division of labour.* New York: SUNY, 1983.

Bristow, P. "Black women in Buxton and Chatham, 1850–65," in P. Bristow, D. Brand, L. Carty, et al., eds., *We're rooted here and they can't pull us up: Essays in African Canadian women's history.* Toronto: University of Toronto Press, 1994.

Brodber, E. "Afro-Jamaican women at the turn of the century," *Social and Economic Studies* 35 (1986): 23–50.

Carbado, D.W. "Motherhood and work in cultural context: One woman's patriarchal bargain," in Adrien Katherine Wing, ed., *Critical race feminism: A reader.* New York: New York University, 1997.

Collins, P. Hill. *Black feminist thought: Knowledge, consciousness, and the politics of empowerment.* 2nd edition. New York: Routledge, 2000.

Dei, G. "Why write 'black': Reclaiming African cultural resource knowledges in diasporic contexts," in Frank Columbus, ed., *Advances in psychology research.* New York: Nova Science Publishers, 2000.

hooks, b. *Ain't I a woman: Black women and feminism.* Boston: South End Press, 1981.

McAfee, K. *Storm signals: Structural adjustment and development alternative in the Caribbean.* London: Zed, 1991

McLaren, P. "Unthinking whiteness, rethinking democracy: Or farewell to the blonde beast; towards a revolutionary multiculturalism," *Educational Foundations* 11 (1997): 5–37.

Mohanty, C.T. "Under western eyes: Feminist scholarship and colonial discourse," in C.T. Mohanty, A. Russo, and L. Tourres, eds., *Third world women and the politics of feminism.* Indiana: Indiana University Press, 1991.

Morrison, T. *Beloved* New York: Alfred Knopf, 1998.

Pierson, R. "Introduction," in R. Pierson and N. Chadhuri, eds., *Nation, empire, colony: Historicizing gender and race.* Bloomington: Indiana University, 1998.

Roberts, D. *Killing the black body: Race, reproduction, and the meaning of liberty.* New York: Pantheon, 1997a.

_____. "Punishing drug addicts who have babies: Women of colour, equality, and the right of privacy," in Adrien Katherine Wing, ed., *Critical race feminism: A reader.* New York: New York University, 1997b.

Williams, P.J. "Spirit-murdering the messenger: The discourse of fingerpointing as the law's response to racism," in Adrien Katherine Wing, ed., *Critical race feminism: A reader.* New York: New York University, 1997.

Chapter thirteen

Bannister, E. Burman, I. Parker, M. Taylor, C. Tindall. *Qualitative methods in psychology: A research guide.* Philadelphia: Open University Press, 1994.

Barnett, B.A. "Invisible southern black women leaders in the civil rights movement: The triple constraints of gender, race and class," *Gender and Society* 1: 2 (1993): 162–182.

Burks, M.F. "Trailblazers and women in the Montgomery bus boycott," in V.L. Crawford, J.A. Rouse, and B. Woods, eds., *Women in the civil rights movement: Trailblazers and torchbearers 1945–1965*. Indiana University Press, 1990.

Cantrow, E. *Moving the mountain: Women working for social change*. Old Westbury: Feminist Press, 1980.

Collins, Patricia Hill. *Black feminist thought: Knowledge, consciousness and the politics of empowerment*. New York: Routledge, 1991.

_____. "Learning from the outsider within: The sociological significance of black feminist thought," in M.M. Fonow and J.A. Cook, eds., *Beyond methodology: Feminist scholarship as lived research*. Bloomington and Indianapolis: Indiana University Press, 1991b.

_____. "The meaning of motherhood in black culture and black mother/daughter relationships," *Sage: A Scholarly Journal on Black Women* 4: 2 (1987).

Clark-Hine, D. "Lifting the veil, shattering the silence: Black women's history in slavery and freedom," in D. Clark-Hine, ed., *The state of Afro-American history: Past, present, and future*. Baton Rouge: Louisiana State University Press, 1986.

Crawford, V. "Beyond the human self: Grassroots activists in the Mississippi civil rights movement," in V.L. Crawford, J.A. Rouse, and B. Woods, eds., *Women in the civil rights movement: Trailblazers and torchbearers, 1945–1965*. Indiana University Press, 1993.

Dickson, L.F. "Toward a broader angle of vision in uncovering women's history: Black women's clubs revisited," *Frontiers* 9 (1987): 62–68.

Dodson, D.J. "Power and surrogate leadership: Black women and organized religion," *Sage: A Scholarly Journal on Black Women* 5: 2 (Fall 1988): 37–41.

Gilkes, C.A. Townsend. "The roles of church and community mothers: Ambivalent American sexism or fragmented African familyhood?" *Journal of Feminist Studies in Religion* 2: 1 (1986): 41–59.

_____. "Together and in harness: women's traditions in the sanctified church. *Signs: A Journal of Women in Culture and Society* 10: 4 (1985): 678–695.

_____. "Going up for the oppressed: Career mobility of black women community workers." *Journal of Social Issues* 39: 3 (1983): 115–139.

_____. "Holding back the ocean with a broom: Black women and community work," in La Frances Rodgers-Rose, ed., *The Black Women*. Beverley Hills: Sage Publications, 1980.

_____. "The role of women in the sanctified church," *The Journal of Religious Thought* 32: 1 (1975).

Glaser, B.G., and A.L. Strauss. *The discovery of grounded theory: Strategies for qualitative research*. New York: Aldine De Gruyter, 1967.

Grant, J. *White women's Christ and black women's Jesus: Feminist Christology and womanist response*. Atlanta, Georgia: Scholar's Press, 1989a.

_____. "Womanist theology: Black women's experience as a source for doing theology, with special reference to Christology," in G.S. Wilmore, ed., *African-American religious studies: An interdisciplinary anthology*. Durham: Duke University Press, 1989b.

Green, B.A. "What has gone before: The legacy of racism and sexism in the lives of black mothers and daughters," in L. Brown and M. Root, eds., *Diversity and complexity in feminist therapy*. The Haworth Press, 1990.

Harley, S. "Beyond the classroom: The organizational lives of black female educators in the District of Columbia, 1890–1930," *Journal of Negro Education* 51: 3 (1982): 254–269.

James, S.M. "Mothering: A possible black feminist link to social transformation," in S.M. James and A.A Busia, eds., *Theorizing black feminisms: The visionary pragmatism of black women*. New York: Routledge, 1993.

Jones, B.W. "Race, sex and class: Black female tobacco workers in Durham North Carolina, 1920–1940 and the development of female consciousness," *Feminist Studies* 10: 3 (1984): 441–453.

Kendrick, R.M. "They also serve: The National Association of Colored Women, Inc." *The Negro History Bulletin* 17 (1954): 171–175.

Lerner, G. "Early community work of black clubwomen," *Journal of Negro History* 59 (1974): 359–364.

Levin, J.S., and R.J. Taylor. "Gender and age differences in religiosity among black Americans," *The Gerontologist* 33: 1 (1993): 16–23.

Lincoln, C.E., and L.H. Mamiya. *The black church in the African-American experience*. Durham: Duke University Press, 1990.

Marshall, C.B. The black church: Its mission is liberation," *The Black Scholar* (December 1970): 13–19.

Morrison, J.D. "The black church as a support system for black elderly," *Journal of Gerontological Social Work* (1971): 105–120.

Murray, S.R. and Harrison, D.D. "Black women and the future," *Psychology of Women Quarterly* 6: 1 (Fall 1981), 113–122.

Omolade, B. *The rising song of African-American women*. New York: Routledge, 1994.

Orleck, A. "Radical mothers in international perspective," in A. Jetter, A. Orleck, and D. Taylor, eds., *The politics of motherhood: Activist voices from left to right*. Hanover: University Press of New England, 1997.

Payne, C.E. "Ella Baker and models of social change," *Signs: A Journal of Women in Culture and Society* 14: 4 (1989): 885–899.

Peebles-Wilkins, W. *Black women and American social welfare: The life of Fredericka Douglass*. Affilia 4 1989.

Reagon, B.J. "Women as culture carriers in the civil rights movement: Fannie Lou Hamer," in V.L. Crawford, J.A. Rouse, and B. Woods, eds., *Women in the civil rights movement: Trailblazers and torchbearers 1945–1965*. Indiana University Press, 1990.

Reagon, B.J. "African diaspora women: The making of cultural carriers," in R. Terborg-Penn, S. Harley, and A. Benton Rushing, eds., *Women in Africa and the African diaspora*. Washington, D.C.: Howard University Press, 1987.

Shaw. "Black club women and the creation of the National Association of Coloured Women," *Journal of Women's History* 3: 2 (1911), 10–25.

Troester, R.R. "Turbulence and tenderness: Mothers, daughters and 'othermothers' in Paule Marshall's *Brown Girl Brownstones,*" *Sage: A Scholarly Journal on Black Women* 1: 12 (Fall 1984), 12–17.

Williams, C., and Williams, H.B. "Contemporary voluntary associations in the urban black church: The development and growth of mutual aid societies," *Journal of Voluntary Action Research* (1997): 19–29.

Chapter fourteen

Cole, Johnetta, and B. Johnetta. *Conversations: Straight talk with America's sister president.* New York: Doubleday, 1993.

Collins, Patricia Hill. *Black feminist thought: Knowledge, consciousness, and the politics of empowerment.* Boston: Unwin Hyman, 1990.

Gill-Austern, Brita L. "Love understood as self-sacrifice and self-denial: What does it do to women?" in Jeanne Stevenson Moessner, ed., *Through the eyes of women.* Minneapolis: Fortress Press, 1996.

Joseph, Gloria, and Jill Lewis. *Common differences: Conflicts in black and white feminist perspectives.* New York: Anchor Books, 1981.

March, Kathryn. "Childbirth with fear," in Maureen Reddy, Martha Roth, and Amy Sheldon, eds., *Mother Journeys: Feminists write about mothering.* Minneapolis: Spinsters Inc., 1994.

Miller-McLemore, Bonnie. *Also a mother: Work and family as theological dilemma.* Nashville: Abington Press, 1994.

Parker, Rozsika. *Mother love, mother hate: The power of maternal ambivalence.* New York: Basic Books, 1995.

Ruddick, Sara. *Maternal thinking: Towards a politics of peace.* Boston: Beacon, 1995.

Silverstein, Shel. *The giving tree.* New York: HarperCollins, 1964.

Snorton, Teresa E. "The legacy of the African-American matriarch: New perspectives for pastoral care," in Jeanne Stevenson Moessner, ed., *Through the eyes of women.* Minneapolis: Fortress Press, 1996.

Stein, Edith. "Essays on woman," in L. Gelber and R. Leuven, eds., *The collected works of Edith Stein.* Washington, D.C.: ICS Publications, 1996.

Chapter fifteen

Bernard, Wanda, and Bernard, Candace. "Passing the torch. A mother and daughter reflect on experiences across generation," *Canadian Women's Studies* 18: 2 & 3 (Summer/Fall 1998): 46–50.

Collins, Patricia Hill. "Black women and motherhood," in Patricia Hill Collins, ed., *Black feminist thought; Knowledge, consciousness and the politics of empowerment.* New York: Routledge, 2000.

Emeagwali, Gloria T., ed. *Women pay the price: Structural adjustment in Africa and the Caribbean.* Trenton, New Jersey. African World Press, Inc, 1995.

Fineman, Martha Albertson, and Karpin, Isabel, eds. *Mothers in law: Feminist theory and the legal regulation of motherhood*. New York: Columbia University Press, 1995.

Fineman, Martha. "Images of Mothers in Poverty Discourse," in Martha Fineman and Isabel Karpin, *Mothers in law: Feminist theory and the legal regulation of motherhood*. New York: Columbia University Press, 1995.

James, Stanlie M. "Mothering: A possible black feminist link to social transformation," in Stanlie James and A.P. Busia, *Theorizing black feminism: The visionary pragmatism of black women*. Routledge, 1997.

Kenyatta, Jomo. *Facing Mount Kenya: The tribal life of the Gikuyu*. London, UK: Mercury Books, 1965.

Kline, Marlee. "Complicating the ideology of motherhood: Child welfare law and First Nation women," in Martha Albertson Fineman and Isabel Karpin, eds. *Mothers in law: Feminist theory and the legal regulation of motherhood*. New York: Columbia University Press, 1995.

Nathani, Njoki. "Sustainable development: Indigenous forms of food processing technologies: A Kenyan case study," Unpublished Dissertation, University of Toronto, 1996.

Mwagiru, W. and Ouko, Riria. "Women in development," in Ahamed I Salim, ed., *Kenya at a glance*. Nairobi. Colorprint Ltd., 1989.

Ogundipe-Leslie, Molara. "African women, culture and another development," in *Recreating ourselves: African women and critical transformations*. Trenton: Africa World Press, 1994.

Omolade, Barbara. "'Making sense': Notes for studying black teen mothers," in Martha Albertson Fineman and Isabel Karpin, eds. *Mothers in law: Feminist theory and the legal regulation of motherhood*. New York: Columbia University Press, 1995.

Robert, Dorothy. "Racism and patriarchy in the meaning of motherhood," in Martha Albertson Fineman and Karpin, Isabel, eds., *Mothers in law: Feminist theory and the legal regulation of motherhood*. New York: Columbia University Press, 1995.

Shiva, Vandana. *Staying alive: Women, ecology and development*. London: Zed, 1990.

Slaughter, M.M. "The legal construction of 'Mother,'" in Martha Albertson Fineman and Karpin, Isabel, eds. *Mothers in law: Feminist theory and the legal regulation of motherhood*. New York: Columbia University Press, 1995.

Stamp, Patricia. *Technology, gender, and power in Africa*. Ottawa: IDRC, 1992.

Wane, Njoki. "Indigenous knowledge: Lessons from the elders: A Kenyan case study," in George Dei, Budd Hall, and Dorothy Rosenberg, eds., *Indigenous knowledge in global context: Multiple readings of our world*. Toronto: University of Toronto Press, 2000.

Wane, Nathani Njoki, and Aferakan T. "Introduction: Theorizing black feminism," in Njoki N. Wane and T. Aferakan, eds., *Theorizing black feminism: A critical reader*. Toronto. Canadian Scholars' Press, forthcoming.

Chapter sixteen

Rich, Adrienne. *Of woman born: Motherhood as experience and institution*. New York: W.W. Norton, 1986.

Badinter, Elizabeth. *Mother love: Myth and reality*. New York: MacMillan Publishing Co., Inc., 1980.

Brown, Lyn Mikel, and Carol Gilligan. *Meeting at the crossroads: Women's psychology and girls' development*. Cambridge, MA: Harvard University Press, 1992.

Caplan, Paula. *Don't blame mother: Mending the mother–daughter relationship*. New York: Harper and Row, 1989.

Chodorow, Nancy. *Feminism and psychoanalytic theory*. New Haven: Yale University Press, 1989.

_____. *The reproduction of mothering: Psychoanalysis and the sociology of gender*. Berkeley: University of California Press, 1978.

Daly, Brenda, and Maureen Reddy. *Narrating mothers: Theorizing maternal subjectivities*. Knoxville: University of Tennessee Press, 1991.

Debold, Elizabeth, Marie Wilson, and Idelisse Malavé. *Mother daughter revolution: From good girls to great women*. New York: Bantam Books, 1994.

de Waal, Mieke. "Teenage daughters on their mothers," in Janneke van Mens-Verhulst, Karlein Schreurs, and Liesbeth Woertman, eds., *Daughtering and mothering*. New York: Routledge, 1993.

Dinnerstein, Dorothy. *The mermaid and the minotaur: Sexual arrangements and the human malaise*. New York: Harper Colophon, 1976.

Dixon, Penelope. *Mothers and mothering: An annotated bibliography*. New York: Garland Publishing, 1991.

Edelman, Hope. *Motherless daughters: The legacy of loss*. New York: Delta, 1994.

Heilbrun, Carolyn. *Writing a woman's life*. New York: Ballantine, 1988.

Hirsch, Marianne. *The mother/daughter plot: Narrative, psychoanalysis, feminism*. Bloomington: Indiana University Press, 1989.

Hite, Shere. *The Hite report on the family*. New York: Grove Press, 1994.

Jackson, Marni. *The mother zone: Love, sex, and laundry in the modern family*. Toronto: Macfarlane Walter and Ross, 1992.

Johnson, Miriam. *Strong mothers, weak wives: The search for gender equality*. Berkeley: University of California Press, 1989.

Kristeva, Julia. *Revolution in poetic language*. Margaret Walker, trans. New York: Columbia University Press, 1984.

Lorde, Audre. "Poetry is not a luxury," in Audre Lorde, *Sister outsider*. New York: Quality Paper Back Club, Triangle Classics, 1993.

Lowinsky, Naomi Ruth. *Stories from the motherline: Reclaiming the mother–daughter bond, finding our female souls*. Los Angles: Jeremy P. Tarcher, 1992.

Luxton, Meg. *More than a labour of love*. Toronto: The Women's Press, 1980.

Mann, Judy. *The difference: Growing up female in America*. New York: Time Warner, 1994.

O'Reilly, Andrea. "'Ain't that love?': Anti-racism and racial constructions of motherhood," in Maureen Reddy, ed., *Everyday acts against racism: Raising children in a multiracial world*. Washington: Seal Press, 1996a.

_____. "'In search of my mother's garden, I found my own': Motherlove, healing and identity in Toni Morrison's *Jazz*," *African American Review* 30: 3 (1996b).

_____. "Talking back in mother tongue: A feminist course on mothering and motherhood," in Paula Bourne et al., eds., *Feminism and education*. Toronto: CWSE Press, 1994.

Pipher, Mary. *Reviving Ophelia: Saving the selves of adolescent girls*. New York: Grosset/Putnam, 1994.

Ruddick, Sara. *Maternal thinking: Toward a politic of peace*. New York: Ballantine Books, 1989.

Thurer, Shari L. *The myths of motherhood: How culture reinvents the good mother*. New York: Penguin Books, 1994.

Westkott, Marcia. "Mothers and daughters in the world of the father," *Frontiers* 3: 2 (1978).

Woertman, Liesbeth. "Mothering in context: Female subjectives and intervening practices," in Janneke van Mens-Verhulst, Karlein Schreurs, and Liesbeth Woertman, eds., *Daughtering and mothering*. New York: Routledge, 1993.

Woolf, Virginia. *A room of one's own*. New York: Granada, 1977 [1929].

Chapter seventeen

Armsden, Gay C., and Mark T. Greenberg, "The inventory of parent and peer attachment individual differences and their relationship to psychological well-being in adolescence," *Journal of Youth and Adolescence* 16: 5 (1987): 427–54.

Bates, Daisy L. "I did not really understand what it meant to be a negro," in G. Lerner, ed., *Black women in white America: A documentary history*. New York: Vintage Books, 1973.

Bogan, Jeffrey. "The assessment of self-esteem: A cautionary note," *Australian Psychologist* 23: 3 (1988): 383–89.

Bond, Selena, and Thomas F. Cash. "Black beauty: Skin color and body images among African-American college women," *Journal of Applied Social Psychology* 22: 11 (1992).

Bowlby, John. "Attachment and loss: Retrospect and prospect," *American Journal of Orthopsychiatry* 52: 4 (1982): 664–78.

Cash, Thomas F. *The multidimensional body-self relations questionnaire manual*. Norfolk, Va.: Old Dominion University, 1994.

Church, Vivian. *Colors around me*. Chicago: Afro-American, 1971/1993.

Colin, V.L. *Human Attachment*. Philadelphia: Temple University Press, 1996.

Easton, Deborah. *Color me proud*. Milwaukee: Identity Toys, 1994.

Greene, Beverly A. "What has gone before: The legacy of racism and sexism in the lives of black mothers and daughters," *Women and Therapy* 9: 1 & 2 (1990a): 207–30.

_____. "Sturdy bridges: The role of African-American mothers in the socialization of African-American children," *Women and Therapy* 10: 1 & 2 (1990b): 205–25.

Grier, W.H., and P.M. Cobbs. *Black Rage*. 2nd edn. New York: Basic Books, 1992.

Hammer, S. *Daughters and mothers: Mothers and daughters*. New York: Quadrangle/New York Times, 1976.

Hare, Bruce R. "Self-perception and academic achievement: Variations in a desegregated setting," *American Journal of Psychiatry* 137: 6 (1980): 683–89.

Hill Collins, Patricia. *Black feminist thought: Knowledge, consciousness and the politics of empowerment*. New York: Routledge, 1991.

Joseph, Joanne M. *The resilient child: Preparing today's youth for tomorrow's world*. New York: Plenum, 1994.

Karen, Robert. "Becoming attached," *Atlantic Monthly* (February 1990): 35–70.

Lykes, M.B. "Discrimination and coping in the lives of black women: Analyses of oral history data," *Journal of Social Issues* 39: 3 (1983): 79–100.

Makkar, Jalmeen K., and Michael J. Strube. "Black women's self-perceptions of attractiveness following exposure to white versus black beauty standards: The moderating role of racial identity and self-esteem," *Journal of Applied Social Psychology* 25: 17 (1995): 1547–66.

McKay, Judith. "Building self-esteem in children," in Matthew McKay and Patrick Fanning, eds., *Self-Esteem*. Oakland, CA: New Harbinger, 1987.

Mruk, C. *Self-esteem research, theory, and practice*. New York: Springer, 1995.

Phinney, Jean S. "The multigroup ethnic identity measure: A new scale for use with diverse groups," *Journal of Adolescent Research* 7: 2 (1992).

Plummer, Deborah. "Patterns of racial identity development of African-American adolescent males and females," *Journal of Black Psychology* 21: 2 (1995): 168–80.

Pyant, Carlton T., and Barbara J. Yanico. "Relationship of racial identity and gender-role attitudes of black women's psychological well-being," *Journal of Counseling Psychology* 38: 3 (1991): 315–22.

Rosenberg, Morris. *Society and the adolescent self-image*. Princeton, N.J.: Princeton University Press, 1965.

Rucker, Clifford E., and Thomas F. Cash, "Body images, body size-perceptions, and eating behaviors among African-American and white college women," *International Journal of Eating Disorders* 12: 3 (1992): 292.

Silber, Earle, and Jean S. Tippett. "Self-esteem: Clinical assessment and measurement validation," *Psychological Reports* 16 (1965): 1017–71.

Singh, Devendra. "Body fat distribution and perception of desirable female body shape by young black men and women," *International Journal of Eating Disorders* 16: 3 (1994): 289–94.

Smith, Althea, and Abigail J. Stewart. "Approaches to studying racism and sexism in black women's lives," *Journal of Social Issues* 39: 3 (1983): 1–15.

Stevenson, Jr., Howard C. "Validation of the scale of racial socialization for African-American adolescents: Steps toward multidimensionality," *Journal of Black Psychology* 20: 4 (1994): 445–68.

Thompson, Vetta L. Sanders. "Socialization to race and its relationship to racial identification among African-Americans," *Journal of Black Psychology* 20: 2 (1994): 175–88.

Wade, T.J. "Race and sex differences in adolescent self-perceptions of physical attractiveness and level of self-esteem during early and late adolescence," *Personality Individual Differences* 12: 12 (1991).

Wade, T.J., V. Thompson, A. Tashakkori, and E. Valente. "A longitudinal analysis of sex by race differences in predictors of adolescent self-esteem," *Personality Individual Differences* 10: 7 (1989).

Chapter eighteen

American Psychiatric Association. *Diagnostic and statistical manual of mental disorders IV.* Washington, D.C.: American Psychiatric Association, 1994.

Caplan, Paula. *Call Me Crazy.* 1996. Script copyrighted by and available from author.

_____. *They say you're crazy: How the world's most powerful psychiatrists decide who's normal.* Reading, Mass.: Addison-Wesley, 1995.

_____. *Don't blame mother: Mending the mother–daughter relationship.* New York: HarperCollins, 1989

Caplan, Paula, and Ian Hall-McCorquodale. "Mother-blaming in major clinical journals," *American Journal of Orthopsychiatry* 55 (1985a): 345–53.

_____. "The scapegoating of others: A call for change," *American Journal of Orthopsychiatry* 55 (1985b): 610–13.

Herrenkohl, Roy C., Brenda P. Egolf, and Ellen C. Herrenkohl. "Preschool antecedents of adolescent assaultive behavior: A longitudinal study," *American Journal of Orthopsychiatry* 67 (1997): 422–32.

Hochschild, Arlie. "A review of sex role research," in Joan Huber, ed., *Changing women in a changing society.* Chicago: University of Chicago Press, 1973.

Siegel, Rachel Josefowitz. "Old women as mother figures," in Jane Price and Ellen Cole, eds., *Woman-defined motherhood.* New York: Harrington Park, 1990.

Chapter nineteen

Lowinsky, Naomi Ruth. "Anasazi woman," *Psychological Perspectives* 19: 1 (Spring–Summer 1988).

Chapter twenty

Childress, Alice. "When the rattle snake sounds," in D.S. Strickland, ed., *Listen children: An anthology of black literature.* Toronto: Bantam Skylark, 1982.

Cocks, J. "Domestic service and education for domesticity: The incorporation of Xhosa women into colonial society," in Cherryl Walker, ed., *Women and gender in Southern Africa to 1945.* Claremont, South Africa: David Philip Publishers, 1990.

Collins, P. Hill. *Black feminist thought: Knowledge consciousness and the politics of empowerment.* New York: Routledge, 1991.

_____. "The meaning of motherhood in black culture and black mother/daughter relationships," *Sage: A Scholarly Journal on Black Women* 4: 2 (1987): 3–9.

Gaitskell, D. "Devout domesticity? A century of African women's Christianity in South Africa," in Cherryl Walker, ed., *Women and gender in Southern Africa to 1945.* Cape Town: David Philip Publishers, 1990.

_____. "Upward all and play the game: The Girl Wayfarers' Association in Transvaal, 1925–1975," P. Kallway, ed., *Apartheid and education: The education of black South Africans.* Johannesburg: Raven Press, 1984.

Goldberg, D.T. *Racist culture philosophy and the politics of meaning*. Cambridge: Blackwell, 1993.

Goodwin, June. *Cry Amadla! South African women and the question of power*. London: Africana Publishing Company, 1984.

Gunner, Liz, and Mafika Gwala. *Musho! Zulu popular praises*. East Lansing: Michigan State University Press, 1991.

Hartshorne, K. *Crisis and challenge: Black education, 1910–1990*. Cape Town: Oxford University Press, 1992.

hooks, bell. *Yearning race, gender and cultural politics*. Toronto: Between the Lines, 1990.

Jensen, J.D. "Curriculum as a political phenomenon: Historical reflections on black south African education," *Journal of Negro Education* 59: 2 (1990a): 195–206.

_____. "In search of liberation pedagogy in South Africa," *Journal of Education* 172: 2 (1990b): 78–87.

Lipman, Beata. *We make freedom, women in South Africa*. London: Pandora Press, 1984.

Marks, S. *Not either an experimental doll: The separate worlds of three South African women*. Pietermaritzburg: University of Natal Press, 1987.

_____. *The ambiguities of dependence in South Africa: Class, nationalism and the state in twentieth-century Natal*. Baltimore: Johns Hopkins University Press, 1986.

Marshall, Paule. *Praisesong for the widow*. New York: Putnam, 1983.

McLaughlin, Andree Nicola. "A renaissance of the spirit: Black women remaking the universe," in Joanne M. Braxton and Andree Nicola McLaughlin, eds., *Wild women in the world wind: Afra-American culture and the contemporary literary renaissance*. New Jersey: Rutgers University Press, 1990.

Meintjes, Sheila. "Family and gender in the Christian community at Edendale," in Cherryl Walker, ed., *Women and gender in Southern Africa to 1945*. Cape Town: David Philip, 1990.

Mogadime, Dolana. "The work of South African-Canadian educator Goodie Tshabalala Mogadime," *Canadian Women Studies* 17: 4 (1998): 98–102.

Nkomo, M.O. *Student culture and activism in black South African universities: The roots of resistance*. London: Greenwook, 1984.

Ravell-Pinto, Thelma M. "Women's writing and the politics of South Africa: The ambiguous role of Nadine Gordimer," in Carole Boyce Davies, ed., *Moving beyond boundaries: Volume 2*. New York: New York University Press, 1995.

Rogers, B. *South Africa: The "Bantu homelands"*. London: International Defence and Aid Fund, 1972.

Russell, Diana. E.H. *Lives of courage: Women for a new South Africa*. New York: Basic Books, 1989.

Shange, Ntozake. *For coloured girls who have considered suicide/when the rainbow is enuf*. New York: Macmillan, 1975.

Troup, Freda. *Forbidden pastures: Education under apartheid*. London: International Defence and Aid Fund for Southern Africa, 1976.

Walker, Alice. *In search of our mothers' gardens*. New York: Harcourt Brace Jovanovich, 1983.

Wilentz, Gay. *Binding cultures: Black women writers in Africa and the diaspora*. Bloomington: Indiana University Press, 1992.

Chapter twenty-one

Althusser, Louis. "Ideology and ideological state apparatuses," in B. Brewster, trans., *Lenin and philosophy and other essays*, New York: Monthly Review Press, 1971.

Arcana, Judith. *Every mother's son: The role of mothers in the making of men*. New York: Anchor Press/Doubleday, 1983.

Bly, Robert. *Iron John*. New York: Vintage, 1990.

Chodorow, Nancy. *The reproduction of mothering: Psychoanalysis and the sociology of gender*. Berkeley: University of California Press, 1978.

Collins, Patricia Hill. "Shifting the center: Race, class and feminist theorizing about motherhood," in Evelyn Nakano Glenn, Grace Chang, and Linda Rennie Forcey, eds., *Mothering: Ideology, experience, and agency*. New York: Routledge, 1994.

_____. "The meaning of motherhood in black culture and black mother–daughter relationships," in Patricia Bell-Scott and Beverly Guy-Sheftall, eds., *Double stitch: Black women write about mothers and daughters*. New York: HarperPerennial, 1993.

_____. *Black feminist thought: Knowledge, consciousness and the politics of empowerment*. New York: Unwin Hyman/Routledge, 1990.

Dinnerstein, Dorothy. *The mermaid and the minotaur: Sexual arrangements and human malaise*. New York: Harper & Row, 1977.

Forcey, Linda Rennie. *Mothers of sons: Toward an understanding of responsibility*, New York: Praeger, 1987.

Friday, Nancy. *My mother/my self: The daughter's search for identity*. New York: Delacorte Press, 1977.

Golden, Marita. *Saving our sons: Raising black children in a turbulent world*. New York: Anchor Books/Doubleday, 1995.

Johnson, Miriam. *Strong mothers, weak wives*. Los Angeles: University of California Press, 1988.

King, Joyce Elaine, and Carolyn Ann Mitchell. *Black mothers to sons: Juxtaposing African-American literature with social practice*. New York: Peter Lang, 1995.

Lorde, Audre. "Man child: A black lesbian feminist's response," in Audre Lorde, *Sister outsider*. New York: Quality Paperback Book Club, 1995.

Moynihan, Daniel P. *The negro family: The case for national action*. Washington, D.C.: U.S. Department of Labor, Office of Policy Planning and Research, 1965.

O'Reilly, Andrea. "'I come from a long line of uppity irate black women': African-American feminist thought on motherhood, the motherline and the mother–daughter relationship," in Andrea O'Reilly and Sharon Abbey, eds., *Mothers and daughters: Connection, empowerment, and transformation*. Lanham, Maryland: Rowman and Littlefield, 2000.

_____. "Across the divide: Contemporary Anglo-American feminist theory on the mother–daughter relationship," in Sharon Abbey and Andrea O'Reilly, eds., *Redefining motherhood: Changing identities and patterns*. Toronto: Second Story Press, 1998a.

_____. "Mothers, daughters and feminism today: Empowerment, agency, narrative," *Canadian Women's Studies* 18: 2&3 (Summer/Fall 1998b): 16–21.

_____. "'Ain't that love?': Antiracism and racial constructions of mothering," in Maureen Reddy, *Everyday acts against racism*. Seattle: Seal Press, 1996.

O'Reilly, Andrea, and Sharon Abbey, eds. *Mothers and daughters: Connection, empowerment, and transformation*. New York: Rowman and Littlefield, 2000.

Pollack, William. *Real boys: Rescuing our sons from the myths of boyhood*. New York: Random House, 1998.

Rich, Adrienne. *Of woman born: Motherhood as experience and institution*. New York: W.W. Norton, 1986.

Ruddick, Sara. *Maternal thinking: Toward a politics of peace*. New York: Ballantine Books, 1989.

Silverstein, Olga, and Beth Rashbaum. *The courage to raise good men*. Viking: New York, 1994.

Smith, Babette. *Mothers and sons: The truth about mother–son relationships*. Sydney: Allen & Unwin, 1995.

Walkerdine, Valerie, and Helen Lucey. *Democracy in the kitchen: Regulating mothers and socializing daughters*. London: Virago Press, 1989.

Wallace, Michele. *Black macho and the myth of the superwoman*. New York: Verso, 1990 [1979].

Wylie, Philip. *A generation of vipers*. New York: Rinehart & Company, 1942.

Chapter twenty-two

Bernard, Wanda Thomas, and Bernard, Candace. "Creative intervention: An Africentric approach to family support services," *The Youth in Care Journal* 13: 1 (1999)

_____. "Passing the torch: A mother and daughter reflect on their experience across generations," *Canadian Women's Studies* 18: 2 & 3 (1998).

Bernard, Wanda Thomas. "Survival and success: As defined by black men in Sheffield, England and Halifax, Canada." Unpublished Doctoral Thesis, University of Sheffield, 1996.

Bryan, Agnes. "Working with black single mothers: Myths and reality," in Mary Longan and Lesley Day, *Women oppression and social work*. London: Routledge, 1992.

Collins, Patricia Hill. *Black feminist thought*. New York and London: Routledge, 1990.

Edwards, A. "Black mothers community mothers." Paper presented at the Mothering in the African Diaspora Conference, York University, Toronto, February 2000.

Franklin, C.W. "Black male–black female conflict: Individually caused and culturally nurtured," *Journal of Black Studies* 15: 2 (1984), 139–154.

Higginbotham, Elizabeth. "Two representative issues in contemporary sociological work on black women," in Hull et al., eds., *But some of us are brave*. New York: The Feminist Press, 1982.

Hutchinson, Earl Ofari. *Black fatherhood II*. Los Angeles, CA: Middle Passage Press, 1994.

_____. *The assassination of the black male image*. Los Angeles, CA: Middle Passage Press, 1992.

Lather, P. "Feminist perspectives on empowering research methodologies," *Women's Studies International Forum* 11: 6 (1988): 569–581.

McAdoo, H. "Black mothers and the extended family support networks," in L.F. Rodgers-Rose, ed., *The black woman*. Beverley Hills, CA: Sage Publications, 1980.

McCray, Carrie Allen. "The Black woman and family roles," in L.F. Rodgers-Rose, ed., *The black woman*. Beverley Hills, CA: Sage Publications, 1980.

Neverdon-Morton, Cynthia. *Afro-American women of the south and the advancement of the race, 1895–1925*. Knoxville: The University of Tennessee Press, 1989.

Rainwater, L. and W. Yancey. *The Moynihan report and the politics of controversy*. Cambridge, MA: MIT Press, 1967.

Stack, C.B. *All our kin—Strategies for survival in a black community*. New York: Harper and Row, 1974.

Staples, Robert. "Masculinity and race: The dual dilemma of black men," *Journal of Social Issues* 34: 1 (1978): 169–183.

Symonds, Terry. "Black mens' roles in preserving the family." *Preserving the black family: Conference proceedings*. Halifax, Canada: Association of Black Social Worker, 1988.

Taylor, R., L. Chatters, B. Tucker, and E. Lewis. "Developments in research on black families: A decade in review." *Journal of Marriage and The Family* 52 (November 1990): 993–1014.

Chapter twenty-three

Beail, N., and J. McGuire. *Fathers: Psychological perspectives*. London: Junction Books, 1982.

Biddulph, S. *Manhood: A book about setting men free*. Sydney: Finch Publishing, 1994.

Blendis, J. "Men's experience of their own fathers," in N. Beail and J. McGuire, *Fathers: Psychological perspectives*. London: Junction Books, 1982.

Bly, R. *Iron John*. Reading, MA: Addison-Wesley, 1990.

Brannen, J., and P. Moss. "Fathers in dual-earner households through mothers' eyes," in C. Lewis and M. O'Brien, eds., *Reassessing fatherhood*. London: Sage, 1987.

Christian, H. *The making of anti sexist men*. London: Routledge, 1994

Cole, J. "Raising sons," *Ms.* (Nov./Dec. 1993): 42–44.

Coltrane, S. *Family man: Fatherhood, housework and gender equity*. New York: Oxford University Press, 1996.

Daly, K. "Uncertain terms: The social construction of fatherhood," in M. Dietz, R. Prus, and W. Shaffir, eds., *Doing everyday life: Ethnography as human lived experience*. Toronto: Copp Clark Longman, 1994.

Demos, K. "The changing faces of fatherhood: A new exploration in American family history," in S. Cath, C. Gurwitt, and J. Ross, eds., *Father and child: Developmental and clinical perspectives*. Boston: Little, Brown, 1982.

Enders, L. "Feminism and mothering of sons," *Feminism and Psychology* 6 (1996): 127–128.

Farber, B. "Marital integration as a factor in parent–child relations," *Child Development* 33 (1962): 1–14.

Greenson, R. "Disidentifying from the mother: Its special importance for the boy," *International Journal of Psychoanalysis* 49 (1968): 370–374.

Hartley, R. "Sex-role pressures and the socialisation of the male child," *Psychological Reports* 5 (1959): 457–468.

Hochschild, A., and A. Machung. *The second shift: Working parents and the revolution at home*. New York: Viking Press, 1989.

Illich, I. *Gender*. London: Marion Boyars, 1983.

Jay, E. "Birthdays. Gaydays," *Feminism and Psychology* 6 (1996): 121–123.

Komarovsky, M. *Women in the modern world: Their education and their dilemmas*. Boston: little, Brown, 1953.

Lewis, C. *Becoming a father*. Buckingham: Open University Press, 1986.

Lewis, C., and M. O'Brien, eds. *Reassessing fatherhood*. London: Sage, 1987.

Livingstone, S. "Rethinking the Oedipal complex: 'Why can't I have babies like Mummy?'" *Feminism and Psychology* 6 (1996): 111–113.

Lynn, D. "The process of earning parental and sex-role identification," *Journal of Marriage and the Family* 28 (1966): 466–470.

Maccoby, E., and C. Jacklin. *The psychology of sex differences*. Stanford: Stanford University Press, 1974.

Maccoby E., ed. *The development of sex differences*. Stanford: Stanford University Press, 1966.

McBride, B., and J. Darragh. "Interpreting the data on father involvement implications for parenting programs for men," *Families in Society* (1995): 490–497.

McGuire, J. "Sons and daughters," in A. Phoenix, A. Woollett, and E. Lloyd, eds., *Motherhood: Meanings, practices and ideologies*, 1991.

McLaren, A. "Working with and against male-dominated culture," *Feminism and Psychology* 6 (1996): 124–126.

Parke, R. *Fatherhood*. Cambridge, MA: Harvard University Press, 1996.

Pleck, J. "American fathering in historical perspective," in M. Kimmel, ed., *Changing men: New directions in research on men and masculinity*, edited by M. Kimmel. Newbury Park: Sage, 1987.

Rich, A. *Of woman born: Motherhood as experience and institution*. London: Virago, 1977.

Rowland, R., and A.M. Thomas. "Mothering sons: A crucial feminist challenge." *Feminism and Psychology* 6 (1996): 93–154.

Ryan, T. "Roots of masculinity," in A. Metcalf and M. Humphries, *The sexuality of men*. London: Pluto Press, 1985.

Segal, L. *Slow motion: Changing masculinities, changing men*. London: Virago, 1990.

Silverstein, O., and B. Rashbaum. *The courage to raise good men*. London: Penguin, 1994.

Spock, B. *Baby and child care*. New York: Duell, Sloan and Pearce, 1945.

Thiele, B. "Ewan—It means 'heart and mind' and heart comes first," *Feminism and Psychology* 6 (1996): 100–102.

Thomas, A.M. "Survival strategies for women in the transition to parenthood: Resisting the myths of motherhood." Paper presented at the Annual Conference of the Association for Research on Mothering, Brock University, St. Catharine's, Ontario, October 1999.

———. "'Men behaving badly?' A psychosocial exploration of the cultural context of sexual harassment," in A.M. Thomas and C. Kitzinger, eds., *Sexual harassment: Contemporary feminist perspectives*. Buckingham: Open University Press, 1997.

_____. "'Boys will be boys?' Resisting the myth of 'essential masculinity,'" *Feminism and Psychology* 6 (1996): 114–117.

Wood, J. "Boys will be boys," *New Socialist* (May/June 1982): 41–43.

Wylie, P. *Generation of vipers*. New York: Rinehart, 1942.

Chapter twenty-four

Bergman, S.J., and J.L Surrey. "Couples therapy: A relational approach," in *Work in Progress, No. 66*. Wellesley, MA: Stone Center Working Paper Series, 1992.

_____. "Men's psychological development: A relational perspective." In *Work in Progress, No. 48*. Wellesley, MA: Stone Center Working Paper Series, 1991.

Boston Public Schools. *Survey of classroom behavioral problems by gender*. Unpublished raw data, 1997.

Brown, L M., and C. Gilligan. *Meeting at the crossroads*. New York: Ballantine, 1992.

Federal Bureau of Investigation. *Uniform crime reports for the US*. Washington, DC: US Department of Justice, 1987.

Gilligan, C. "The centrality of relationships in human development: A puzzle, some evidence, and a theory," in G.G. Noam and K.W. Fischer, eds., *Development and vulnerability in close relationships*. Mahwah, NJ: Lawrence Erlbaum, 1996.

Gilligan, J. *Violence*. New York: Vintage Books, 1996.

Jenkins, Y.M. "Diversity and social esteem," in J.L. Chin, V. De La Cancela, and Y. Jenkins, eds., *Diversity in psychotherapy: The politics of race, ethnicity, and gender*. Westport, CT: Praeger, 1993.

Jones, M.B., D. R. Offord, and N. Abrams. "Brothers, sisters and antisocial behavior," *British Journal of Psychiatry* 136 (1980): 139.

Jordan, J.V., ed. *Women's growth in diversity*. New York: Guilford, 1997.

_____. "Relational development: Therapeutic implications of empathy and shame," in *Work in progress, No. 39*. Wellesley, MA: Stone Center Working Paper Series, 1989.

Lewis, D.O., R. Lovely, C. Yeager, et al. "Toward a theory of the genesis of violence: A follow up study of delinquents," *J Am Acad Child Adolesc Psychiatry* 28 (1989): 431–436.

Miller, J.B. *Toward a new psychology of women*. Boston: Beacon Press, 1976.

_____. "What do we mean by relationships?" in *Work in progress, No. 22*. Wellesley, MA: Stone Center Working Paper Series, 1986.

_____. "Connections, disconnections and violations," *Work in progress, No. 33*. Wellesley, MA. Stone Center Working Paper Series, 1988.

Miller, J., and I. Stiver. *The healing connection*. Boston: Beacon Press, 1997.

Piaget, J., and B. Inhelder. *The psychology of the child*. New York: Basic Books, 1969.

Resnick, M.D., et al. "Protecting adolescents from harm: Findings from the National Longitudinal Study on Adolescent Health," *Journal of the American Medical Association*, 278: 10 (1997): 823–832.

Silverstein, O., and B. Rashbaum. *The courage to raise good men*. New York: Penguin, 1994.

Stein, N., and L. Sjostrom. *Bullyproof: A teacher's guide on teasing and bullying for use with fourth and fifth grade students*. A joint publication of The Wellesley College Center for Research on Women and the NEA Professional Library, 1996.

Stiver, I.P. "Beyond the Oedipus complex: Mothers and daughters," *Work in progress, No. 26*. Wellesley, MA: Stone Center Working Paper Series, 1986.

_____. (1998). Personal communication.

Touchpoints project manual. Boston, MA: Child Development Unit, Children's Hospital, 1998.

Tronick, Edward. *Touchpoints project manual*. Child Development Unit, Children's Hospital, Boston, MA, 1998.

Chapter twenty-five

Blakey, Mary Kay. "Who are we this time?" in Andrea O'Reilly, ed., *Mothers and sons: Feminism, masculinity and the struggle to raise our sons*. New York: Routledge, 2001.

Gilligan, Carol. *In a different voice: Psychological theory and women's development*. Cambridge, MA: Harvard University Press, 1982.

Jackson, Marni. *The motherzone: Love, sex, and laundry in the modern family*. Toronto: MacFarlane, Walter, and Ross, 1992.

Lee, Claudette, and Williams, Ethel Hill. "Masculinity, matriarchy and myth: A black feminist perspective," in Andrea O'Reilly, ed., *Mothers and sons: Feminism, masculinity and the struggle to raise our sons*. New York: Routledge, 2001.

Lorde, Audre. "Man child: A black lesbian feminists response," in Audre Lorde, *Sister outsider: Essays and speeches*. New York: Quality Paperback Book Club, 1993.

O'Reilly, Andrea, ed. *Mothers and sons: Feminism, masculinity and the struggle to raise our sons*. New York: Routledge, 2001.

Smith, Babette. *Mothers and sons: The truth about mother–son relationships*. Sydney: Allen and Unwin, 1995.

Wells, Jess. "Lesbians raising sons," in Andrea O'Reilly, ed., *Mothers and sons: Feminism, masculinity and the struggle to raise our sons*. New York: Routledge, 2001.

Contributors' Notes

Christina Baker is a professor of English at the University of Maine at Augusta. She has published on feminism, women's history, and labor history. Baker is the author of *In a generous spirit: A first-person biography of Myra Page*, and the co-author (with her daughter Christina Baker Kline) of *The conversation begins: Mothers and daughters talk about living feminism*. Baker received the Presidential Outstanding Teacher Award from the University of Maine (1992) and the Trustee Professorship for University of Maine at Augusta (2000). Most recently, she completed three terms in the Maine State Legislature. She and her husband have four daughters and six grandsons.

Wanda Thomas Bernard is an African Nova Scotian mother and othermother. She has a B.A. from Mount St. Vincent University, an M.S.W from Dalhousie University, and a PhD from the University of Sheffield (England). Dr. Thomas Bernard is an associate professor and director at the School of Social Work, Dalhousie University. She has done extensive research work with black men, and is currently conducting research on the impact of racism and violence on the health and well being of African-Canadian men, their families, and communities in Halifax, Toronto, and Calgary. Previous research projects have explored topics such as Africentric perspectives in social work, race relations in the education sector in Nova Scotia, and issues of addiction and health care services with African Nova Scotian women.

Petra Büskens is a PhD candidate and sometimes lecturer in the sociology program at the University of Melbourne, Australia. Her research engages with questions of maternal identity in the contemporary West through an empirical study on mothers who leave. She has published essays on motherhood, social structure, individualism, and sexuality. In 2001, she was Visiting Scholar at the Centre for Research on Mothering, York University, Toronto. For this research she was awarded the Australian Federation of University Women (WA) Foundation Bursary. Petra lives in Daylesford, Australia, with her nine-year-old daughter, Mia. She can be contacted at: petra.b1@bigpond.com.

Paula J. Caplan is a clinical and research psychologist, and Adjunct Professor at Brown University and at Washington College of Law, American University. She is the author of twelve books, including *Don't blame mother: Mending the mother–daughter relationship*; *The myth of women's masochism*; *Lifting a ton of feathers: A woman's guide to surviving in the academic world*; *You're smarter than they make you feel: How the experts intimidate us and what we can do about it*; and, with her son, Jeremy B. Caplan, *Thinking critically about research on sex and gender.*

Dawn Comeau is working on a PhD in women's studies and a Master's degree in public health at Emory University. She is currently researching lesbian and bisexual women's health and access to care. Comeau received her Master's degree in women's studies from San Diego State University, where her research project focused on lesbian families.

Sharon Anne Cook is Professor and former Director of Teacher Education at the University of Ottawa. She is the author of eight books in Canadian, women's, addictions, and educational history, and has edited a recent collection in women's history (with Lorna McLean and Kate O'Rourke, 2001)—*Framing our past: Canadian women's history in the twentieth century*—that won the award from the Canadian Association of Foundations of Education for the best book in educational foundations in Canada for 2002. She is cross-appointed to the Faculty of Education and History where she teaches history pedagogy, the history of education, and moral movements.

Cate Dooley is Co-director of the Mother–Son Project and a faculty member at the Jean Baker Miller Training Institute of Wellesley College's Stone Center. She is Campus Consultant for Eating Disorders at Brandeis University Student Health Services and has been the Stone Center's relational consultant for T. Berry Brazelton's Touchpoints Project at the Child Development Unit, Boston Children's Hospital. From 1977 to 1993, Ms. Dooley codirected the Eating Disorder Program in the Cognitive Behavior Therapy Unit at McLean Hospital, Belmont, Massachusetts. She later worked as a trainer and program developer for the Women in Prison Project at Wellesley College's Stone Center. She has twenty-five years of experience in the field of psychology, doing clinical work and research projects, designing treatment programs, and supervising clinicians. Ms. Dooley is also in private practice in Newton and Watertown, Massachusetts. Ms. Dooley has co-authored several publications including: "An inpatient model for the treatment of anorexia nervosa" in *Theory and treatment of anorexia nervosa and bulimia* (1985); *Mothers and sons: Raising relational boys* (1998); *Relational and social diversity training in a prison setting: A training manual* (1995); and *Workplace training: Relational intelligence and action* (2000).

Arlene E. Edwards is a community psychologist whose professional interests include the engagement of black women's familiar knowledge of their communities as a means of designing interventions. Her focus is primarily on community mothering in its many forms, and on the ways in which black women in particular practice this type of mothering in different venues, including the community, churches, and academic institutions. As a community psychologist she attempts to infuse intervention design, program evaluation and applied research with the methods and strategies that black women engage as they address the maintenance and survival needs of their communities. Current research efforts center on the use of qualitative research methods to investigate the experience of health disparities in minority communities and ways by which black women's community knowledge and strategies may be used to address this issue.

Juanita Ross Epp came to teacher education after fifteen years as a classroom teacher at all levels (kindergarten to high school) in Canada, Yugoslavia, and Great Britain. She has been a professor at Lakehead University for twelve years and has served as President of the Canadian Association for the Study of Women and Education (1994–1996), Lakehead University Faculty Association (1999–2000), and the Ontario Council of University Faculty Associations Status of Women Committee (1997–2000). Dr. Epp's current position is Chair of Undergraduate Studies in Education at Lakehead University (June 2000 to present), where she teaches in the area of educational administration and school law. Her recent research is focused on alternative delivery methods for teacher education with an emphasis on language arts and early reading.

Rachel Epstein coordinates the LGBT (lesbian/gay/bi/trans) Parenting Network of the Family Service Association of Toronto, and is a doctoral candidate in education at York University. She has been researching, writing, and teaching on issues related to queer parenting for about twelve years and also works as a mediator, assisting LGBT parents and prospective parents to work out parenting arrangements and the conflicts that can arise when people are engaged in the passionate act of parenting children.

Nikki Fedele graduated from Cornell University College of Arts and Sciences in 1972 with a B.A. in psychology and biology. She concentrated her psychological studies on physiological psychology and her biological studies on neurobiology and behavior. Dr. Fedele received her M.A. (1979) and her PhD (1983) in clinical and community psychology from Boston University. She began her studies of parenting with her dissertation on differences in parenting styles between mothers and fathers. She has spoken nationally on parenting, women's development, and application of the relational model. Currently she is Co-director of the Mother–Son Project at the Jean Baker Miller Training Institute at the Stone Center for Developmental Studies, Wellesley College. Dr. Fedele is also Assistant Clinical Professor of Psychology in Psychiatry at Boston University School of Medicine and teaches residents about a relational model of group psychotherapy at Harvard Medical School. Dr. Fedele has twenty-two years of clinical experience working with men, women, couples, groups, and children. She is also the mother of two sons.

Jacqui Gabb is currently undertaking an ESRC-funded D.Phil research project into lesbian families with children in Yorkshire, England She was formerly a senior lecturer in media specializing in the areas of female spectatorship, lesbian, gay, and queer media. She has published in *Journal of Gender Studies; Journal of the Association for Research on Mothering;* and *The media in Britain: Current debates and developments* (Palgrave Macmillan, 1999).

Fiona Green is a mother, an assistant professor, and the coordinator of the women's studies programme at the University of Winnipeg. Her interdisciplinary dissertation (women's studies, education, and sociology), entitled *Living feminism: Pedagogy and praxis in mothering*, draws upon Adrienne Rich's *Of woman born*. Other work related to her doctorate is published in various issues of the *Journal for the Association of Research on Mothering*. Her current research investigates how female university students use campus washrooms to nurture consciousness raising and to celebrate and participate in political activism. Dr. Green is Chair of the Margaret Laurence Women's Studies Centre in downtown Winnipeg.

Erika Horwitz holds a PhD in counselling psychology. She is a feminist therapist, public speaker on mother empowerment, and an university instructor. Her research interests are focused on finding ways to enhance the experience of mothers and women by understanding social discourses and constructions of motherhood. She has run programs to promote maternal, family, and child well being in both Canada and in Mexico, where she was born. She is currently writing a book on maternal resistance to the Western dominant discourse on mothering. She has two amazing daughters, Leigh-Ann and Stephanie.

Erica Lawson is a PhD candidate in the department of sociology and equity studies at OISE/UT. Her research interests include anti-racism theory and practice, indigenous knowledge, anti-colonial thought, and black feminist thought. Her dissertation focuses on how black mothers and their daughters produce knowledge about sex and sexuality in the context of their relationship. She examines the silence and secrecy that black women generally experience around these issues, and the implications for the mother/daughter relationship.

Noami Lowinsky is a Jungian analyst, a member of the San Francisco Jung Institute, a poet, and poetry and fiction editor for *Psychological perspectives*. Her book, *The motherline: Every woman's journey to find her female roots*, was published by Putman in 1992. She has a private practice in Berkeley, California, has grown children and stepchildren, and grandchildren.

Dolana Mogadime is an assistant professor in the faculty of education at Brock University. Her current research interests include enthnography in urban schools and the inclusion of African-Canadian history, and the diaspora experience within the context of the official school curriculum. Her work has been published in various feminist journals including *Canadian Woman Studies* and *Journal of the Association for Research on Mothering*.

Andrea O'Reilly is an associate professor and award-wining teacher in the School of Women's Studies at York University, founding president and director of the Association for Research on Mothering—the first feminist association on motherhood with 500-plus members plus worldwide—and editor-in-chief of the *Journal of the Association for Research on Mothering*. She is author of *Toni Morrison and motherhood: A politics of the heart* (2004), and editor of six books on mothering including: *Mothers and sons: Feminism, masculinity and the struggle to raise our sons* (2001); *From motherhood to mothering: The legacy of Adrienne Rich's Of woman born* (2004); and *Mother matters: Motherhood as discourse and practice* (2004). She and her common-law spouse are the parents of a nineteen-year-old son and two daughters, fourteen and seventeen.

Joanna Radbord is a lawyer with the firm of Epstein Cole, and is a lesbian mother. Her practice focuses on family law and gay and lesbian rights, and she is particularly interested in the legal regulation of lesbian mothering. Radbord was involved with *M.* vs. *H.*, the first Supreme Court of Canada decision to successfully challenge the definition of "spouse" as restricted to opposite-sex couples. She is currently co-council to the eight same-sex couples seeking the freedom to choose civil marriage in Ontario.

Alison Thomas is an assistant professor in the sociology department at the University of Victoria, where she teaches courses on the sociology of families and on qualitative research methods. Her research interests encompass diverse aspects of the broad topic of "gender relations" and include a major study of the impact of university sexual harassment policies, as well as her more recent work on the nature and extent of fathers' participation in family life. Amongst her publications are a book on sexual harassment (*Sexual harassment: Contemporary feminist perspectives*, 1997, co-edited with Celia Kitzinger), and a special feature for *Feminism and Psychology* on "Feminists mothering sons" (1996), co-edited with Robyn Rowland. As the mother of a teenage son and daughter (twins), her interest in mothering and the issue of work/family conflict is more than merely academic.

Trudelle Thomas is a professor of English at Xavier University, a Jesuit university in Cincinnati, Ohio, where she teaches courses in writing and literature. She writes creative non-fiction as well as academic essays. She has published in *College Composition and Communication; The International Journal of Children's Spirituality; The Journal of the Association for Research on Mothering*; and elsewhere. Her book on maternal spirituality, *Mother spirit*, is forthcoming from Paulist Press. She lives in Cincinnati, Ohio, with her partner and son. She is an avid power walker and literacy volunteer.

Barbara Turnage earned her PhD in 1998 in social work at Tulane University, where she was awarded a four-year Regent's Fellowship. A practitioner and academician, Dr. Turnage has presented and participated in regional, national, and international conferences. Currently, she teaches social work at Arkansas State University.

Njoki Nathani Wane is an assistant professor in sociology and equity studies in education at the Ontario Institute for Studies for Education of the University of Toronto. She teaches both in the graduate and pre-service program. Her research and teaching areas include: black feminism, African feminisms, anti-racist studies, women and development, and indigenous knowledge.

COPYRIGHT ACKNOWLEDGEMENTS

"Feminist Mothers: Successfully Negotiating the Tensions between Motherhood As 'Institution' and 'Experience'" by Fiona Green was originally published in *From Motherhood to Mothering: The Legacy of Adrienne Rich's* Of Woman Born, edited by Andrea O'Reilly. New York: The State University of New York Press. © 2004 State University of New York. All Rights Reserved. Reprinted by permission.

"'We Were Conspirators, Outlaws from the Institution of Motherhood:' Mothering Against Motherhood and the Possibility of Empowered Maternity for Mothers and Their Children" by Andrea O'Reilly was originally published in *From Motherhood to Mothering: The Legacy of Adrienne Rich's* Of Woman Born, edited by Andrea O'Reilly. New York: The State University of New York Press. © 2004 State University of New York. All Rights Reserved. Reprinted by permission.

"The (Male) Advantage of a Feminist Mother" by Juanita Ross Epp and Sharon Cook was originally published in the *Journal of the Association for Research on Mothering* 2(2). Reprinted by permission of the authors.

"Telling our Stories: Feminist Mothers and Daughters" by Christina Baker was originally published in *Mothers and Daughters: Connection, Empowerment and Transformation*. Lanham, MD: Rowman and Littlefield Publishing Group. © Rowman and Littlefield Publishing Group, 1998. Reprinted by permission of the author and publisher.

"From Perfect Housewife and Fishnet Stockings and Not Quite Back Again" by Petra Büskens was originally published in the *Journal of the Association for Research on Mothering*, Spring/Summer 2002. Reprinted by permission of the author.

"Imag(in)ing the Queer Lesbian Family" by Jacqui Gabb was originally published in the *Journal of the Association for Research on Mothering*, Fall/Winter, 1999. Reprinted by permission of the author.

"Our Kids in the Hall: Lesbian Families Negotiate the Public School System" by Rachel Epstein was originally published in the *Journal of the Association for Research on Mothering*, Fall/Winter 1999. Reprinted by permission of the author.

Dr. Andrea O'Reilly is Director of the Association for Research on Mothering, and Associate Professor of Women's Studies at York University.